THE BRITISH SUBMARINE

by Commander F W Lipscomb OBE, RN

with an Introduction by
Vice~Admiral Raikes, Flag Officer Submarines

CONWAY MARITIME PRESS
GREENWICH

© 1975
Conway Maritime Press

Published by
Conway Maritime Press Limited
7 Nelson Road, Greenwich, London SE10
ISBN 85177 086 X

First edition 1954
Second, revised and expanded edition 1975

Designed by Jon Blackmore Design, London
Typesetting by Jaset, London
Printed and bound in Great Britain by
Garden City Press, Letchworth

Authors note

In order to emphasize the fact that all submarines (except the *K* Class) referred to in Part I were fitted with some form of internal combustion engine, including the latest *Porpoise* and *Oberon* Classes, I have alluded to them frequently as *conventional* submarines. This modern term has been used mostly in the chapters describing how a submarine works, and questions relating to it. Here the present tense has been retained as in the First 1954 Edition because the subject matter is best suited to this style.

Part II deals exclusively with the revolutionary leap into the Age of the Nuclear Powered Submarine. This Part has been completed up to *November 1974.* In the subsequent months up to publication, there have been some changes in matters of detail. For example, where some officers mentioned have been promoted to higher rank and have received appropriate decorations. Again, because of the constant progression of science, some 'Rates' have had to be abolished and new ones introduced appropriate to the new developments and the responsibilities involved.

In a standard work of this kind it has been necessary to rule up at a certain point, and this has been done at the above date.

By reprinting the original work, and updating it to include the nuclear age, the book contains a fully comprehensive and authenticated account of the history of British Submarines from their inception to the present day.

Contents

PART I   1901 TO 1958

Plates

Acknowledgements

In bringing *The British Submarine* up to date from 1954 to 1974 I have received the most expert and willing help from all whom I consulted. Unfortunately it is not practicable to list the names of everyone who assisted me, and I hope those whose names do not appear below will accept my grateful thanks for their kindness and interest in this abbreviated form.

My thanks firstly are due to Vice-Admiral I G Raikes, CBE, DSC the present Flag Officer Submarines for honouring me by writing the Introduction to Part II. This is particularly gratifying to me as I served with his father in submarines when he was Captain (S/M) of the two flotillas on the China Station in 1926, and again in HMS *Dolphin* when he was Flag Officer Submarines and I commanded the Instructional School in 1938.

My thanks are specially due to Vice-Admiral J A R Troup, DSC recently Flag Officer Submarines, who set me on my path with every possible facility that an author could require. The whole of the arrangements were placed in the hands of Mr John Chambers, Public Relations Officer to the Flag Officer Submarines, to whom I am very specially indebted, not only for this but also for his very considerable help with the manuscript without which I could not have completed the task. The following officers in HMS *Dolphin*, Fort Blockhouse, gave me expert guidance and their personal interest for which I am most grateful: Captain A J Whetstone, Chief of Staff to Flag Officer Submarines; Captain L H Oliphant, DSC Flag Captain to Flag Officer Submarines and Captain S/M 1; Commander D Leggatt, Commander Training; Commander J Salt, Director of Studies; Lieutenant-Commander M R Todd, MBE, Escape and Diving Officer. I am also indebted to Fleet Chief Petty Officer D F C Jones, BEM for much painstaking instruction on many aspects of modern submarine technique and on Polaris Submarines.

At the Clyde Submarine base I received all possible help from the following officers to whom I am very grateful: Commodore A J Cooke, Commodore Clyde; Captain R R Squires, Captain S/M3 (Fleet Submarines); Captain M C Henry, Captain S/M10, (Polaris Submarines); Captain R G Fry, OBE, Captain Sea Training; Lieutenant-Commander S Watson, Instructing Officer, Polaris School.

All officers and civil servants in the Ministry of Defence (Navy) to whom I turned for help most kindly did all and more than I asked of them. First of all my warmest thanks are due to Admiral of the Fleet Sir Michael Pollock, GCB, MVO, DSC for so kindly contributing to the book, and in this connection I acknowledge the permission of the Editor *Janes Fighting Ships* to reproduce extracts of an article by Admiral Pollock which appeared earlier in that publication; Rear-Admiral P E C Berger, MVO, DSC, Assistant Chief of the Naval Staff, (Policy), most kindly advised me on naval strategy and I am grateful to him and his Staff for the work they did on my paper.

For guiding me on matters connected with the Polaris Executive I have to thank Vice-Admiral Sir Hugh Mackenzie, KCB, DSO, DSC. On Dockyards, my thanks are due to Sir Rowland Baker, Royal Corps of Naval Constructors, and Rear-Admiral T C Ridley, CB, OBE. I am very indebted to Captain Kenneth Dunlop who helped me considerably on the above two subjects and gave me much of his time on general matters concerning nuclear submarines.

The following officers in the Ministry of Defence (Navy) helped most willingly with the illustrations and I am very grateful to them: Commander B E Bulbeck and Mr R A Karn, both of the Chief Polaris Executive; Mr D J Newton and Mr S W Howell, both of the Ministry of Defence (Navy) Public Relations; Mr J A Bagshaw, Office Services; also Mr D A F Scrivener of the Central Office of Information Photo Library.

Acknowledgement is made to the following for permission to reproduce photographs: The Admiralty for the Crown Copyright photographs in plates 4(top), 5(top), 7,10,11(top), 12,13,17(left), 19(top),

22,25,26,27,29(left), 31,33(top), 34(top), 35,36,37,38(top), 39,40,41(bottom), 43,44; Stewart Bale, plate 6(bottom); Imperial War Museum, plates 2,3,4(bottom), 9(top), 19(bottom), 24; Times of Malta, plates 8,9(bottom); Popperfoto for all other photographs.

Others who have helped me in their special spheres of activity and to whom I am most grateful are Mr Roger Varney of Rolls-Royce and Associates Ltd; Professor J M Ward, Research Manager, Central Electricity Generating Board Research Laboratories Leatherhead; and Commander D Wixon of the Department of Nuclear Science and Technology, Royal Naval College, Greenwich. For much typing and retyping of the manuscript my thanks are due to Mrs H Swanson of High Park Avenue, East Horsley.

Finally my warmest thanks go to my wife who, as my usual editor and critic, has contributed so much to the presentation of the book.

Extract from the foreword

The advent of the submarine as an integral part of the navies of the world occurred during the opening years of this century. This profoundly influenced maritime strategy and tactics which in their turn have demanded sweeping changes in the types of ships and composition of naval forces, calling for the utmost ingenuity on the part of constructors and scientists.

Commander Lipscomb has written this book to show in a broad historical and simple technical manner the evolution and achievements of the Submarine Branch of the Royal Navy. He is well qualified to do so having made submarines his career and having served on the staff of Flag Officer Submarines during World War II. He has been tireless in his efforts to check and re-check the accuracy of his work and has had the ready assistance of the Admiralty and full access to the Submarine Records. He has also had the full co-operation of the Submarine Headquarters.

I feel that Commander Lipscomb has succeeded in placing before the public an interesting and authoritative narrative of the developments and events which cover our submarine history from its start.

Rear-Admiral G W G Simpson CB, CBE — Foreword to the First Edition

'Of all branches of men in the forces,
there is none which shows more devotion and faces grimmer
perils than the submarine ... Great deeds are done
in the air and on the land, nevertheless
nothing surpasses your exploits.'
Winston Churchill 1943

PART I
1908 TO 1958

A British conventional submarine at sea

Chapter one
Early history 1901-1904

'Close attention has been given by the Admiralty to the subject of submarine boats.' So said Viscount Goschen, First Lord of the Admiralty, in April 1900. The Parliamentary Secretary added in a statement to the House: 'The Admiralty are not prepared to take any steps in regard to the submarines because this vessel is only the weapon of the weaker nation. If, however, this vessel can be rendered practical, the nation which possesses it will cease to be weak and may become really powerful. More than any other nation we should have to fear the attacks of submarines.'

Nearly a hundred years previously Lord St Vincent had called 'Pitt the greatest fool that ever existed' and overrode Pitt who considered buying the American designer Fulton's submarine plans. British policy of suppressing the submarine as it threatened our immense maritime superiority, did not waver from that of the nineteenth century, but in December 1900 the Admiralty were concerned to note the additional provision for submarine boats in the French naval programme.

Faced with a submarine expansion of our traditional enemy, it was decided to change our policy and bring submarines into the British Fleet. As we had no designs of our own it was necessary to purchase them from abroad. The country selected was America, and the Admiralty asked Captain de Chair, the Naval Attaché in Washington, who later became Admiral de Chair, to choose a design from existing American boats.

One April day in 1901, Lord Selborne, First Lord of the Admiralty, made a statement in the Naval Estimates to the Commons. 'Five submarine vessels,' he announced, 'of the type invented by Mr Holland have been ordered, the first of which should be delivered next Autumn. What the future value of these boats may be in naval warfare can only be a matter of conjecture, but experiments with these boats will assist the Admiralty in assessing their true value.'

The report of the Naval Attaché in Washington, Captain de Chair, had been accepted and the Holland design had been ordered, but for experiment only.

Before these experiments were possible, as outlined by Lord Selborne, news reached these shores which pointed a warning finger at British maritime supremacy. The French battleship *Jauréguiberry* had just slipped her moorings to follow the main French Fleet out of Ajaccio harbour. The *Jaureguiberry* was the pride of the Fleet and suddenly a dummy torpedo struck her. In the *Daily Express* of 5 July 1901, the naval correspondent wrote: 'After every deduction has been made there is no disproving the fact that the submarine has proved

its tremendous possibilities in warfare.' The submarine was the *Gustav Zède,* a French submarine despatched from Toulon for the express purpose of giving the navies of the world the greatest shock of those times.

At Greenwich, the advanced school for naval officers, a young Captain, R H S Bacon, was studying war. He had heard that five of Mr Holland's boats had been ordered for the British Navy and he wondered who would be the first to command them. He was a torpedo specialist, so thought that he might be a suitable choice. Application was made and the appointment granted. On taking up his duties he met with a strange attitude of mind. Admiral Sir Arthur Wilson was advocating treating submarine crews in war as pirates, and hanging them! Sir William White, Director of Naval Construction had advised Sir Arthur never to go below water, and Sir John Durston, Engineer-in-Chief, had washed his hands of anyone who contemplated running a petrol engine in a confined space. It is a wonder that Bacon managed to tide these storms, but in many ways the attitude of these gentlemen was the best thing that could have happened, because he was left to his own resources and thereafter dealt direct with Messrs Vickers Son and Maxim who had secured the drawings of Mr Holland's submarine, and were building the first boat at Barrow-in-Furness for Britain.

In the construction of ships, a task in which nearly all naval officers take part in their careers, try as one may, there nearly always appears some curious indefinable happening which 'throws a spanner in the works' at one stage or another. Similar things occur year after year and much of what took place in the early days of submarines, applies today. By remembering these points the reader can visualize some of the difficulties which may be happening in the construction of submarines in modern times. Some of these instances are not large, but they are enough to make themselves felt. In the case of the first Holland boat, Captain Bacon, his title now being Inspecting Captain of Submarines, found the drawings of the Holland boats to be very extraordinary in many particulars and naturally he protested that they could not be correct. Nevertheless in spite of his heated and commonsense arguments the building continued as shown on the drawings. At Bacon's instigation an experienced officer was sent from America. He too could not believe these were the correct drawings of the Holland submarine. Nevertheless, work proceeded and it was not until a complete boat nearly turned on end in dock trials, with both Bacon and the American officer on board, that the Admiralty approved any modification of the design. Further, Captain Bacon was given authority to work out a design of his own. So far as it is known, the peculiarities of these drawings were never cleared up!

So it came about that before the first Holland boat had been modified and launched, Captain Bacon had been given a room in the Drawing Department of Messrs Vickers Son and Maxim and British brains had conceived a design for a submarine of our own, and *A1* was approved, and the keel laid down.

The home of these first pioneers who undertook Lord Selborne's experiment

in 'Hollands' was initially a floating one. This was HMS *Hazard,* a gunboat. She arrived at Barrow-in-Furness in late 1901 together with ten stalwart volunteers whose names are already recorded in a book written by the late Admiral Sir Reginald Bacon, KCB, entitled *From 1900 onwards.* These names are surely worthy of repetition if this story is to be complete.

Lieutenant F D Arnold Foster
Lieutenant S Bowle- Evans
Lieutenant J B Moreton
Engineer Robert Spence
William R Waller, Petty Officer First Class
F C Knight, Petty Officer First Class
Joseph B Rees, Petty Officer First Class
Ernest E Neville, Petty Officer First Class
William J Robinson, Engine-Room Artificer Third Class
William Muirhead, Engine-Room Artificer Third Class

The voyage to Portsmouth of the modified Hollands was not without incident. Holland 1 and Holland 2 left Barrow-in-Furness together with HMS *Hazard* to look after them, but they had not gone far before they broke down. The petrol engines gave trouble and thus began the never ceasing battle of the engineers to find a reliable and suitable engine for surface propulsion. The battle was to go on until Diesel electric drive became standard practice. HMS *Hazard* took the submarines in tow after a journey best described by the depot ship's own name! Sea voyages round our west coast are always contingent with adventure if undertaken in small ships. This journey was carried out with a fortitude and enterprise typical of all that has been accomplished by submarines in the years that followed. In fact it gave the standard by which all submarine work in all the years which have passed might be judged. Heavy seas around Land's End in these tiny ships with no freeboard, not even bridges, gave Captain Bacon some days and nights of acute anxiety. He need not have worried however, because the standard had been set and his men saw to it that every danger would be accepted or overcome if humanly possible. In addition it should not be forgotton that the early 'submariners' were looked on with suspicion by their own service contemporaries. Admiral Sir Arthur Wilson's words were uttered in all seriousness and the Navy as a whole felt that submarines 'hit below the belt' and were very un-British. Not only then were these early pioneers faced with many unknown dangers, but they had to stand the criticism which this new weapon evoked throughout the Navy. Every thinking naval officer remembered Lord St Vincent's warning to Pitt in 1809 when the American Fulton demonstrated his submarine before a Royal Commission. He urged Pitt to have nothing to do with the submarine as its development would threaten our sea power more than any other invention.
On looking at the picture of *Holland 1* it will be seen at once how elementary

these first submarine boats were. It is odd to reflect how people in those days thought a submarine could make a reasonable passage at sea without any form of bridge at all. However, it must be remembered that the First Lord of the Admiralty told the House that these submarines had been ordered from America only as an experiment.

In the photograph the long tube like a mast is the periscope. Originally in the American design this submarine had no periscope at all. The only way of seeing the situation when the submarine was being operated was to break surface and look through one of the scuttles in the small conning tower. In any sea at all this was a most difficult proceeding for the commanding officer. The idea of the periscope was first thought of and designed for our submarines by Captain Bacon, in conjunction with Howard Grub, head of a firm of opticians in Dublin. This periscope did not rise up and down vertically when in use, and it could only be in two positions; either fully extended vertically, or housed horizontally by a ball and socket joint on the hull of the submarine when not in use. Also when the submarine captain was looking ahead the object he saw was upright and when he looked astern the object was upside down. Similarly, when he looked on the beam the object was on its side. Nevertheless this invention was a tremendous step in the evolution of the submarine and although the French were the first to design and fit periscopes, let it be recorded that a British naval officer gave us our own and it was Bacon's periscope which was adopted in the American Navy.

The dimensions of *Holland 1* were very small. She had one propeller driven by a petrol engine on the surface, and by an electric motor submerged. When dived, the vessel could be controlled perfectly at any speed. She carried only two officers and five ratings.

Eventually the remaining three Holland boats were also towed to Portsmouth, and a series of trials and experiments were undergone. The most interesting of these to the modern reader was a projected trip round the Isle of Wight. All five boats started, three were out of the picture by the time they got to the Spit Fort which is not far from the South Parade Pier, Southsea, one broke down about half way to Cowes and the fifth finally came to grief opposite the Royal Yacht Squadron. It was obvious there was much to be done before British submarines could become in any way operational, but, let it not be thought that these Hollands never really got going. In time their engines were made astonishingly reliable, enabling the boats to carry out a very large number of exercises both on the surface and submerged. Sometimes they were towed to Queenstown in Ireland, or to Milford Haven, where they took part in important tests to see whether they were effective as 'night torpedo boats' and many other tactical ideas were given trials. Their position as men-of-war was assured when, during the passage of the Russian Baltic Fleet through the North Sea, on its way to utter defeat by the Japanese at Tsushima, the Russians opened fire on our North Sea trawlers, and the Hollands were towed to Dover and east coasts ports ready for action. Warheads were put on the torpedoes

for the first time in our British submarine history. In passing, the Hollands never lost a man from any cause.

Meanwhile, our own design, *A 1,* chiefly made by Captain Bacon, was going well and the autumn of 1903 and the spring of 1904 saw the completion of the submarine not, however, without those indefinable delays already mentioned, which are so often attendant on the building of submarines. Weeks went by with engine trouble taking place and other nagging difficulties taking their toll of time, but those working on her and in particular Captain Bacon, were not to be put off, no matter how exasperating things were. Also before leaving the works of Vickers Son and Maxim at Barrow there occurred in *A 1* the first explosion due to a pocket of hydrogen gas which fortunately was not sufficiently bad to wreck the whole ship, but served as a warning to all submarine officers from that day to this. Again, when on passage off Land's End, the sea played its part, and one night, the engines being unreliable, the submarine was taken in tow like the Hollands; *A 1* rolled in very heavy seas and water entered the batteries and the submarine was filled with chlorine gas, choking the crew who had to abandon their ship. This served as yet a further warning to the future. Captain Bacon put into Falmouth for quick repairs and the Chloride Company who had made the batteries sent their representative to profit from the experience gained. After a short stay, *A 1* proceeded under tow to Portsmouth.

On arrival, the submarine was berthed alongside HMS *Latona* in the northern and remote part of the harbour, so that this 'dangerous craft' could do as little damage as possible if she blew up!

In the photograph of *A 1* the first advance in construction can be seen. Quite a high conning tower had been built, an openwork bridge had been constructed round it, three ventilating pipes had been supplied, and a periscope had been fitted.

It would not be right to tell the early story of British submarines without mentioning the start of their home for about the last fifty years. Fort Blockhouse, the ancient western Fort at the entrance to Portsmouth harbour, was chosen to be the first shore base and was taken over in 1904 by Sub-Lieutenant Little (later Admiral Sir Charles Little). This was a selection of considerable foresight. The Fort is near enough to the Royal Portsmouth Dockyard to enjoy its amenities, while being on the opposite side of the water, it can remain an entirely separate entity. The creek running up to Haslar has adequate water and there is sufficient land on the peninsular for recreational facilities. The fact that this base has been in operation for submarines for over   half a century is evidence of the wisdom put to this important step. When Little took over there was no ceremony. It so happened that he was Duty Officer in HMS *Hazard* that day and was ordered to mount a Naval guard in the Fort. Having exchanged formalities with a party of Army Mining Engineers, he returned to carry on his duties in the depot ship.

By the summer of 1904 it was felt that the British Navy, equipped now with

five Holland submarines, whose teething troubles had been greatly overcome, and with the new first British-designed *A1*, some manoeuvres could be carried out against the Fleet. Two weeks in all were devoted to these special Fleet exercises, culminating with five whole days of attacks arranged in the vicinity of the Isle of Wight, and during which each submarine had two crews and was worked continually. In the first four days the Holland boats principally carried out attacks on various units of the Fleet and by the end of the fourth day claimed to have sunk two of the larger ships in spite of the Fleet being protected by torpedo boats, picket boats and pinnaces patrolling everywhere. This was an outstanding achievement for the 'experimental' boats and more will be heard about it later. *Holland 1* had her periscope pulled out of her with a wire from a torpedo-boat but the exercises continued with undiminished enthusiasm. Captain Bacon, who was controlling the submarines from a surface ship had great hopes of a spectacular success by *A1* on the final day, and in accordance with his plans he despatched the vessel to attack a battleship manoeuvring not far from where the Nab Tower now stands, which is seaward of the entrance to Spithead. Unfortunately, the SS *Berwick Castle* was going into Southampton and the commanding officer had not sighted this ship through the periscope. The SS *Berwick Castle* passed right over *A1* striking her conning tower, and the vessel sank. This was the first submarine disaster in the British Navy. To prevent the recurrence of an exactly similar disaster all submarines have been fitted since with a second conning tower hatch leading from the control room to the conning tower, so that if the conning tower only is holed, as in the case of *A1,* the water can be prevented from entering and flooding the pressure hull.

Naturally the tragic loss of *A1* caused very great concern throughout the country. Not only had we lost our first entirely British submarine, but with it some stalwart pioneers who believed so strongly in this new arm of the Navy. It is remarkable also that the part played by the elements at this first disaster has so often been repeated in subsequent accidents. For example, although the boat's position was known through the bubbles coming to the surface, salvage was seriously delayed due to the weather. A sea swell arose and then a gale blew. Eventually salvage vessels got wires slung under the submarine, but when they took the strain both the wires broke. One can imagine that the comments of people all those years ago were much as they are today, if not brought up in the ways of the sea. One of the most difficult things to do is to salvage a submarine, and this is discussed fully in another chapter of this book. Eventually, in the case of *A1*, it was decided that the best way to raise the vessel was to give it positive buoyancy, a lesson which is shown in the diagrams. To do this it was necessary to blow high pressure air into the top of the submarine and to have a hole in the bottom of the vessel for the water to come out. Before this could be done the conning tower hatch had to be cemented down so that it would not lift, and the cracks in the conning tower itself made by the SS *Berwick Castle* also had to be repaired to withstand an intern-

al air pressure. This was successfully done and the submarine was eventually raised, though it took a month.

One might almost say that the first stage of British submarine operations had now ended. The experimental time with *Holland 1* had passed, the difficulties of submarine work had been experienced, including even a disaster, and in a very few years the submarine crews of that day had undergone many of the trials which have befallen the Submarine Service in the years that have followed.

The *A 1* disaster served to accentuate the antagonism to submariners and their calling, but the more discerning studied the 1904 summer exercises and in them they saw that this arm of the Navy must be accepted, that the men were valiant pioneers, and that the strength of British sea power would have to face the challenge of the submarine. Previously, submarine officers had been drawn from all branches of the Navy, such as gunnery officers, navigators, torpedo specialists as well as non-specialists. Many of those officers had given up because they thought there was no future in the submarine since it was considered as an advanced form of defensive mining, and also they bowed to the criticism of their contemporaries. The 1904 manoeuvres changed all that. The submarine had 'arrived'. Here lay adventure and progress, a close-knit comradeship and not the lest of all possibilities, early promotion.

Chapter two
The opening of the door
1904-1914

Phase two in the story and development of our submarines covers the period from 1904 to the beginning of the First World War. This story might have been one of progress limited simply to bigger hulled submarines, deeper diving ability, longer endurance and higher surface speeds. However, the advance of submarines in all countries, and of course in ours, was suddenly given great impetus. For a long time experts had been studying a safer method of propelling the submarine on the surface other than by the petrol engine, and although experimental diesel engines had found their way into one or two boats, no submarine had yet been specifically designed in this country to be equipped with a diesel.

Hitherto all submarines, except where an occasional experimental diesel had been tried, were fitted with petrol engines, they all had one propellor each, their submerged speed had not exceeded 6 to 7 knots at full power and at best their surface speed in the latest class gave them just over 12 knots. As the ballast tanks for destroying the buoyancy were fitted *inside* the actual submarine's hull, space in the interior of the boat for machinery and living conditions were terribly cramped. None of these submarines had an armament bigger than two bow torpedo tubes and none of them had a gun. The one development which had really made progress was the fitting of hydroplanes instead of trying to control the boat submerged by a simple form of horizontal tail rudder only.

With all these limitations it is easy to see how the minds of people reacted to their operational value and believed them capable only of extending the coast defences. Few officers before 1904 visualized submarines operating by themselves on very long journeys, but in that year one or two people had such progressive ideas and the most important of these people was Admiral Sir John Fisher, the well-known 'Jackie' Fisher of later days.

This officer was Commander-in-Chief Portsmouth in 1904 and made a note on January 5 of that year in which he wrote: 'Satan, disguised as an angel of light, wouldn't succeed in persuading the Admiralty or the Navy, that in the course of some few years the submarine will prevent any Fleet remaining at sea continuously either in the Mediterranean or the English Channel'.

Later, after the 1904 manoeuvres in which *A1* was lost but the primitive 'Hollands' claimed having torpedoed two battleships, he wrote a letter at Admiralty House, Portsmouth and in some notes he left about this letter he says: 'Now follows a letter which I wrote to a high official in 1904 and which I had forgotten until I came across it recently. It is somewhat violent but so

true. I went as First Sea Lord shortly after so was able to give effect to my views.'

Admiralty House
Portsmouth
20 April 1904

My dear friend,
I will begin with the last thing in your letter, which is far the most important, and that is our paucity of submarines. I consider it the most serious thing at present affecting the British Empire. That sounds big, but it is true. Had either the Russians or the Japanese had submarines the whole face of their war would have been changed for both sides. It really makes me laugh to read of Admiral Togo's eighth attack on Port Arthur! Why! Had he possessed submarines it would have been all over with the whole Russian Fleet caught like rats in a trap. Similarly, the Japanese Admiral Togo outside would never have dared to let his transports, full of troops, pursue the even tenor of their way to Chemulpo and elsewhere!
It is astounding to me, perfectly astounding, how the very best amongst us fail to realize the vast impending revolution in naval warfare and naval strategy that the submarine will accomplish! (I have written a paper on this but it is so violent I am keeping it!) Here, at Portsmouth, just to take a single instance, is the battleship *Empress of India* engaged on manoeuvres and knowing of the proximity of submarines, the Flagship of the Second Admiral of the Home Fleet, nine miles beyond the Nab Light (out in the open) so self-confident of safety and so oblivious to the possibilities of modern warfare that the Admiral is smoking his cigarette, the Captain is calmly seeing defaulters on the half-deck, no one caring an iota for what is going on, and suddenly they see a Whitehead torpedo miss their stern by a few feet! And how fired? From a submarine of the 'pre-Adamite' period, small, slow, badly fitted, *with no periscope at all,* and yet this submarine followed that battleship for a solid two hours under water, coming up gingerly about a mile off every now and then like a beaver! Just to take a fresh compass bearing on her prey and then down again.
Remember that this is done (and I want specially to emphasize the point) with a Lieutenant in command of the boat out in her for the first time in his life on his own account, and half the crew never out before either. Why, it is wonderful! And so what results may we expect when bigger and faster boats and periscopes more powerful than the naked eye (such as the latest pattern one I saw the other day) and with experienced officers and crews and with nests of these submarines acting together?
I have not disguised my opinion in season and out of season as to the essential, immediate, vital, pressing, urgent (I cannot think of any more adjectives) necessity for more submarines at once—at the very least twenty-five in addition to those now ordered and building and a hundred more as soon as practicable,

or we shall be caught with our breeches down just as the Russians have been!

And then, my dear friend, you have the astounding audacity to say to me: 'I presume you only think they (the submarines) can act on the defensive!!' Why, my dear fellow, not take the offensive? Good Lord! If our Admiral is worth his salt he will tow his submarines at 18 knot speed and put them into the hostile port (like ferrets after the rabbits) before war is officially declared. Just as the Japanese acted before the Russian naval officers knew that war was declared.

In all seriousness I don't think it is even *faintly realized the immense, impending revolution which the submarine will effect as offensive weapons of war.*

When you calmly sit down and work out what will happen in the narrow waters of the Channel and the Mediterranean—how totally the submarines will alter the effect of Gibraltar, Port Said, Lemnos and Malta, it makes one's hair stand on end.

I hope you don't think this letter too personal.

Yours

J A Fisher.

When later the First Lord of the Admiralty introduced the Navy Estimates for 1905-6 he made a statement in the House which is worth recording. This is what he said:

'A naval officer of great distinction, Captain Bacon, was appointed to have sole charge of the submarine for some time and he and Messrs Vickers Son and Maxim together were authorized to supervise the construction of the submarine and to improve the type. So ably did they deal with this matter that even before the first Holland submarine was launched they had already evolved and laid down what is known as the *A* type—the first type of submarines. After the *A* class there has been a still further development to the *B* class. We have now thirteen of these boats on our Navy list, exclusive of the five original Holland pattern. Also there are ten more in an advanced stage of construction. These boats have been constantly at work during the last two years, subject to manoeuvres of very great severity but on all occasions they have proved themselves very reliable.

The House would not expect, of course, that I should enter into any detail as to our intention with regard to the submarines or their distribution. But I may state generally that amongst those nations who use submarines in war, their role will be supplementary to the surface torpedo craft ... You may classify a submarine as a daylight torpedo boat of moderate speed and very considerable radius of action. Certain areas in wartime, by the use of surface torpedo craft by night and submarines by day might be practically denied to large ships.

There is one other immediate and very important function of the submarine and that is the defence of our ports, harbours and coast. It is quite clear that

the use of the submarine extends the range of the defence far beyond the range of the guns of the Forts defending the harbour. These vessels will not only defend the ports but link up the defences and the possession of a sufficient number of them would greatly reduce the anxiety of any Admiral entrusted with the defence of our coasts.'

The unforeseeing Admiralty view was soon to be shattered, firstly by the arrival of Admiral Sir John Fisher at the Admiralty as First Sea Lord, secondly through the untiring efforts of the submariners themselves, and thirdly through *D1*. This was the first British submarine to be fitted with diesel instead of petrol engines.

Admiral Fisher took over on 20 October 1904 and made the submarine his 'child'. *B* and *C* classes of submarines had been established by now, and they began to go on cruises. In 1907 the Nore Submarine Flotilla went on a month's cruise in the North Sea along the east coast of Scotland. They visited various ports on the English and Scottish coasts and made a few days' stay in the Firth of Forth. The *Daily Telegraph* of 9 July 1908 says:

'In the morning the flotilla of seventeen submarines put into Granton Harbour from Dover and were berthed at the inside of the west breakwater. This is the second visit of the submarines to the Firth of Forth, a few having come north about a year ago. The voyage of the flotilla from Dover was a notable performance and marks the successful development of the policy of maintaining sea-going submarine flotillas. It was accomplished in the remarkably short time of about forty hours and is stated to be the longest non stop run ever made by a flotilla of submarine boats.'

D1 (whose commanding officer was Lieutenant-Commander Little) was revolutionary in construction. This boat was ordered in 1906 but was not completed until 1908. She survived the whole of the First World War and was finally scrapped in 1919. The submarine was fitted with diesel engines, a German invention, by a designer of that name. Thus the petrol engine era was ended and with it the danger from petrol fumes. Experimental diesel engines had been fitted as far back as *A13* but no class of submarines had been constructed with this type of propulsion. Of even more importance was the fact that *D1* had far better endurance than the previous boats, having a range of 2500 miles, and could do a steady 14½ knots on the surface at full speed and could work up to short bursts of 10 knots submerged. She was the first British submarine with twin screws. Moreover her ballast tanks were not inside the hull but fitted on the *outside* as 'saddle tanks'. She carried two 18 inch bow torpedo tubes like the earlier *C* class but in addition had one 18 inch tube in the stern because it was supposed a submarine could not be turned quickly enough to ensure the captain always getting in a shot from the bow. Then again, although *D1* had no gun, some boats of this class were fitted with a 2 pounder, *D4* being the first. No British submarine had previously carried guns. Such a weapon had been advocated repeatedly but was turned down by the Admiralty, and ever since that day there has been controversy about the gun. It can be seen

that this innovation alone was sufficiently revolutionary in itself to cause a stir in submarine circles. Much thought was put to the *D* class, and *D 1* in particular, to gaining better sea-keeping qualities. This class became the first 'Overseas' type of submarine as opposed to the 'Coastals', and *D 1* made, which was for those days of 1910, an adventurous voyage, by herself, from Portsmouth to the west coast of Scotland. In spite of engine trouble this vessel arrived to take part in the Fleet manoeuvres under her own power. She patrolled for three days without her presence ever being suspected, and torpedoed two of the Blue Fleet's cruisers as they left their harbour on the last day of the exercise. *D 1* was by then commanded by Lieutenant-Commander Laurence.

The advantages of the *D* class were capped by the fitting for the first time of wireless. Previously boats had fitted their own receiving sets but no receiving or transmitting set had been incorporated in the design of a class of submarines. With this improvement some interesting facts emerged which are still facing submarine experts with difficulties today. Submarines of the *D* class had wireless aerials rigged to their masts. Before diving, this mast had to be lowered by hand and the wireless aerial stowed away carefully along the side of the vessel. This practice was continued until the middle 1920s, but the important factor which came out of the carrying of wireless was that signals could not be transmitted when submerged unless a mast was projected above the surface of the water. Also in those early submarines it was not possible to receive signals under water, but this was only because there was not yet the advance in transmitting that came about in the late 1920s.

Again in connection with *D 1* it is interesting to note the care which the Admiralty and Vickers took to conceal her from enquiring people. Something of this nature might well be copied even in these days though people are generally schooled in security. The *Western Daily Mercury* of 19 May 1908 gives the reader an interesting paragraph: 'True to their present policy of rigid secrecy, the Admiralty have just brought forth a new design of submarine concerning which it is scarcely an Irishism to say nobody knows anything. The new craft, which will presumably be the first of the group provided for in the 1907-8 Naval Estimates, was launched on Saturday last from the yard of Messrs Vickers Son and Maxim. She had been reared in a private and strictly guarded shed and the men who had been employed upon her are all sworn to secrecy. The ceremony of bringing forth the new submarine was confined to the departmental heads of the great Barrow firm and to several of the officers of the cruiser *Mercury* which is moored off the yard. Immediately on taking the water, the mysterious submarine was hurriedly towed to a wharf, barricaded on land and rendered invisible from the sea by a huge pontoon. Here she will be darkly and furtively brought to completion. All that has leaked out concerning her is that she is substantially larger in every way than her predecessors and in certain features she differs from any other craft of this sort in the world. It is expected that she will possess a greatly extended radius of action

and indeed may be regarded as the first specimen of an ocean going submarine class.'

One more note about this vessel. The *Daily Telegraph* of 26 August 1908 in discussing this ship says: 'There is scarcely standing room in the widest part of the *Cs* but in the new ship which it is rumoured will be the *D 1* there is ample clearance.'

This, of course, was because the main ballast tanks had for the first time been placed outside the submarine proper. For the officers and men the added space was well used because, for the first time, an attempt at providing accommodation was made.

These articles prompted the *Liverpool Daily Post* to remark on the very important development in connection with the submarine branch of the Navy, and what was reported at the time gave a very true picture of the position in 1909.

'Hitherto of course, the role of the submarine has been entirely defensive. It was expected to protect harbour mouths, estuaries, ports and so forth, replacing the old submarine mines. Latterly an extended view has been taken and this found ample justification during recent manoeuvres which proved that submarines can knock about for days together in the North Sea and make long trips along the coast. It is safe to say that before long we shall have more than one flotilla of submarines capable of crossing the North Sea and for daily work hundreds of miles from their harbours. Even the older boats have a pretty good radius of action. The newest boats, with larger fuel capacity and more powerful engines and better sea qualities will easily prove this. One has only to glance at a map of the North Sea to understand what powers of defence are conferred by an extended radius like this. The significance is obvious. The submarine fleet which we have been building up so steadily will be available not only for direct home defence but to strike a blow in the enemy's waters.'

The story of the *Ds* would not be complete without mentioning Lieutenant Horton. The name of Horton was inseparable from submarines for the next forty years. Not only was he one of the most outstanding officers of the First World War but in the Second World War he commanded the Submarine Service during the most difficult years and was promoted to full Admiral before leaving his Command. He commanded *D 2,* and dived outside May Island in the approaches to the Firth of Forth. During this exercise there were destroyers, battleships and a good deal of traffic in the Forth but in spite of this and the strong tides, he succeeded in passing under the Forth Bridge submerged and finally travelled so far towards Rosyth Dockyard that he was able to torpedo his own submarine depot ship lying there at a buoy.

Captain Bacon had left submarines in 1904 and had been succeeded by Captain E Lees who in turn had been relieved in 1906 by Commander S S Hall. It was a year before Hall was promoted to Captain so that the Submarine Service, even in 1907 was placed for twelve months on Commander level. Many

of the advances described in this chapter were the responsibility of the last-named officer whose genius was a by-word in those times. Captain Hall was relieved by Captain Roger Keyes in 1910, but before he left he had proved that even the *C* class, in spite of petrol engines and being only about half the size of the great *D 1,* could give a strong pointer to the future by making an ocean passage, though admittedly escorted by surface craft, all the way as far as Hong Kong. This journey was carried out in April 1910, the voyage was really very risky for those days and is recorded here because it was a great adventure which included crossing the Indian Ocean.

To give an idea of what those *C* class endured, one recalls the stories about fishermen along our coasts in the early days who, whenever they were near a submarine, used to throw fishes overboard to these 'sea monsters'. This was done because, according to the fishermen, the men on board seemed to be more in the water than out of it even when these submarines were steaming on the surface! However, it may be taken as a compliment to the hardiness and determination of those early submarine crews.

The arrival of Captain Keyes in 1910 as Inspecting Captain of Submarines, although he had no previous knowledge of submarines, meant that there was at the top someone who would push forward our Submarine Branch of the Service with the greatest energy. Keyes realised his lack of knowledge and appointed a sub-committee to advise him. These names are well worth recording here:

Commander P Addison
Commander C Little
Lieutenant-Commander Laurence
Lieutenant-Commander Nasmith
Lieutenant-Commander Craven
Engineer Commander Skelton

Eventually the first four became Admirals, and each commanded the Submarine Service. Lieutenant Craven became Managing Director of Vickers Armstrongs as Sir Charles Craven, and Engineer Commander Skelton became the Engineer-in-Chief of the Navy.

The difference between Keyes and his predecessor Hall was most marked. Whereas the latter was a great technical expert, Keyes was the showman. Both officers' qualities were of the greatest value to the new branch of the Service. Hall by his genius had seen to it that the British submarine worked well, but the Navy as a whole still needed convincing of the fact that the submarine had 'arrived', and this Keyes was able to do. Nevertheless, he did not succeed in getting his hopes translated into hard cash in the Estimates. What Keyes wanted was to improve the 'Overseas' submarine and to have more of that type. Under the existing system of placing contracts, Vickers had the monopoly of submarine building in private yards of any Admiralty design and it required

Plate 2

The American designed Holland 1, the first submarine built for the British Navy

A1, the first all-British submarine

Plate 3

D 1 entering harbour. Fort Blockhouse in the background

E 11 returning from one of her exploits in the Sea of Marmora

two years to terminate these arrangements. Keyes did in fact bring about the end of the Vickers monopoly, and there has been some play on this point in the past, some people explaining that Keyes could not proceed with his pro- gramme of 'Overseas' submarines until the Vickers monopoly had been broken. However, this was not altogether true, as there were always the three Royal Dockyards for building ships, had the Admiralty given special priority to the submarine programme. Further, Vickers has always been the friend of the Submarine Service, a great debt is due to this splendid firm, and if the broad policy of the Navy had been different Vickers would not have stood in the way. Nevertheless, the frustration which Keyes felt at the time and his anxiety to speed submarine building, persuaded him to go abroad for what he believed might be better engines and better designs, and at any rate would bring other British building firms into the field of production since there was no monopoly on these foreign designs. He was influenced in this decision by his own exper- ience as Naval Attaché, Rome, a short while before. Accordingly, orders for submarines of foreign designs were placed with some of our other building firms. This was perhaps not very expedient because these foreign contracts were only really in their infancy when war broke out in 1914, and it was then no longer possible for us to get the machinery for these vessels. Keyes had been fully warned of this possibility but allowed his enthusiasm to over ride his judgment.

Some of the submarines that resulted from Keyes's policy are worth recording here. Firstly there was the *S* class. This was built in Messrs Scotts' yard to the design of the Italian, Laurenti. These boats were not a great success because they were unsuitable for the peculiarities of the North Sea weather. This sea when rough stands up very high and has a peculiar forceful break of its own. Naturally the Italians who worked in the Mediterranean did not allow for this. Secondly there was the *W* class. They were built at Messrs Armstrongs to a design by the Frenchman, Laubeuf. They too were not really satisfactory. Their conning towers were too low, they did not have the sea-keeping qualities that we needed here, and it is recorded that our own Admiralty officers who visited the Schneider Company at Toulon before these vessels were ordered, said that they would not be suitable for work in northern waters. However, on the principle 'better something, than nothing' Keyes got his way and at least the Service gained submarine knowledge. As only two of this class were built no great harm was done.

Then came the *Nautilus,* sometimes known as *N 1.* This was actually a Vickers boat. The idea was to have a submarine which had good sea-keeping qualities for extended operations in all conditions of weather and it was hoped to get some higher speed out of the vessel. When laid down this submarine was twice the size of any existing boat in our Service. She was 240 feet long and 26 feet beam. With all this extra length she was only 3 knots faster than existing boats

This firm was not amalgamated with Messrs Vickers until some years later.

and never really achieved anything. She spent most of her short life in dock-yard hands and was a failure. When completed in October 1917 after years of delay she was out of date, and finally was scrapped in 1919.

The Keyes policy cannot pass without reference to the *Swordfish*. This sub-marine was built at Messrs Scotts to another Laurenti design and was the first steam driven submarine in the British Navy. It was hoped that she would do 18 knots, and have a radius of action of 3000 miles at 8½ knots. She was not quite as big as the *Nautilus*, being 231 feet long and had 1300 tons displace-ment when submerged. Nothing came of this vessel either, except that much was learnt about steam propulsion. In the end the submarine had to be con-verted into a surface patrol boat.

Meanwhile another and better design of our own was brought forward. This was the famous *E* class, which was an improved *D* class, and went to show that perhaps it was better in the long run to make steady improvements than to go off at tangents in the hope of striking something better. The knowledge and skill of our constructors was quite sufficient for the task, and this was proved in the *Es* which eventually bore the brunt of the First World War. Perhaps it is fair to say that these were the most successful 'Overseas' sub-marines which we possessed in the first twenty years of this story.

When Keyes started as Inspecting Captain in 1910 he had fifty-seven submar-ines. They were, eleven *A* class which were already obsolete, eleven *B* class, thirty-three *C* class and two *D* class.

It is interesting to reflect that at this time the Germans had only fifteen sub-marines. At the outbreak of war in 1914 Keyes had seventy-four submarines built, thirty-one building and fourteen ordered or projected, while the Ger-mans had thirty-three built and twenty-eight building. The difference here lay in the fact that of our total, only eighteen were *D* and *E* class 'Overseas' boats whereas the Germans possessed twenty-eight of the 'Overseas' type. It seems sad in retrospect that with all Keyes's energy, and advised by his sub-committee, we had fewer 'Overseas' type of submarines at the outbreak of war than the Germans. In fact we had not the number of these boats necessary to main-tain a continuous blockade of the Heligoland Bight.

Opinion just before the war was still very mixed, and in May 1914 a Special Committee, having been able to study by now the first exercises, where des-troyers screened the heavier ships and where attacks had successfully been made by submarines on the Battle Fleet under the destroyer screen, came to the following conclusions:

1 No effective means of direct attack on a submarine submerged has yet been produced. (The depth charge had not been invented.)

2 The best means of attacking a hostile submarine lying on the surface is for another submarine to stalk and torpedo her.

3 The development of the submarine, rather than reducing the necessity of defensive mining has necessitated a revival.

Progress as ever was not made without sacrifices and the story up to the

beginning of the 1914 war would not be complete if the tragedies were not mentioned. There was an explosion in *A 5* in February 1905 due to petrol fumes, and lives were lost. *A 8* was sunk at the breakwater at Plymouth Harbour while changing over crews for instruction. Her hatches had been opened to facilitate this, and the submarine suddenly took an angle bow down and filled with water. All except two or three of the crew lost their lives, though the submarine was later salved. Admiral Sir Dunbar Nasmith in October 1905, when a lieutenant, nearly lost *A 4* when the wash of a passing ship sent a sudden inrush of water through one of the ventilators. Through tremendous pluck and calmness Nasmith brought his boat back to the surface. Nevertheless he was court martialled and found guilty of hazarding his vessel. A charge of negligence was quashed 'taking into consideration his great calmness and presence of mind under exceptionally trying conditions'. There was also the tragic loss of *C 11* in 1909 when she came into collision with a steamer called the *Eddystone,* with the result that the submarine sank. It is not without significance, at any rate to submarine people, that the *Eddystone* herself sustained no damage of any consequence. This shows how easy it is to hole a low buoyancy ship like a submarine, sinking her at once. On the whole, however, with all the risks taken, and the experiments that these submarines carried out, commanded by men of great dash who were anxious to show the value of the submarine in attacking a battle fleet, the total losses by hazard up to the start of the 1914 war were remarkably few.

Finally, to end this story, it is not a little remarkable to read that Queen Alexandra and Princess Victoria went into the interior of *A 3* in 1905 and had all the mechanism explained to them. This was shortly after the loss of *A 1* and is surely typical of the Royal Family in the encouragement they have given and the interest they have always shown in the Navy. Earlier, and before the loss of *A 1,* the Prince of Wales had actually been to sea and submerged in a submarine.

Chapter three
Submarines in the First World War 1914-1918

The first part of the mechanical age naturally brought into prominence those weapons which were entirely the products of such advances. There had been submarines of primitive design as far back as the time of James I, and in the American War of Independence the British Fleet had been attacked by a submarine invented by the American, Bushnell, but no really effective damage had been done by this craft. There was no method of mechanical propulsion and, equally important, no weapon with which a satisfactory blow could be struck at an enemy ship even if the submarine was able to manoeuvre into a position to do so.

Metal submarines, the internal combustion engine, the electrical battery and the locomotive torpedo, changed all this. In 1914, for the first time, submarine warfare was to be waged and while there had been many exercises carried out by the fleets of the world to test the power of the submarine, no one really knew how this newcomer to war would meet the test. How the submarines met this challenge is contained in various publications in detail but it is the purpose of this chapter to gather together the principal features of British submarine operations and the advances made in their construction and design.

Britain started the war with seventy-four submarines, but as has been explained in the preceding chapter, not many of these were of the Overseas type. When Admiral of the Fleet Lord Fisher returned to the Admiralty as First Sea Lord in October 1914 after four years in retirement, he noticed that our submarine strength was no better than when he left the same office in 1910. Though Captain Roger Keyes and his committee had tried to make progress, we as an island nation required at that time, first and foremost, a battle fleet of capital ships, so it would be wrong altogether to blame Keyes for so moderate a submarine building programme. At the same time the inadequacy of the Overseas type was the direct result of going abroad for designs. Lord Fisher was very incensed. However, in retrospect, our slow progress in numbers, particularly of Overseas types, may have been the saving of our country. Had we built a large submarine fleet then Germany would most certainly have done the same and started the war with a sufficiency of the one weapon which could most surely bring us to surrender. Fortunately for us, the Germans had not foreseen the use to which they could finally put their submarines in the war, and by the time they had made up their minds to this course, we were just able to bring in the convoy system coupled with the necessary surface forces to beat the U-boat campaign—but only just.

Except for three submarines on the China Station, three at Malta, and a further three at Gibraltar, all our seventy-four boats were in home waters when war broke out. At the beginning of the war they were divided into three groups to fulfill three separate roles. The Overseas *Ds* and *Es* took up station on the east coast of England to carry out Overseas Patrols in the Heligoland Bight. Most of the *B* and *C* classes joined with the Surface Patrol Flotillas which were arranged to work from the principal ports, the most important of these being the Dover patrol, which was instituted to cover the passage of the Expeditionary Force to France. The remaining submarines, chiefly the old *As* were attached to the Harbour Defence Flotillas. In these modern days it is heartening to reflect that even the Overseas submarines were, when possible, towed part of the way to their patrol positions while the Dover flotilla actually secured at buoys, specially laid across the Straits, to conserve the submarine endurance, the boats remaining at these moorings until an 'enemy report' was received.

Lieutenant-Commander A C M Bennett wrote of his experience at Dover: 'On 27 August *B3* commenced the Dover patrol which consisted of a surface patrol in positions situated between Dover and Calais. Three sets of buoys equidistant across the Channel marked the positions of the line of patrol ... A, B and C. All boats worked three days at sea followed by two in harbour. First day out at A, second at B and third at C. The object of the patrol was to form a line across the Channel to guard our lines of communication to France from surface craft. In this organization the menace of enemy submarines was apparently ignored, as six of the submarines on patrol were ordered to secure to buoys at the billets to save their engines, the remaining three patrolling at slow speed at the billet. On Sunday 27 *B3* was at position A together with two other submarines, the torpedo boat *Attentive* being with us. At 2.30 pm the *Attentive* was attacked by an enemy submarine, the torpedo passing ahead of her. This caused great excitement. Anti-submarine organization was absent. All ships and submarines immediately returned to harbour, whereupon they were all then ordered to proceed to sea to search for the enemy. Needless to say the search proved fruitless and the flotilla returned to harbour at 6-7 pm.

That night there was much discussion in the wardroom. The occurrence, however, served a useful purpose. From that day, vessels of the Dover patrol did not remain stopped, and submarines no longer secured to the mid-channel buoys.'

Of the three-fold role of our submarines, it will be seen as the story progresses that the second and third roles died a natural death in the course of the war, never to be revived, and it was soon evident that emphasis was almost entirely on the first role, the Overseas type of submarine. From the beginning, these boats showed their great value in war and it was in a boat of this type that one of our most famous submarine commanders was soon at work. In mid-September, Lieutenant Horton in *E9* sank the German cruiser *Hela* and on

6 October he succeeded in the far more difficult task of sinking a German destroyer *S116*. From the enemy too there were other very definite indications that it would be the Overseas submarine which would be remembered in this war. Already the cruiser *Pathfinder* had been sunk by a U-boat when the German officer Otto Weddigen in *U9,* an enemy type of Overseas submarine, in September 1914 brought disaster to the British Navy by sinking the three cruisers *Aboukir, Cressy* and *Hogue* during a time when our destroyer escorts had been forced to shelter from heavy weather. Later in October there were over twenty incidents involving German U-boats covering positions from the Straits of Dover to the Orkneys.

By the autumn of 1914 some stocktaking was necessary. This was carried out both on the spot and at the Admiralty. Captain Roger Keyes's own analysis was based on active sea experience, as he had been conducting submarine operations almost continually from the destroyer *Lurcher.* While he was reluctant to give up such an idea, it was becoming more and more apparent that the Senior Submarine Officer would have to remain ashore. Communications were much of the trouble; Lieutenant-Commander C P Talbot of *E6* gives some idea of the limitations obtaining even a year later when describing how he passed a message at long range:

'On one occasion in the Heligoland Bight in August 1915, having important news to communicate and being out of W/T range, I despatched four pigeons, each with the same message, from off Terschelling. The pigeons were sent off at 0400. They had to fly 120 to 140 miles, about WSW, wind SSE, about 15 mph to their traps, be found there by their owners, the message removed and taken to the nearest post office, telegraphed from there to Admiralty, decoded and re-transmitted to HMS *Maidstone* at Harwich, and again decoded. Captain (S) *Maidstone* received the signal about 1530.' At sea, *Lurcher* was under even greater handicaps for receiving information.

But this method was by no means always so successful, as Lieutenant-Commander Keble White of *C12* found. He reported:

'At about 1030 on 19 August, a fine sunny but hazy day, we were about ninety miles ESE from Hartlepool when we saw a Zeppelin, which passed over us at about 1500 feet without apparently noticing us. We did our best to get an enemy report through by carrier pigeon, which was the only means of communication. Unfortunately, the O C pigeons was a member of the crew who was very fond of animals. He had fed them too well, and one and all in succession were loth to leave their happy surroundings in the fore peak'.

Also, another source of trouble was that though the submarines could perfectly well remain at sea, in fact never returning to harbour for bad weather, *Lurcher,* in common with most of the destroyers, frequently had to take shelter. The facts combined to force Captain Keyes to become shore based.

Keyes could already look back on submarine successes but he knew that these would have been even greater if British torpedoes had not been 'running under' their targets. The moral effect of lack of confidence in the torpedo had to be

checked, and there were other worrying problems as well. On occasions, when operations had been planned in conjunction with Commodore Tyrwhitt's Light Forces, based on Harwich, it had not always been clear when submarines sighted surface forces whether they were friend or enemy. Captain Keyes had also noted that local commanders of ports lacked imagination in the placing of submarines and had failed to use them to the best advantage when our coasts were raided by German battlecruisers. Also our submarine losses had to be considered. *E 3* had been sunk by a German submarine, *D 5* had hit a mine and *D 2* had gone off on patrol never to be heard of again.

Out of all that had been learnt in the first three hectic months of the war, Captain Keyes was certain of one thing, namely that it was essential to maintain the distant submarine patrols despite increased enemy counter measures and fewer targets, because our submarines formed the vital outer tentacles of the British Grand Fleet, now based in far northern waters.

Meanwhile in the Admiralty tremendous pressure was placed on submarine affairs. On 28 October 1914, in one of his now famous minutes, Churchill, the First Lord of the Admiralty, wrote this to Lord Fisher:

'Please propose without delay the largest possible programme of submarine boats to be delivered in from twelve to twenty-four months from the present time. You should assume for this purpose that you have control of all sources of manufacture required for submarines, that there is no objection to using Vickers' drawings, and that steam engines may be used to supplement oil engines. You should exert every effort of ingenuity and organization to secure the utmost possible delivery. As soon as your proposals are ready, which should be in the next few days, they can be considered at a conference of the Sea Lords. The Cabinet must be satisfied that the absolute maximum output is being worked to in submarines. We may be sure that Germany is doing this. Third Sea Lord's Department must therefore act with the utmost vigour, and not be deterred by the kind of difficulties which hamper action in time of peace.'

The Third Sea Lord's Department was responsible for placing the contracts with building firms. Lord Fisher's conference to take action on this minute, called forty-eight hours later, was dynamic to say the least of it, and resulted in the immediate order of twenty Overseas submarines to be built within eight to twelve months. In addition, orders for submarines were sent to America and a programme of construction of American designed boats was arranged to be carried out in Canadian yards. Some details are surely worth quoting. The final November 1914 War Emergency Programme gave us thirty-eight *E* class, five of which were to be fitted for carrying twenty mines each, all built in this country; seven *G* class again built in our yards; ten *H* class built in Canada and five in America. The *Gs* were no improvement on the *Es,* the *Hs*, however, although half the tonnage of the *Es* and thirty feet shorter, were the first submarines in the British Navy to carry a bow salvo of four tubes and proved a very successful type.

The year 1914 saw yet one more typical 'Winston touch' in which submarines co-operated. New ideas requiring imagination coupled with drive were always attractive to the First Lord and amongst these was the Naval Air Service. A raid by seaplanes on the Zeppelin sheds at Cuxhaven was planned for 23 December. Eleven Overseas submarines proceeded to positions off the north German coast to 'stand by' and in the event rescued three pilots from their seaplanes which force-landed.

The first campaign which brought our submarines into prominence was in support of the Russians in the Baltic. As early as 18 October 1914, three submarines attempted to enter the Baltic. Lieutenant-Commander Laurence in *E 1* and Lieutenant-Commander Horton in *E 9* succeeded, but *E 11* with Lieutenant-Commander Nasmith, who was the third to try, found the alarm had been given to such an extent that he could not get through. *E 1* and *E 9* were joined in 1915 by three other submarines making a total of five *E* boats in the Baltic. Besides these, the Submarine Command, never lacking in ideas, shipped four *C* class to Archangel, also in 1915, having first removed their batteries and other particularly heavy but moveable parts. From Archangel the boats were taken by canal and river to Petrograd, their batteries and machinery were re-installed and they then joined up with the *Es*.

This Baltic flotilla of submarines caused far greater confusion than was ever hoped for and showed how valuable submarines could be when targets were available and when handled by such resolute commanders as Horton. Before the first submarines had been more than a day or two in the Baltic they were taking toll of enemy naval ships to such an effect that the Germans launched expeditions to search them out and destroy them either at sea or in harbour. In the event, these expeditions proved costly to the enemy without any further effort on the part of our submarines as some of their ships hit mines and others broke down. Not only was the German Naval Command thoroughly embarrassed by our submarines but the valuable iron ore trade to Germany from Sweden virtually stopped, and there was considerable dislocation of shipping generally in those waters.

From the first our submarines placed themselves under the command of the Russian Admiral, but finding the Russian submarine crews backward and inefficient they took more and more independence upon themselves. It was not that the Russians were averse to getting to grips with the enemy but the orders to their naval forces considerably restricted initiative. This situation obtained until the Revolution in 1917 when co-operation with the Bolshevik Russian Navy, although at first both parties tried their best, became impossible.

It was then decided that the need for good submarine crews at home overruled any further efforts in the Baltic. Most of the crews returned to England by way of Archangel, and the submarines were withdrawn from Reval to Helsinki. The 'care and maintenance' party left behind tried valiantly to keep things going so that operations might once again be started when the situation was more settled, but when the Bolsheviks concluded a separate peace with

the Germans at Brest Litovsk in 1917, the Germans demanded the surrender of the British boats, and there was nothing left to do but take the submarines to sea one by one and sink them. Added to this, German forces were already ashore in Finland and might have overrun this last submarine base at any moment.

One man of whom the public may not have heard but who played a hero's part throughout the Baltic campaign was Commander Cromie of *E 19*. He remained in Russia attached to the British Embassy instead of returning home after the final sinkings, telling his nearest friends that he had further work to do. Not long afterwards he was murdered on the steps of the British Embassy in Petrograd.

Apart from the actual war effort, this campaign emphasized how versatile submarine officers must be. One instance was the difficulty of acting correctly with regard to neutrals, mistakes with whom might easily have serious consequences. Another instance was competing with the arctic conditions of a Baltic winter. No British submarine had ever operated in this area before. The effect of ice on the various and complicated machinery of submarines was untried. Another condition to contend with was the necessity of keeping well abreast with the international situation in spite of considerable difficulty in communications, both with England and Petrograd. The crews themselves were from time to time anxious about their future and the long intervals between mails from home were very testing, particularly when breakdowns or winter conditions forced inactivity, but morale remained high due to superb leadership. These were some of the problems dealt with and successfully solved by the men on the spot and notably by Horton who returned to England at a later date as a Commander with a DSO and bar, and also wearing a number of the highest Russian decorations.

While the Baltic campaign was in progress the Dardanelles campaign had begun and with it the entry of submarines, both British and French, in December 1914, into the sea of Marmora. Much has been written about the submarine exploits against the Turks in those waters. Here the story must be confined to a broad summary, but this does not mean that the efforts of those heroes who took part are in any way belittled. The object of sending submarines into the Marmora was to cut the communications of the Turkish Army which was operating on the Dardanelles peninsular against our forces landed there with the intention of capturing Constantinople. That the sea communications were cut by our submarines there is no shadow of doubt. Sometimes weeks passed when the Turks were too frightened to send any supplies to their hard pressed forces by sea routes. At times it was possible also to interfere with communications ashore either by landing demolition parties or by bombardment, but these were not operations which produced lasting results. Unfortunately, the campaign as a whole failed and evacuation had to be carried out. In consequence on 2 January 1916, the last British submarine was recalled from the Marmora. This was *E 2*. It would have been a great triumph for British submarines

if the evacuation could have been prevented through their exploits in the
Marmora, for their work deserved positive results. In spite of the immense
hazards of the passage of the Narrows, where nets, land fortifications bristling
with guns, surface patrol craft and strong tides all combined to deter even the
most daring of submarine commanders, there was not a day during the campaign when a British submarine was not behind the enemy's lines. These boats
if not actually sinking ships, by their very presence induced sufficient fear into
the enemy that transport of their men and materials by sea was only undertaken under extreme necessity. From the passage through the nets few submarines emerged without some hair-raising experiences as the following extract from an account by an officer shows, though the operation did work to
plan sometimes.

'By 7 am we were off Seddl Bahr approaching the Narrows, our presence entirely unobserved and no hindrance to our passage. At 8.30 am the captain
brought the boat to 25 feet and made his final observation before going deep
to break through the chain boom and net defence at Nagara Kalessi. Having
put the vessel on a course at right angles to the now visible boom pontoon
supporting the nets we went to 80 feet again and increased speed.

At 8.47 am we struck the obstruction and were temporarily held up, the boat
rising to 60 feet. Additional ballast was taken in to keep the boat down, and
in a few seconds the net defence broke, cables passing overhead and along the
starboard side with much jarring and scraping. By 8.48 after one minute's excitement, all was peace again and the trim of the boat corrected, course and
speed being maintained to pass through the second net defence. This, the old
one, was passed without feeling anything, and soon after 9 am the obstructions
were behind us and speed was reduced, the boat proceeding as before after a
check of our position by periscope observation.'

The total positive sinkings by British submarines were 2 battleships, 1 destroyer, 5 gunboats, 9 transports, 30 steamers, 7 ammunition and supply ships
and 188 sailing vessels. Added to this the Golden Horn had been penetrated, a
feat which had not been accomplished for over 500 years by a belligerent
power.

The British submarine balance sheet from this campaign showed five losses.
Not unnaturally there emerged heroes of this truly overseas operation by our
submarines. Lieutenants Holbrook and Boyle, both of whom won the Victoria
Cross, were the first to make the double passage of the Narrows. Lieutenant-
Commander Nasmith, of *E 11* who also won the Victoria Cross, was soon well
known to the public for his outstanding exploits.

While both the Baltic and Dardanelles campaigns were in progress, 1915 brought
a change in command for the Submarine Branch. Lord Fisher recalled S S Hall
and made him Commodore in succession to Keyes who went as Chief of Staff
of the Dardanelles operations. Shortly afterwards a disturbing rumour that
German submarines could steam at much higher speeds than ours on the surface, started to circulate. We have a peculiar trend of crediting others with

greater achievements than our own, while history shows that we are seldom behind hand in progress and often well ahead of others. This rumour was, however, sufficiently strong to force serious consideration of the matter and at the same time colour was lent to the idea through suggestions from many responsible quarters that some submarines should have enough surface speed to work with the main fleet.

It will be remembered we had two submarines building which were designed to go faster than other types. They were the *Nautilus,* a diesel engine type, designed for 17 knots, and the *Swordfish,* a steam engine type, billed for 19 knots. The sudden impact of war on the building firms of Vickers and also Scotts had considerably retarded progress on these two vessels, both of which embodied a good many experimental ideas, so it was decided in the case of our first really fast boats to start with a clean slate. Naturally steam propulsion seemed an attractive proposition in many ways, but there had recently been the case of the French submarine *Archimede* which had been caught in the precarious position of being unable to dive for twenty minutes due to trouble with the funnels in rough seas.

Accordingly the risk of steam propulsion in this project was ruled out and it was decided to build diesel engines which should be able to drive a submarine on the surface at 19 knots. The size of the hull, to give a reasonable chance to such engines, would have to be twice as long as any other submarine at present in service. All this was agreed to and the *J* class came into being, of which six were completed by 1916. By that time it was clear that the original rumour regarding the high speed of German submarines was quite unfounded; moreover, further study showed that 19 knots was not fast enough for submarine operations in company with our Grand Fleet so they were sent to join the *Ds* and *Es* as fast patrol boats.

Determined, however, to meet the speed of the Fleet and in spite of the fears of what might happen with steam engines and funnels, the Admiralty ordered the *K* class with a requirement of steam surface propulsion giving 23 knots and a maximum diving time of five minutes.

So many new designs now faced the Admiralty that rather than build more new classes as ideas came along, a Submarine Development Committee was formed in May 1915 to thrash out future policy.

The Development Committee quickly collected together all existing ideas on submarine design and thus had before them six proposed types: coastal submarines, patrol submarines, fleet submarines, cruiser submarines, minelaying submarines and monitor submarines. It will be seen there was no lack of ideas. The Committee did good work and sorted matters out on the following lines.

'Coastal' submarines were already in existence and it was decided to continue the type as required. 'Patrol' or 'Overseas' submarines were bearing the brunt of the war and it was decided to continue building these boats, improving them as much as possible. 'Fleet' submarines were recognized as being necessary but

that no large programme should be undertaken until the full trials of the first of the steam *K* class had been studied. The Committee considered 'Cruiser' submarines to be perfectly practicable but there appeared to be no requirement for the type at that time. 'Minelaying' submarines were already building and more could be ordered if the Naval Staff found them to be necessary. At that time there were no such things as 'Monitor' submarines but it was considered such a type should be built. The reasons being:

1 That a submarine with a 12 inch gun would find its own opportunity for action in the North Sea, if the enemy became active, which in 1915 was considered to be a very likely future event.

2 That if the gun failed there still remained a good submarine with torpedo tubes.

3 That great surprise would be effected on the enemy.

4 That we should be, at any rate, abreast of any enemy development in that direction.

Lord Fisher also records his own reasons for favouring a 'Monitor' type submarine. In his view submarines were finding increasing difficulty in bringing off successful torpedo attacks due to the high speed and zigzag course of the enemy and the low speed of torpedoes of that day (24 knots) did not allow commanding officers any latitude for errors. He adds 'No case is known of a ship of war being torpedoed when under way at a range outside 1000 yards'. This statement did not hold true for long but it played its part in bringing into being the *M* class fitted with one 12 inch gun.

There were Monitor surface ships in existence but these were really floating gun batteries. They carried not more than two very large guns, they were extremely slow because they had broad hulls which made good gun platforms and they were used for bombarding the flank of the German Army positions in Flanders.

Churchill once again at this time lent his foresight and drive to further submarine interests. Two of his minutes speak for themselves.

'I await a special report on the fitting of 'Overseas' submarines and selected destroyers with special long distance wireless. It is indispensable that a submarine should be able to communicate with our receiving stations when operating in the Heligoland Bight. It is also necessary that a certain number of destroyers should have the special faculty of long distance communication in order that they may be used in connection with submarines.'

As a result of this minute some of the *E* class had one beam torpedo tube removed in order to fit a suitable wireless cabinet.

And the second:

'... The system of sound signalling, enabling one submarine to communicate with another, has been toyed with for a long time, and it is necessary now to produce practical results, even if of a crude and imperfect character, which can be made rapidly effective. A report should be furnished within three days, stating what is possible and making proposals for action.'

In spite of the money available and the energy and brains put to the problem, the underwater speaking devices of the First World War were rather disappointing. Talking was achieved by the 'Fessenden' which was nothing more than a plate which could be vibrated to give off sonic waves. Its range was limited to a few miles, it was not directional and could be heard by enemy submarines just as easily as by friendly ones. The listening device was the hydrophone. So much faith was placed in this invention that it was heralded as being the means of driving enemy submarines from the high seas, but like so many of these sensational inventions of which we have seen a number in recent years, it finally found its level in the general scheme of things as progress was made in other ways. Both the Fessenden and the Hydrophone were British inventions, and, while stressing their primitive nature, it is as well to remember that they were great advances in their day and must take their rightful place among the long list of first steps in the various fields of science.

In home waters the patrolling of the North Sea continued throughout the war, and became more difficult and costly as every month went by. Perhaps the most trying aspect was the intense boredom from lack of targets coupled with the very difficult conditions and some periods of terrible weather. It is interesting to reflect that the conditions were typical of these waters in the Second World War. Another typical feature is given in an account by an officer:

'There were shoals of porpoises in the Bight, and more than once, my heart lost a beat when a glowing, torpedo-like object came at us at full speed through the sea and then turned away with a jaunty wave of its tail.' Almost every submarine officer has experienced this 'lost beat'.

The naval war now centred on the possibility of fleet action coupled with the danger of invasion or raids on our coast. The Overseas submarine patrols, though forced to withdraw to the approaches to the Heligoland Bight, continued ceaselessly. At the same time a large number of submarines were held in ports in readiness for defence against invasion. This was in accordance with the views held by some senior officers at the beginning of the war that the role of the submarine should be to help protect our shores. Unfortunately, when the enemy raided our coasts their movements were so uncertain that interception was extremely difficult to achieve.

In May 1916 a Naval plan was formed to try and lure the enemy High Seas Fleet to sea on 2 June and bring it to action with our Grand Fleet. Part of this plan provided for three submarines to be in the vicinity of the Horns Reef from 1–3 June. On 30 May German signalling indicated that the German Commander-in-Chief, Admiral Scheer, might make a sortie at once so the British plan was cancelled and dispositions made to meet the new situation. The positioning of the three submarines had been most satisfactory but tragically there was no method of informing them of any new orders, and they had been told to remain on the bottom as much as possible until 2 June when they might expect to sight the German Fleet.

During the daylight action of the Battle of Jutland, although a large number

of submarines had put to sea for patrol areas, the course of the battle did not give them any chance to attack. By nightfall the crux of the situation was the possibility of enemy heavy ships slipping through to the eastward, either ahead or astern of our Grand Fleet, which was by then well placed between the German Fleet and its base. In the event, the Horns Reef passage was chosen by the retreating enemy, and unknown to the three submarines nearly all the German High Seas Fleet passed close to them during the night of 1 June while they waited on the bottom in accordance with their instructions.

After the Battle of Jutland the new Commander-in-Chief of the Grand Fleet, Admiral Beatty, gave orders for a more realistic submarine policy as there was in his opinion no longer any possibility of invasion. This gave the submarines freedom to put to sea in greater numbers and to maintain more continuous patrols and also to act earlier on intelligence in the hope of intercepting enemy surface forces.

There were, however, many disappointments. Sometimes the submarines were unable to reach their allotted positions in time, often the weather deteriorated at the vital moment and there was always difficulty in receiving messages on inadequate wireless sets. The greatest of all disappointments was the reluctance of the enemy to come out of his bases, but the second half of 1916 pro- a few successes.

In August, the 18 000 ton battleship *Westfalen* was torpedoed by Lieutenant-Commander Turner in *E23* but the vessel did not sink. In October Lieutenant-Commander Jessop in *E 38* hit the light cruiser *München* and in November, Commander Laurence in *J1* torpedoed the battleships *Grosser Kurfurst* and *Kronprinz*. Again both battleships managed to return to harbour but were out of action for some months. All these attacks were close to the enemy's bases in the North Sea. By this time the Germans had had enough of surface ship warfare and scarcely a target was seen from the end of 1916 for over a year. In the sorties of German heavy ships from the first raid on Galston off the Thames estuary, to the last which ventured only as far as the south coast of Norway, our submarines always hoped to cripple one or two big ships far from their base. This would force the German Admiral to delay his return to harbour, unless he elected to desert the damaged ships, and thus he would be compelled to give action to our own Grand Fleet which could then reach the scene, in time, from its far off base at Scapa Flow.

Throughout the submarine story it has been quite clear that there were fertile minds at play and many were the schemes put forward to exploit the use of this vessel. For example, when Zeppelins became a nuisance Churchill ordered two submarines to be equipped with four 6 pounder anti-aircraft guns each and go into Heligoland Bight to hunt the 'Zeps'. There were encounters between them but no Zeppelin was brought down. In fact the Zeppelins generally succeeded in bombing the submarines and it is worthy of note that one Zeppelin commander on sighting a submarine, opened fire with an anti-aircraft gun, and in spite of the vulnerability of his airship, turned towards

the boat and made a spirited attack with bombs, forcing the submarine to dive hurriedly.

Commander G F Bradshaw described a similar incident graphically:

'G 13 whilst diving at sunrise some miles SW of Horns Reef sighted a patrolling Zepplin to the northward.

It was a flat calm beautiful day with good visibility.

Gun action stations were ordered and the boat was surfaced. The gun's crew tumbled up in record time and brought their gun into action. It was extraordinarily difficult to estimate the range but fire was opened with five rounds in rapid succession while G 13 got under way with her engines.

The effect on the Zeppelin was peculiar and startling—the tail dropped until she was at an angle of 35 degrees by the stern and she started to zigzag about in the most eccentric way.

After several more rounds the Zeppelin with a special effort got on an even keel only to overbalance again, this time by the bow. She lost height rapidly and turned away from G 13.

After about five minutes she came roaring back on a level keel. She steamed round G 13 in a large arc and, in spite of every effort on G 13's part eventually took up a strategic position dead astern of the submarine where the gun would not bear. G 13 was placed so that she was forced to dive when the Zeppelin was a short distance astern leaving the airship in possession of the air and the surface of the sea.

During the day any attempt on the part of G 13 to surface was greeted with one or two bombs.

Towards evening several bombs were dropped and the captain of G 13 decided to surface on the chance that the Zeppelin had dropped all her bombs and would afford a target. On coming to the surface it was found that the Zeppelin had gone home.'

Ideas were also coming forward to meet the ever-growing threat to our supplies by this time dangerously reduced through unrestricted submarine warfare by the Germans. Amongst these was a scheme for towing submarines by trawlers. Thus when a German U-boat attacked what appeared to be a harmless fishing trawler the submarine was slipped from the tow and in theory sank the enemy. This scheme had varying success but naturally when the Germans became wise to the idea there was no point in continuing it.

One successful attack was made by Lieutenant-Commander Taylor in C 24 when he sank UC 40. Lieutenant-Commander G J Mackness describing the event writes:

'When going on those trawler towing patrols the submarine and trawler used to leave Aberdeen separately, well before dawn. Also the trawler used to be berthed in the harbour well away from the submarines so as to try to prevent any unauthorized person from finding out that we were working together.

We used to pick up the fishing fleet separately, and then get in tow of the trawler and start diving before it was light. The towing wire was secured to

the towing slip in the bows of the submarine, and the end of the telephone cable was spliced to a short length of cable which was led through a water-tight connection in one of the ventilating shaft caps. When slipping the tow it was hoped that this splice would carry away—it being the weakest part of the cable.

When towed we used to dive at about 40 feet. As soon as we were in good trim we used to set a watch of one officer and two men at the diving planes. We rang up the trawler at regular intervals to make certain that the telephone was working all right.

We had been diving for about two hours on our first patrol when the trawler rang us up to say a German submarine had appeared on the surface and was firing at her to force the crew to abandon ship.

We went straight to action stations. As soon as Taylor had got a rough position from the trawler he gave the order to slip the tow. We then found that the wheel working the horseshoe securing the hinged pin could not be moved at all. We put all the pressure on it we dared, but it refused to budge. When Taylor realized it was hopeless to do anything from our end, he told the trawler to slip the tow from their end. As soon as they had done this, we of course began to sink heavily by the bow. However, Taylor caught the trim and got to periscope depth. In the meantime the bow tubes were got ready. We had an absolutely sitting shot at the German as she was stopped beam on to us. When she sank we blew and came to the surface to pick up survivors. Immediately afterwards I found that we couldn't move our propellor as the telephone cable had floated aft and had got properly wrapped round it and the shaft. The trawler had to take us in tow and return to Aberdeen.

We were rather pleased with ourselves as the torpedo which sank *UC 40* was, I believe, one of the oldest in use at the time—Mk V, Number 10. The commanding officer of the German submarine who was one of the survivors, told me that it made such a small explosion that he thought he had been sunk by an internal explosion, and that when we came to the surface he thought we had just come to the surface by coincidence. His Number One, who was a survivor, was most indignant with him for not having kept on the move when on the surface, a point with which I am in entire agreement.'

Such departures from the normal patrolling in the North Sea gave a break from the tiring and seemingly endless work in mine infested waters, heavily patrolled by surface craft and offering few targets, coupled with mounting losses. By this time, of the first eighteen *E* boats, twelve had been lost, taking with them some of the pioneers who did so much to give the Submarine Branch of the Navy the reputation it so rightly won.

Each year there had been Emergency War Building Programmes and by 1916 the *L* class had reached the drawing office stage, over thirty boats being ordered. These submarines were first intended to be 'Improved' *E* class but their improvements were so marked they were given a letter of their own. They represented an all round increase in performance over the *Es* in 'habitability',

speed, endurance and armament. Perhaps their only disadvantage was rather a large silhouette. Proof of their fine qualities is the fact that one or two survived to take part in the first patrols of the Second World War.

Also in this year the five *E* boats equipped to lay some twenty mines each (ordered in the 1914 War Emergency Programme), were by now completed. There was some good hearted rivalry as to which boat would be the first British submarine to lay mines. Actually *E 24* won the race and sailed for the mouth of the Elbe on 4 March 1916. The trip was designed to mine one of the lanes used by the U-boats when coming in and out of the Bight. The submarine was entirely successful but on her next trip, sad to relate, *E 24* did not return. The work was very hazardous as it consisted of sealing enemy swept channels in existing minefields and in the prevailing conditions there were inevitably errors in navigation which on such work were almost bound to prove fatal.

By 1917, with the U-boat offensive at its height, not only were more and more submarines turned to the anti-U-boat task but it was decided that there should be a special type of submarine with very high underwater speed built solely for this kind of work. This was the *R* class; they were small boats and designed for 15 knots submerged. Everything was done for speed, even to putting the main ballast tanks again inside the pressure hull, so as to obtain the best shape of hull for underwater speed. They reverted to 18 inch torpedo tubes so that six could be fitted, numbers being more important than size when attacking a U-boat. The submarine having a single propeller, some officers wondered whether, by the time the boat was going full speed, the propeller might stand still and the submarine be turning round the propeller, due to the tremendous torque; happily such a terrible thing never happened! Only one *R* boat had the opportunity of attacking a German submarine and this effort failed due to reasons beyond the control of the captain.

From 1916 to 1918 a flotilla of our submarines worked in conjunction with French and Italian submarines in the Adriatic where it was decided no surface forces should be sent. Perhaps the most notable thing about these operations was that we were fighting the Austrian Navy, a forgotten fleet these days. However, as their ships seldom left port little opportunity was afforded the submarines and the only attack on an enemy warship was when *H 4* sank a German U-boat in the spring of 1918.

Of the fast *K* class which were to operate with the Main Fleet seventeen were completed and in 1917 some of them formed the Twelfth and Thirteenth Flotillas attached to that part of the Grand Fleet based on Rosyth. No opportunity came to test these ships as a tactical unit in war. Many were the times they went to sea with the Fleet and, so far as keeping up with the big ships and taking up tactical positions required by the Commander-in-Chief, they were an unqualified success, but when it became clear there would not be an opportunity for another fleet action such as at Jutland, some of the class were fitted with depth charge throwers and relegated to the anti-submarine war. A

tribute here is due to Sir Arthur Johns the Director of Naval Construction whose design was so good that this class of submarine went into production without trials. This was an amazing feat. Finally, it must be remembered that the *Ks* were asked for by the Grand Fleet; they were not the product of the Submarine Branch nor were they the submariners' idea of what a submarine should be.

By now the submarine fleet had expanded so rapidly that it is hardly surprising that with so great a dilution of crews and the rapidity with which men had to be trained for the war emergency programmes, some accidents happened. Perhaps the worst disaster was what has come to be called the 'Battle of May Island'. This island is at the entrance to the Firth of Forth leading to Rosyth.

At six o'clock in the evening of 31 January 1918, the Grand Fleet units based on Rosyth sailed for a rendezvous off the Norwegian coast where later they would meet the rest of the Fleet from Scapa Flow.

Leaving harbour were two *K* class flotillas, destroyer flotillas, cruiser squadrons, battlecruisers and battleships. The speed of the Fleet was 20 knots, the ships showed no lights, and the winter's night was very dark. The various flotillas and squadrons were all spaced apart in a specified order, each unit steaming in line ahead.

The whole disaster has never been fully explained, but briefly what happened was this. *K 14*, avoiding small craft, turned out of line. Her helm jammed and she struck *K 22*. Five minutes later, before these two could disentangle themselves and get clear of the other ships, the battlecruisers were on them and the *Inflexible* struck *K 14*. Moments later the other flotilla of submarines came up and their surface ship leader, the light cruiser *Fearless*, cut *K 17* of the leading flotilla in half, sinking her. This submarine had turned round to stand by *K 14*. Then *K 4* which was astern of the *Fearless* had to haul out of the line to avoid running into her leader, as also did *K 6* but on hauling out *K 4* stopped engines. *K 6* did not reduce speed and cut *K 4* in half. This submarine also sank like a stone. In all, two large submarines were sunk and two large submarines and a light cruiser were badly damaged. Many heroes of the war lost their lives in this terrible tragedy.

People may wonder how on earth this could all have happened without gross inefficiency somewhere. Those who have steamed in formation at night in war, without lights, and in mid-winter conditions, understand how quickly disaster can overtake a ship. Surface ships have run down other surface ships on similar occasions in both the First and Second World Wars. It is always a heavy anxiety to an admiral, even in these days of radar-fitted ships, to handle a fleet at night or in low visibility when steaming at high speed.

Other accidents were *K 13* which sank on trials in a Scottish loch but happily, through superhuman efforts, there was a large number of survivors, and a *J* class submarine was sunk by one of our own Q-ship submarine decoys which mistook the 'J' on her conning tower for the letter 'U'. It is a wonder that the

known list is not greater since throughout the war there were numbers of cases of mistaken identity, a problem still occupying the minds of experts even today with all that modern science has brought to bear on the problem.

In April 1918 the German Fleet made a last sortie with the object of intercepting one of our convoys coming from the north of Norway. As ever our submarines were busy in the approaches to the Bight. *J 6* sighted these forces but having been warned there might be British surface ships operating in this area, made no report. Nothing came of this final enemy sortie because the battlecruiser *Moltke* broke down completely off the south west corner of Norway and the German Admiral Scheer, decided he must call off the operation and cover the battlecruiser's passage home under tow. *E 42* with Lieutenant Allen in command managed to fire some long range shots at these forces as they entered the swept channels of the Bight, one torpedo hitting the already damaged *Moltke.* This brought one of the hottest destroyer concentrations of the war on *E 42* but Allen managed to get away safely.

Another important part played by submarines in the war at this time was the use of *C 1* and *C 3* as blockships at the Zeebrugge operation in 1918. Only *C 3* got to the allotted position, namely wedged in the viaduct connecting the mole to the mainland, but that was sufficient for the task. Lieutenant Sandford blew up his boat exactly at the right moment and in the right place thus contributing immensely to the success of the operation. Sandford was awarded the VC.

Earlier in the year the German battlecruiser *Goeben,* which had been at Constantinople since 1914, endeavoured to make a breakout. A report was received at Mudros that the vessel had gone aground off Nagara Point and *E 14,* Lieutenant-Commander White, was immediately despatched to force the Narrows of the Dardanelles and torpedo the *Goeben* while she was in a helpless condition. He never found the battlecruiser but torpedoed another vessel, in the course of which the submarine was damaged and had to run the gauntlet on the surface of guns on both sides of the Narrows. White remained alone on the bridge throughout and was killed by a shell just as the submarine was beached, thereby giving the crew a chance to save their lives. He was awarded the VC posthumously.

From this account of five years of submarine war, mention must be made of the three *M* class or Monitor submarines previously ordered. Only *M 1* was completed in the war. Construction of the others and to a certain extent of *M 1* was deliberately delayed because at the time it was felt we might have conceived an idea which would be more useful to the enemy than to us. *M 1* was entirely successful, but was never used operationally in war. Her gun fired perfectly well and instead of doing alarming things to the submarine when it recoiled, the boat behaved splendidly. Further, *M 1* was a very good diving boat because at the beginning of the dive she had the full weight of the gun to help her down, but when the gun became submerged its buoyancy came into play which served as a most suitable brake helping to check the dive at about 20

feet depth exactly as the crew wanted.

The war ended for the Submarine Service with two events. Firstly a signal from the Commodore Submarines and secondly the covering of the surrender of the German Fleet. Commodore S S Hall's signal read:

'Now that a general Armistice is in force, I wish to lose no time in tendering my personal tribute to the officers and men of the Submarine Service. Having had a good deal to do with this Service in its early stages, it has been a great pleasure to command it in war, and it must be a source of great pride and satisfaction to you, as it is to me, that our peace organization and training have withstood the supreme test, and that you have so splendidly carried out the many and varied services demanded of you.

Submarines were the first at sea on the outbreak of war; they have been continually in action while it lasted; they will be the last to return to harbour.

You have, in addition to the valuable outpost, patrol, minelaying, fleet duties, and other services, the sinking of 54 enemy warships and 274 other vessels to your credit, and you have done more to counter the enemy's illegal war upon commerce than any other single means; at the same time you have been called upon to man new and intricate types of submarines, demanding the highest standards of knowledge and efficiency. Your steadiness and grit, whilst the toll of your gallant fellows was heavy, have been beyond all praise, and will form glorious pages in naval history when this comes to be written ... the result was certain. We leave the war with a record as proud as any that war has ever produced.'

It was very true. Submarines were the last home as they were stationed in positions to torpedo the German High Seas Fleet if, on 21 November when they came out to surrender, they had doubled back. The toll of these gallant fellows of which the Commodore spoke was great, 54 submarines being lost out of a total of 203. Their successes, however, were outstanding. These make glorious pages of submarine naval history and the valour of the officers and men remain an inspiration to all who serve in submarines.

The following officers and men were awarded the Victoria Cross for service in submarines during the First World War:

Lieutenant N D Holbrook, VC, RN,
of B 11 for service in the Dardanelles, 1914
Lieutenant-Commander E C Boyle, VC, RN,
of E 14 for service in the Dardanelles, 1915
Lieutenant-Commander M Dunbar-Nasmith, VC, RN,
of E 11 for service in the Dardanelles, 1915
Lieutenant-Commander G S White, VC, RN,
of E 14 for service in the Dardanelles, 1918
Lieutenant R D Sandford, VC, RN,
of C 3 for service at Zeebrugge, 1918

Chapter four
The inter-war period: design and experiment 1919–1938

Peace came, and with it the heartbreaking reductions which have to be made, the scrapping of large numbers of ships and the loss of employment to many very worthy officers and men.

Counting all our submarine flotillas, large and small, there were sixteen in existence over the face of the globe. Within a year these had been reduced to ten; five years later the strength was down to six. Large numbers of the submarines were scrapped. This list of them is a formidable one, and is included to impress on civilians and service people alike the tremendous upheaval of the advent of peace, on the prospects and careers of service professional men.

The surviving boats of the following early classes were scrapped:

	Class	Number		Class	Number
1919	A	10	1919	E	29
	B	9	to 1924	F	All boats
	C	27		G	All boats
	D	3		W	All boats
				H	Large number
				K	Nearly all

Not only were those in the Naval Service affected by the reductions, work stopped on new construction in the Royal Dockyards at Chatham, Portsmouth and Devonport and the principal private firms such as Vickers, Scotts, Armstrongs, Thornycrofts, Beardmores, Whites, John Browns and Cammel Lairds.

With the arrival of the surrendered German submarines in our ports, the principal naval bases appeared full of underwater craft, but within a few years nearly all had disappeared. Memories became short and there were voices in some responsible circles saying that after all the submarine had 'shot its bolt'.

Nevertheless, the Naval Staff and the best brains in the Submarine Branch were soon at work planning and designing for the future, convinced, in face of all the cynics, that the submarine would continue to influence naval tactics.

The new designs started with the *M* class or the 'Mutton Boats' as they were nicknamed. It will be remembered that in 1916, as part of that year's War Emergency Programme, *K 18, K 19, K 20* and *K 21* were ordered, but no more than their keels had been laid down when the Admiralty Committee working on submarine development made their decision to build monitor submarines.

The four hulls changed their numbers to *M 1, M 2, M 3,* and *M 4* but the completion of these boats was delayed, since it was realized that the idea would be of more use to the enemy than to ourselves. *M 1* was completed just before the end of the war but she never got a chance to prove herself in action. The Naval Staff ordered extensive trials which were most successful and there is little doubt, had these boats seen action in war they would have damaged the enemy, as well as giving them something new to think about. The target could be approached submerged, with the gun loaded. As it passed, the submarine could be brought to the surface sufficiently to clear the muzzle of the gun from the sea, and the gun fired. This operation of 'bobbing up' from below took about twenty-five seconds. As soon as the gun had been fired and the muzzle shut off, the submarine submerged again. This second operation took about fifteen seconds. In these circumstances the enemy could have no time to take avoiding action.

Attention was next turned to *M 2* which started her life as *K 19.* It was decided that this boat should be converted into a submersible seaplane carrier. During the war *E 22* had carried a seaplane on her upper deck casing into the Heligoland Bight to try and shoot down Zeppelins. Obviously this was not a satisfactory method of transport for the seaplane as it could only be carried and launched in calm weather and had to be abandoned if the submarine was forced to dive.

The 12 inch gun was removed from *M 2,* the gun house converted into an aeroplane hangar, and in front was a catapult. The aeroplane which was carried had to be of a small design to fit into the hangar, and Messrs Parnell provided a suitable machine named the Parnell 'Peto'. Like *M 1,* the *M 2* experiment was a success and the submarine was very handy under water, could dive quickly and could come to the surface from periscope depth, open the hangar door, catapult the 'Peto' into the air, shut the hangar door and dive again in five minutes total time. The seaplane could only get back to the submarine if the sea was fairly calm, as it had to alight on the water alongside and be hoisted in. On operations this was not a necessity because the aircraft could return to a shore base, or in war, if need be, it might have to be considered expendable. It must be borne in mind that the submarine had considerably increased the radius of action of the aircraft, by taking it unseen close to its objective.

M 3 was converted to an experimental minelayer. The submarine minelayers of the *K* and *L* classes could only carry a limited number of mines in chutes let into the main ballast tanks. This was not sufficiently effective, besides being clumsy and requiring special mines to fit into the chutes. In *M 3* a mine rail was fitted on top of the hull for two thirds of its length. The mines, of standard pattern, were laid by moving them along the rail until they reached the stern, when they were dropped. This could be done either with the submarine on the surface or submerged, and a much bigger casing than usual was built to cover the whole arrangement. This casing formed the best 'upper deck' of any submarine in any of the world's fleets, and inspired one commanding

officer of *M 3* who was a Scotsman, to arrange for the bagpipes to be played when entering or leaving harbour, there being sufficient space for a kilted sailor to march up and down! *M 3* could carry one hundred mines of standard pattern and was the forerunner of a class of large minelayer submarines.

It is sad to relate that both *M 1* and *M 2* came to disastrous ends. *M 1* was rammed by a merchantman when on diving patrol in the Channel, and *M 2* sank while carrying out the 'flying off' procedure. Happily *M 3* lived to a ripe old age and was scrapped in 1933. *M 4* was never completed.

The three converted *Ms* represented forethought well in advance of other countries and it was a pity that such achievements had to be 'written down' as they were deemed more useful to an enemy than to ourselves.

Although the big steam-driven *K* class had been unable to prove themselves in war, experience with them justified ordering five improved *Ks* in 1918. When the war ended all but one of this class, *K 26* was scrapped. *K 26* was building in Chatham Royal Dockyard and it was decided to complete her. The chief points of improvements over the earlier *Ks* were better sea-keeping qualities at high speeds on the surface, and better diving time and these were mainly achieved in this very large and fine submarine. Although *K 26* might have been considered a 'cruiser' submarine she was not designed for that purpose.

There were people who held the opinion that the 1915 Committee who thought a 'cruiser' submarine feasible but found there was no requirement for such a type in the British Navy at that time, should be tested in their views. Pressure was sufficiently strong to have a 'cruiser' design included in the 1921-2 Naval Estimates. The result was *X 1* the largest submarine in the world at the time of her completion in 1925. This submersible cruiser was 363 feet long, displaced over 3000 tons, had a maximum surface speed of 18½ knots from twin diesel engines, and could go half way round the world without refuelling. The principal features of her cruiser armament were four 5.2 inch guns in twin turrets. Many improvements resulting from war experience and from trials in the surrendered German submarines, were incorporated in this design. Moreover, opposition which had been greatly overcome when the vessel was placed in the estimates had increased by the time *X 1* went to sea and feeling was strong that like *M 1* she would be of more value to an enemy than to ourselves. As her engines gave a considerable amount of trouble, *X 1* spent most of her life in dockyard hands until she was placed in reserve in the late twenties. If it had not been for the adverse criticism she might have been given more attention and made some interesting voyages worthy of recording in this story. The submarine really had a lifetime of trouble because special provision had to be made for her in the London Treaty, which limited the size of submarines to 2000 tons. When in 1937 she was scrapped the tonnage was used to build several new smaller submarines within the main Treaty limits. All the same it is as well to remember that the British Navy built a cruiser submarine as long ago as the early twenties and proved to the world that it is practicable to dive a 3000 ton ship under water.

While these experiments with different types of submarines were in progress our politicians were taking a hand in their future. There were in the twenties a series of disarmament conferences and the Government of the day took each opportunity to press for the abolition of submarines. Such a step would have been very much to our advantage. As an island power dependent on overseas supplies, the one weapon at that time which might bring us to our knees if ruthlessly used by an enemy, was still the submarine. However, hope for such an agreement was very slight and never once was any real progress made towards this goal. The submarine is a cheap weapon as armaments go, yet it has a hitting power capable of destroying the biggest ships afloat. In these circumstances few countries would listen to arguments for its abolition.

To help in the design of the new submarines the Admiralty appointed an experienced submarine officer, Commander J F Hutchings, as 'Experimental Officer'. At the experimental station on an isolated spit of land in the northern part of Portsmouth harbour, scale model submarines ran trials submerged in a tank while being studied from above by means of a kind of bicycle in which the Experimental Officer sat, which ran on rails the length of the tank. Here submarines of any design could have model trials with the position of their hydroplanes altered, their rudders changed in size and shape, or their conning towers switched from one position to another.

Data of all kinds were produced which was useful, particularly coming from an expert who had himself commanded submarines in war, with distinction. Such work, going on unobtrusively while our flotillas were reduced to three operational commands, was invaluable when the time came to lay the foundations for expansion and standardization of designs for the next war. Meanwhile, the few submarines comprising the three operational flotillas of the 1920s were divided between the Home Fleet, the Mediterranean Fleet and the China Squadron.

About this time there came on the scene a device called the ASDIC. The asdic was a great advance on the hydrophone. Being more sensitive, supersonic and directional, it gave a strong punch to anti-submarine vessels, as an instrument by which surface hunting craft could use a 'searchlight' underwater. It also gave the submarines a method of talking to each other underwater without being heard, except by an asdic-fitted ship, and it gave to commanding officers an accurate method of assessing the tactics of hunting craft. The balance was therefore not all on the side of the anti-submarine craft. Nevertheless, here was something which was a very great potential danger to submarines. Such an invention which might prove to be decisive in a future submarine campaign against us, had to be developed. A special school was opened and submarines were soon co-operating in training anti-submarine officers and men, in asdics, while at the same time learning how best this invention could be put to their own purposes. The most important consideration was that no possible future enemy should discover the secret. The asdic was fitted in almost every ship other than battleships and aircraft carriers and its full secrets were remarkably

well kept until early in the Second World War.

The first of the fully post-war designs was the *O* class and the first boat the *Oberon*. As the Anglo-Japanese treaty had not been renewed, the possibility of war in the Pacific had to be considered. The *L* class were thought to be of too short endurance for operations in the Far East, so this new design was given an endurance of 6500 miles at 10 knots on the surface. The 200 tons of fuel necessary for this range was all carried in the external ballast tanks in the upper sections; this particular boat was never a success as the light plating leaked and the boats were constantly battling against leaving an oil trail. The actual pressure hull of these boats was greatly increased in strength to give protection from depth-charging and for deeper diving. The fact that only the lower half of the external ballast tanks was used to destroy the buoyancy of the vessel gave a quick initial diving time as the tanks flooded up very quickly. *Oberon* was the first British submarine to have more than one stern tube and she was also the first submarine to be fitted with asdic. Another of the various new ideas incorporated, were 40 foot periscopes which meant that the vessel could be deep enough at periscope depth to be safe from ramming by any but very large ships. Also the tranquility at that depth was certainly an advantage.

These boats ran into a veritable field of teething troubles until *Oberon* herself became almost a joke. All the same the boat lasted with credit until 1945 though she only spent a few months on operations at the very beginning of the Second World War.

In 1926 an improved *O* class was ordered, six boats in all being built. They had asdic domes fitted into their keels which could be raised and lowered. They were big boats, being 283 feet long and nearly 2000 tons displacement. Naturally, since designed for the Far East, they went to the China Station and served all their time there until recalled to the Mediterranean at the beginning of the Second World War where, in unaccustomed surroundings, they suffered heavy losses.

Next there followed the *P* and the *R* classes which were very slight improvements on the later *Os*. Also at this time it was decided to try a fast fleet submarine, using diesel engines as opposed to the earlier steam-driven *K* class. They were the *River* class submarines and were a success until the speed of battleships jumped to 30 knots. Only three of these submarines were built: *Thames, Severn* and *Clyde*. All these classes suffered from leaking external fuel tanks and it was realized that something different must be built. The whole problem of future design was thoroughly thrashed out in the light of the considerable experience now gathered during the previous ten years, and a very sound policy was arrived at which stood the test of war extremely well.

It was decided to build all future boats with their fuel tanks *inside* the pressure hull. It was also agreed that the time had come to standardize on two main types; a medium size patrol type for operations in the North Sea, and a larger type to replace all the *Os, Ps* and *Rs*.

The first of these types were the *S* class. They were 202 feet long, 735 tons surface displacement, with speed of 14 knots on the surface and 10 knots submerged. Their diving depth was 200 feet and everything was done to make the internal design simple. These boats were ordered in late 1929; they were a great success, did very well at the beginning of the war and were the forerunner of improved *S* classes which again were all good boats, and operated throughout the war.

The larger boats to replace the *Os, Ps* and *Rs* were the *T* class, 269 feet long, 1300 tons surface displacement with speeds of 16 1/2 knots on the surface and 8 3/4 knots submerged. Their diving depth was 300 feet. Even greater efforts were made with this class to keep them simple, not to expect too much from the engines and above all to concentrate on reliability. Both the engines and the electrical gear of the *Os, Ps* and *Rs* needed simplifying and drastic measures were taken. At the same time a really heavy armament was provided of ten torpedo tubes; this was the most powerful salvo mounted by any submarine, British or foreign. Two factors prompted this action. Firstly it was considered that improved anti-submarine tactics and instruments would entail a submarine firing at longer ranges than hitherto and therefore a bigger salvo seemed advisable, and secondly, battleship construction in foreign countries pointed to the need for obtaining six or eight hits to sink any modern very heavy warship. A salvo of ten torpedoes should give a fair chance to the submarines. These boats like the *S* class, were an immense success and proved as reliable as any one could hope. They served in the Second World War in every part of the globe with distinction and a few were still in commission in the 1950s.

At first it was intended to equip some of the *Ts* with minelaying gear but this was scrapped to ensure simplicity and give room for the large salvo of torpedoes.

About this time much attention was paid to harbour defence against submarines. At the end of the First World War the best device that had been tried was a form of electrical loop. This worked on the principle that when a submarine passed over it the needle of a galvanometer moved in a control hut ashore and this movement was also shown on a screen. When the light on the screen was moved a maximum, the submarine was immediately over the loop. The position along the loop was also indicated and the operator had merely to press a button and explode those mines nearest the submarine. Improved loops were the subject of tests in which submarines took part and it was decided there were ample grounds for the retention of this form of defence. Following this investigation, anti-submarine nets came under review. If the loops were evaded, could a modern net stop a submarine of the latest type? Extensive trials were undertaken to arrive at a true answer. Not only the Admiralty, but private firms had devised various types of nets and it was decided to test all those which appeared to give a reasonable chance of success. The trials were arranged under the general direction of the Boom Defence Organization at Rosyth and one of our most modern and efficient submarines, at that

time *Regulus*, was selected.

After careful consideration and some practical tests, two nets were finally chosen for 'live' trials. One of these was the Admiralty design. A half mile of these nets were laid across part of the Firth of Forth. They were hung with weights to simulate mines and the surface buoyage was fitted with rockets and flares to give the alarm when the submarine struck. The nets were not anchored to the sea bed so that there would be plenty of 'give' when the submarine struck.

The boat was fitted with special net cutters and with hardened steel edges to all projecting parts. Guards were arranged around the propellers and the hydroplanes and the hull was streamlined in every way possible. In the presence of Rear-Admiral Submarines (at that time Admiral Nasmith who had successfully negotiated countless nets during the Dardanelles campaign) and members of the Board of Admiralty, the submarine submerged to 100 feet and attacked a double line of nets at full speed. The boat shot through the first net with little difficulty but in doing so had lost some speed. This was a vital factor and when the bows struck the second net it held. Being over two miles long and freely suspended the net was carried forward by the submarine until it took up the shape of a V. Inside the boat the motors were kept at full speed in an endeavour to force a way through, and tanks were flooded and blown liberally to apply the pressure at various points in the net. At one time the submarine's bows were below 100 feet and at another they were very near the surface. However, the net remained unbroken and when the submarine had carried it forward to the limit of its yield, and the speed of the propellers had dropped through loss of battery power, both the net and the submarine in it began to move back to the original position of first impact. Not only this, the tide had by now begun to make, with the result that the stern of the boat was swung round and while still running at full speed one propeller struck the net. There was a brilliant flash in the motor room as the fuses blew and now the submarine was held fast at 60 feet depth by over thirty turns of net wire round the propeller shaft. After consulting with the surface ships by asdic it was decided to surface the submarine in the net. This was successfully carried out in spite of the whole boat being wrapped in the heavy net and one large buoy actually wedged in the bridge. Experts immediately came on board and cut away part of the net but it was impossible to remove it all. Accordingly, tugs and trawlers took both net and submarine in tow back to Rosyth Dockyard, an operation which could only be done at a speed of 3 knots. Eventually, by using the floating dock, the submarine was brought clear of the water and oxyacetylene cutters freed the propeller shaft. Fortunately not much damage had been done to the submarine, while our boom defence experts received really useful data which could be quickly applied in the event of war.

Also towards the late twenties there appeared in submarines an invention which at first caused some controversy. This was the Davis Submerged Escape Apparatus. The invention of Sir Robert Davis, head of the firm of Siebe, Gorman

and Company Limited, the apparatus provided an adjunct to escaping from a sunken submarine. By this device it was believed possible that men might escape up to a depth of 300 feet dependent on the pressure which each individual person's body could stand. It was felt that escapes up to half that depth could be made by almost all fit men without much difficulty. As a whole chapter in this book is devoted to escape and salvage a detailed description of the apparatus will not be given here. All that need be said is that there was insufficient knowledge in the late twenties about the effects of breathing oxygen under pressure.

The impact of this new apparatus influenced submarine design immediately, and had a great bearing on submarine thought. In future designs, space was surrendered to provide two strengthened chambers with escape hatches over them, one between the foremost living compartment and the torpedo stowage compartment, and the other between the engine-room and the after living compartment. Lockers were also provided for 'sets' of the apparatus, throughout the boat, in spaces where men were most likely to be at the time of emergency. While recognizing the value of those arrangements in saving life, there was criticism. People said that submarines could ill afford to sacrifice valuable space for a safety arrangement, that two more hatches piercing the pressure hull would tend to weaken the boat, and some went so far as to say that the fighting efficiency might be impaired. High policy prescribed, however, that space must be provided, and the necessary hatches were fitted. At the same time, with all this thought for the safety of the crew, time has shown that in every disaster they do their job without thought for their personal safety until the time arises for escaping.

Returning to the development of submarine construction the *Narwhal* class of large submarine minelayer was built to carry ordinary mines. The first of this class was ordered in 1933 and orders were repeated up to 1936. There were five in all, only one surviving the war, but all did good work and functioned perfectly well in the role for which they were intended. In addition they did splendid cargo carrying work, particularly to Malta in the days of the siege. As soon as a means was found of laying mines with a specially designed mine through a submarine's torpedo tube, there was no longer a requirement for the *Narwhal* type of minelayer. All submarines thereafter, when required, were able to lay their mines through their torpedo tubes.

Three years before the Second World War a proposal was made to build small unarmed submarines for training surface ships in anti-submarine work. This idea resulted in the *U* class, which were begun in 1936 but owing to international developments during their construction they were armed and became operational submarines. These boats were 191 feet long and 630 tons surface displacement with speeds of 12 knots on the surface and 8 1/2 submerged. Somehow the constructors managed to squeeze four internal torpedo tubes into the design and two external, giving six in all. These submarines were very handy and came in most useful at the beginning of the war before the main

construction got under way.

Thus we had in 1939 some very sound and satisfactory submarines in the Fleet. In fact, in design, we could hardly have been better equipped. By 1939 we were well into construction with improved *Ts* and *Us* and we had designs for improved *Ss* which could be put in hand at once. Vickers built most of the *Us* and *Ts* while Cammel Lairds concentrated chiefly on the *S* class. Scotts and the Royal Dockyards all took a helping hand and with such satisfactory and simple classes, expansion in war was made easy and rapid.

Chapter five
Submarines in the Second World War 1939–1945

SUMMER 1939 TO DECEMBER 1939

Following the 1938 crisis, the situation in the Fleet in the summer of 1939 was one of great activity. By the Reserve and Auxiliary Act 1938, large numbers of officers and men were called up progressively from 15 June. By the end of July the Reserve Fleet was fully manned and proceeded for exercises, culminating on 8 August with an inspection in Weymouth Bay by HM The King. The Submarine Branch in conjunction with all other naval forces, was able to man all submarines that were fit for operational work in war. Many of these went to sea for two or three days' practice patrol to accustom the crews to long periods of diving and give a thorough test to the older boats. By the middle of August, Rear-Admiral B C Watson, commanding the submarines, had moved the Home Fleet operational boats to their war stations. The large modern depot ship *Forth*, together with the Second Submarine Flotilla, consisting of eight *S* class, three *T* class, also the *Thames, Oberon* and *Oxley,* went to Dundee, while the old depot ship *Titania* proceeded to Blyth and berthed alongside the same jetty which she had occupied in the closing stages of the First World War. She had with her the Sixth Flotilla made up of three *Us,* three *Ls* and one *H* boat. In all, there were only twenty-one operational submarines available in home waters and five of these were over ten years old. The Fifth Submarine Flotilla, made up of eight *H* class, remained at Portsmouth for training. The other four flotillas were all on foreign stations and a number of adjustments were made which are recorded later. So far as the Home Station was concerned it was decided to create another flotilla, to be known as the Third Flotilla, by bringing home the four *S* class from Malta and basing them on Harwich with the old depot ship *Cyclops.* Further, the minelayer *Narwhal* happened to be off station at home and was retained, while two more minelayers, the *Cachalot* and *Porpoise,* then in the Mediterranean, were ordered to return to the UK.

Meanwhile, the international situation was rapidly deteriorating. On 23 August Germany signed a non-aggression pact with Russia and by 28 August Great Britain felt bound to reaffirm her pledge to Poland. On this latter event the submarines prepared for patrol, and at 4.0 pm on 31 August sailed for pre-arranged positions in the Heligoland Bight and off the south-west coast of Norway. The reason why some submarines were placed on a patrol line off the south-west coast of Norway was to augment Coastal Command's air patrol line Aberdeen-Obrestadt.

At 11.0 am on 3 September the submarines at sea received the signal: 'Com-

mence hostilities with Germany forthwith.' Thus this branch of the Navy once again was first on the job and this time right against the enemy's coast the minute war began.

Four minutes after 11.0 am *Spearfish,* Lieutenant J H Eaden, was attacked by a German submarine but fortunately the torpedo missed. Thus the submarines were also the first warships to make contact with the enemy. On 10 September the first British casualty occurred when, through the hazards of war, on a dark night and with a heavy sea running, one of our own submarines torpedoed the submarine *Oxley,* only the commanding officer and one rating surviving.

The problems facing the submarines at the beginning of the war were very similar to those of the First World War. Germany possessed a fair sized surface fleet of which the most powerful unit was the *Bismarck,* a battleship said to be built within the 1935 Naval Treaty limits of 35 000 tons, but actually far heavier and superior in fire-power and armament to any ship in the British Navy. Her sister ship the *Tirpitz* was still completing. Two battlecruisers, the *Gneisenau* and *Scharnhorst,* three pocket battleships, and five heavy cruisers made up the main fleet. The most important of the lighter units were five 6000 ton cruisers. All these ships might at any time appear singly or together in the Heligoland Bight or Skaggerak and the larger ones might attempt a breakout into the Atlantic to augment the work of their U-boats which began unrestricted submarine warfare from the outset.

At this time we were able to keep a battle fleet in northern waters capable of dealing with a full scale enemy sortie, but the balance of power was too close for comfort and thereby offered a great opportunity to any submarine commanding officer who, with one blow, could alter this considerably in our favour.

German submarines leaving their home ports for the Atlantic offered most important targets, and there was always the anxiety of an attempt by the enemy to interfere with the passage of the Expeditionary Force to France, warning of which might be provided by the submarines.

Behind the higher direction of the submarines there stood Winston Churchill, once more back at the Admiralty, as First Lord, exercising his energy and knowledge to the great benefit of the Navy.

As in the First World War one of the immediate matters requiring attention was an Emergency Building Programme. By the 1937 estimates seven *T* class were due to complete in 1939 and four in 1940. By the 1938 estimates there were only three *T* class, two due to complete in 1940 and one in 1941. In addition, *Thetis* had been raised and renamed *Thunderbolt.* This number was nothing like enough for a major war and the day after hostilities began action was taken to build up the submarine fleet. Seven *T* class and twelve *U* class were ordered at once and arrangements were made to augment this programme early in 1940.

The events of the next six months were many and varied, and in nearly all, British submarines played their part. It is inevitable in a broad survey of this

nature that details are omitted which might appear important in the eyes of some people. This story must be balanced to give the correct influence of submarines on each major event and so while individual stories of adventure and heroism cannot be given as fully as their accomplishment merits, it must be remembered that underlying the whole picture, the most stirring individual tales were being unfolded through the work of these small but immensely powerful underwater weapons.

Operating so close to the enemy's shores, while having the advantage of offensive action, could on rare occasions also be a liability, since a submarine might get into difficulties. This was soon instanced on 26 September when the *Spearfish,* Lieutenant J H Eaden, reported she was damaged by depth charging. After she had managed to evade her attackers and make the signal reporting her distress she had to be escorted home. Such an operation involved the two cruisers *Aurora* and *Sheffield* proceeding well into the approaches of the Skaggerak, two battleships, the *Nelson* and *Rodney,* two battlecruisers, *Hood* and *Repulse* with air cover provided from the *Ark Royal,* all steaming towards the Norwegian coast to cover the cruisers—in fact a major fleet operation. In the event *Spearfish* was brought safely home but not before the heavy ships had been attacked by enemy aircraft 150 miles off the Norwegian coast.

By the middle of October it became apparent that neither Blyth nor Dundee were likely to have sufficient anti-aircraft defences in reasonable time to warrant their continuance as submarine bases. Accordingly both the Second and Sixth Flotillas were ordered to Rosyth and HMS *Forth* left Dundee on 14 October to act as the principal depot ship to the whole concentration. On the afternoon of 16 October the German Air Force raided the Firth of Forth. Happily no damage was done to the submarines, which were alongside in the dockyard itself. It was said that the pilots in the initial raid had been told not to bomb the dockyard so as to avoid killing civilians. This has subsequently been confirmed from captured documents.

At the same time Harwich, which played such a great part as a base in the First World War, had by now come into its own with the *S* class back from the Mediterranean based there with the depot ship *Cyclops* forming the Third Submarine Flotilla

While many people, particularly in inland districts, were saying they hardly knew there was a war on, submarine patrols continued under most trying conditions. The autumn of 1939 came in with a strong wind and wild weather continuing well beyond Christmas. The submarines saw few targets to relieve the battle with heavy seas and long periods of intense boredom, but all submarines saw plenty of mines which had come adrift from their moorings in the appalling weather. The Germans had declared a large area of the North Sea in which they announced it was their intention to lay mines. Submarine patrols in the early days were mostly to the eastward or German side of this area. The lack of action was most trying to the submarine crews operating under the strain of winter conditions and in mined areas. Any event helped

Plate 4

M 1, showing the 12″ gun

K 26 our largest steam driven submarine

Plate 5

M 2 flying off aircraft

X 1 entering Malta. The largest British conventional submarine ever built

to brighten the outlook. One such event was the arrival of two Polish submarines, the *Wilk* and the *Orzel.* The escape of the *Orzel* from the Baltic was one of the great stories of that time. She was at Gdynia when the Germans attacked Poland and left on 1 September to cruise in the Baltic. On 16 September she put into Tallin, Estonia, to land her sick captain. The Estonian authorities made the surprising decision to intern her and removed her charts and the breech blocks of her guns. However, after overpowering the Estonian guards at night, she got away, cruised in the Baltic and later passed through the Sound between Sweden and Denmark, thence through the Kattegat and Skaggerak into the North Sea, she navigated without charts and was hunted continuously by German sea and air patrols. On 14 October she managed to get through a faint wireless message to a British station giving her estimated position, and not many hours later she was escorted into Rosyth by a British destroyer. A few days earlier the Polish submarine *Wilk* had come to Rosyth having broken out of the Baltic without trouble, and there began the Allied Flotilla under British command which continued until the end of the war. Another event which was quite heartening was the torpedoing on 20 November of a German anti-submarine trawler in the Skaggerak, by *Sturgeon,* Lieutenant D G A Gregory. This was in fact the first British submarine success of the war.

Meanwhile the first of Hitler's secret weapons, the magnetic mine dropped from aircraft, had made its appearance in the Thames Estuary and Lieutenant-Commander Ouvry had carried out the coolest act of bravery so far in the war, when he waded through the mud and removed the detonators, thereby allowing the secrets of the mine to be studied and the antidote worked out. The Submarine Branch will always remain indebted to Ouvry for this brilliant action. The passage of submarines to their patrol areas and their return journey could only be made safe or reasonably so without hazard, through such men as Ouvry who could place in the hands of the minesweepers the knowledge required to free the channels of danger.

On 4 December, a U-boat now known to be *U 36* was sunk off the approaches to the Skaggerak by *Salmon,* Lieutenant-Commander E O Bickford, and on 13 December *Salmon* attacked a German squadron 130 miles west of Jutland. Bickford in his report said that on 4 December he first sighted what he thought was a box but as it did not move with the waves he took a shot. It was a long one and matters did not go very well after firing, as one torpedo broke surface and the submarine lost trim temporarily. However, Bickford was able to regain normal trim in time to see a U-boat 'Blown to small fragments which rose at least 200 feet into the air'. It was a week later when the Officer of the Watch reported a Heinkel 70 just after dawn. *Salmon* dived and Bickford was at once suspicious that something special was happening. He was right, as not long afterwards the liner *Bremen* was seen crossing astern at a range of 2000 yards. Bickford looked for offensive armament in the liner but seeing none surfaced and made the international signal to stop. His intentions were to fire torpedoes

if the *Bremen* opened fire on him or to use the gun if she refused to stop but did not open fire. Before any action could be taken, however, a Dornier 18 appeared and *Salmon* had to dive. The next time Bickford was able to have a look, *Bremen* was too far off for anything to be done. It was shortly after those exciting moments and ones during which the commanding officer had to act entirely on his own initiative, that Bickford intercepted a signal to *Ursula* telling her that *Bremen* was not a target. In the absence of other instructions Bickford had held rigidly to international law.

The very next day at 9.45 am *Salmon* sighted a squadron of five destroyers supported by three light cruisers *Nürnberg, Leipzig* and *Köln.* The destroyers had been on a minelaying operation with the object of closing the entrance to the war channel off Newcastle, and the cruisers had been sent out to cover their return. At first both the cruisers and destroyers were too far off to allow an attack to be developed but at 10.30 am the cruisers turned nearer to *Salmon.* Bickford fired a salvo at long range from which *Nürnberg* and *Leipzig* were each struck by one torpedo. At that distance Bickford believed that the destroyers he had sighted were larger ships including battle-cruisers, pocket battleships and 8 inch cruisers. This was not so, however, as at that time, it has since been established, the battlecruisers *Gneisnau* and *Scharnhorst,* the pocket battleship *Deutschland* and the 8 inch cruiser *Hipper* were all in dockyard hands, and the pocket battleship *Admiral Scheer* and the 8 inch cruiser *Blücher* were both undergoing trials in the Baltic, while the pocket battleship *Graf Spee* was that day in action with our cruisers off the River Plate.

Following this, on 14 December, *Ursula,* Lieutenant-Commander G C Phillips, attacked the damaged cruiser *Nürnberg* in the Heligoland Bight, while she was being escorted into harbour by numerous small craft. The torpedoes from *Ursula* missed the cruiser, but two escorts, a torpedo boat, *F 9,* and a gunboat were sunk.

This was the submarine contribution to the Christmas fare of news for England. Winston Churchill personally broadcast the news and both officers were promoted to the rank of Commander and each awarded the DSO.

These successes were more than timely as the *Rawlpindi,* an armed merchant cruiser had been sunk by the German battlecruisers in the Denmark Strait on 13 November. People wondered how two big battlecruisers could evade our submarine patrols in the Heligoland Bight and Skaggerak. These sorties by German warships were undetected due to the small number of British submarines on patrol and the scarcity of long-range aircraft in Coastal Command.

1940 HOME STATION

At this time it was decided to bring Vice-Admiral Sir Max K Horton back to the kind of work in which he had excelled in the First World War, and he assumed command of the submarines on 9 January 1940. Rear-Admiral Watson handed over a rapidly expanding submarine force which had gained in

experience and confidence, and in the previous month had had important successes against the enemy. With the arrival of Admiral Horton who had won fame in 1915 by his Baltic campaign, it was natural that minds were concentrated on the possibility of having a British submarine flotilla once again in the Baltic. Plans to carry out such an operation were drawn up but after consultation with the Polish officers who had recently brought their submarines out of the Baltic, it was decided not to proceed with the idea. This is only mentioned as many people have since asked whether Admiral Horton had considered a return to the Baltic feasible in the Second World War.

Unfortunately, concurrently with Admiral Horton taking over command, the Submarine Service suffered a severe loss when three boats, *Seahorse*, Lieutenant Massy Dawson, *Undine*, Lieutenant-Commander Jackson and *Starfish*, Lieutenant Turner, failed to arrive at Blyth on 10, 11, and 12 January respectively. We now know how these boats were lost: it was through attacks by increased numbers of German anti-submarine vessels patrolling east of the German declared minefield area. *Undine* scuttled on 6 January after a depth charge attack by German minesweeping trawlers. *Seahorse* was sunk by depth charges from the German First Minesweeping Flotilla and *Starfish* scuttled after a depth charge attack from the German minesweeper *M 7*. They were the first British submarines to be sunk by enemy action in the war. Shortly afterwards the patrols were withdrawn to the approaches to the Bight in the same way as in the 1914 war, it being considered that anti-submarine measures in the Bight itself were too hazardous.

Despite these losses, the Submarine Branch was finding its feet. The whole setting in the flotillas had taken on firmness and confidence. In some ways, at the beginning there had been a tendency to overestimate the enemy, patrolling was very much a matter of going into the unknown. Now much had been learnt. Of these lessons, the effect of the air had been most marked. While in the First World War submarines had been able to move on the surface in daylight without undue anxiety, commanding officers now kept their boats submerged on passage during daylight because of enemy aircraft. This considerably slowed up the timetable. It meant that a boat which might reasonably be at sea for three weeks took the best part of a week of that on passage. Nevertheless it was a most necessary precaution, as any submarine on the surface in the North Sea and approaches to the Skaggerak in daylight was sure to be attacked by aircraft before long. Also another change of considerable moment to the Submarine Branch had taken place. Admiral Horton had called for a review of the ages of the commanding officers and formed the opinion they were much too high in many cases. With every indication that this war would be longer and certainly more strenuous than the First World War, he relieved many of the senior commanding officers and replaced them by much younger men. Some experience may have been lost in this way but serving in submarines in war is essentially a younger man's game.

In the early days of the war our submarines had to face many problems involv-

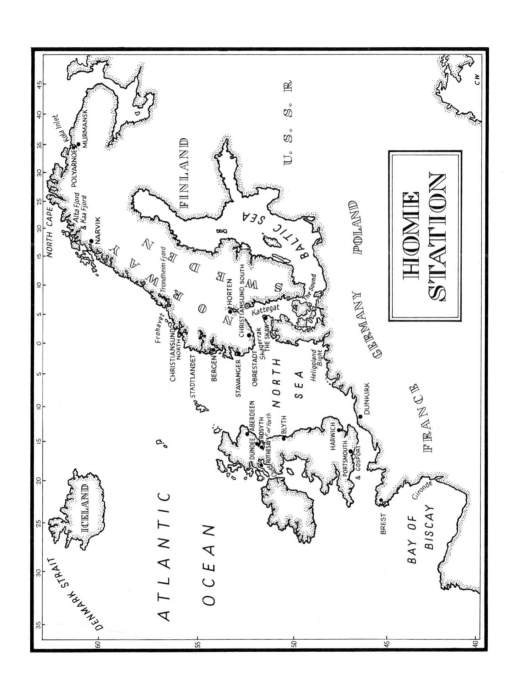

HOME STATION

ing international law. At this time the iron-ore trade from Scandinavian countries to Germany was still running and often merchant ships showing neutral flags were in fact under German control. A submarine is a difficult type of ship from which to visit and search a neutral for contraband. Nevertheless one night in the Kattegat, *Ursula*, Commander G C Phillips, stopped the Norwegian SS *Oscar Jarl* and after an exchange of messages released her. Shortly afterwards he intercepted the *SS Heddernheim*, eight miles east of the Skaw; the ship was known to be in the iron-ore trade. This ship tried to escape by giving her nationality as Esthonian and employing delaying tactics. However, a shot over her funnel soon produced the required result and the crew abandoned ship into their boats. As soon as Phillips was sure that the men were safe in their boats, the weather being dead calm, he torpedoed and sank the merchant vessel. Calling one of the boats alongside he found the members to be German. They told him that the captain of the merchant vessel had shot himself. Phillips singled out the senior officer in the boat and took him prisoner. This officer said that the *Heddernheim* was in fact carrying 7000 tons of iron-ore. Shortly after *Ursula* had moved off, an unknown ship, burning searchlights, approached the lifeboats and picked up the crew. There were other somewhat similar occasions when our submarines investigated ships suspected of being concerned in the iron-ore trade.

A second interesting incident was when *Triad*, Lieutenant-Commander Jonas, who had put into Norwegian waters to repair damaged hydroplanes, remained at Stavangar for 48 hours. Neutral States may forbid the entry of belligerent warships altogether, as did Sweden, Norway and Denmark in the Russo-Japanese War. The Hague Convention lays down that belligerent vessels, if permitted entry, must leave within 24 hours unless they obtain permission to stay longer for provisioning or repairs. In this case Norway gave every facility to *Triad*.

One of the most difficult problems which had emerged from the war so far, was the arrangement to prevent our own aircraft bombing our own submarines. One submarine looks very like any other from the air and because of the speed of modern aircraft coupled with the very short time a submarine takes to dive, neither dared wait to establish recognition. Lieutenant Gregory in *Sturgeon* when making his arrival signal on returning from one of the early war patrols said: 'Expect to arrive 2300 if friendly aircraft stop bombing me.' Lanes had already been instituted in which the submarines were not permitted to be bombed. These lanes were adjusted every twelve hours or so as the submarine concerned moved position on passage. When there were large numbers of submarines on passage the arrangements were most complicated and necessitated considerable signal traffic. Experience showed that aerial navigation in wintry conditions meant that pilots often did not know where they were to within at least twenty miles. Thus, the width of these 'bombing restriction lanes' had to be as much as twenty miles or more. Even then mistakes were made, nearly always unavoidable but everything was done to eliminate them

as far as possible. The worst aspect was the possibility of a U-boat unknow-ingly sailing in a restricted area and thereby obtaining immunity from air at-tack, but this condition had to be accepted.

On 23 March by arrangement between our two governments, the French depot ship *Jules Verne* and eight French submarines joined the Harwich submarine force and a further five including the minelayer *Rubis* went to Dundee, this port now being better prepared for defence against air attack. There were two types of French boats; the large 1500 ton boats went north to operate in the fairly open waters while the 600 ton boats which were very comparable to our own *S* class submarines now operating in the more confined waters of the southern North Sea, were more suitable, therefore, to join forces at Harwich. It is interesting to note that the ages of the French crews, and particularly of their commanding officers were widely divergent. There were some quite young men while others were over forty. A British Commander, R M Gambier, was appointed Liaison Officer to the French Flotillas and each submarine carried a British lieutenant, a signalman and a telegraphist. While with us at this time the French flotilla lost one submarine, *Doris*, in a patrol position west of the German declared minefield.

By early spring, the war was really beginning to make itself known to many who had not yet felt its clutches severely even among neutrals. *Unity*, Lieuten-ant J F B Brown, on her way to the Heligoland Bight on 28 March came across, and took on board, eight Dutch seamen of the trawler *Protinus*. They had been over a week in an open boat since their ship had been sunk by a German night bomber on 18 March.

Towards the end of March, Admiral Horton made a full appreciation of the situation with particular regard to a possible invasion of Norway and Sweden by the enemy. The three main questions were: 'When would Hitler attack?' 'Would both countries be invaded?' 'Would he use the ports or the beaches?' As no submarines had been passed through to the Baltic there was nothing the Submarine Branch could do if Sweden was invaded, so all thought was concentrated on the Norwegian aspect. It was decided to cover the exits from the Kattegat and the Heligoland Bight, east of the German declared mining area, together with selected points on the Norwegian coast itself, including the entrances to Oslo and Christiansund South. Admiral Horton sailed every available submarine in the first week in April to augment those already in the area and this brilliant appreciation meant that nineteen submarines were ready to meet the threat. Since the submarines could not stay at sea indefinitely, had this appreciation been wrong in the timing, it might well have happened that there would have been more submarines on passage home instead of taking up patrol positions on the day of the invasion.

From 8.45 am on 7 April reports began to come in of enemy movements and at 12.59 pm the Admiralty sent the following signal: 'Recent reports suggest a German expedition is being prepared. Hitler is reported from Copenhagen to have ordered unostentatious movement of one division in ten ships by night

to land at Narvik, with simultaneous occupation of Jutland. Sweden to be left alone. Date given for arrival at Narvik 8 April. All these reports are of doubtful value and may well be only a further move in the *war of nerves.*' Whatever happened Admiral Horton had committed his entire force to patrol and was convinced that he was right.

First news came when at 7.59 am on 8 April the destroyer *Glowworm,* which had become detached from the screen of the battlecruiser *Renown* at sea off the coast of Norway, slightly north of Trondheim fjord, sighted two enemy destroyers and engaged one of them. Surface ship dispositions were made to intercept these enemy ships and others reported during the day, but no contacts were made except by the submarines in the Skaggerak. The excitement was started by the Polish submarine *Orzel* which at twelve noon sank the transport *Rio de Janeiro* off Christiansund South, full of troops. An hour later *Trident,* Lieutenant-Commander A G L Seale, off the Skaw sank the tanker *Poseidonia.* With nineteen submarines perfectly positioned it was clear that if full scale invasion took place they would take a heavy toll of the enemy. Accordingly when at 5.0 am on 9 April German troops invaded Denmark and Norway a steady flow of reports began to come in. From the submarine point of view it was vital at this moment to ensure that commanding officers knew they were free to sink at sight every enemy ship of any type which passed their way. Flag Officer Submarines, represented this matter most urgently to the Admiralty. Naturally, the question was a difficult one and some agonising hours passed while consultations took place. Cabinet approval to sink transports at sight was given at 1.24 pm on 9 April and at 7.56 pm on 11 April permission was given to sink any ship on sight within ten miles of the Norwegian coast.

These were magnificent days in the story of British submarines. So often and for so long denied any targets, here at last was an opportunity to show their worth. Nothing like this had been seen in the First World War and the commanding officers went to work to make submarine history. The names of the submarines which were first on the spot due to Admiral Horton's foresight, are surely worth recording. They were: *Clyde,* Lieutenant-Commander R L S Gaisford; *Sealion,* Lieutenant-Commander B Bryant; *Seawolf,* Lieutenant-Commander J W Studholme; *Shark,* Lieutenant P N Buckley; *Severn,* Lieutenant-Commander B W Taylor, *Snapper,* Lieutenant W D A King; *Spearfish,* Lieutenant-Commander J H Forbes; *Sunfish,* Lieutenant-Commander J E Slaughter; *Triad,* Commander E R J Oddie; *Truant,* Lieutenant-Commander C H Hutchinson; *Triton,* Lieutenant-Commander E F Pizey; *Unity,* Lieutenant J F B Brown; *Thistle,* Lieutenant-Commander W F Haselfoot; *Ursula,* Lieutenant-Commander W A Cavaye; *Tarpon,* Lieutenant-Commander H J Caldwell; *Sterlet,* Lieutenant G H S Haward; *Trident,* Lieutenant-Commander A G L Seale; and the Polish *Orzel.* Later they were joined by *Tetrach,* Lieutenant-Commander R G Mills, and *Swordfish,* Lieutenant P J Cowell.

The waters in the Kattegat and along the extended coast of Norway at many

points offered splendid opportunities for minelaying. There were three British minelaying submarines available, *Porpoise,* Commander P Q Roberts; *Narwhal,* Lieutenant-Commander R J Burch; *Seal,* Lieutenant-Commander R P Lonsdale, and the French submarine *Rubis;* all these were early at work and achieved successes. *Porpoise* in addition to minelaying, sank the German submarine *U1.*

In the spring the conditions of light in the southern Skaggerak leave little time for a submarine to come to the surface and charge its batteries at night. Also much of this water is shallow and there are times when there is a stillness on the face of the water which is all against the submarine commanding officer as he hardly dares to raise his periscope. Many submarines had narrow escapes. *Swordfish,* Lieutenant P J Cowell, was hunted by anti-submarine craft from dawn till dusk on 20 April, and *Tetrarch,* Lieutenant-Commander R G Mills, had to endure depth charge attack continuously from 6.45 pm on 23 April to 8.0 am on the 24 and it was not until 9.30 pm on the 24 that he was able to surface after being submerged for 43 hours from his original dive in the early hours of the 23. The experiences in *Tetrarch* were very similar to those of other boats but the long hours which *Tetrarch* had to endure were exceptional. Owing to the varying density of the water the submarine sometimes lost trim through no fault of her own. Constant depth charging and bombing caused leaks and stiffness in the glands through which the shafting passed, the hydroplanes had to be worked by hand involving considerable physical effort in conditions almost of desperation; sometimes the submarine took on the most alarming angles, water sloshed in the bilges and leaks in the stern necessitated forming bucket chains to pass the water forward to maintain the balance of the boat. Oxygen was resorted to in order to help keep the men going. Most of the crew had violent headaches, many of them were physically sick, no one was ever hungry; not a soul ate anything for thirty hours, until finally, when the submarine reached the surface free of her attackers and fresh air was admitted to the boat, two-thirds of the crew became physically drunk on the freshness of the atmosphere.

By now British landings had taken place in the Narvik area and at Namsos and Andalsnes, but by 29 April the first evacuations had already begun. Our submarines made heroic efforts to stem the tide of German reinforcements but conditions in the southern end of the Skaggerak forced a withdrawal from that area and increasing numbers of anti-submarine craft coupled with the long hours of light made their task well nigh impossible, so that at one time, in spite of the immense damage inflicted by our submarines, enemy troop reinforcements were arriving at Trondheim at the rate of 5000 a week.

During the course of the early days signals were made telling the submarines of the great part they were playing, amongst which was one on 11 April from the Admiralty which read: 'You are all doing magnificent work'. That this was so is shown in the following table of known sinkings during the Norwegian invasion, 1940:

Tonnage sunk by Submarines

	Date	Name of Ship	Tonnage	Sunk by
APRIL	8	*Rio de Janeiro*	5 261	*Orzel*
		Poseidonia	8 100	*Trident*
	9	*Karlsruhe* (cruiser)	6 000	*Truant*
		Amasis	7 129	*Sunfish*
	10	*Friedenau*	5 219	*Triton*
		Wighert	3 648	*Triton*
		Rau. 6	354	*Triton*
		Antares	2 593	*Sunfish*
	11	*August: Leonhardt*	2 590	*Sealion*
		Ionia	3 102	*Triad*
	12	*Moonsund*	321	*Snapper*
	13		3 000	*Sunfish*
	14	*Florida*	6 148	*Sunfish*
		C. Jancen	472	*Snapper*
		Behrens	525	*Snapper*
	15	*Brummer* (gunnery training ship)	2 400	*Sterlet*
	16	*U1* (submarine)	250	*Porpoise*
	18	*Hamm*	5 874	*Seawolf*
MAY	1	*Buenos Aires*	6 097	*Narwhal*
	2	*Clare H. Stinnes*	5 000	*Trident*
	4	*Monark*	1 786	*Severn*

75 869

Tonnage sunk by Mines laid by British and Allied Submarines

	Date	Name of Ship	Tonnage	Sunk by
APRIL	13	*Deutschland* (M/S trawler)	432	*Narwhal*
		M.1701 (M/S trawler)	250	*Narwhal*
		M.1702 (M/S trawler)	218	*Narwhal*
	30	Four trawlers	1 200	*Narwhal*
MAY	4	*Vogesen*	4 240	*Seal*
		Aimy	200	*Seal*
		Skandia	1 248	*Seal*
	10	*Kem*	1 706	*F.S. Rubis*
	27	*Kyvig*	763	*F.S. Rubis*

10 257

86 126

Altogether it is fair to say that close on 100 000 tons of enemy shipping had been sunk and with it at least one division of troops. One cruiser, the *Karlsruhe,* had been sunk by *Truant,* Lieutenant-Commander Hutchinson, and the pocket battleship, *Lutzow,* (Ex-*Deutschland,* renamed 24 January 1940), damaged by *Spearfish,* Lieutenant-Commander Forbes. Nevertheless the story of the Norwegian campaign might have been crowned with far greater success had there not been four circumstances which deprived the submarines of the cream of the targets. Firstly, Lieutenant-Commander Bryant, in *Sealion,* had to withdraw slightly to seaward from a close inshore patrol to charge his batteries, and during this time one of the main invading forces passed through his patrol position. Secondly, Pizey, in *Triton,* had cruel luck when, just as he had fired a full salvo at a battlecruiser, the target increased speed by 10 knots. Thirdly, the enemy force which subsequently went to Narvik spent a night in dense fog close to three of our submarines which in those early days had no radar and could not develop an attack. Fourthly, it had been Admiral Horton's intention to place a submarine off 'Horten' at the entrance to Oslo fjord, but in the event, international considerations prevented his wish being fulfilled and the enemy force which entered Oslo escaped!

This hectic month did not go by without losses on the British side. Three submarines were sunk and one was captured. On 10 April the German submarine *U 4* torpedoed and sank *Thistle,* Lieutenant-Commander W F Haselfoot, when south-west of Stavangar. On the 14, *Tarpon,* Lieutenant-Commander H J Caldwell, was sunk in the approaches to the Skaggerak by the German minesweeper *M6,* and *Sterlet,* Lieutenant-Commander G H S Haward, was destroyed by three enemy corvettes, *UV 126, UV 125* and *UV 128* on 18 April in the difficult submarine area north-east of the Skaw. *Seal,* Lieutenant-Commander Lonsdale, was captured in the Kattegat after receiving damage by mine and aircraft. This event greatly shocked the Navy and particularly the Submarine Branch *at the time,* and some account of the circumstances is necessary.

The problem set to *Seal* was to lay mines in the Kattegat on the probable route of enemy transports proceeding from Germany to Norway. While dived and laying her minefield, there was an explosion outboard of the submarine and a compartment at the after end of the boat was flooded. The vessel immediately sank to the bottom of the sea.

After considering the position with particular regard to surfacing in enemy waters in daylight, Lonsdale decided to rest on the bottom until dark. After some hours, when darkness had fallen, main ballast was blown. The boat immediately took up an acute angle by the bow, being anchored on the bottom by the flooded compartment. The situation was then one which all submarines hope to avoid, namely to have used precious compressed air to regain buoyancy, without obtaining the required result. Furthermore, when on the bottom through accident, it is vital to conserve the energy of the crew both from their own personal point of view and from the necessity to conserve air generally. With the submarine at a very steep angle every movement was a considerable

effort. There could be no question however of re-flooding main ballast to rest on an even keel, as the buoyancy already obtained was extremely important.

All through the night efforts were made to regain buoyancy aft, but without success. Towards the afternoon of the next day the air in the boat was getting very foul and all attempts at further work were out of the question. Lonsdale had always been a man of high ideals and it was his will-power which kept him going. He now determined that the time had come for one last desperate effort. He therefore first called his crew to prayers in the control room. Only six of the crew of fifty-four had the strength to get there.

After prayers Lonsdale ordered a final check on the compressed air remaining in the boat. A small amount was found in one of the engine-room compressed air bottles and applied to the after tanks. To his amazement the boat at once responded and shot to the surface where she lay in a state of considerably reduced buoyancy.

Lonsdale managed to open the conning tower hatches and fresh air came into the boat. He immediately ordered the engines to be run, both with the intention of ventilating the boat and in order to run for neutral waters on the Swedish coast. After some little time one engine was started, but as the stern of the boat had been damaged the submarine only moved round in a circle. The engine was therefore stopped.

A German seaplane appeared over the boat at this moment and attacked with machine-guns. Lonsdale, the First Lieutenant, the Navigator and one rating were on the bridge and all were wounded except Lonsdale. The First Lieutenant was very badly hit. While the seaplane was circling for another attack, the wounded were passed down to the control room where their presence added to the distressed state in which most of the crew were still in. Meanwhile, however, somebody had passed up a Lewis gun which Lonsdale immediately took and proceeded to return the fire of the enemy aircraft until the gun jammed.

On seeing the submarine stop firing the German aircraft landed on the water nearby and at about the same time a German trawler appeared and closed the submarine. The airmen beckoned for someone from the submarine to come over to them.

By this time strenuous efforts had been made in the submarine to destroy everything which might be of value to the enemy. This was carried out most successfully including the wireless, whereby *Seal* never received a signal sent to her by the Flag Officer Submarines to the effect that the safety of the crew was the first consideration. Nevertheless Lonsdale had already made up his mind similarly on this important matter.

The sea was icy cold and as both the First Lieutenant and the Navigator were wounded, Lonsdale decided that he would swim over to the seaplane himself, to parley and gain more time. He managed to do this and by the time the trawler arrived there was only a bare hull and broken bits for the enemy to take over, together with a totally exhausted crew. Years later after the war

Lonsdale was court martialled, and was defended by Captain G C Phillips. Lonsdale was honourably acquitted.

The defence rested to a great extent on the physical condition of men subjected to slow suffocation and acute mental strain. Giving the figures to a scientist of the cubic capacity of the submarine, the number of men in it and the time they were submerged, Captain Phillips asked in what condition the men would be. The answer showed that when Lonsdale called for prayers, most of the crew would be in a dying condition, and only superhuman strength of mind could keep anyone going, and that clear thinking would be almost impossible. Another side of the evidence came from the crew. Every man stood by his captain without reservation. Eventually, when the Court assembled to read the verdict, this fine submarine crew marched in *en bloc.* When it was seen that the hilt of the sword was pointing towards their captain it was all they could do to withhold a cheer.

One more submarine was lost in April. *Unity,* Lieutenant F J Brooks, was sunk in collision with a Norwegian merchant vessel in low visibility. Lieutenant J N A Low who remained below to shut bulkhead doors was awarded the George Cross for his action. He lost his life, together with three ratings.

The German invasion of Holland, Belgium and Luxembourg on 10 May 1940 had been anticipated and by 4 May the submarines had been redisposed. Only the larger boats of the *T* class, the minelayers, also *Severn* and *Clyde,* together with the Polish *Orzel* and French minelayer *Rubis* were left to compete with the work off the Norwegian coast. All the remaining submarines were given defensive patrol positions to intercept enemy forces emerging from the Skaggerak and the Heligoland Bight and a special concentration took up positions off the Dutch coast. Training submarines at Portsmouth of the *H* and *L* classes were brought forward to full operational status. Thus once again Admiral Horton had disposed in time and had a concentration of maximum strength in the right places. In the event, the enemy funked the sea passage possibly due to the great losses he had suffered during the invasion of Norway, but had he augmented his westward dash in that way he would have met with as strong an opposition as he did a month earlier on his passage to Norway.

With the invasion of Holland, Dutch submarines quickly made their way to Portsmouth. This was a situation unprecedented in our history and there were no directions as to how to treat such crews. At this time the words 'Fifth Column' were in everybody's minds and when a flotilla of submarines arrived at a British port and men from the bridge gave orders and called out in a foreign language, the position needed handling with great firmness and sound judgment. Fortunately, the situation was in the hands of Admiral Darke, one of our most experienced submarine officers who had come back from retirement to take over the important command at Portsmouth.

The first that the Admiral saw of the arrival of the Dutch flotilla was the strange sight of a number of submarines which he knew were not his own, coming towards the entrance to Portsmouth harbour from Spithead. These

Plate 6

Early S Class submarine

Improved S Class submarine

Plate 7

Submarine minelayer

U Class submarine

submarines turned into the creek where our own submarines were lying, at Fort Blockhouse.

Admiral Darke without any hesitation greeted the newcomers as allies. Naturally, many of the Dutchmen were still suffering from the shock and horror of the enemy blitz on their homes but they were soon steadied, and set to work to prepare their boats for operations.

The Dutch submarine crews were fine reliable men and from their arrival there began a number of personal friendships which have continued ever since. Their boats were of good design but rather naturally intended for work in the Far East and therefore not suitable for close work in the Channel.

Accordingly it was decided in the first instance to operate them from Dundee to augment our patrols in the open waters around the Norwegian coast. It is sad to record that *O 13* was lost on passage from Portsmouth to the north. Floating mines abounded in the North Sea and one of these may have been the cause.

The memorable evacuation from Dunkirk, operation 'Dynamo', which was carried out between 26 May and 4 June, did not directly affect the submarines. The patrols were continued, particularly along the coast of Holland, but no targets presented themselves. During the operation however, the Submarine Command was able to help. It happened, at the time when every possible small ship was needed to help get our men away from the beachhead, that a number of these small ships were diesel-driven and of these, some were barges lying in the Thames. At Admiral Horton's personal command submarine engineers were sent to get these small craft engines going in cases where the personnel of the vessels themselves were not available. At one time the Admiral telephoned the manager of a factory in the midlands in the middle of the night and to the astonishment of this gentleman, told him his diesel barges in the Thames would shortly be sailing for Dunkirk!

Immediately after the evacuation from Dunkirk the Admiralty reviewed the dispositions in Home Waters, especially of the light forces. On 7 June the First Sea Lord, in a telegram to the Home Fleet, said it appeared that during the next few weeks the Fleet should be disposed to deal with the following possible eventualities:

1 Invasion of the East Coast.
2 A breakout of German ships to the northward as a diversion.
3 Attack on Iceland.
4 A break through into the Channel to cover an invasion of the South Coast from the Channel ports.

To meet the possibilities outlined in this appreciation, there was little change needed in the submarine dispositions in the North Sea and off the coast of the Low Countries. When France collapsed, however, on 21 June, more responsibility fell on the Portsmouth Flotilla, as patrols had to be extended along the Channel ports and as far down as the French Biscay ports. At this time air reconnaissance was stretched to the utmost; there were not enough aircraft

for the job, and often poor visibility made air reconnaissance unreliable. The submarines did their best to fill the gap.

The position was well described by Winston Churchill who by that time had left the Admiralty to become Prime Minister. He said in a broadcast: 'What General Weygand called the Battle of France is over. I expect that the Battle of Britain is about to begin. Upon this battle depends the survival of Christian civilization. The whole fury and might of the enemy must very soon be turned on us. Hitler knows he will have to break us in this Island or lose the war.'

With the rapid advance of German forces through France, the French Admiralty recalled their flotilla of submarines which had been working with us. The minelayer *Rubis* by special request was allowed to carry out one more mine-laying patrol. This submarine was commanded by Capitaine de Corvette L de V G Cabanier, a man of great ability and courage who did splendid work for the Allies under our direction, continuing after the fall of his country.

The French submarine *Minerve* also remained in the United Kingdom as she was refitting in Portsmouth dockyard.

When the fall of France was imminent, the question of the prevention of French naval units from falling into enemy hands now became a pressing matter. French ships were urged by us to make for the nearest British ports. On 18 June many started to come over, and among these ships were the large French submarine *Surcouf* and six other submarines.

On 22 June the Armistice terms between France and Germany were arranged.

The French Fleet, except part of it left for the safeguard of French interests in their colonial empire, was to be collected in ports, demobilized and disarmed. Both Marshal Petain, and Admiral Darlan, commanding the French Navy, declared that no unit of the French Fleet would be allowed to fall into enemy hands. While we had no doubt of the good faith of this solemn statement, we doubted their ability to stand by it.

In accordance with the general policy of the Government at this anxious time regarding all French naval forces their submarines in British controlled ports were taken over by us on 3 July. Looking back one is forced to ask if there could have been a more difficult situation devised by the circumstances of war. It is no exaggeration to say that the action which British naval personnel had to carry out was extremely distressing to them and like their surface force contemporaries the submarine officers and ratings entrusted with this part of the task felt their position most keenly.

Here were Frenchmen, already their country invaded for the third time by an enemy, who had come over to a foreign country to continue the fight, only to find their ships boarded and taken over by their ally. The work was not completed without tragedy on both sides and the loss of two first class British submarine officers was a shock which went deep in people's minds.

At Porstmouth the procedure was different. Once again Admiral Darke found himself in a strange position. On the morning of 3 July, the Admiral woke at

5 am to hear a commotion on the other side of the harbour in the main dock-yard. On making enquiries he found that the French surface fleet was being boarded. Having a nucleus of French submarine crews under his command at Blockhouse and nearly two hundred officers and men of an anti-submarine flotilla it was quite clear there had been a slip and the Admiral had not been informed of the taking over of the French Fleet and that he therefore would have to act without any definite instructions, and at once.

Accordingly he sent for the French officers at 8 am. He told them the position, namely that their ships would be taken over by us or alternatively he would arrange for the immediate return of personnel to France. He gave them two hours to see their men and bring back an answer. At 10 am the answer came that all except a handful desired to remain under British command. During all these anxious hours no one, either British or French, had been armed; all had been arranged through straight and firm dealing and in a spirit of co-opera-tion.

At Dundee when the order of 3 July came to take over the French ships, Commander Gambier had the thankless task of entering the *Rubis* with a sup-perior force and ordering her capitulation. Cabanier and his crew were given 24 hours in which to consider their position after which Cabanier saw Gam-bier and made the wishes of himself and his crew clear. He was very co-operative about being boarded and pointed out that so far as he and the majority of his submarine crew were concerned, they would not be repatriated but would just like to work for the Allies under Admiral Horton. This friendly and very agreeable arrangement was accepted by us and the splendid story of the French submarine *Rubis* under Admiral Horton's command began. Only five of Cabanier's crew had elected to go home and this was accordingly arranged.

While the stirring events of the invasion of France were taking place there was still much activity in the North Sea and off the Norwegian coast. In June, *Narwhal*, Lieutenant-Commander R J Burch; *Trident*, Lieutenant-Commander G M Sladen; *Severn*, Lieutenant-Commander B W Taylor; *Sealion*, Lieutenant-Commander B Bryant; *Taku*, Lieutenant-CommanderV J H Van der Byl;*Spear-fish*, Lieutenant-Commander J H Forbes; *Tetrarch*, Lieutenant-Commander R G Mills and *Truant*, Lieutenant-Commander H A V Haggard, all reported successful attacks on enemy vessels. Also the French submarine *Rubis*, and our own *Narwhal* and *Porpoise*, carried out minelaying operations in the 'Leads' running between the mainland and the islands along the Norwegian coast. So far as the *Rubis* was concerned this was the special lay for which she had re-mained behind just before the fall of France.

On 20 June there was very cheering news as *Clyde*, Lieutenant-Commander D C Ingram, in difficult conditions off the Norwegian coast, attacked an enemy force consisting of one battlecruiser, a pocket battleship and a destroyer. A hit was obtained on the *Gneisenau*. She had left Trondheim at 4.12 pm on 20 June and was torpedoed at 11.35 pm. She managed to creep back to

Trondheim Roads on the 21 but was out of action for many months.

The time of this attack is interesting as it illustrates the long periods of light in those latitudes at that time of the year which made submarine operations so difficult. By 9 July, because of the long days, coupled with the arrival of large numbers of enemy hunting craft and stronger air patrols our submarines had to be withdrawn temporarily from the focal areas such as the approaches to Trondheim. Offensive action was, however, continued in other ways. *Seawolf*, Lieutenant-Commander J W Studholme, landed two Norwegian naval officers on Ullers Island on 4 July and took them off again five days later. This was one of the first of many operations when Norwegians were taken back to their own country for a short time to encourage the 'underground' movement, provide war supplies, obtain intelligence and often carry out demolitions on their own. In those days and at intervals throughout the war, submarines came across Norwegians escaping to this country in yachts, open boats and fishing trawlers. Many of these brave people were brought safely to this country by British submarines.

With the whole of the Biscay coast of France now in enemy hands, the big ports of Brest, St Nazaire, and Bordeaux all needed careful watching. As early as July two submarines, *Tigris*, Lieutenant-Commander H F Bone, and *Talisman*, Lieutenant-Commander P S Francis, were off this coast and began a relentless watch which was continued by the Submarine Command until the day of liberation.

As ever, these various activities brought their losses. On 5 July, *Shark*, Lieutenant Buckley, reported she was unable to dive. Assistance was sent at once to her position in the approaches to the Skaggerak, but nothing more was heard. *Shark* had been attacked by enemy flying-boats carrying, for the first time, depth charges, and later, aircraft bombed her until the boat was forced to the surface, and then machine-gunned her crew. *Shark* fought back for five hours but the long hours of daylight were against her and when all but three of her crew had been wounded she scuttled and the crew were picked up by a trawler and taken prisoner.

On 14 July, *Salmon*, due at Rosyth from patrol in the North Sea, never turned up. This famous submarine had been on normal patrol work and may have struck a mine. On 22 July the minelayer *Narwhal* left the Humber to lay mines in the southern approaches to Trondheim and nothing more was heard of her. Also on 22 the large *River* class submarine *Thames*, Lieutenant-Commander W D Dunkerley, left Dundee for patrol and did not return, and on 4 August the Germans correctly claimed *Spearfish*, Lieutenant-Commander J H Forbes.

Some of these losses were possibly due to the courageous manner in which some commanding officers of submarines pressed home their attacks.

On 6 August, *Sealion*, Lieutenant-Commander B Bryant, was lucky to escape disaster when attacking an important convoy well into the Skaggerak. Having sunk the leading transport, his attack was so close that the next ship of the

convoy passed right over him, breaking his periscopes.

The Battle of Britain began on 8 August and while submarines took as much rest as they could afford in the light of intelligence received, there were few days when the majority were not at 'Immediate Notice', but as time went on the incredible appeared to be taking place and when, on 15 September, a record number of aircraft were destroyed, Admiral Horton felt he could release some of his submarine force for longer periods of rest. Two days earlier the possibility of a large scale invasion had appeared imminent and our submarines had been either at sea or at immediate call. Much concern had been felt at the possibility of the enemy invading forces being supported by heavy ships in the North Sea and it was here that the Admiralty particularly looked to the submarines for their greatest efforts. Had there been invasion, let there be no doubt, the submarines, including all the oldest training boats, would have been in the thick of it. Happily, on 27 October, the Admiralty were able to announce that the immediate danger of invasion had passed for the time being. This had been a trying time and during it calls had been made on certain submarines which might well have been on the scrap heap by rights. *H 49*, Lieutenant R E Coltart, on 1 October reported attacking a convoy of six merchant ships 9 miles off the Texel, Holland, and it is sad to relate that later in the month this old, little boat, with her brave Company, was lost on patrol in the same area. Ordered in the War Emergency Programme of summer 1917 and built by Beardmores, she had been completed in 1919 only to be lost in another war 21 years later. But all credit to those who built her and to the engineers who had kept her running so efficiently that she was an effective unit in war so many years later.

The pause following the successful outcome of the Battle of Britain gave Admiral Horton time to review the building programme. Work had been started on a number of hulls and orders for engines had been placed with suitable firms widely spread about the country. The final programme was confined to three classes—now almost standard in the British Navy—but opportunity was taken as each submarine was laid down to improve the class within the general framework of the basic design. New submarines in hand by this time were eighteen *S* class, sixteen *U* class and a further nine *T* class. These were all in addition to the immediate orders for submarines placed the moment war broke out.

Dispositions were also adjusted to meet the new situation of enemy occupied seaboard stretching along the Northern and Biscay coasts of France. A small operational flotilla was formed at Portsmouth to carry out patrols in the Channel and a much larger flotilla was based in the Clyde on the depot ship *Forth*, which had been brought round from Rosyth. This flotilla's operational area included the Bay of Biscay. Harwich as a base was 'wound up' and the submarines all went to the Clyde where the *S* class joined the flotilla based on the *Forth* and the old *H* class augmented the boats in the Clyde area which were employed in training our anti-submarine escorts fighting the Battle of

the Atlantic.

In the Channel the Portsmouth flotilla submarines saw plenty of enemy shipping moving along the coast, particularly off focal points like Cherbourg, and nearly all ships were well escorted, both by anti-submarine vessels and aircraft. The enemy escorts, of which the Germans had plenty, were principally E- and R-boats, of a size similar to our motor torpedo boats. To protect their convoys further, they soon began to lay mines along the seaboard and as our submarines had to close the coast to obtain fixes, owing to the difficulties of navigation in the strong tides, the commanding officers had a difficult and hazardous task. In the Bay of Biscay there was less coastal traffic but it was obvious that German submarines and possibly Italian, would soon be operating from Biscay ports and would be open to attack. This was soon proved when in August *Cachalot*, Commander J D Luce, sank *U 51*. *Cachalot* was employed laying mines in the Bay but it was soon decided that there was insufficient traffic moving along the coast to warrant continuance of such a policy there; also, the laying of a minefield denied waters to ourselves for some weeks, and in the circumstances this could not be accepted.

Besides the new Channel and Biscay patrol areas, in the early autumn the idea was put forward that the Axis powers might attack the Azores and establish a base there for U-boats and raiders. Accordingly a submarine patrol was established off the Islands. The Azores were not attacked, and the patrol was abandoned after a period of one month.

The broadening of the war also took submarines across the North Atlantic. Some boats of the Second Flotilla now in the Clyde, were ordered to Halifax to reinforce the surface escort of North Atlantic convoys. This was quite a new departure in submarine work and was instituted to deter the enemy's surface raiders. On this point the Admiralty issued a memorable instruction to the effect that there must always be a battleship or a submarine with every convoy. War produces strange ideas; this was both strange and sound. It was amusingly termed by the French, 'scarecrow effect', and in fact the French can claim to be the originators. The long passage across the Atlantic placed an unexpected strain on the submarines' diesel engines: nevertheless, they stood up to it well, and in practice the strain really fell on the bridge personnel who had to face the long hours of fierce Atlantic weather on the low bridges of their submarines. The reason for this novel role to submarines was because German surface raiders were at large in the oceans. *Deutschland* (renamed *Lutzow*, 24 January 1940) and *Admiral Graf Spee* were in the Atlantic at the beginning of the war, although the former returned to Germany in early December 1939 for repairs, and the latter was scuttled after the action off the River Plate. Many others left Germany during 1940, the majority being specially powerful armed merchant cruisers. They were: *Atlantis* (left Germany March 31); *Orion* (April 4); *Widder* (May 6); *Thor* (June 6); *Pinguin* (June 22); *Comet* (July 9); *Admiral Scheer* (October 23); *Admiral Hipper* (November 30); *Kormoran* (December 3).

Apart from the possibility of torpedoing any of these ships if they attacked convoys, the presence of our submarines, it was hoped, would be a deterrent to the enemy and a source of confidence to our merchant seamen. The *Jervis Bay* action, when that armed merchant cruiser turned from a position at the head of her convoy in an endeavour to fight off the battlecruiser *Scharnhorst*, will live in the memories of seamen for many years to come. Commander Fegan—who was given the Victoria Cross—showed by his action that the Navy would always stand by their charges, but obviously such a one-sided situation, without either battleship or submarine support, could not be allowed a repetition.

Such new dispositions and tasks brought in their train many and varied individual events of special interest to submarines. *Truant*, Lieutenant-Commander Haggard, was on passage to the Mediterranean as part of the 'build-up' there when she intercepted in the Bay of Biscay the Norwegian motor vessel *Tropic Sea*, of 5700 tons, which was proceeding to Bordeaux with a German prize crew on board. The *Tropic Sea* had been captured by the German raider *Orion* on 19 June 1940 in the Pacific. She had on board the captain and crew of the British SS *Haxby* which had been sunk by the raider on 24 April. The *Truant* took on board the captain and his wife, the crew of the *Haxby*, and the captain from the *Tropic Sea*. The German prize crew scuttled the *Tropic Sea* and took to the boats themselves. On arrival at Gibraltar on 6 September, Lieutenant-Commander Haggard, reported to the Admiral Commanding North Atlantic that a woman had been on a trip in a submarine for the first time in history!

Meanwhile, attention had been paid to the restrictive conditions imposed on our submarines operating off the Norwegian coast and instructions were issued to sink merchant vessels on sight up to a depth of 90 miles from the coast, 'with the exception of such neutral ships of whose movements the Admiralty has been informed'. These new arrangements though, did not mean that our submarines would no longer operate in confined waters, and this was well demonstrated in September by *Sturgeon*, Lieutenant-Commander Gregory, who, while patrolling the Skaggerak, boldly penetrated an enemy mine barrier in order to attack the principal convoy route between Germany and Norway. He was immediately successful and sank the transport *Ponier*.

The autumn brought further successes to the new dispositions. *Trident*, Lieutenant-Commander Sladen, in October, missed by torpedo *U 31* in the Bay of Biscay, but in a spirited attack chased her on the surface, and managed to damage her severely by gunfire. In November *Taku*, Lieutenant-Commander Van der Byl, sank the tanker *Gedania*, also in the Bay of Biscay, and in December, off the mouth of the Gironde, *Thunderbolt*, Lieutenant C B Crouch, sank the Italian submarine *Tarantini*. *Tuna*, Lieutenant-Commander Cavenagh-Mainwaring, sank an 8000 ton supply ship off the Gironde, and a tanker escorted by two destroyers. Fortunately, losses were reduced this autumn, but *Swordfish*, Lieutenant M A Langley, which had left Portsmouth on 7 November

to relieve *Usk* off Brest, failed to return.

By Christmas, patrolling off Norway, in the Channel and the Bay of Biscay had settled down almost to a routine which, except on occasions in the Channel, continued for the rest of the war.

MEDITERRANEAN 1940

In the Mediterranean, after the outbreak of war, Italy being neutral at that time, the strength of our submarine fleet there had been reduced to two *O* class for anti-submarine training. On 27 March 1940, the Admiralty informed Commanders-in-Chief that it was necessary to concentrate considerable forces at short notice in that area. During April and May ten submarines arrived and by the time Italy declared war on 10 June 1940, the First Submarine Flotilla included twelve submarines, six at Alexandria with the depot ship *Medway* and six shore-based at Malta. These forces had come from China and the East Indies. Those with the depot ship were four *P* class and the minelayer *Rorqual*, all from China, while Malta reinforcements were made up from four *O* class from the East Indies, the minelayer *Grampus* and the two original *O* boats, also from China.

The signing of the Armistice between France and Germany on 22 June, following Italy's entry into the war twelve days earlier, completely altered the naval situation in the Mediterranean, Formerly, all coast lines were either allied or neutral and the Anglo-French Fleets had complete command of the seas. Now, all coasts except those of Egypt, Palestine and Cyprus in the east, Malta in the centre and Gibraltar in the west, were closed to the Royal Navy, until Greece entered the war four months later. The Allies had lost the services of the French Fleet and also had arrayed against them the Italian Fleet of five capital ships, twenty-five cruisers, ninety destroyers and ninety submarines. The Italian Air Force was reputed to number 2000 first line aircraft. With the Mediterranean supply lines closed except for special convoys involving major fleet operations, the replenishment of stores to the Mediterranean theatre became a heavy draw on shipping, covering a sea trip round the Cape of two or three months. Further, the oil pipe line from Iraq through Syria was closed down as it passed through the French Mandate. In the western Mediterranean the situation was equally serious. The Flag Officer North Atlantic stationed at Gibraltar pointed out there was no force between the Rock and the main Italian Fleet bases. He asked for reinforcements, notably including submarines. Indeed, in these circumstances, and until some measure of parity in surface naval forces and in the air had been established, the submarine was once again the obvious unit which could carry the war immediately to the enemy's shores. Had we possessed a large and modern submarine fleet in the Mediterranean at this moment, much of our anxiety in these waters would have been lessened.

In a message to the Admiralty on 23 May 1940, the Commander-in-Chief said his initial objective would be to secure control of communications in the

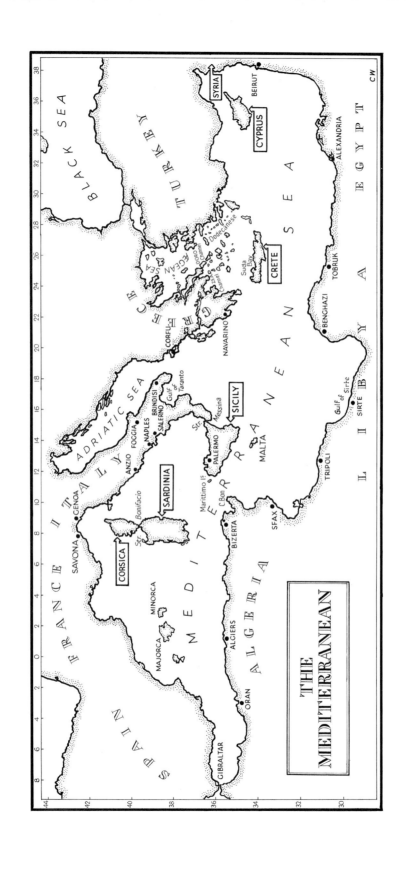

THE
MEDITERRANEAN

eastern Mediterranean and the Aegean and cut off enemy supplies to the Dodecanese. This limited objective did not envisage cutting Italian sea communications with Libya and illustrated the lack of naval strength in this area.

On 11 June, the day Italy entered the war, our submarines from Malta and Alexandria immediately sailed for patrol positions close to the enemy's shores. Most unfortunately, three submarines were lost during the first fortnight. The *Grampus*, Lieutenant-Commander C A Rowe, which on 13 June had laid mines off the entrance to Port Augusta was reported overdue on the 17. On 26 June both *Odin*, Lieutenant-Commander K M Woods, and *Orpheus*, Lieutenant-Commander J A S Wise, were presumed lost. This wiped out half of the Malta flotilla. The Commander-in-Chief believed that the loss of all three was due to deep mining by the Italians in depths up to 200 fathoms. We now know that this was not so. The submarines were all sunk by surface anti-submarine ships and the assumption that the loss was due to mines showed that we had over-estimated the mining ability of the Italians. Also there was a contributory cause from the fact that these submarines came from the Far East where they had been accustomed to ocean conditions and had not readjusted themselves to the confined and narrow waters of the Mediterranean.

After the entry of Italy into the war, air raids began on Malta. The defences of the island at this time were described by the GOC General Sir William Dobbie as 'woefully meagre and include no aircraft'. By 30 June there had already been fifty raids on the island. Long before the war, submarine officers had pointed out the great possibilities of underground shelters in the rocks of the island ideally constructed for such a scheme. One proposal put forward by the Submarine Command included shelters and canteen arrangements for 10 000 Maltese in addition to the submarine personnel. While these ideas received sympathetic hearing nothing was done, and in an event on 7 July a bomb hit the *Olympus* in dry dock and put out of action a submarine of value in pounds-shillings-and-pence greater than the cost of the shelter scheme. Later in the campaign such a scheme would have been the source of saving millions of pounds, let alone many lives, and adding to the effectiveness of the submarine effort in the Mediterranean generally.

The first sinking by a British submarine in this theatre of war was by *Parthian*, Lieutenant-Commander M G Rimington, who sank the Italian U-boat *Diamante* in June. This success was shortly followed by the *Pandora*, Lieutenant-Commander J W Linton, a submarine based on Alexandria which took part in operations against the French Fleet at Oran. She sank the French surface mine-layer *Rigault de Genoully* which, together with other units, was trying to break back to France.

By late July, convoys to Libya from the Italian mainland had begun. The intensity of enemy air attacks on Malta limited the degree of interference that the Navy could offer. The following incident illustrated this. At 3.30 pm on 31 July, the submarine *Oswald*, Lieutenant-Commander D A Fraser, reported

a convoy of three ships, thought to be troopships, escorted by six destroyers, passing through the Straits of Messina. Next day the Admiralty asked Vice-Admiral, Malta, to report what action was taken. The reply was 'None' as the enemy report was not received until 9.45 pm, also the only aircraft available were Swordfish and the enemy would have been beyond the range of these aircraft by first light. The Commander-in-Chief remarked that the Admiralty did not appear to appreciate the situation clearly. It was evident that transports were making for Benghazi and that they would be beyond the range of Malta Swordfish by daylight. In any case, it would not be possible to get a surface force to the central Mediterranean in time to intercept. 'If and when the defences of Malta are such as to allow it to be used as a base by our light forces, our power to attack these convoys will be greatly improved.' Thus once again the offensive rested in the hands of the submarines.

Much help was given to the submarines when in mid-July the Admiralty gave authority to sink without warning within 30 miles of the Libyan coast, ships of any nationality. Italian shipping was to be sunk without warning within 30 miles of any Italian territory.

On 31 July, *Phoenix,* Lieutenant-Commander G H Nowell, failed to return from patrol off Augusta and *Oswald,* Lieutenant-Commander D A Fraser, having made an enemy report of cruisers passing through the Straits of Messina was sunk by an Italian destroyer. Fifty-two of her crew of fifty-five were, however, rescued. Mines, the disparity of forces, coupled with the offensive action in all theatres, were bound to take their toll, but all the time, when few other forces were able to bring the naval war home to the enemy, the submarines brought back with them stories of successes vitally needed in the first year of the war and at the time when we stood alone. Many submarines had attacked convoys and already some damage had been done to Italian shore bases by submarine gunfire.

As July turned into August, the first of a long series of operations took place. Aircraft reinforcing Malta were flown from carriers which approached from the westward and retired again when the aircraft were within flying distance of the island. Submarines were stationed to cover these operations, but the equally important stores and RAF personnel were convoyed to the Island Fortress in submarines. In his first operation *Pandora,* Lieutenant-Commander J W Linton and, *Proteus,* Lieutenant-Commander R T Gordon-Duff, successfully brought their precious cargoes into Malta.

Meanwhile other reinforcements had been arriving in the Mediterranean but in spite of these welcome additions, including the aircraft carrier *Illustrious,* the Mediterranean Fleet was inadequately equipped with surface ships. On 15 September there were only ten sound destroyers out of twenty-two, such was the position two days after the Italians launched their invasion of Egypt.

Once again the submarines were able to keep up active operations against the enemy with success, just at a time when encouragement was most needed. During a patrol in the Adriatic, *Osiris,* Lieutenant-Commander J R Harvey,

sank the Italian destroyer *Palestro* near Brindisi on 22 September and on the same day *Truant,* Lieutenant-Commander Haggard, sank a 3000 ton supply ship off Naples. *Pandora* had a similar success off Benghazi and *Triton,* Lieutenant B Watkins, sank a 5000 ton ship heavily escorted by light craft off Genoa. *Triton* followed this by bombarding a factory at Savona and the gasworks at Vado. *Regent,* Lieutenant-Commander H C Browne, also reported successes, and *Rorqual,* Lieutenant-Commander R H Dewhurst, kept up a steady run of minelaying operations on the Libyan convoy routes.

While these operations were going on, events for Greece were taking a serious turn, culminating on the morning of 28 October, when General Metaxas was handed by the Italian Minister an ultimatum (to expire three hours later), demanding the occupation of certain unspecified strategic points in Greek territory. The Prime Minister refused to accept the Italian demand and Greece was immediately invaded. Welcome as was the entry of an ally in the Mediterranean theatre, bringing with it the provision of a fuelling base at Suda Bay in Crete, it also brought fresh commitments for the already overburdened Mediterranean Fleet, including the submarines.

Two days later, ships in the western entrance to the Admiralty harbour at Gibraltar were attacked by two Italian midget submarines, each manned by two persons. No damage was done. An Italian officer and rating were picked up and one of the attacking machines was salved by the Spaniards. This was the first appearance of such a weapon in this war. People asked whether the British Navy had similar craft. At that time there were none, but they were in the mind of Admiral Horton and already on the drawing boards.

In a summary of events from September to November inclusive, the Commander-in-Chief, Mediterranean, remarked that as expected, the Mediterranean proved a dangerous place for submarine operations. Both sides had experienced heavy losses and results had been comparatively small. Inadequate air reconnaissance prevented us from finding the Italy-Libyan traffic routes with any certainty and our submarines, though they achieved some successes had not been able to obtain really good results. The losses referred to by the Commander-in-chief were *Rainbow,* Lieutenant-Commander L P Moore, and *Triad,* Lieutenant-Commander G S Salt, in the Gulf of Taranto, taking with them six officers and fifty ratings in each vessel. Unfortunately, in December, *Regulus,* Lieutenant F B Currie, also was lost in the same area and *Triton,* Lieutenant B Watkins, did not return from the Adriatic. Thus in six and a half months from Italy's entry into the war, the Mediterranean submarine flotillas lost nine boats with a total personnel of 41 officers and 407 ratings.

Total British losses in the whole Submarine Branch of the Navy for the first sixteen months of the war up to December 1940, was twenty-five boats, a figure which emphasizes the risks which commanding officers took and the way in which the war had been carried to the enemy's shores. These figures do not include those of our Allies working with us. So the relentless struggle went on, while for a year Britain withstood the onslaught alone.

The story of 1940 cannot be ended without reference to the Free French submarine *Narval*. This old submarine of 1000 tons laid down in 1923 and reconditioned, arrived at Malta shortly after France had capitulated. After a good fitting-out and some working up she carried out a simple patrol quite successfully and might well have been given a more difficult area for her second venture but Commander Mills, in charge of the Malta submarines, decided to give her another fairly straightforward operational area. Her second patrol was carried out in December and from this she did not return. It was particularly distressing to the British crews to learn of the loss of this brave Company. Her example was a brave and splendid effort contributed at a time when the addition of one submarine meant more to us possibly than at any other time in the war.

HOME STATION 1941

The year 1941 opened with all eyes focused on the U-boat war being waged by our enemies in the Atlantic. In contrast with the observance of international law exercised by our own submarines, the enemy's unrestricted warfare reached a new low level with the sinking of the *Arandora Star*, 15 000 tons, sailing independently with German and Italian refugees from Liverpool to Halifax. There was heavy loss of life. There were some who felt that our submarines should have practically no restrictions placed on them, by way of retaliation. In point of fact this had been done, but in a reasoned and just fashion. Our declared policy of sinking at sight all shipping within 90 miles of the Norwegian coastline was already in operation and as an example of our policy, *Sealion*, Commander B Bryant, in February had intercepted the Norwegian *SS Fylke* while exposing herself to enemy air and anti-submarine forces. The passengers and crew of the *Fylke* were first evacuated, and then the vessel set on fire with high explosive shells from the submarine's gun.

When later in the year further horrors were accomplished by the enemy, notably in the sinking of the Dutch liner *Volendam* off Malin Head at the end of August with 320 children on board, and also the *City of Benares*, in mid-September in heavy weather, with 100 adults and 100 children, our submarine policy was so strongly in contrast to that of the enemy, that the effect on neutrals could be said to have sealed their attitude in our favour. Happily, all the children in the *Volendam* were saved by magnificent organization.

Some reference has already been made to German raiders and the early part of 1941, so far as Home and Atlantic waters were concerned, might be called the era of the raiders. The *Admiral Hipper*, the *Scharnhorst* and *Gneisenau*, the *Admiral Scheer* and six armed merchant cruisers were all at work in the oceans. *Thunderbolt*, Lieutenant C B Crouch, *Talisman*, Lieutenant-Commander Francis and others all took part in the search for these ships, the two mentioned were particularly employed in conjunction with a vast array of surface ships and aircraft looking for the battlecruisers. Eventually *Hipper* arrived in Brest in mid-February and the battlecruisers docked there on 28

March. Submarines had laid mines in anticipation of this move but no success was achieved, possibly due to the German minesweeping. *Snapper*, Lieutenant G V Prowse, one of the boats waiting off the French Biscay coast never returned from patrol.

The change in the disposition of enemy heavy ships demanded corresponding readjustment to our own forces, on the one hand to counter any move by the ships in Brest, and on the other hand to watch for, and if possible prevent a break out from Norwegian waters of other German ships, including the new battleship *Bismarck*.

Owing to the employment of submarines to cover Atlantic convoys against the enemy heavy ships, few had been available for patrol covering Brest, and some concern was felt that these important units had not been attacked. It was appreciated that they might make a move towards their home ports, either up the Channel or round through the Denmark Strait. In either event they had to emerge from Brest and accordingly immediate steps were taken to try and seal the port.

Every submarine possible was brought into this operation including the training flotilla of *H* class, now based on Rothesay, in the Clyde. The concentration was an exceptional event in submarine history both from the point of view of establishing this closely concentrated blockade, and the submarines which took part, many of which should never have been in existence, let alone on operational patrol in the Atlantic. That the submarines could, in the conditions off Brest, maintain position in a close concentration was most questionable. Nevertheless, by disallowing our submarines to attack enemy submarines, for fear of failure in recognition, some measure of safety was arrived at. The dangerous aspect of this 'Iron Ring', as it was called, lay in the neat pins stuck in maps in operations rooms, which appeared to show that the port was well blocked, when in effect it is doubtful whether half the submarines could keep their exact position, as they were unable to surface in daylight to obtain a fix. However, in the situation prevailing, the effort had to be made and it is worth recording the submarines which took part.

They were: from Portsmouth, *L 27*; from the Clyde, *Torbay, Tuna, Taku, L 26;* from Rothesay, *H 31, H 32, H 33, H 44, H 50*, Dutch *O 9, O 10;* from Dundee, *Undaunted*, Polish *Sokol;* from Blyth, *Sealion, Sunfish, Sturgeon;* diverted on passage to Gibraltar, Dutch *O 24*.

It will be seen from the above, that submarines were actually drawn from the east coast of England as far away as Blyth to make up numbers; Falmouth had to be used as an advance base. The concentration was kept up for a month and no longer, and lasted from early March until 10 April, when it died its own death from sheer inability to keep going with so many lame ducks. The strength of the patrol at its maximum was eighteen but this often fell to eleven, and by early April numbers were even less. With regard to the German ships, the attentions of the RAF and the difficulties of making good repairs in a foreign port, kept them there until 11 February 1942.

These special submarine operations affected from their point of view the next major event at sea, there being no question of a second concentration off Brest so soon after the strain of the April operations. The German battleship *Bismarck* accompanied by the *Prinz Eugen* broke out from Germany on 21 May, the force was off Trondheim on the morning of the 22 and entered the Denmark Strait the same evening.

So far as the submarines were concerned the general policy on the Norwegian coast had been to withdraw from close patrols owing to the long hours of light which made charging most difficult. The position had been aggravated by increased enemy anti-submarine activity. When the important break-out by the two German heavy ships took place, there was only the Free French submarine *Minerve* many miles off Stadlander (the French submarines were kept from patrolling off their own coasts in the channel and Bay of Biscay), and a new British submarine, *P 31,* on passage for her first patrol was given a wide area to the north of *Minerve.* Although we knew from reports from the British Naval Attaché in Stockholm that the *Bismarck* and *Eugen* had passed through the Kattegat, and later our own aircraft had photographed them in a fiord near Bergen, the submarine force was obviously too thin to entertain any real hope of success. This was most disappointing, as the operations against these two heavy ships were among the most important of the war. They provided a searching test of British naval dispositions, and when eventually the *Bismarck* was sunk on 27 May, all chance for our submarines which had reverted to their normal patrols in the Bay of Biscay, had gone, nor had they sighted the *Prinz Eugen* which had escaped the surface trap and arrived safely at Brest.

The sally of the *Bismarck* had been strongly urged by Admiral Gunther Luetjens, whose Flag she wore, following his great success earlier in the year when he commanded the battlecruisers *Scharnhorst* and *Gneisenau* and sank 115 122 tons of shipping in one cruise, before sheltering at Brest. That the *Bismarck* was at last sunk was a major event in the war at sea, but there was no concealing the disappointment in the British submarine service that they had not had the good fortune to assist in her destruction.

By this time new submarines were coming forward from the War Emergency Programme, already well advanced. They had been allotted Job numbers in the various building yards, all of which began with the letter 'P'. Thus there was *P 31* a *U* class submarine built at Vickers, *P 216* an *S* class built at Cammell Lairds, and *P 321,* a *T* class boat, also of Vickers construction. When these submarines began to do their trials the officers and crews wanted to know by what names they would be known. On being told that the programme was so vast it had been decided to leave the boats with numbers only, there was consternation in some flotillas. Here and there, submarines assumed names given them by their crews and shortly these names became so well used that they crept into official papers. The intentions of submarine officers and men were clear, and on the realization of this all flotillas and the staff at Headquarters

compiled lists of suitable names. Unfortunately, some of the familiar names had already been taken over by destroyers when it was thought that submarines did not want to be named, but in the end enough names were thought of, although some of them were rather far-fetched. So *P 31* became *Uproar*, *P 216* took the name of *Seadog* and *P 321* was called *Trespasser*. Altogether quite an earnest view was taken of this matter as it meant more to sailors than many had imagined, in spite of the fact that submarines of the First World War were all numbered. At one time there was talk of launchings taking place without the traditional ceremony, but this was very soon overruled. No submarine began life afloat without a bottle of wine, if only of Empire vintage, being broken across her bows with due ceremony, generally carried out by the wife of someone connected with submarines. Fifty-three submarines were ordered in 1941, and this programme was supported by the addition of nine United States submarines lent under Lease-Lend and four retained by us which were building at Vickers for Turkey. One more submarine was unexpectedly brought into the fleet during this year; she was the German *U 570* which was captured in August by an anti-submarine trawler when operating in waters off Iceland, and renamed *Graph*. When *U 570* was on her first patrol from Germany after two or three days of terrible weather she surfaced and found herself under a Hudson aircraft. She was immediately bombed and although no serious damage was inflicted Lieutenant-Commander Hans Rahmlow and his crew had no further stomach for the fight. No attempt was made either to dive or scuttle, and the U-boat surrendered without a fight to the trawler *Northern Chief* which was sent to the scene on the report of the Hudson.

Included in the 1941 programme was a new type of submarine, the *V* class. It was an improved *U* class with a deeper diving depth. It was, however, overshadowed by the faster and more heavily armed and improved *S* class, whose keels were laid down at the same time.

So far, the submarines when in their bases in the United Kingdom had been remarkably free from the effects of bombing and even those in the building yards had had little interference. It was the home of all submarines which first felt the shock of the Luftwaffe. On the night of 8-9 April HMS *Dolphin*, Fort Blockhouse, was attacked with bombs and incendiaries as part of a general raid on Portsmouth. This was again repeated on the night of 27-28. Fires were started, and one bomb hit the torpedo workshop. Though other bombs fell in the creek, no submarines were damaged Unhappily, the fires destroyed part of the instructional rooms and with them some original photographs which had not been sent away for safety.

Early on the morning of 22 June, Germany launched an attack on Russia. For a year Great Britain had stood alone. Now ranged alongside was this vast Union of which we knew comparatively little. One thing was certain, however: Winston Churchill had immediately promised our support to the hilt.

Co-operation with Russia on the submarine side presented some difficult

Plate 8

The visit to Malta of Admiral Sir Max Horton, Flag Officer Submarines, seen here with
Captain G W G Simpson, of the 10th Flotilla

Lieutenant-Commander M D Wanklyn

Plate 9

The submarine base at Malta

Malta under bombardment. A 1000 kilo bomb falling on the submarine base

problems without compensating advantages. Two submarines were detailed at once for service in North Russia. *Tigris,* Commander H F Bone, and *Trident,* Commander G M Sladen, left Scapa on 28 July and 1 August respectively, for the Russian base at Polyarnoe. They began operations at once against the German seaborne supplies along the northern Norwegian coast to Kirkenes. By mid-August the first northern convoy to Russia had completed loading and amongst the cargo were torpedoes and stores for the British submarines. So once again, the first naval forces to implement the policy of our government were the submarines, and in so doing they showed our allies how submarine operations should be carried out. In return, the Russians made varying and spasmodic efforts to align their operations to ours.

The place where our submarines were based was Polyarnoe, situated at the entrance to the Kola inlet which leads to Murmansk. Polyarnoe itself is little more than a village and lies on the mainland facing a small island, which makes a useful naval base, affording good shelter between the island and the village. The main portion of the submarine base was on the mainland.

The first British officer to taste the delights of Polyarnoe was Commander G P S Davies. He had been sent out to the British mission in Moscow when a treaty between Great Britain and the USSR was being discussed. On the invasion of Russia by Germany, Davies went to Polyarnoe arriving there four days before *Tigris.* Davies had a staff of four whose first duty was to attend to signals. By much improvization they managed to get in touch with the Admiralty after a day or two and by dint of even greater efforts actually spoke direct to *Tigris* before her arrival. This was just as well because the Russians demanded that submarines should arrive at a spot in the sea 30 miles due north of the Kola inlet, at one precise moment. Any submarine not complying with this strict rule would be sunk immediately. It was soon obvious that the Russians did not have the first idea of the navigational difficulties, nor had they any practical approach to such matters. Nothing had been fixed about recognition signals, and without our direct wireless communication things might have been really serious. However, *Tigris* arrived safely and on time.

The conditions which these pioneers encountered were exceptional. In the summer the days are very long, and, in fact, there is no complete darkness during three or four weeks in June. By August when *Tigris* arrived there was just a little darkness around midnight. The days were similar in temperature to early springtime in England, warm but with a nip in the air. The British party were given a block of flats. These quarters were filthy beyond all description and the whole place took one month to put into a condition in any way suitable for habitation.

The actions of the Russian officers and men appeared to be controlled by the political Commissars. Generally speaking the officers were interested to see our submarines and ready to accept an invitation to walk round. Their difficulty seemed to be in making arrangements for a return party. In consequence

these exchanges were few and far between. Food was chiefly reindeer and potatoes coupled with caviare and vodka; the latter two items the British sailors could not stand after a very short time. Nevertheless, the purpose for which our submarines were sent was very worthwhile.

At Kirkenes the most easterly port of Norway which was now in enemy hands, were six German destroyers, two torpedo boats and about six U-boats, employed on raiding our north Russian convoys and protecting the enemy coastal traffic around the north coast of Norway. In Norway much of this traffic from one town to another had to go by sea. There were any number of small ships passing round the coast, their tonnage being in the neighbourhood of 1000—2000 tons each. These supply ships did not always have to come out into the open sea and they could only be attacked reasonably well when passing through the open waters of an inlet, of which there were quite a number to be crossed. In the summer when it was light almost all the time, our Russia-based submarines had to retire some 30 miles to seaward of their patrol positions in order to charge, and often it so happened that with having to dive against German aircraft and patrols, they were only able to spend an hour or two out of twenty-four on their actual billets. Conversely in winter, the indescribable conditions of weather prevented more than occasional glimpses of targets. It was a matter of supreme physical endurance to keep a submarine at sea at all. During the winter when a boat surfaced, the upper deck gear froze completely at once, and constant howling gales took their toll of gear both outside and inside the boats. Weeks of such weather called for the utmost determination amongst the crews subjected to such intense cold, violent storms and almost continual darkness. Some of the patrol areas were 400 miles from Polyarnoe, entailing long and tedious passages.

Added to these facts, was a curious sensation felt by some of our men, due to being in such northern parts, which seemed to affect their nerves. This became more marked in the winter when conditions were so particularly depressing and there was daylight only for about one hour, and no more. There were other aspects too, of these arctic regions, which Englishmen felt more keenly than people might imagine. For example, after the green fields and woods of Britain, the absence of trees added greatly to the desolate outlook of the surroundings and when by October there was thick snow, many found the endless wastes affected their nerves.

The Russians had some of their large *K* class submarines at Polyarnoe in addition to a number of smaller types. The submarine crews were the pick of their navy and much ahead of their destroyers. Although the Russians seemed content to live in rough conditions ashore, their submarines were amazingly smart. The officers, however, had no background in naval tradition and worst of all, the commanding officers had not the slightest idea of attacking or how to fire a spread salvo, and a dozen other equally important factors were quite beyond their experience and in some cases their understanding too.

It was not long before our submarines, *Tigris,* Commander Bone, and *Trident,*

Commander Sladen, were showing our new allies how things should be done. Reports of successful attacks against supply ships were soon coming in. This put the Russians on their mettle, and they achieved some successes, but when the disparity became too great they fell into the unfortunate way of making claims far in excess of the truth.

There were certain things, however, about the Russian sailors which our crews had to admire. The Kola inlet is the entrance to the ice-free port of Murmansk. When the gales are not blowing there is invariably dense fog. Yet ships coming to the inlet on passage to Murmansk were cleverly handled and passed up the inlet under most difficult conditions with skill and energy, notably our 10 000 ton cruiser, *London,* in the autumn of 1941 with Anthony Eden on board, which was piloted by the Russians. On the other hand the destroyers refused to put to sea when conditions were at all rough and this behaviour was only checked when the Captain of the flotilla was liquidated in the usual manner!

In due course *Sealion,* Lieutenant-Commander G R Colvin, and *Seawolf,* Lieutenant R P Raikes, relieved Commanders Bone and Sladen, and they were followed by others in their turn. This went on until the day came when the Germans finally evacuated Norway.

At the time of the invasion of Russia by Germany, there were five submarine flotillas in Home Waters. They consisted of the Second Submarine Flotilla of two *T* class and one Dutch *O* class with their depot ship *Forth* under Captain Menzies, at Halifax, and employed in Atlantic escort duties. The Third Flotilla in the Clyde, commanded by Captain H M C Ionides, had the old *Titania* for a depot ship, having moved from the east coast. This flotilla was being built up for the Biscay patrols and consisted principally of *T* class, and when one could be spared, a submarine minelayer. The Fifth Flotilla, was at Fort Block-house, Gosport, a welcome event to all submariners. This flotilla was small, and in mid-1941 consisted of two *S* class, one *U* class working up, and the Polish *Sokol,* but it was able to augment the Biscay patrols and occasionaly have a boat in the Channel. Rear-Admiral R B Darke was the Captain of the flotilla. The Sixth Flotilla was a remnant at Blyth, entirely for submarine training, and had one or two *T* class submarines only. The Seventh, was a large flotilla based at Rothesay and had the old *Cyclops* as its depot ship, under the command of Captain R L M Edwards. There were two tenders, *Alecto* and *Breda,* six *H* class submarines, two *L* class, two of the original *O* class, including *Oberon,* and two Dutch *O* class submarines. All this large flotilla was employed in training our anti-submarine escorts for the Atlantic convoys. The Ninth Flotilla was based at Dundee, and was called HMS *Ambrose,* under Captain J G Roper, and consisted primarily of the Allied submarines. These were the Polish *Wilk,* the Dutch *O 14,* the Free French *Minerve* and *Rubis,* the Norwegian *Uredd* and at times a couple of British boats. This was not an easy flotilla for Captain Roper to administer but it was achieved with great success and operated at sea in northern waters with keenness and efficiency.

The second half of 1941 showed a more even tempo; gone were the fears of

invasion, and the blitz had eased up entirely. Thus a steady build up was achieved without much interruption and happily without many losses, though *Umpire* was lost during this period due to a collision with a surface vessel when on passage up the east coast of England. The swept channel running the whole distance of our coast and inside our own mine barrier was nearly always full of shipping, and in low visibility and on dark nights, although escorted by a surface ship, a submarine on passage often had an anxious journey, and on the whole one loss such as *Umpire,* Lieutenant M R G Wingfield, was understandable. Most of the crew, including the captain survived. A number of escapes were made from the sunken submarine, both with and without the use of DSEA from a depth of about 60 feet.

It was on 4 September when the US Navy Department informed the Admiralty that two United States submarines out of the promised nine were available for immediate transfer to Britain under Lease-Lend Act. The offer was gratefully accepted and one of their *R* class and one of their *S* class were transferred. The latter was lent by us to the Polish Navy and renamed *Jastrzab.* Both left St Johns, Newfoundland, on 21 November for Great Britain, and on 10 December the Flag Officer Submarines reported to the Admiralty that they had arrived without a single defect. He asked for an expression of gratitude to be conveyed to the Commander Submarines US Atlantic Fleet. Two more of the *R* class were transferred and commissioned in the Royal Navy but these arrangements were not long-lived except in the case of the first two mentioned, because when America found herself at war after Pearl Harbour on 7 December, she immediately asked for the return of some of the vessels which had been handed over to us under Lease-Lend.

Before the year was quite out, certain possibilities disturbed this build up of flotillas. In December, with the long dark nights combining a moonless period, there were indications from photographs that the German battlecruisers and heavy cruisers in the French west coast ports might break out for a raid on convoys. This time, rather than being placed in a close concentration off Brest itself, and possibly including La Pallice, the submarines were given more room, and stretched over most of the southern half of the Bay of Biscay. Once again every submarine available, large and small, was brought into the operation. There were two concentrated periods, 19 to 21 December, and again 26 to 30. Looking back, it seems astonishing that in this concentration, our small *H* boats were able to spend their Christmas and New Year in the Bay in midwinter, when they had been active in a war twenty-five years previously. Nevertheless it was done. In the event, the German ships decided to spend their festive season in port, in the time-honoured manner, and as some submariners remarked: 'Was our journey really necessary?' One of the gallant band of *H* boats, *H 31,* Lieutenant E B Gibbs, did not return from this operation.

THE MEDITERRANEAN 1941

To describe the events of 1941 in the Mediterranean, in relation to submarine operations, would take a book in itself. The pages which follow must necessarily be inadequate even on the principal events, and more so in the mass of smaller operations which are almost daily occurrences. They are, however, a broad summary.

While the tide of war went to and fro, the submarines kept up a constant attack on the enemy supply routes particularly in the central Mediterranean. Some successes taken from official records and reproduced, show the steady flow of sinkings and damage to enemy ships and it must be borne in mind that there were others not recorded and which may never be traced even with the aid of captured enemy documents. These operations kept the enemy in a constant state of alarm and forced him to provide escort on a scale which drained his resources, in spite of beginning the war with many hundreds of destroyers and small craft.

The First Flotilla at the eastern end of the Mediterranean was being strengthened as quickly as possible when boats came from the building yards and had been worked up. The depot ship was HMS *Medway* commanded by Captain S M Raw, and by the middle of the year there were five of the new *T* class, three *R* class, two *P* class, one of the remaining *O* class and the minelayer *Cachalot*, all at Alexandria.

At Malta in the central Mediterranean under Commander G W G Simpson, who relieved Commander Mills in January, was the Tenth Flotilla, consisting of four *U* class. This number was steadily increased and by June consisted of ten submarines amongst which were such famous names as *Upholder, Upright, Utmost* and *Urge*.

At the western end of the Mediterranean the Eighth Flotilla was formed at Gibraltar on 1 January, to act as a working-up flotilla for the Mediterranean and to provide submarines to reinforce the surface escort of the United Kingdom–Gibraltar convoys. The flotilla was shore-based and named HMS *Pigmy* until 29 March when the depot ship *Maidstone* arrived.

For the Submarine Command the year started strangely. On 10 January, without previous warning, four British officers and sixty other ranks from the Second Battalion Commandos reported to the Commanding Officer Submarines at Malta. They brought with them a letter stating that they had come to carry out a special operation. These men had arrived in a convoy from Gibraltar, and so far as the submarines were concerned, were a most welcome addition to the Submarine Command and played an important part in future activity. Later in January the Commando staff arrived by air to prepare the first parachute operation ever carried out by the British in war. The object was to cut the aqueduct south-west of Foggia which supplied the heel of Italy with fresh water. Although there is adequate water in the heel of Italy it was believed that the supply not carried by the aqueduct is so charged with magnesium that if the population had to resort to this source for supplies, two million

Italians would be very ill for the rest of the war.

A special party arrived in early February, and on the 6 the weather was suitable for the operation. About forty parachutists and their guide, who was the brave chef of the Savoy Hotel, London, left Malta in eight Whitley aircraft. Four aircraft made perfect drops and four were detailed to make a diversion. Unfortunately, information somehow leaked through to the enemy and further, the details and information about the aqueduct were faulty, with the result that the explosion only cracked the supports and did not demolish the aqueduct. Major T A G Pritchard, who commanded the parachutists, and his men were made prisoners of war, but the chef of the Savoy was shot, as being Italian, he was treated as a traitor.

These events are mentioned not only because the Submarine Branch had the honour of housing the first parachute men to make a drop in the Second World War, but because the return of these men depended on a submarine. It was agreed with Major Pritchard that a submarine should be sent to bring the party back. Here, from *The Red Beret,* the story of the Parachute Regiment, is quoted an account of this incident:

'His Majesty's submarine *Triumph* was ordered by the Admiralty to be lying off the mouth of the River Sele on the night of the 15—16 February. Since the operation was due to take place on the 10—11 it was hoped that the parachute troops would have ample time to reach the rendezvous on foot, for though the country was mountainous the distance to be traversed was not more than 50 miles ... even if the various parties had been able to reach the mouth of the Sele, disappointment, and not a submarine, would have awaited them. Two of the Whitleys which took off from Malta were ordered to bomb Foggia. One succeeded, the other developed engine trouble. Its pilot sent out a signal that he was about to make a forced landing. By a coincidence no novelist would dare to use, he chose the sandy mouth of the River Sele.'

This unfortunate event put the Italians on their guard and made them realize the possibility of this beach being used for the evacuation of the parachutists. Captain Simpson had to make the decision whether to risk sending *Triumph* or not. He decided against it. It was a most difficult order to give, but in the event, no member of Pritchard's party ever got to the mouth of the Sele. Such decisions have to be made in war, and even if the parachutists had reached the beach-head, the almost certain capture of the thirty commandos was outweighed by the likely destruction of a large modern submarine and all her crew.

Militarily the year began well with the capture of Benghazi, following a particular success at Bardia where over 25 000 prisoners were taken, including many generals, and also much equipment. These events, however, coupled with the reverses inflicted on the Italian Army by the Greeks, and the feeble showing of the Italian Fleet, provoked action by the Germans which affected the British submarine force very closely. Between 6 and 10 January, operation 'Excess' which was a Malta convoy passing from west to east took place. It

had been known for some time that the German Air Force was using aero-
dromes in Southern Italy as a training ground and there had been anxiety
whether the G A F in the toe of Italy would take a hand in Mediterranean
operations. It did not surprise the Allies when German aircraft attacked the
Malta convoy but the fierceness and strength of the German attack wrote the
dates 6-10 January indelibly in the minds of those serving in the central Mediterranean in 1941. Following on the attack on the convoy, dive-bombing attacks on Malta began on 18 January, and in addition, the numbers of Axis
minelaying aircraft were increased. On the military side, German ground
troops soon began to cross to North Africa, and commanding them was their
now famous General Rommel.

If our slender hold was to be kept on Benghazi, it fell mainly to the submarines to cut the sea lines of communication bringing these reinforcements
to the Italians. Surface action against these enemy convoys was practically
ruled out as air reconnaissance from Malta had not sufficiently improved, while
the G A F dive-bombing attacks made the harbour untenable for light surface
craft.

In these circumstances the odds against our submarines proved too great,
and the advance position of our Army became even more precarious when
calls were answered for land forces to be diverted to Greece. In spite of every
effort by the submarines at Malta, German armed forces soon appeared in
strength in the Gulf of Sirte region, and began to move forward under General Rommel's energetic direction. An Axis full scale land offensive was
launched at the beginning of April, Benghazi fell and soon afterwards 9000
British troops and three British Generals were captured. On 12 April the
enemy were again at Bardia and the Army of the Nile was in full retreat to
the frontier of Egypt.

In describing the early months of 1941, the Commander-in-Chief Mediterran-
ean remarked that the new *U* class submarines which had just arrived at
Malta were inexperienced and in consequence important units got through to
Tripoli. Nevertheless, in January and February alone, *Regent, Upholder, Truant,
Utmost, Rover, Upright* and *Ursula* all had successes including eleven supply
ships sunk, while *Upright*, Lieutenant E D Norman, included 'in the bag' the
Italian cruiser *Armando Diaz*, and *Rorqual*, Commander R H Dewhurst, sank
the Italian U-boat *Capponi* in March.

Mention of *Rorqual* brings to mind the outstanding work of Dewhurst. This
officer had been employed minelaying for most of the war up to that time.
It is not spectacular work but it means going right into the enemy's normal
traffic lanes and it requires very expert navigation for accuracy of lay. In the
Mediterranean in particular it is always hazardous to take a large minelayer
like *Rorqual* into well patrolled enemy routes and off harbours. Apart from
casualties to the enemy from the mines, the knowledge that certain waters
were dangerous forced the enemy to change his routes, and in the case of convoys to Libya brought them nearer to positions at which our aircraft could

strike at them. Commander Dewhurst managed to vary his minelaying activities by effective use of both gun and torpedo. In the northern Adriatic he encountered a large armed tug towing a floating battery of field artillery arraigned on a large flat-topped lighter. He surfaced at close range and attacked this formidable gun opposition with his single 4 inch gun, and by exploiting surprise and changing his target frequently from tug to battery and thus engaging in turn that unit which was becoming most offensive, he effectively · silenced the sea-borne field artillery and left the tug in a sinking condition. His sinking of the Italian U-boat *Capponi* was described by a senior submarine officer as a model of its kind.

During these important early months of 1941 there were never less than four submarines at sea on operations from Malta. This at once appears to be a very small number but it constituted 50 percent of the force available in the central Mediterranean and every submarine officer and rating knows full well the great strain imposed when so high a proportion of a flotilla has to remain at sea continually. Some support was given from the eastern Mediterranean but this was necessarily limited by important operations in the Aegean, by the long line of nearly 1000 miles from Alexandria to the Libyan coast and by the fact that no submarine proceeded on the surface in daylight. Submarines from the First Flotilla at Alexandria only worked the Benghazi and Navarino areas and could not normally come further west for the reasons already given. Occasionally an extra submarine could be used on the central Mediterranean patrols because both the First Flotilla and the Tenth were being augmented. Those passing through to the First Flotilla called at Malta and would possibly carry out a patrol on their way to the eastern Mediterranean. A limitation placed on this handful of submarines responsible for delaying the Afrika Corps was the number of torpedoes available. There had been a fair stock of torpedoes in Malta at the time of the outbreak of hostilities but as time went on this grew less, and replenishment was only possible by submarine. Nor was it altogether acceptable to the general overall command that only submarine torpedoes should be brought, as supplies of 18 inch torpedoes for the Fleet Air Arm and R A F torpedo-bombers were also necessary. Thus orders had to be given to the submarines to conserve their own torpedoes. They were told not to fire on north-bound merchant ships and never to fire a salvo of more than three, unless attacking a major war vessel. While there way very naturally great disappointment in submarine circles that more could not be done to help the Army of the Nile at so critical a time, their work in March and April was recognized by the Commander-in-Chief who informed the Admiralty in April that the submarines from Malta 'were beginning to get their hand in' and he added that the most successful boat was *Upholder* commanded by Lieutenant-Commander Wanklyn. In this connection it can be said that from the very start of the operations *Upholder*, Lieutenant-Commander M D Wanklyn, *Utmost*, Lieutenant-Commander R D Cayley, and *Upright*, Lieutenant E D Norman all found

their feet soon after arrival and their efforts were augmented by some of the submarines passing through, notably *Truant,* Lieutenant-Commander Haggard, whose entry into an enemy harbour on 19 March was an example of daring. *Truant* ran into the roadstead of Buerat El Sun on the Libyan coast and fired two torpedoes at a tanker. Both torpedoes ran under the target, which had been unloaded by then, but they blew up the quay. In order to get out of the harbour the submarine had to surface, and with luck and daring she was able to escape unscathed. Consternation was caused in Italian naval circles by this very close attack. That success can be obtained by resolute action was also shown by *Upholder,* Lieutenant-Commander Wanklyn, on 12 April, while returning to Malta having expended all torpedoes, she sighted a south-bound convoy of five large ships escorted by destroyers. It was night, so *Upholder* fired star shells from her 12 pounder gun and this was sufficient to turn the convoy back to Italy as the Italians thought this was preliminary to an attack by surface forces.

With these examples before them, commanding officers soon began to make submarine history. The run from Malta to the Axis supply line between the heel of Italy and Sicily and the Libyan coast was only 60 miles, to that submarines could proceed quickly if needed in support of those at sea, after reconnaissance showed that a particularly important convoy was in transit.

Unfortunately, in April the help provided by the eastern Mediterranean flotillas had to be reduced, thereby placing even more responsibility on the Tenth Flotilla at Malta. This was because earlier in the month German forces had invaded Greece and Yugoslavia, and by 21 April it was decided to withdraw all British forces from Europe. In consequence still more coastline had to be patrolled along the enemy occupied Mediterranean area.

These German land successes had offset to a great extent the surface naval success at the Battle of Matapan which had taken place at the end of March. No submarines took part in Matapan although *Rover* and *Triumph* were disposed off Suda Bay and to the south of Milo respectively in case the Italian Fleet intended to carry their forces into the Aegean.

Meanwhile the enemy advanced into Yugoslavia and the British evacuation brought adventure to *Regent,* Lieutenant-Commander H C Browne, who was ordered to Kotor in the Adriatic to try to bring away Ronald Campbell, British Minister to Yugoslavia, and his staff. *Regent* left Malta on 17 April and arrived at Kotor five days later where she found the place in Italian hands, an armistice having been arranged between the Yugoslavs and the Axis. Having discovered that Campbell was probably at Zeleika the submarine went on to this small port and discussions were opened with Italian and Yugoslav officers. These led to an arrangement for an Italian officer to be held in *Regent* as a hostage while one of *Regent's* officers landed to find Campbell who was now said to be at Ercegnovi, 3 miles away. Thus 'a tense and farcical situation' as it was later described in an Admiralty communiqué, continued for nine hours. In the evening two German aircraft arrived and bombed *Regent.*

They also attacked the submarine with machine-guns, wounding the Captain and First Lieutenant and a petty officer. *Regent* got under way and dived, having been fired on by shore batteries. Negotiating her way through mine-fields she cleared the Gulf of Kotor and arrived at Malta on the 26 April. Following this an exchange of British and Italian officers was arranged, and later Campbell and his staff were evacuated through the normal diplomatic arrangements!

The difficulties of operating submarines from Malta at this time cannot be over-emphasized. The situation was well described in a signal made by Vice-Admiral, Malta, on 30 April in which he said that a heavy air raid had been in progress for six hours by about sixty bombers and he felt anxiety about the submarine crews getting sufficient rest while in harbour. The situation was a trying one, but it was handled by careful organization. Normally, the commanding officer of a ship on arrival in harbour from patrol, went imme-diately to a rest camp away from the main bombing targets. During the day-time while raids were in progress the submarines were dived in the harbour and were manned by half their crews taking turn about. Sometimes, if it so happened that it was the turn of a very junior officer when heavy raiding de-veloped a more senior officer had to be withdrawn from his rest camp, but generally speaking the routine was run without change and the submarines had considerable immunity from damage in consequence of this policy of remaining submerged.

During the months when the submarines were still 'getting their hand in', twelve of them reported successes, and these included a higher proportion of troop transports than hitherto; *Utmost*, Lieutenant-Commander R D Cayley, sank three of which one was a 12 000 ton ship. *Urge* accounted for one large one, and a tanker, while *Upholder* capped this month by sinking the *Conte Rosso*, a 21 000 ton ship full of troops. The Malta Flotilla lost, how-ever, on 3 May *Usk*, Lieutenant G P Darling, when on patrol off Cape Bon. *Undaunted*, Lieutenant J L Livesay, and *Union*, Lieutenant R M Galloway, were also lost at this time during patrols off Tripoli.

Submarine activity in June was on an even larger scale; many boats were ex-perienced now, and the bag increased day by day. In this month too, the First Flotilla from Alexandria had been able to add much more weight to the task. *Clyde*, Commander D C Ingram, *Torbay*, Lieutenant-Commander A C C Miers; *Triumph*, Lieutenant-Commander W J W Woods, and *Severn*, Lieutenant-Com-mander A N G Campbell, all made successful attacks on convoys, and *Tri-umph* sank the Italian submarine *Salpa*. This was most heartening after the tragic days of the loss of Crete which reduced the active Mediterranean Fleet by about half, leaving little which could be employed on any offensive sur-face operations. Greek submarines had by now joined the First Flotilla and made a very welcome addition; they had all been trained by the British Naval Mission and were anxious to show their worth.

Throughout the summer the same names of the Malta based submarines appear

again and again in the list of successes, including *Urge,* Lieutenant-Commander Tomkinson;*Upholder,* Lieutenant-Commander Wanklyn; *Unbeaten,* Lieutenant E A Woodward; *Upright,* Lieutenant-Commander Norman; *Utmost,* Lieutenant-Commander R D Cayley; all sank supply ships and in addition *Upholder* obtained a hit on the small cruiser *Garibaldi.* On 24 July *Upright,* now commanded by Lieutenant J S Wraith, took the chance of firing at an unusual target, a floating dock under tow and escorted by anti-submarine craft. Wraith actually thought he had sunk the dock, but in point of fact one torpedo exploded on the tow wire, making it appear that he had hit the dock. It is now known that the dock reached harbour safely. Four days later, one of our big minelaying submarines *Cachalot,* when off Benghazi, was rammed and sunk by the Italian destroyer *Generale Achille Papa.* The commanding officer and crew survived.

By this time Syria — which was pro-Vichy France — was proving a thorn in the side of our Middle East forces. Already there had been a pro-Axis rising in Iraq and it was decided to shut this 'back door' by land invasion. Some experience had been gained by now of the varying attitudes of the French naval forces and not unexpectedly, those at Beirut resisted the Allied forces. We sent submarines on patrol along the Syrian coast and on one of these operations *Parthian,* Commander Rimington, sank the Vichy submarine *Soufleur.* Happily the Syrian campaign was short and it was not long before our submarines were relieved of the unpleasant duty of attacking warships of our late ally.

In the second half of 1941 patrolling from Malta became more regular. Submarines were able to go to sea for about a fortnight at a time and were adjusted in position by the Command ashore on information received. As previously, when important convoys were passing to Libya, those submarines at sea were augmented by others which were brought to readiness at short notice. But generally speaking, the Command was able to settle down to a fairly steady routine.

At the eastern end of the Mediterranean larger submarines carried out definite patrols. Normally they were given fairly large areas of operations, although at times the Captain of the flotilla adjusted their positions on information received. A typical patrol was carried out by *Torbay,* Lieutenant-Commander Miers, in July. Leaving Alexandria she proceeded on the surface via the Kaso Strait and arrived in position off Phalconera Island where she joined a special patrol line. At 8.45 p m on 30 June she sank a laden caique; on 1 July she proceeded to the Zea channel to intercept the Italian tanker *Torsello.* The following morning 2 July, she hit one of two merchant ships escorted by a destroyer and aircraft and was hunted and depth charged. On 3 July, off Mykoni, she sighted an anti-submarine trawler and at 2.0 p m on the same day she saw two merchant ships but they were out of range. On the 4 July, now off the Island of Doro, she sank a caique by gunfire and also a schooner; both were wearing the Nazi flag and were laden with troops and stores. On the 5 she sank the Italian submarine *Jantina* and following this she made a

reconnaissance of Syra Harbour. On the 8, off Cape Malea another caique was sunk by gunfire, full of troops and stores. On the 9 a convoy of one schooner and three caiques was encountered north-bound from Crete. All were wearing the Nazi flag and contained troops, petrol and captured British ammunition. *Torbay* sank the schooner and the two caiques, one of which was boarded and blown up by TNT.

On the 10 July she sank the Italian tanker *Strombo* escorted by a destroyer and aircraft in the Zea channel, after which she was depth charged heavily but got away. During the following night she was twice forced to dive through hunting craft approaching, and on the 11 a destroyer escorting two merchantmen was sighted but by this time *Torbay* had no torpedoes left and practically no ammunition, so she returned to Alexandria.

The month of August recorded further heartening series of successes. In the Commander-in-Chief's own words this month 'laid the seeds of the acute shortage of the sinews of war which so greatly assisted our advance in December into Libya'. To achieve this high praise the submarines had put every effort into their patrols. The principal successes were *Upholder*, Lieutenant-Commander Wanklyn, and *Utmost*, Lieutenant-Commander Cayley, who sank two supply ships of 6000 tons each. *Upholder* on a further patrol sank a 2000 ton merchant ship and a tanker. *Rorqual*, Lieutenant L W Napier, attacked a convoy of two ships sinking the first and being rammed by the second, but fortunately without serious damage to herself. *Severn*, Lieutenant-Commander A N G Campbell, sank the Italian submarine *Bianchi. Triumph*, Commander W J W Woods, hit the cruiser *Bolzano*, and was heavily depth charged. She had on board a Commando unit which the next day, in wonderful fettle following their experience of depth charging, landed near Palermo and most successfully blew up a railway viaduct! It was tragic that the rescue operations of these brave men were unsuccessful, due to low mist on the water, which prevented *Triumph* from finding them when she went to the pre-arranged position, before they were rounded up by enemy patrols. In addition to this Commando success, Appollonia was bombarded and two highly successful Fol-boat (small collapsible rubber boats) landings were made from submarines off Sicily where trains were blown up. Finally, 130 Allied soldiers were rescued from the hiding places in Crete.

By September the Commander-in-Chief submitted an appreciation to the Chiefs-of-Staff after referring to the depleted surface forces still licking their wounds from Crete or carrying out major refits off station. The Commander-in-Chief stated that: 'Twenty-two ships of the enemy had been sunk during August, excluding those *probably* sunk or damaged. Of these the submarines had sunk ten, the Fleet Air Arm torpedo-bombers augmented on occasions by R A F torpedo-bombers had sunk five, medium bombers of the R A F had sunk four, and three enemy ships were destroyed in harbour by heavy R A F bombers. Expressed in terms of tonnage, the submarines had sunk 44.5 percent of the total tonnage sunk by submarines and aircraft which was

Plate 10

His Majesty King George VI inspecting crews of X-Craft on board their depot ship Bonaventure

A group of commanding officers of X-Craft. From left to right: Lieutenants T L Martin, RN;
K Huspeth, RANVR; B M McFarlane, RAN; B C Place, RN; D Cameron, RNR

Plate 11

An X-Craft, or midget submarine under way on the surface

A Chariot being hoisted out from the depot ship

25 percent of the traffic making passage between Italy and North Africa, and represented 83 780 tons of a total of 339 800 tons. In playing their part in this vital work *P 33,* Lieutenant Whiteway Wilkinson; and *P 32,* Lieutenant D A Abdy, were both lost off Tripoli. Abdy and two ratings escaped from a depth of 210 feet by coming up in the bubble of air through the conning tower, no DSEA was worn. One rating died on reaching the surface but Abdy and the other rating survived. This was a remarkable escape from such a depth.
September produced an order from Hitler to the effect that more attention must be paid to the security of convoys to Libya carrying German soldiers. The Fuhrer made this quite clear to Il Duce in a personal letter. The reply of the British submarines was most spectacular. *Upright,* Lieutenant Wraith, sank the enemy anti-submarine destroyer *Albatross.* This was the first time a submarine had deliberately attacked an anti-submarine destroyer and it created confidence in the flotilla. Another source of great stimulus was a patrol carried out by *Unique,* temporarily commanded by Lieutenant Hezlet, on a patrol off Tripoli when she sank the Italian troop transport *Esperia* which was closely escorted by MTBs. Also towards the end of the month, reconnaissance showed that a particularly large and important convoy was to make the passage. Accordingly Captain Simpson sent *Upholder,* Lieutenant-Commander Wanklyn; *Upright,* Lieutenant Wraith; *Ursula,* Lieutenant Hezlet, and *Unbeaten,* Lieutenant-Commander Woodward, to intercept. This episode is clearly given in the Admiralty pamphlet on submarine work (issued in 1945). 'The submarines were spread on a line in the vicinity of the expected course of the enemy, 150 miles north-east of Tripoli. The *Upholder* was seriously handicapped by a gyro compass failure. When the convoy was sighted in the darkness at three o'clock in the morning, Lieutenant-Commander Wanklyn closed at full speed on the surface, using the magnetic compass. The submarine was yawing when he fired his first torpedoes, and he had to spread them over the full length of the target by giving the order 'fire' and anticipating the amount of swing between the moment the order was given and the time the torpedo left the tube. This had to be repeated six times. By skilful timing he covered the target accurately and two of the ships were hit.' (These were the 19 000 ton liners *Neptunia* and *Oceania*) 'Dawn showed one of them still afloat with a heavy list; the third, the *Vulcania* of 24 000 tons, had escaped and was out of sight. Having reloaded his tubes, *Upholder* approached the stopped troop transport, submerged, Lieutenant-Commander Wanklyn did not know that at the same moment *Unbeaten,* also submerged was approaching the transport from the same side. As Wanklyn was about to fire he was forced deep by a destroyer. In doing so he passed under the damaged ship and came up to periscope depth on the other side. Here he fired two torpedoes, both of which hit and the ship sank a few minutes later. *Unbeaten* had just time to hold her fire'. In the words of Captain Simpson, 'September culminated in a record water carnival for the enemy's military force'.
On returning to harbour, Lieutenant-Commander Wanklyn was morose and

disgusted, and on being asked why he should behave like this after so successful an attack, and particularly since he had sunk the *Oceania* and the *Neptunia*,
he replied that it was only luck, as he had fired by eye. This purist was never
satisfied unless he had done the perfect attack where luck played no part!

In addition to this brilliant concerted attack, September brought useful successes to the Dutch submarines working from Gibraltar where they had joined the *Maidstone* flotilla.

In October, Admiral Sir Max Horton flew out from his Headquarters in
London to visit his Mediterranean Flotillas. He was able to congratulate
them on the part they were playing in cutting the enemy's supply lines to
North Africa.

During the autumn the submarines increased their activity which reached a
peak concurrently with the Army's attack in Libya on 18 November. This
was a time of real harvest as a small cruiser force had now been established
to work from Malta following the departure of much of the G A F for the
campaign in Russia. This cruiser force had immediate success and forced the
Italians to provide cruiser escorts for their convoys; for our submarines this
was most welcome. *Utmost,* Lieutenant-Commander Cayley, attacked and
damaged the cruiser *Duca Degli Abruzzi, Upholder* sank the destroyer *Libeccio,*
and *Truant,* Lieutenant-Commander Haggard, sank another destroyer, the
Alcione. Added to these successes were, one might almost say, the usual number of supply ships.

From the further end of the Mediterranean, *Torbay,* and *Talisman* Lieutenant-Commander M Willmott, were selected to carry out a combined operation with the Scottish Commando against Rommel's lines of communication, immediately prior to our next offensive. The leader of the attack was
Lieutenant-Colonel Keyes, son of Admiral of the Fleet Sir Roger Keyes, of
submarine fame in the early days. *Torbay* landed her party successfully but
Talisman had difficulty in deteriorating weather conditions and not all got
ashore. Thus all the planned objectives could not be undertaken. The story
goes that had Rommel been in his headquarters that day he could not have
escaped being killed. Such a claim cannot be substantiated but there is no
doubt that much havoc and interference to enemy communications was achieved. Lieutenant Colonel Keyes was killed in circumstances of great bravery
for which he was awarded the Victoria Cross. *Torbay* remained to re-embark
the men, which she did successfully, bringing off all those who were able to
make the foreshore.

In November our Army of the Nile resumed the offensive and by 9 December
the siege of Tobruk was raised and the submarines could at last see the splendid results of their work. However, just as the burden of responsibility looked
as though it might recede for a while from the Submarine Command, the
two flotillas found themselves once more with an even greater burden on
their shoulders. The aircraft carrier *Ark Royal* had been sunk on 13 November, following this on the 25 of the same month, the battleship *Barham* was

sunk in two minutes by a U-boat. Next, the cruiser force working from Malta ran into a minefield when proceeding to intercept a convoy. *Neptune* was sunk, *Aurora, Penelope* and the destroyer *Kandahar* were all seriously damaged. Nor was this all, because the Italian human torpedoes attacked the Fleet at Alexandria on the 19 December and put both the battleships *Queen Elizabeth* and *Valiant* out of action for months. As if these reductions to the Mediterranean Fleet were not enough to contend with, some units were already on their way by now to the Far East following our declaration of war against Japan on 8 December, the day after Pearl Harbour. Amongst the Fleet units which had left the station was the submarine *Trusty,* and *Truant* was preparing to leave also.

Nevertheless, faced with these events, the Tenth and First Flotillas did great things and in addition to a large number of merchant vessels sunk, the Italian battleship *Vittoria Veneto* was hit by three torpedoes from *Urge.* Lieutenant-Commander Tompkinson. As ever, offensive operations carried out close to the enemy's coast line and penetrating convoy escorts, brought their toll of losses, and *Perseus,* Lieutenant-Commander E C F Nicolay, was lost in December off Argostoli, and *Tetrarch,* Lieutenant-Commander F H Greenway, never arrived at Gibraltar when on passage from Malta.

THE FAR EAST 1941

From the outbreak of war in Europe until early December 1941, active naval operations in the Far East were on a very minor scale compared with contemporary happenings elsewhere. No shot was fired. For the Submarine Command it was a case of rapid movement to other theatres, notably the Mediterranean, where action was soon joined.

During the whole of this period the general background in the Far East was continually under the influence of a growing arrogance and encroachment on the part of the Japanese, while there took place a steady diminution of our own forces.

In September 1940, after the collapse of France and the concentrated German bombing assault on Britain, the feeling throughout the Far East was that our defeat was only a matter of months. Historians may well wonder why leaders in Japan did not seize this moment to attack.

At Hong Kong we had three small old destroyers, a flotilla of eight MTBs and a flotilla of auxiliary patrol vessels. The whole of the submarine force had long been withdrawn to Mediterranean waters thereby depriving the Commander-in-Chief in eastern waters of any operational striking force. Even at Singapore there were only local defence vessels, again led by old *S* class destroyers, and three twenty-two year old *D* Class cruisers, *Durban, Dauntless* and *Danae.* As regards possible help from other sources, the Netherlands authorities in the East Indies were negotiating with Japan at the time and were naturally hesitant on the subject of co-operation, while the United States only went as far as allowing a Commander in plain clothes to attend a

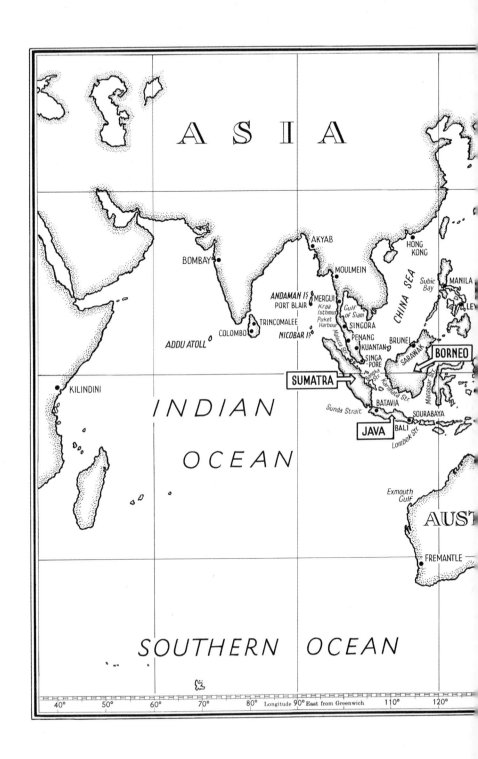

ASIA

AKYAB

BOMBAY

MOULMEIN

HONG
KONG

Subic
Bay

MANILA

ANDAMAN IS
PORT BLAIR

MERGUI

*Kraa
Isthmus*

*Gulf
of Siam*

LEY

TRINCOMALEE

*Puket
Harbour*

SINGORA

CHINA SEA

COLOMBO

NICOBAR IS

PENANG

KUANTAN

BRUNEI

ADDU ATOLL

Malacca Str.

SINGA
PORE

SARAWAK

BORNEO

SUMATRA

Bangka

Karimata Str.

KILINDINI

BATAVIA

Macassar Str.

SOURABAYA

INDIAN

Sunda Strait

JAVA

BALI

Lombok Str.

OCEAN

*Exmouth
Gulf*

AUST

FREMANTLE

SOUTHERN   OCEAN

40°   50°   60°   70°   80°   Longitude 90° East from Greenwich   110°   120°

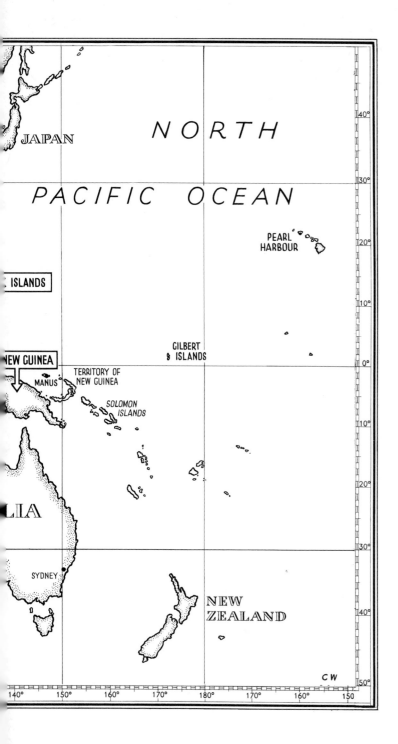

NORTH

JAPAN

PACIFIC OCEAN

PEARL
HARBOUR

ISLANDS

GILBERT
& ISLANDS

NEW GUINEA

TERRITORY OF
NEW GUINEA

MANUS

SOLOMON
ISLANDS

LIA

SYDNEY

NEW
ZEALAND

C W

40°

30°

20°

10°

0°

10°

20°

30°

40°

50°

140° 150° 160° 170° 180° 170° 160° 150°

Defence Conference, having sent him to Singapore ostensibly on a visit to his
medical adviser!

By the Spring of 1941 the toll of Axis successes in Libya, Greece and Crete,
further discouraged our friends and heartened our enemies, and it was with
some astonishment that the Far East suddenly heard of Hitler's attack on
Russia. This opened new fields for consideration and Russia's unexpectedly
prolonged resistance to the attack coupled with some increase in our strength
in the Far East began to show its effect. Japan, in fact, on looking round began to feel she was being encircled.

By September, Duff Cooper arrived at Singapore on a mission to examine the
direction of affairs in the Far East. He was still in Singapore when hostilities
broke out. From the moment of his arrival he had brought together our allies
and co-ordinated their ideas in a manner far in advance of anything which
had previously been achieved, with the result that considerable progress was
made with regard to preparations for the event of war, and by the time hostilities broke out on 7 December with the bombing of Pearl Harbour, the
Allied forces were in readiness within the scope of their small numbers.

Early in 1941, the Admiralty had decided to reinforce the Far East and ap-
point a Commander-in-Chief who would command the units of the British
Main Fleet on passage to the Far East and after their arrival would assume
general command of our naval operations in that theatre. Vice-Admiral Sir
Tom Phillips had been selected for this command and was given the appointment of Commander-in-Chief Eastern Fleet. He arrived at Singapore on the
29 November 1941, having flown from Colombo in advance of his heavy ships,
the *Prince of Wales* and *Repulse*. He took over immediately from Admiral
Sir Geoffrey Layton who had been the Commander-in-Chief China Station.
Four days later Admiral Phillips went to Manilla to confer with the Commander-in-Chief U S Asiatic Fleet and he was still there on 7 December, the
day of Pearl Harbour. The first Japanese invasion moves on Malaya began
immediately and he at once returned to Singapore.

On Monday, 8 December, the heavy ships and all available destroyers proceeded to sea with the object of attacking enemy transports off Singora, a
small port in the Thailand part of the Kra Isthmus, north of the Malay peninsula. The Air Officer, Far East, had been consulted previously about fighter
protection and at one time he thought this might have been arranged, but
eventually as the ships sailed, he informed them there was no air cover and
left no doubt in Admiral Phillips's mind on this point. On Wednesday, 10 December, after learning from intelligence reports that matters were going very
badly ashore, and that the danger from enemy air was considerably increased.
the fleet turned from Singora with a view to returning to Singapore. In the
meantime a landing having been reported at Kuantan, a port on the east
coast of Malaya itself, a divergence was made by our fleet in that direction,
and a destroyer sent in to investigate. While this was in progress, and shortly
after daylight, an enemy reconnaissance plane sighted our fleet. The destroyer

which examined Kuantan found it to be normal and the whole force then turned back temporarily to the north east to investigate a steamer and some junks. Between 11.15 am and 1.15 pm the Japanese attacked with five squadrons, each of nine twin-engined torpedo-bombers, as a result of which both the *Prince of Wales* and *Repulse* were sunk and Sir Tom Phillips lost his life. The destroyers, however, suffered no damage and were able to rescue a small percentage of the crews of both ships.

The above background to the Far Eastern war may seem somewhat remote so far as the submarines are concerned but it will serve to remind the reader of the tragic position at that time.

Admiral Sir Geoffrey Layton had relinquished his command entirely on the arrival of the new Commander-in-Chief Eastern Fleet. Twenty minutes before he was due to leave Singapore in the SS *Dominion Monarch* for the United Kingdom, he heard the news of the disaster to the fleet and the death of Admiral Phillips, and reassumed command both of the remainder of the Eastern Fleet and of the China Station. Thus there was on the spot a man with unrivalled submarine experience from the First World War. Also Admiral Layton had been one of the principals in the various conferences up to the beginning of hostilities. At these conferences in the late autumn of 1941, the Dutch had been more forthcoming and had promised to send to Singapore for operation by the British Commander-in-Chief, two of their six submarines which were based at Sourabaya. The Americans had given it as their intention in the event of capture of the Phillipines by the Japanese, that the submarines based on Manilla, consisting of the Second and Twentieth US Squadrons, a total of twenty-nine submarines, would fall back on Singapore and be operated by the British Commander-in-Chief, pending clarification of the situation.

On assuming command so unexpectedly and suddenly in a rapidly changing naval situation, Admiral Layton found the entire military position far worse than had been envisaged in the planning days before hostilities had broken out. Not only had the keystone of the foundation of an Eastern Fleet been removed and the assembly of a useful force been put back for months, but more important at the moment was the fact that the US Asiatic Surface Fleet was falling back on the Solomons and Gilbert Islands and their submarines to Sourabaya instead of Singapore. It seems reasonable to say that if the US submarines had been based on Singapore under the British Commander-in-Chief, although their size restricted their diving operations in shallow waters, they might have executed great destruction on the invading forces and considerably improved the position in Malaya.

In the event, this work was left to the handful of Dutch submarines which did all they could manfully, but were insufficient for the task. Admiral Helfrich, the Dutch Naval Commander-in-Chief, was a man of great energy and determination and he, too, suffered considerable disappointment from the new dispositions of the United States Navy. Nevertheless, it must be remembered

that no one could have visualized a situation such as faced the Americans after the Pearl Harbour attack, annihilating much of their fleet and rendering preconceived plans meaningless. Naval strategy in the Far East now had to be entirely revised.

On Wednesday, 10 December, the Dutch submarines *K11, K12, K13, K17,* and *O16,* which had all placed themselves under the British Commander-in-Chief, were ordered to begin a sweep towards the Thai coast, *K17* and *O16* had already been operating from Singapore, being the two submarines which were originally promised to the British by the Dutch, and the other three automatically joined on hostilities being opened.

On Thursday, 11 December, two more Dutch submarines, *O19* and *O20* were placed under the orders of the Commander-in-Chief Eastern Fleet and left Batavia for Singapore. On this day, too, Admiral Layton expressed his policy to the Admiralty and amongst the points he made were, that in order to hold as much of Malaya as possible and to secure Singapore as a base for the Eastern Fleet, he required all possible reinforcements of submarines, in addition to destroyers and air reinforcements which it might be possible to provide.

From this time for the next fortnight, the submarine effort to save Singapore was entirely carried out by Dutch boats, seven being under the direction of Admiral Layton. They distinguished themselves well. *O16* carried out a very successful night attack off the Kra Isthmus, torpedoing and sinking four transports, one of which blew up. The attack was made trimmed down on the surface in 26 to 30 feet of water. After four torpedoes from the bow tubes had been fired, a further attack was made with the stern tubes. This action was carried out with great skill and determination and Lieutenant Commander Bussemaker received the immediate award of the DSO. He estimated the total ships sunk at 40 000 tons and the number of troops on board at 4000.

Almost daily there were reports of large enemy convoys at sea escorted by warships. This was the submarine officer's dream, and it was agonizing that there was not a really strong submarine force to take advantage of such targets. One particular report gave six Japanese heavy ships and supporting vessels south of Indo-China, a glorious opportunity if only the necessary boats had been available. The Dutch did all they could, their Commander-in-Chief even hurrying thirty-six torpedoes to Singapore at a time when he could ill afford to spare them himself, but the number of boats was hopelessly inadequate to the task.

Inshore operations are often particularly hazardous and it was not long before the inevitable losses began. *O20* was sunk by enemy anti-submarine vessels and aircraft in the Gulf of Siam. Also a most tragic event took place when the Dutch *O16* which had done such splendid work, struck one of our mines. All hands were lost except one. Her fate was unknown until this survivor arrived at Singapore five days later and *K13,* unfortunately, had a serious

battery explosion killing three of her crew.

On the 19 December the welcome news came through that the first British submarine reinforcements had been ordered to the Far East. These were *Trusty,* Lieutenant-Commander W D A King, and *Truant,* Lieutenant-Commander H A V Haggard, from the Mediterranean. The Admiralty had also ordered the Dutch *O24* to leave the North Atlantic Command and proceed to the Far East. Offsetting this news was a telegram from Washington saying that the United States Asiatic Fleet was now withdrawing irrevocably south west from the Phillipines towards Australia rather than towards Singapore. Not only did this mean the end of any possible joint operation at sea in the Malay area but even that mining could not be carried out because only the American submarines had the mines available at that time.

Meanwhile, Churchill had gone to America and was setting in motion a series of negotiations which recast the scheme of co-operation in the Far East.

Just before Christmas the Japanese sent a very large expedition against Sarawak and Borneo. All available submarines were directed from their patrols to counter this move, and those in harbour, whether rested or not, were sailed for the area. *K14* got in a good attack on the main convoy sinking three transports and a tanker, and *K16* sank a destroyer. The numbers against the submarines were, however, overwhelming and the Japanese proceeded with their landing without serious interruption. From these operations *K17* and *O20* did not return. The captain of *K14* was recommended for an immediate award and received the DSO.

By the end of December the submarines had been on patrol or making good defects, without rest since the first hostilities, and crews were feeling the strain. With the background of advancing Japanese troops, the evacuation of civilians and the desperate efforts to bring relief convoys to stem the many invasions, also the constant reports of large enemy landing all over the South Pacific, one can realize that the steady work of the Dutch submarines was carried out under the most trying conditions. It is tragic to think that through weight of enemy numbers, their successes hardly affected the Japanese advance in any way.

HOME STATION 1942

The year at home started with attention focused on the German battleship *Tirpitz.* There were indications from photographs that she might move from Germany and, on 23 January, our aircraft spotted her in a fjord near Trondheim in Norway. The Submarine Command immediately disposed boats to try and catch her if she moved further north off Norway, or out to sea as the *Bismarck* had done. Hardly were these arrangements made when attention shifted to the *Scharnhorst, Gneisenau* and the *Prinz Eugen* at Brest where there appeared to be special activity. Early February would produce two moonless nights, and the escapes of the big ships back to Germany seemed possible. So far as the Submarine Command was concerned, *Sealion,* Lieut-

enant-Commander Colvin, now home from Russia, was ordered to reconnoitre the approaches to Brest, and three submarines were disposed to seaward of the approaches. In spite of these dispositions, the German heavy ships succeeded in slipping out under cover of complete darkness on the night of 11 February. They returned to northern waters, proceeding through the Straits of Dover.

Of these events, *The Times* said 'The German Vice-Admiral Ciliax has succeeded where the Duke of Medina Sidonia failed; nothing more mortifying to the pride of sea power has happened in home waters since the seventeenth century'.

Purely from the submarine angle, perhaps the most prominent feature in the minds of submarine officers was the difficulty of patrolling in the extremely strong tides off the Normandy and Brittany coasts. It is difficult for the public to realize the problem of operating a submarine off these rocky coasts in mid-winter and in tides of 3 to 4 knots. Suffice it to say that accurate position-keeping is almost an impossibility, and visibility is so frequently impaired that large areas of the sea must remain entirely unwatched.

By the escape of the battlecruisers and the *Prinz Eugen*, the situation in home waters had profoundly changed. While the threat to North Atlantic convoys was diminished, there was a prospect of a concentration in northern waters. *Tirpitz*, already at Trondheim, could be reinforced by two battlecruisers, two pocket battleships and three 8 inch cruisers. It was not surprising, therefore, when on 21 February, the pocket battleship *Admiral Scheer* and the heavy cruiser *Prinz Eugen* were reported by aircraft steering north through the Kattegat. Four submarines additional to those already on the coast, were immediately disposed off the southern entrance to Trondheim. Early on 23 February, *Trident*, Commander Sladen, reported having attacked the enemy off Christiansand about 40 miles to the southward. She had fired three torpedoes at 1500 yards and scored a hit on the cruiser. The Home Fleet returned to base on hearing that the German ships had taken shelter.

While news of these exciting events was being studied, a report of an unfortunate incident on 19 February was received, which deprived the Allies of a vessel of very special interest. This was the Free French submarine *Surcouf*, the largest submarine in the world, with a surface displacement of 2800 tons, which besides heavy torpedo armament, carried two 8 inch guns. *Surcouf* had left Bermuda on 12 February to proceed to Tahiti via the Panama Canal but failed to arrive in the Canal Zone. Concurrently, the SS *Thompson Lykes* made a report that on the night of 19 February she had accidentally rammed and sunk a large submarine. This was undoubtedly *Surcouf* and not only was the Submarine Command deprived of the services of this vessel but some British liaison personnel were also lost.

From the concentration of German heavy ships in northern Norway it was evident that every effort was to be made by the Germans to stop the North Russia convoys. On 6 March, *Seawolf*, Lieutenant R P Raikes, reported an

enemy ship, possibly *Tirpitz,* in Fro-Havet, steering north. Fro-Havet is the wide inlet leading to the fjords around Trondheim. This looked dangerous for the convoy PQ 12 to Russia, and the Home Fleet put to sea. *Tirpitz* was attacked by Fleet Air Arm aircraft and she put into Narvik. A few days later *Seawolf* still on watch, reported a U-boat steering on a course taking her northwards and not into the Atlantic. These circumstances prompted the Admiralty to send an appreciation to senior officers on the Home Station emphasizing the importance of guarding the Russian convoys. The immediate appreciation covered three things in order of priority:

1. To keep Russia effectively in the war. (This meant sending war material by convoy to north Russia.)
2. To prevent Germany and Japan from joining hands in the Indian Ocean.
3. To stop further Japanese advances either to India or towards Australia and the South West Pacific.

The Submarine Command bent all its energies at home to the first priority. PQ 14 had been severely hit, only eight ships out of twenty-three arriving at Murmansk. PQ 15 was a little more fortunate but the Polish submarine *Jastrzab* which was one of the escorts, had got over a 100 miles out of position and *Seagull* and *St Albans,* anti-submarine vessels, had sunk her. Two officers and twenty-eight men were saved. Surface escorts were very 'trigger happy' and it was an anxious time, not only from the point of view of keeping Russia effectively in the war, but our own submarines in the close escort were a source of great anxiety to the Submarine Command. Much concern was also felt for those disposed along the Norwegian coast, where navigation in winter is often difficult and failure to maintain position would result in further disasters. The weather off the north coast of Norway in 1942 was specially foul. There were few good days, and if it did not blow, then there were dense fogs. The enemy base 1000 miles from England and 400 from Polyarnoe precluded maintaining a constant watch. Indeed, on many occasions the submarines left the United Kingdom and proceeded to their patrols off the north Norwegian coast, stayed there a few days and then went on to Polyarnoe. A reverse process was instituted for the return journey. The time on patrol was necessarily short and this factor coupled with the weather greatly reduced the chances of an interception of enemy main units when they made their sorties.

Discussion took place at this time on the question of withdrawing the submarines from the close escorts and using them on anti-U-boat patrols, because on 1 April it was estimated that Germany had a total of 270 U-boats in commission and was adding to them at the rate of about twenty a month. The successes of our submarines against German U-boats in the First World War was recalled and it seemed almost a necessity that the Submarine Command should take as big a hand as possible in the anti-U-boat war, now that the enemy's numbers were so alarmingly high.

Added to the great U-boat menace, reports kept on coming through of

raiders in the South Atlantic. These vessels might at any time break back
to the Biscay ports, so there were calls for even more submarines to patrol
these approaches. Some balance was found to meet the many urgent and
heavy commitments but the point was clear that in every sphere of naval
warfare there were calls for more and more British submarines.

The first priority, however, remained that of escorting Russian convoys. PQ
16 lost seven ships out of thirty-five and when our escorting submarines arrived
in the Kola Inlet, they were greeted by an air attack. Matters were 'warming
up' and reached their peak in the ghastly events of the passage of PQ 17. At
this time our submarines were specially disposed along the north coast of
Norway and there were two in the close escort of this convoy which included six destroyers, two anti-aircraft ships, three rescue ships, eleven corvettes,
nine minesweepers and trawlers and the two submarines all under the command of Commander J E Broome in the destroyer *Keppel* The close convoy
escort was covered by the cruiser force *London, Norfolk* (British), *Tuscaloosa*
and *Wichita* (American) and three destroyers under Rear-Admiral Hamilton.
The battle of fleet under Sir John Tovey consisted of the *Duke of York*, the
USS Washington, the aircraft carrier *Victorious,* the cruisers *Nigeria, Cumber-
land* and *Manchester,* with attendant destroyers — about sixty naval units in
all. It was our policy never to escort the convoys with our heavy ships further
than Bear Island which took the merchant ships two thirds of their journey.
Beyond that owing to enemy torpedo-bombers based on northern Norway,
we could not risk sending the only ships capable of preventing a breakout
of the *Tirpitz* into the Atlantic.

At noon on 3 July a photographic reconnaissance of Narvik showed that the
Tirpitz, Hipper and four destroyers had left. At 9.11 pm on the 4, owing to
the threat of this extremely powerful enemy force which could have destroyed our cruiser force, they were ordered to withdraw west, and at high speed.
The battle fleet having arrived at its appointed limit off Bear Island, had
already turned back. The withdrawal order to the cruisers was followed
twelve minutes later by a signal from the Admiralty which said, 'Owing to
threat from surface ships, convoy is to disperse and proceed to Russian
ports', and thirteen minutes later another signal which said, 'Convoy is to
scatter'. The destroyers with the convoy escort were also ordered to turn
back and join the cruiser force. The two lone submarines were told to remain and attack the enemy and the other escorting ships were ordered to
proceed to Archangel.

Meanwhile the enemy force which had left Narvik on the 3 July, joined
Scheer in Altafjord and were still there when the convoy scattered on the
evening of the 4. They sailed at midday on the 5.

Shortly after clearing the fjords, *Tirpitz* was attacked by the Russian submarine *K21* which later claimed two hits but this was never substantiated.
The British submarine *P54* also sighted the enemy but could not get within
range and no other submarine had any better luck. This was not surprising

owing to the vast spaces of those northern waters.

As soon as the German High Command heard the submarines making their reports they knew that their heavy ships had been sighted. Remembering the fate of the *Bismarck* and fearing attack by our Fleet Air Arm they ordered the German heavy ships to return to harbour.

In spite of this, twenty-three merchant ships of the convoy were lost out of thirty-four, by attack from German aircraft and U-boats. As a result of this disaster, no convoy was sent to Russia in August but the decision was partly influenced by the loan of Home Fleet ships to assist in a convoy to Malta.

During the quiet period in August the *Admiral Scheer* made a cruise in the Barentz-Kara seas, but quite rightly, the submarines were resting, prior to going off again to try and help PQ 18 through to Russia in September. In this convoy again there were two submarine escorts and a large force stationed round the Norwegian coast. The French submarine *Rubis* had laid mines in Alten fjord where the German ships were now disposed on the northern coast of Norway. However, the Germans made no attempt to attack the convoy by surface ships but they sent instead sixty to seventy torpedo-bombers on one day, followed by forty to fifty on the next and the convoy lost thirteen out of forty ships.

As a result of the passage of PQ 18 a full conference on policy was called and in spite of the strongest representations from Russia and much high talk about keeping Russia in the war, it was decided that no further convoys would be sent to Russia until December. Indeed, it would have been hard to cover such convoys because at this time we were hoping to land in North Africa, concurrently with our attack on Rommel by the Army of the Nile, and every ship possible was needed for this operation.

Some merchant ships were sailed independently to Russia but the submarines were not required to continue unbroken watch off the Norwegian coast. Opportunity was taken to do some working up patrols of new submarines and they were disposed between the Shetlands and Norway, with the object of sinking U-boats. Amongst these *P247, Saracen,* Lieutenant Lumby,· torpedoed *U335* and it seemed a profitable way of training our new-comers!

This summer the submarines were informed that the British minesweepers had by now swept 5000 mines since the beginning of the war. Naturally, with all the comings and goings of submarines in and out of harbour, everyone from the Submarine Branch joined in sending messages of thanks for this splendid work of their friends in the minesweepers.

It will be remembered that in 1941 the Italians made an attack on Gibraltar with human torpedoes and that people began to ask whether we had made any advance with this weapon. Admiral Horton had, in fact, put in train plans for three types of special craft. They were:

1. The Welman. Invented by an Army Colonel. This was a one-man submarine.
2. The Chariot. A two-man human torpedo, run by electricity and fitted with buoyancy chambers.

3. The Midget submarine of X craft. A four man small submarine.

The Welman attacked its foe by attaching small limpet mines magnetically to the hull. The Chariot attached its explosive head mechanically to the hull of the enemy ship using buoyancy chambers to keep the trim of the remainder of the Chariot. The X craft were solely to attack the *Tirpitz* in harbour and carried two explosive chambers or charges which were deposited underneath the vessel while she lay at anchor.

Welman craft had to reach objective by being towed by motor torpedo boats and then released outside the enemy's harbour. Chariots were carried in pressure-tight containers specially welded on to the outside of large submarines and released from the submarines near the enemy's harbour. X craft were towed by submarines, both being submerged, and behaved rather like airborne gliders, only operating in water. Special diving dresses were required for the crew of all these small craft. These suits were successfully designed by the Navy's diving section under the command of Commander W Shelford, advised by Admiral Darke and perfected and constructed by Siebe Gorman & Co.

All three craft had to negotiate the enemy's nets. The first two had to juggle their way round the edges and push through. The X craft actually released a man from inside while dived, through a special chamber. This man walked forward on his craft and cut a hole in the net allowing the craft to move gently forward through the net. Having done this he returned into the craft again by the special chamber and resumed his duties with the other three members of the crew. While on the job of cutting the net he could talk to his captain by telephone. A feature common to all was that they had after hydro-planes only.

Welman craft were built at Welwyn Garden City. They took a long time to make progress and actually came into operation the last of the three types of special craft. The design was watched over by Lieutenant-Commander Selby Hall.

Chariots were built at Bath in the works of Stothard and Pitt. Prototypes were tried out by Commanders Fell and Sladen in Portsmouth harbour.

X craft were built on the Hamble River near Southampton at Varley's works. Commander Varley and Commander Scott Bell carried out the trials on the Hamble.

All crews were volunteers. Mostly they were R N V R officers but there was a sprinkling of officers from the R N and R N R and some long service R N ratings.

All the initial training was carried out at Rothesay on the Clyde at H M S *Varbel*, named after Commanders Varley and Bell. Chariots and X craft had advanced training quarters. For the Chariots the old Depot Ship *Titania* was called into this service. The X craft had to have a ship big enough to hoist them inboard. This necessitated 100 ton cranes. The *Bonaventure* was found to fill the requirements and was commissioned under the White Ensign. Captains Ingram and Banks were in charge of the X craft Flotilla.

In this summer of 1942 progress with the Chariots suddenly leapt ahead. Assembled in their secret hideout in Scotland the crews had become so proficient and their determination and confidence was so inspiring that it was decided to make an attack on the *Tirpitz* which had by then returned to her anchorage behind nets in the fjord north of Trondheim. The operation was launched in October. The scheme was to lash two human torpedoes underneath a Norwegian fishing trawler; the crews of the Chariots were to be hidden in a special double bulkhead in the trawler. All this was arranged and the trawler proceeded to Trondheim. There were three check posts through which the trawler had to pass before reaching the more open waters of the fjord in which the *Tirpitz* lay. All went well at these check posts although the Nazis searched the ship from top to bottom and often looked over the side into the clear water. Fortunately they never looked far enough to see the Chariots, nor did they tap the bulkheads to see if there were any secret compartments. Eventually the trawler turned the corner from the narrow sheltered lead into the big fjord and the crews began to prepare their Chariots. As so often happens in land-locked waters, suddenly from a dead calm, the wind blew and a furious storm produced a wild sea with breakers. The trawler pitched and tossed, the Chariots got out of hand and had to be abandoned. The crews got ashore and made their way into Sweden. This was a terrible disappointment as the venture was so near to completion but the experience gained was very great. It was decided that no further Chariot operations would be carried out until all improvements had been incorporated. This meant that no further attacks would be made in home waters in 1942, as the temperature of the water in the autumn would preclude men working in diving suits for long periods.

There was a moment at the submarine headquarters when a report from a reconnaissance aeroplane caused considerable excitement. This plane had flown over the *Tirpitz* on the day allotted for the Chariot attack. The photographs apparently showed oil floating round the *Tirpitz* and the vessel appeared to have a slight list. Admiral Horton at one moment considered going to Buckingham Palace to tell the King, but eventually decided to await further confirmation. As it happened, further photographs showed the *Tirpitz* to be normal and fortunately no claim to such a pronounced success was made!

Through the temporary abandonment of convoys to North Russia it was possible to reinforce Biscay patrols and this was most necessary because numbers of merchant ships in the southern seas and the Indian Ocean had failed to reach their ports. There was little doubt that raiders were off the Cape of Good Hope and in the Indian Ocean, and if these could be caught returning to their Biscay ports it would be some compensation. *Unbeaten*, Lieutenant D E Watson, was unfortunately lost on these Biscay patrols, having landed some Commando men in fol-boats to attack shipping in Biscay ports. She had intercepted a supply ship successfully on 6 November and then on 11 November one of our Wellington aircraft, fitted with special anti-U-boat searchlight equipment, reported bombing a submarine in an area where there were total

bombing restrictions. It seems almost certain that this, tragically, was *Unbeaten* on the surface charging, and presuming herself to be entirely safe, at any rate from our own aircraft.

On 9 November Admiral Sir Max Horton relinquished his command of the Submarine Service to take up the vitally important post of Commander-in-Chief Western Approaches. Admiral Horton had steered the submarines successfully through three most arduous and difficult years of their history, a fitting climax to a brilliant submarine career. He was relieved by Rear-Admiral C B Barry, also a submarine officer who, as captain of HMS *Queen Elizabeth* in the Mediterranean, had seen the work of our submarines in that theatre of war first hand.

The year ended with a resumption of convoys to Russia in December. Four submarines watched the entrance to Alten fjord and on 31 December *Hipper* came out and attacked a convoy; *Lutzow* was also in this operation, but neither ship was seen by submarines. The convoy was saved by the personal bravery of Captain Sherbrooke in the destroyer *Onslow* and he received the Victoria Cross for his services.

THE MEDITERRANEAN 1942

This most momentous of all years began with a long list of further submarine successes, described by the Commander-in-Chief as the outstanding feature of the month of January in the Mediterranean, and he added, 'hardly a day passed without some loss to the enemy which must have complicated his supply problem.' Enemy submarines also came in for a drubbing. *Upholder,* Lieutenant-Commander Wanklyn, sank the Italian submarine *St Bon; Unbeaten.* Lieutenant-Commander Woodward, got the German U-boat *U 374,* and *Thorn,* Lieutenant-Commander Norfolk, sank the Italian submarine *Medusa* 1942, however, was to prove the hardest year our submarines had to bear. The successes were supreme, but the losses were heartrending, beginning in January with the loss of *Triumph,* Lieutenant Huddart, in the Aegean, and in February of *Tempest,* Lieutenant-Commander W A Cavaye, and *P 38,* Lieutenant Hemingway. The loss of *Tempest* was particularly felt because Cavaye had begged to be given a second period in command following his long and successful first period, and against the usual practice, this request had been granted.

At the same time the situation in Malta was rapidly deteriorating because the G A F had returned to their training ground in Southern Italy and bombing was extremely heavy. The submarine flotilla at Malta suffered considerable damage and loss while boats were in harbour for rest and repairs.

During the first four months of the year the period of alert averaged more than twelve hours out of every twenty-four. The submarine shore messdecks, officers' quarters and the submarine base hospital were demolished. There was fortunately little loss of life as all but essential personnel were able to use the rock shelters. The submarines *P 31, P 36, P 39* and *Una* were all damaged while at the submarine base, and it was decided in early March that all boats were

to remain dived during daylight hours except the one at the base repair wharf. It was at this wharf that *Sokol,* Commander Boris Karnicki, a British *U* Class submarine manned by a Polish crew, was near missed and damaged. Her subsequent efforts to effect repairs in the dockyard while under constant aerial bombardment covered one month during which she received further damage, but nevertheless lived a charmed life. That she was eventually able to leave for patrol was almost entirely due to the determination and personal bravery of her officers and men, assisted by both officer and rating volunteers from the naval barracks at Fort St Angelo, the crews of British submarines whose boats had been bombed beyond repair, and units from commandos stationed in the Island.

While undergoing major repairs in the dockyard from previous bombing, *P 39* also was bombed, and broke her back; later she was bombed again and became a total loss. *Pandora,* on arriving in harbour with stores received two direct hits and was sunk before she could discharge all of her cargo. At the same time *P 36* was near missed at the submarine base while on the surface, and took on a list. Valiant efforts to get her on an even keel were unavailing and she rolled over into fifty feet of water. Even *Unbeaten,* while actually submerged in harbour, was near missed and received damage to her bows.

At this time, realizing that the German air effort had steadily increased during January, February and March, Captain Simpson considered the possibility of moving the flotilla away from Malta temporarily. However, in view of the fact that withdrawal from the Island virtually meant stopping the offensive operations against Rommel's supply lines, and since the Tenth Flotilla was the only remaining means of preventing the enemy from bombarding Malta by heavy naval forces, also bearing in mind the bad effect on local morale a move would have caused, it was decided to remain.

At sea even greater efforts were asked of our submarines and they had responded in March with a list of nineteen ships sunk, totalling 45 000 tons. *Upholder,* Wanklyn never failing, having sunk an Italian U-boat in January, got the double in March by sinking the U-boat *Tricheco:* so did *Unbeaten,* Lieutenant-Commander Woodward, by sinking the Italian submarine *Gugliemotti. Ultimatum,* Lieutenant Harrison, also sank an Italian submarine the *Ammiraglio Millo.* Attacks were pressed home and every means at the disposal of the submarine commanding officers were used. A notable example was an attack by *Uproar,* Lieutenant-Commander J B Kershaw, who sank the supply ship *Marine Sanudo,* 5081 tons, firing four torpedoes aimed by Asdics while he was directly under an Italian destroyer.

By April matters were made even more unpleasant in Malta by the G A F, and during this month the climax of the Luftwaffe bombardment was reached with an intensity which was not previously attained, or subsequently repeated. This aerial bombardment was aggravated by the lack of fighter defences, which had become reduced to a comparatively few Hurricanes, and a shortage of A/A ammunition which necessitated an order that the A/A defence could

only engage bombers.

In the first week of this month three blocks of flats now being used as officers' quarters were demolished and the Greek submarine *Glaucos,* nearing the completion of a long refit, received a direct hit and was sunk. Electric light and telephones were constantly failing and the rest camps were daily machine-gunned and finally bombed.

There was, however, still some hope of better conditions, as in the middle of the month the American aircraft carrier *Wasp* was expected to fly off reinforcements of Spitfires for the island. Meanwhile, in spite of the great difficulties under which the submarines worked, a further list of successes was obtained. *Urge,* Lieutenant-Commander Tompkinson, sank the 6 inch cruiser *Bande Nere* and other submarines brought back a long list of sinkings and damage to enemy supply and warships.

On the 18 of this month, the Malta Flotilla and the whole Submarine Branch suffered the most serious of all losses. *Upholder,* Lieutenant-Commander Wanklyn, who by now held the VC and the DSO was sunk on patrol. He had a record of achievement and efficiency without parallel. Of this brilliant officer's work two points illustrate his character as well as any. The first was when at night he encountered an enemy U-boat on the surface; the enemy turned towards him and opened fire with his gun. Wanklyn instantly dived, knowing the enemy could not do likewise with a complete gun's crew on the upper deck casing. Wanklyn only had one torpedo left and true to his methods, quickly and at the same time with the greatest method and accuracy in spite of obtaining his data at night through the periscope, fired his one torpedo at 800 yards and sank the Italian U-boat. The other picture of Wanklyn is towards the end of his time. He had often asked to have a run up the Adriatic as a change from the Italy-Libya convoy work and this had been granted when in March he went to patrol off Brindisi and in typical manner closed the port to a mile and a half, and sank a U-boat.

There was a sad twist of fate about Wanklyn's next and last patrol. He had asked to return to the area off Brindisi, but Captain Simpson was worried about this because he knew that those waters must be well mined, and when Wanklyn made his request, Captain Simpson, knowing that this was to be Wanklyn's last patrol on the station, persuaded him to have one more run in a familiar area off Sfax. While we shall never know the exact facts, *Urge* later reported that depth-charging was heard from six in the morning until five at night in Wanklyn's area. When *Upholder* was lost, the boat had carried out twenty-four patrols, in all of which she was commanded by Wanklyn except once when Lieutenant C P Norman took her out. During all these patrols two destroyers and two submarines had been sunk, one cruiser had been damaged, 82 000 tons of shipping sunk and damaged, and two special operations had been carried out.

On 19 April *Wasp* brought forty-eight Spitfires to a position south of Sardinia from where, with the assistance of long range tanks, they flew to Malta. The

outcome of this air reinforcement was awaited by the Submarine Command with intense interest, but for logistic reasons it was decided to employ only twelve of the Spitfires airborne at any one time, and in the event this proved inadequate. Thus the initial battle against seventy or more Messerschmitts was lost and within forty-eight hours the Spitfire reinforcement had been so reduced that the German air supremacy was re-established. This meant that the aerial mining and the minelaying by German E-boats based at Licata in southern Sicily, continued unhampered and as all the minesweepers had been sunk, the submarine flotilla was virtually hemmed in. Moreover, bombers had begun to direct their attacks against submarines lying submerged in deep water; *P 34* was near missed and only surfaced with difficulty.

Thus Captain Simpson considered that submarines would be unable to operate from Malta without overwhelming and fruitless loss, and recommended to Vice-Admiral, Malta, that there must be a temporary withdrawal of the Tenth Flotilla until minelaying had been checked and the recently laid fields cleared. Captain P Ruck-Keene who had just taken over the First Flotilla at Alexandria from Captain S M Raw, flew to Malta and was in full agreement that the submarine situation was now untenable due to enemy minelaying. Submarines sailed for Alexandria from late April until early May, and the staff of the Tenth Flotilla flew there from Malta on 5 May.

Two more submarines were lost before the trials of these last four months were over. *Olympus,* carrying a large number of personnel for passage to Alexandria in accordance with the temporary withdrawal, including the entire crews of two *U* Class submarines, was mined, and there were only nine survivors. A few days later *Urge,* Lieutenant-Commander Tompkinson, also sailed for passage to Alexandria and was not heard of again. It is presumed she, too, was mined.

When *Urge* was lost she had been on eighteen patrols, all of which Tompkinson had commanded except one when Lieutenant J D Martin took command. One cruiser and one destroyer had been sunk, one battleship and one cruiser damaged, 26 000 tons of shipping sunk and 37 000 tons damaged. The boat had also taken part in two special operations.

From Alexandria, Captain Simpson sent a report of the events in Malta to Sir Max Horton, in which he wrote these words, 'The exemplary conduct of all and their determination to get on with the job despite difficulties, loss of kit and amenities, deserves remark. The exceptional work of the repair parties was outstanding, no circumstances daunted them, and I never heard a complaint.

'The Flotilla is now dispersed, damaged, and has suffered heavy loss but it is notable that the essentials at Malta for the operation of the submarines remain. It is hoped that the day is not far distant when the Flotilla can reassemble and continue the fight.'

Meanwhile, from Alexandria the First Flotilla had been keeping up a steady offensive in the Aegean and adjacent waters.

There were two spectacular patrols which are worthy of special mention. The first was by *Thrasher,* Lieutenant H S Mackenzie, off Crete; she attacked a well-escorted 3000 ton merchant vessel which was entering Suda Bay, and sank her, after which she was counter-attacked by anti-submarine vessels supported by two aircraft. Having evaded her attackers she surfaced after dark, only to find two unexploded bombs in her casing. Lieutenant P S W Roberts and Petty Officer T W Gould, the Second Coxswain, volunteered to crawl into the casing and remove the bombs. The risk was very great as apart from the fact that the bombs might explode at any time, circumstances might force the submarine to dive instantly, trapping these two men in the casing. In the event, however, Roberts and Gould managed to pull the bombs along the casing until they could get them on to the upper deck.   There they calmly proceeded to measure the bombs for statistics, and then, placing them in canvas bags, lowered them successfully over the side to the bottom of the sea. For their action both men were awarded the Victoria Cross.

The second patrol which must be mentioned was by *Torbay,* Commander Miers. Operating in the Corfu-Taranto-Messina area, the submarine began her patrol by attacking a small convoy with her gun; a 1000 ton merchant vessel was sunk, and a trawler and another vessel only escaped because *Torbay* was forced to dive due to firing from shore batteries. Later she sighted four large troopships heavily escorted, but being unable to get in an attack, Miers appreciated that the troopships might possibly shelter in Corfu harbour. He proceeded right into the harbour, making a forty mile passage in confined waters to do so. On arrival he was disappointed not to see the troop transports, but there were two supply ships there, of 5000 tons and 8000 tons. He waited until night, then surfaced in the harbour to charge his batteries. Four times he was forced to dive hurriedly to avoid patrol craft but after hours of unequalled suspense completed the task. At first light he torpedoed both the supply ships and also fired at a destroyer, but missed. As he had now spent seventeen hours inside an enemy harbour and had a forty mile run in confined waters to get clear, Miers decided to withdraw. For this spirited and daring action he was awarded the Victoria Cross.

In spite of the combined efforts of the First and Tenth Flotillas their successes were not sufficient to prevent the Germans assuming the offensive in Libya on 25 May.

In June the call came for all available submarines to be sailed to cover the convoy to Malta, on which hung the future of the island. The operation was divided into two parts, one 'Harpoon' coming from the westward and the other 'Vigorous', approaching Malta from the eastward. The former was mounted in the United Kingdom and the latter at Alexandria. This activity was perhaps the best thing after the trials of the previous months and every available submarine went to sea.

The importance of the convoy was such that the Italian Main Fleet sailed to intercept it, and *Umbra,* Lieutenant Maydon, damaged the battleship *Vittorio*

Veneto and sank the cruiser *Trento.* Maydon was deprived of achieving what
might have been one of the greatest submarine successes of the war by a
matter of about twenty seconds. Before these two large scale convoy operations were launched, plans for co-operation by the submarines were discussed.
At Alexandria, from where the submarines operating in the eastern basin of
the Mediterranean were being controlled, it was decided to place the *U* Class,
which were slow on the surface, on diving patrol on a line across which the
Italian Fleet would probably pass, if it ventured to attack the eastern convoy,
'Vigorous'. The *T* Class which had a good surface speed, were to accompany
this convoy, placing themselves between the merchant ships and any enemy
attacking force. It so happened that the Italian Fleet came towards the patrol
position occupied by Maydon in *Umbra* and he immediately developed his
attack. Not more than half a minute before his sights came on, when he would
have sent six torpedoes speeding towards the leading Italian battleship, the
Vittorio Veneto, out of the sky and entirely unannounced so far as the submarines were concerned, a rain of high explosive from RAF bombers fell
around, and upon some of the Italian ships. The leading ships including the
Vittorio Veneto at which Maydon was about to fire, put their helms hard over
and began to describe a large circle. There was nothing Maydon could do but
hold his fire and hope to get in a long shot if the Italian Fleet continued their
turn through more than ninety degrees. This they did, and Maydon fired a
salvo at long range hitting the *Vittorio Veneto* with one torpedo. By now the
cruiser *Trento* had almost stopped, having been seriously damaged by the
bombers. Seeing this, Maydon at once reloaded his torpedo tubes, manoeuvred towards the stricken cruiser and finished her off. Meanwhile *Turbulent,*
Commander Linton, fell in with an enemy supply convoy and sank the destroyer *Pessagno,* also a supply ship, and a schooner full of fuel and ammunition. The torpedoing of the *Pessagno* was unexpected as one of Linton's salvo
failed to run on its intended course towards the supply ships, and in describing a circle of its own choosing, hit the destroyer escort.
Of the Allied convoys, the one from the east under Admiral Vian was forced
to turn back, and it will be remembered the Admiral saved the convoy from
the main Italian Fleet by the spirited handling of his much lighter escorting
forces. The portion coming from the westward, however, got through in part,
and the safe arrival of these relief ships at Malta between the 12 and 16 June
was the beginning of the turn of the tide in the Mediterranean.
It was not long after this that the German Air Force had to be called off in
part for other operations, and the Vice-Admiral, Malta, made the welcome
signal that in his view the scale of mining and air attacks would now allow
the Tenth Flotilla to return to the island. This was taken up with great enthusiasm, and by the middle of July the submarine offensive from Malta had
begun again.
A tribute here is due to the minesweepers. Vice-Admiral, Malta, reported that:
'In recent weeks 206 mines had been swept up chiefly by four hastily repaired

local minesweepers manned mostly by Maltese naval ratings who had faced up to this dangerous and most difficult task with indomitable spirit.'
This new situation once again permitted submarines to carry supplies of petrol, aircraft torpedoes and ammunition for the garrison; *Otus*, Lieutenant R M Favell; *Rorqual*, Lieutenant L W Napier, and *Clyde*, Lieutenant R S Brookes, all made successful trips. Newspapers at this time in England were referring to these operations under the heading of 'The Magic Carpet'.
The Germans had driven as far as El Alamein by the end of June and the whole position of the Allies in the Middle East was once again threatened. *Medway*, the depot ship at Alexandria, was sailed for Haifa. She was torpedoed on passage and sunk on 30 June, but fortunately there was little loss of life. Many of the First Flotilla submarines were at sea when this event happened and on their return from patrol they went to Beirut, now in our hands after the Syrian campaign, where they found that a shore base had been prepared for them in an amazingly quick time. In reply to this loss the submarines reaped a particularly heavy harvest. *Unbroken*, Lieutenant Mars, damaged the two cruisers *Bolzano* and *Attendolo*, and in the month of August alone ten other submarines sank or damaged supply ships totalling over 80 000 tons.
An anniversary kept by some people is 30 August, because on this day the Army of the Nile definitely halted Rommel's advance towards Cairo and also deprived Mussolini of riding into Egypt on his white horse! This day is complementary to Alamein but is not so widely remembered. Marshal of the Royal Air Force, Lord Tedder, in his book, *Air Power in War*, comprising a series of lectures delivered at Cambridge University, says of the days following: 'The question was would the Eighth Army be ready in time before sufficient supplies had evaded our blockade to set Rommel on his feet again ... The story goes that Rommel saw the last of his tankers sunk by our torpedo bombers before his eyes at the entrance to Tobruk harbour.' Two events in the submarine story are also closely connected with 30 August and with Alamein. On 29 June just at the time when Rommel needed petrol more than any other commodity, Lieutenant-Commander H S Mackenzie, in *Thrasher*, torpedoed and sank the *Diana* of 3337 tons. This ship was a vital link in Rommel's build up. She was steering south for Tobruk at high speed and was escorted. Mackenzie fired six torpedoes of which four hit the target. From the resultant explosion there seemed little doubt that she carried cased petrol. This event undoubtedly had a bearing on the operations on land on 30 August. Again Mackenzie was off Tobruk on 4 September and this time he sank the *Padenna* of 1580 tons and once more the indications were that this ship was carrying cased petrol. Of course *Thrasher* was by no means the only submarine at sea in these vital days and there were other successes against Rommel's supply line, but these two successes by Mackenzie appear to have had a special significance in relation to the great events in the desert.
Very close patrols were maintained off Marittimo, the small island west of Sicily, and Tobruk, throughout the second half of 1942 and it was on these

operations that we lost *Talisman,* Lieutenant-Commander Willmott, and *Thorn,* Lieutenant-Commander Norfolk. The Malta flotilla also lost two boats, *Unique,* Lieutenant R E Boddington, and *Utmost,* Lieutenant J W D Coombe, who had relieved Lieutenant-Commander Cayley in this famous boat.

By this time Generals Alexander and Montgomery, working together with the Army of the Nile, had decided to launch their major offensive early in November. Also at home a decision had been reached to land a force in North Africa concurrently with the attack in Egypt. In view of these two forthcoming large scale operations, the Eighth Submarine Flotilla at Gibraltar, now under the command of Captain G B H Fawkes in *Maidstone,* had been built up to ten of the improved *S* Class, four *T* Class and the *Regent.* In addition, submarines from the First Flotilla at Beirut at the eastern end of the Mediterranean were detached to augment the Tenth Flotilla at Malta, and later on augmented the Eighth Flotilla as well. Thus from August onwards the tempo of submarine operations in the western basin of the Mediterranean had been increased.

During the early autumn submarines from the Eighth Flotilla reconnoitred the beaches and landing places for the Allied invasion of North Africa and two important tasks had to be carried out prior to the actual landings. The first one was to land the American General Mark Clark in North Africa and bring him off again. On 19 October, General Mark Clark, Brigadier-General Lemmitzer, Colonels Holmes and Hamblen, together with Captain Wright, all of the United States Forces, were embarked at Gibraltar in *P 219,* Lieutenant N L A Jewell. This party was landed by fol-boats on the north coast of Africa about fifty miles west of Algiers. They made contact with various French Generals, and through them arranged for co-operation when the time came for the Allied landing to take place.

For the second task *P 219* (later named *Seraph*) sailed from Gibraltar on 27 October and proceeded to La Fosette, some twenty miles east of Toulon, where on 6 November she picked up General Giraud, his son, his Aide-de-Camp and a staff officer, Major Beauffre. The next night, *Sibyl,* Lieutenant E J D Turner, who had followed *P 219* to the French coast, brought off Madame Beauffre and some more officers of General Giraud's staff from another rendezvous.

When General Giraud reached Gibraltar he refused to co-operate unless he was made Supreme Commander; later however, he modified his attitude and made a broadcast to the French people. *Sibyl* took her party to Algiers, as the landings had taken place on the 8 and the port was able to receive ships immediately. There she met four other submarines of the Eighth Flotilla which had acted as navigational beacons to guide the landing forces.

All the remaining submarines of the Eighth Flotilla and the whole of the Tenth Flotilla from Malta, augmented by others from the First Flotilla, had covered the landings from possible interference by the Italian Fleet. These special dispositions were coordinated by Captain Simpson at Malta. In the

event the landings took the enemy by surprise. Strategical surprise could not be achieved once the convoys were in the Mediterranean, but complete tactical surprise was gained by the enemy believing the concentration was for the relief of Malta or destined for Benghazi.

Meanwhile, seven days earlier, at the other end of the Mediterranean, the great day had dawned for which the Army of the Nile had trained so long, and the Axis forces had been defeated at the Battle of El Alamein.

No great harvest was reaped by the submarines while these stirring events were taking place on land, but *Unbending*, Lieutenant E T Stanley sank the destroyer *Da Verrazzano*, *Unruffled*, Lieutenant Stevens, damaged a *Regolo* Class cruiser and there were some useful successes against shipping, notably by *Safari*, Commander B Bryant, who by this time was building a reputation comparable to those of Wanklyn and Miers.

Soon after the landings in North Africa had taken place, the *Maidstone* with three escorts left Gibraltar and proceeded to Algiers. She was attacked twice by U-boats on the way and narrowly escaped the fate of *Medway*. In the first attack, which was made at night, torpedoes fired from a U-boat on *Maidstone's* port beam missed ahead, and instead hit the escort on the starboard bow, the *Porcupine*. This little ship was cut in half and the two portions, which were soon christened *Porc* and *Pine*, were later towed into Oran. For a short and anxious period *Maidstone* was left with only one escort and again the same night sighted torpedoes which passed ahead. However, adequate help was soon on the way, and by the time she arrived at Algiers, *Maidstone* had no fewer than fifteen escorts. Her safe arrival meant a great deal to the success of the subsequent operations in the western basin since she was to have thirty-eight submarines in the Eighth Flotilla before the campaign on land had been won.

The effect of the landings on the Mediterranean naval situation was very soon evident, and on the 19 a large convoy, 'Operation Stoneage', arrived safely at Malta, after which the island was no longer in danger.

For the remainder of the year the whole of the submarine fleet in the western and central Mediterranean was concentrated on the Axis supply lines in support of their armies in North Africa and Libya. The route from Palermo to Bizerta was particularly heavily attacked and here the submarines had to contend with very closely escorted convoys sometimes employing as many as eight destroyers. Nevertheless a heavy toll was taken of enemy shipping, the Eighth Flotilla vying with the Tenth for the honours. Thus once again the initial offensive operations at sea were left entirely to the submarines as the whole of the surface fleet was switched to defensive operations in support of the army.

Naturally the Axis knew at once the great seriousness of their position, and so the Italian Fleet, supported by its submarines, was persuaded to risk itself far more than hitherto. Opportunity was taken by our submarines to make every use of this more aggressive policy by the enemy, and *Saracen*, Lieutenant

Lumby, torpedoed the Italian U-boat *Granito,* this making his double, and *Tigris,* Lieutenant-Commander Colvin, also sank an Italian U-boat, the *Porfido;* and *Splendid,* Lieutenant McGeogh, sank the Italian destroyer *Avierre* and the ammunition ship *Santa Antiocha.* The month of December saw the first chariot operation being planned under the direction of Commander G M Sladen, and before the year was out *Thunderbolt,* Lieutenant-Commander Crouch and *Trooper,* Lieutenant J S Wraith had sailed to launch an attack on Palermo harbour. As the individual chariot attacks were made in January 1943 they are described in that section later. *P 311,* Commander Cayley, also sailed with chariots to attack two Italian cruisers reported in Madallena harbour, Sardinia. It is sad to relate that Cayley was lost on this patrol. It is known that he passed safely through the Sicilian Straits and it is thought that the northern current running up the east coast of Sardinia took him further north than he expected and that he ran into the minefield east of the Bonifacio Straits. This was a tragic loss to the Submarine Command as Cayley had had a brilliant career and was one of the original commanding officers who had built up the great reputation of the Malta Flotilla. Cayley will be specially remembered for volunteering to find a clear passage through an Italian minefield in which he led the way for *Urge* and *Upholder,* and was completely successful.

Traveller, Lieutenant-Commander St Clair Ford, was also lost in December during a patrol off Taranto. Up to this patrol *Traveller* had been successfully commanded by Lieutenant St John. It was tragic that she should run into disaster on St Clair Ford's first patrol. Another loss in this month was *P 222,* Lieutenant-Commander A J MacKenzie; she left Gibraltar for patrol off Naples and the last signals from her were received on the 7. It is now known that she was sunk by depth charges from an Italian torpedo boat.

In December Captain Simpson had completed two years in command at Malta and was relieved by Captain G C Phillips. During these two years in the Mediterranean the submarines had been a vital factor in the land campaign. Besides keeping up a continuous offensive from both ends of the Mediterranean they had also operated from their central base at Malta except for the one short break of ten weeks. Although with the passage of time it is hard to realize what their patrols really meant in achievement, there is no doubt that the whole Mediterranean offensive can be regarded as the finest work ever accomplished by British submarines. Their part in the great decisive battle of El Alamein, was one of the cornerstones of victory.

On the other side of the picture, the losses of fourteen submarines, totalling 70 officers and 720 ratings, were irreplaceable, both in experience and skill, but their great valour and devotion to duty remained as an inspiration to all who came after them. Four Victoria Crosses had been won, together with many other decorations and amongst these were some given by foreign powers.

FAR EAST 1942

By the second week in January 1942 Singapore had become the target for

aerial bombing, and accordingly the Dutch submarines returned to the Netherlands base at Sourabaya. *Trusty,* Lieutenant-Commander W D A King, and *Truant,* Lieutenant-Commander H A V Haggard, were now well on their separate ways from Alexandria to join the Eastern Fleet, and *Trusty* was told she might sink any surface craft sighted in the Malacca Straits, north of two degrees north. After calling at Singapore she proceeded for a patrol in the Gulf of Siam and the China Sea. Here she found all manner of targets, and mostly they could be attacked with the gun. Some of the ships were small merchant vessels carrying one 4 inch gun which generally had a bullet-proof shield. Many of these small ships were used for carrying motor transport, and others had been converted into tankers or landing craft. Attacks were always attended by surprise as the submarine could surface unexpectedly a few hundred yards from the enemy ship and fire a few rounds before the enemy armament could be brought into action.

Such rest for *Trusty* as there was, after patrol, was taken at Sourabaya but as the dockyard there could not carry out repairs, all resources being required for Dutch ships she only got a quick docking. Unhappily, this revealed considerable underwater damage due to having grounded at Alexandria on passage out, and from near misses from bombing at Singapore. As Singapore had by this time fallen, *Trusty* proceeded to Colombo.

Truant on arrival in Far Eastern waters went to Batavia first and then to Sourabaya, as Singapore was out of the question. The temperature in the submarine was 103 degrees F, air raids were frequent, and at one time bombs fell in the basin where *Truant* was lying. It was with some relief therefore that *Truant* heard from the Dutch Commander-in-Chief that there were Japanese convoys off Bali and immediately sailed to see what could be done. No other intelligence was available and worst of all *Truant* had no idea whether there were any United States submarines operating in the area. When *Truant* arrived off Bali the coast was infested with ships. She had an exciting time dodging anti-submarine vessels and destroyers and eventually got in an attack on a cruiser escorting a convoy. Although six torpedoes were fired and two were heard to strike the cruiser none appeared to explode. After all the trials and tribulations through which the submarine had passed, this was bitter disappointment. *Truant* was hunted after this attack but managed to get away; later she sighted a number of submarines on separate occasions but never dared fire as she did not know whether they were American. As Singapore was now in enemy hands and there were no facilities for British submarines at Sourabaya, *Truant* rightly decided to return to Ceylon. This had also been decided for her by a high level conference which arranged for the Commander-in-Chief, Eastern Fleet, now in Ceylon, to take both *Truant* and *Trusty* under his command and establish a patrol in the Malacca Straits. However, *Truant* needed general repairs as well as having a main motor out of action and being reduced to 11 knots surface speed. For the time being, therefore, the Malacca Straits patrol was left to *Trusty* alone.

Anyone can see that if there had been a strong force earlier in this theatre, great destruction could have been carried out. Indeed, with such a strong force in action Sir Tom Phillips might have felt that he need not, in December 1941, risk his fleet, deprived as it was of any air cover; furthermore, the advance of the enemy down the Malay peninsula might have been sufficiently delayed to have allowed adequate land and air reinforcements to be sent to the area.

By early March, Colombo had become the collecting centre of what was left of the Allied naval forces after the Japanese advance through Malaya and the Dutch East Indies. Vice-Admiral Helfrich arrived by air and set up his headquarters there, being appointed to command all Dutch forces in the Far East on land, sea and air. The Dutch submarines, however, continued to operate under British command. Meanwhile, Admiral Sir Geoffrey Layton who had assumed the additional duties of Commander-in-Chief, Ceylon, set about putting the island into a state of readiness to meet the expected Japanese attack. As a measure to provide him with some warning, he had *Truant* and *Trusty* for the Malacca Straits patrol, although two submarines could never do the job adequately. The remnants of the Dutch flotilla were too exhausted and too badly in need of refit to help, although one boat did go to the northern ends of the Straits for a short while. The Dutch were, however, slightly better off by now as their new depot ship *Colombia* had arrived, and they had good accommodation, but unfortunately this ship had very poor workshops and did not compare with the modern British counterpart.

Colombia brought out Commander Gambier who very shortly after arrival took over the old British depot ship *Lucia* and the operational command of the British and Dutch submarines.

On 26 March Admiral Layton relinquished his command of the first Eastern Fleet, such as it was, to Admiral Sir James Somerville who had arrived at Colombo with hastily collected reinforcements which included the old *R* Class battleships, two *County* Class cruisers and an aircraft carrier.

This was perhaps the first date on which it could be said that the newly-formed Eastern Fleet existed as such, which was 108 days from the outbreak of hostilities with Japan. In turning over to Admiral Somerville, Admiral Layton explained that as soon as Singapore fell it became important to establish a patrol of submarines at the northern end of the Malacca Straits, to watch for, and attack enemy forces debouching into the Indian Ocean, but it was some time before he could extract *Trusty* and *Truant* from the South Pacific area and thus it was not until 23 March that the first patrol had begun and then with only one submarine on duty at a time.

As regards bases for the submarines, one of the main results of the fall of Singapore and Java was that we had no naval base capable of maintaining the Eastern Fleet near its sphere of operations. Colombo and Trincomalee were both very inadequately defended but offered the best prospects. At this time it was still intended to develop Addu Atoll as the principal base. This last named place can best be described as an area of water surrounded by coral

reefs at the southern end of the Maldive Islands. A very great deal of work was required before the base would be suitable and in fact the submarines never operated from there, even though they were depot ship based, and were fairly mobile.

On 5 April an attack by enemy aircraft operating from carriers, was made on Colombo. Sir Geoffrey Layton who now had the sole appointment of Commander-in-Chief, Ceylon, had been working for six weeks to two months to make some preparations for this expected attack and it was through his foresight that shipping had been widely dispersed and the defence of the island coordinated with the Ceylon Government. Admiral Somerville, the Commander-in-Chief, Eastern Fleet, had been at sea for three days previously, looking for these very forces which were expected to make the strike against the island, but he had to return to Addu Atoll to refuel and it was at that moment that the blow was struck. The attackers met stronger opposition than they had expected and although some naval ships were sunk, including the aircraft carrier *Hermes*, sufficient damage was inflicted on the Japanese aircraft to deter them from an immediate repetition of the raid. So far as the submarines were concerned, the old depot ship *Lucia* was hit by a small bomb which passed right through the ship without exploding, and only the fore mess deck was flooded. For a major air raid the submarine side of things was not seriously affected.

Following the Japanese fleet air arm attack on Ceylon, it was appreciated that the enemy could take one or both of two courses, namely they could attack Ceylon or south India, or both, It was felt, however, that they were unlikely to undertake two such big operations, knowing as we did, that the Americans were putting further pressure in the South Pacific in the enemy's rear. It was thought that if the Japanese did strike again they might try to establish themselves in southern India as a first move rather than in Ceylon itself.

It was natural at this time that high level conferences should take place to discuss the situation and one of these, at which General Wavell presided, Admiral Somerville, and Admiral Layton, with a large number of other high ranking officers in all Services, attended. The point arose as to the availability of submarines, particularly for reconnaissance work, to which the Commander-in-Chief, Ceylon, had to point out that there were at present far too few to provide reconnaissance of sufficient strength to give warning of the enemy's intentions. In a general discussion on the use of submarines it was realized that in the position then obtaining, only one submarine could be on patrol at any one time and that in the Malacca Straits. Even this one patrol was invaluable both to provide information of enemy activity in that area and to act offensively as an embarrassment to enemy shipping moving up to Burma and the Indian Ocean. Everyone agreed that the strengthening of this patrol was highly desirable.

About this time the latest submarine depot ship, a vessel of 15 000 tons building at Harland and Wolff at Belfast, was nearing completion. One of the

youngest Captains in the Navy at that time, and a most experienced submarine officer, Captain R S Warne, was appointed in command. This vessel, the *Adamant,* was to relieve the *Lucia* as the depot ship in the Far East and begin the build up of our submarine strength in that theatre. Matters, however, turned out differently. Admiral Somerville realized that he would be unwise to base his surface fleet on either Colombo or Trincomalee and accordingly divided his forces between Bombay and Kilindini, the port of Mombasa. As at Kilindini he had no facilities for fleet repairs he therefore ordered *Adamant* which was herself a 'floating repair shop', to join the fleet there, and act for his surface ships only, thus robbing the submarines of their repair ship and base. The Dutch took very similar action. They sent their precious *Colombia* to South Africa and some of their submarines to refit in UK.

While this action was definitely necessary it threw the submarine aspect of the eastern war into the doldrums. *Truant* and *Trusty* having carried out, one or two more patrols in the Malacca Straits were sent home to refit, leaving only the remnants of the Dutch still under our operational control, to keep up the all-important patrol in the Straits. This patrol was indeed kept going by these stalwart Dutchmen but through lack of numbers there was no watertight closing of the Straits. It was only possible to arrange that one boat went out after the other had arrived in port.

The year ended with the remarkable position that there were no British submarines at all in one of the most momentous theatres of operations in this world war. Nevertheless, on Captain Warne returning to the United Kingdom from Kilindini, never having given an operation order to a submarine after a year in command of our biggest depot ship, instructions were given that the *Adamant* was to be brought over to Colombo as soon as possible. This move was sanctioned on the sailing from the UK of the new fleet repair ship *Hecla* to Kilindini. Accordingly *Adamant* sailed for Colombo and a glorious month was spent in that port turning over to the new depot ship from the old *Lucia.* However, hardly had this been accomplished when the *Hecla* was sunk by a German U-boat while on passage, and *Adamant* was ordered to return to Kilindini as surface repair ship again!

HOME STATION 1943

At the beginning of 1943 the Germans had in Norway the *Tirpitz, Lutzow, Admiral Hipper, Nurnberg, Koln* and eight destroyers. Also about twenty U-boats were based there, thus saving the long run back to Germany. In addition, *Scharnhorst, Prinz Eugen,* two small cruisers and eleven destroyers were in the Baltic ready for service. In January Admiral Donitz succeeded Admiral Raeder. The former had been head of the German Submarine Service, and now gave it as his intention to place the entire resources of the German Navy to their submarine war.

British submarines in home waters found themselves faced with a formidable proposition. Numerous ports and fjords along the Norwegian coast from

Stavanger to Narvik, and from Narvik along the north coast to Kirkgnes, were available to the enemy in which they could either concentrate or disperse their forces at will. All could not be watched by our submarines, particularly bearing in mind that at least three submarines, and more probably four, are generally required in order to keep one patrol billet filled at a long distance from the base. Not only this, the lengthy hours of darkness were a severe handicap and the weather beyond description. On one occasion this winter the *Sheffield,* one of our large 6 inch cruisers, lost the top of her foremost turret in a gale, numerous destroyers were damaged and sometimes merchant vessels turned back to port because the weather was too much for them. No submarine ever returned to port before her scheduled time due to weather, a remarkable tribute to officers and men, the building yards, and the designers.

Early in March, more changes in German Naval High Commands were announced. These were changes to younger men mostly around Donitz' own age and they presaged a period of great naval energy by the enemy.

At this time *Tirpitz* left Trondheim and proceeded further north where she joined the other German heavy units. This put them out of reconnaissance range from the United Kingdom, and offered surprise if they broke out. The greatest threat was to convoys now running again, to north Russia. For their part, the submarines could now concentrate their watch on the northern coast of Norway, but the conditions of weather, although happily improved with spring, were often such that the visibility favoured the enemy too strongly and there could be no guarantee of warning by the submarines. The Commander-in-Chief, Home Fleet, Admiral Sir John Tovey, informed the Admiralty that the enemy concentration was too strong for the cruiser escorts and that furthermore, because of enemy shore-based aircraft, he was not prepared to take his battle fleet so far east to support the cruisers. Accordingly, once more, Russian convoys were called off, and this released the submarines for duties elsewhere.

There was plenty of scope for our submarines as not only were the anti-U-boat patrols increased in the Shetlands area, but attention could be paid to the Bay of Biscay. Here as early as January, a United States submarine, the *Shad,* had torpedoed the blockade runner SS *Nordfels* off Bilboa and there was a number of useful patrol positions in the Bay often untenanted. There was one United States squadron of submarines (this corresponded to a flotilla) operating under Admiral Bany at this time. When these vessels first came over they were very anxious to carry out inshore patrols for much longer periods than British submarines had been accustomed to. British submarine officers wondered whether, after all, they were to be shown how things might be done, but it was not long before the Americans admitted that the type of patrolling which the British submarines were doing was quite different to what they had been accustomed to in the Pacific, and they too cut their time from sailing to return, to about three weeks.

Two submarines were lost in the Home Command during the first quarter of 1943. The Norwegian *Uredd,* ex-British *P 41,* which left Lerwick on 5 February to carry out two landing operations on the coast of Norway, did not return. Then on 28 February, *Vandal,* Lieutenant J S Bridger, did not return from exercises in Kilbrennan Sound near Inchmarnock on the west coast of Scotland; the reason is unknown to this day.

There are always certain teams of enthusiastic people who scheme special operations in war. The submarine is their ideal man-of-war for these purposes, and at the time there is naturally a great temptation to loan submarines for these ingenious and plausible schemes. That the north Russian convoys were no longer running was an opportunity for these gentlemen to state their claims at Submarine Headquarters. Some of these proposals were approved, and the spring and summer of 1943 saw a number of these operations carried out. Whether the results justified all the elaborate planning and the use of such valuable warships as submarines on matters not precisely for which they were designed, is always a debatable point, but useful information was gained, particularly of radar stations and gun positions.

For example a submarine would take a small number of secret agents to a prearranged point on the coast of Norway and sometimes a commando party would be included in the operation. The parties would be landed at night and would have settled on meeting the submarine again at another carefully selected point probably after two or three days. If the operation was successful it might result in the blowing up of an oil fuel tank, the destruction of a gun position and the capture of some useful maps. A member of the local underground movement might elect to come over to England for a short while and one or two members of the party landed by the submarine might equally well elect to stay until a much later date. These 'story book' exploits were full of excitement, and men captured by the enemy were given no second chance. The operations certainly kept the enemy guessing and made him maintain larger guards than would otherwise have been normal throughout the long coastline.

Amongst other diversions Spitzbergen had been occupied by the Allies and reliefs for the party were carried by submarines. The Germans also occupied part of. Spitzbergen from time to time, and on one occasion when a party from our base at Barentsburg had been operating against an enemy meteorological station, they were attacked by a U-boat, and one officer and fourteen men were left stranded and unable to return to their base. The *Seadog,* Lieutenant C R Pelly, was then sent and rescued the party.

The additional British submarines diverted to patrol in the Bay of Biscay did not have any luck, but the United States *Shad* again got in an attack, this time on the SS *Pietro Orselo* which was escorted by four destroyers and was running for the Gironde. The vessel was damaged but made harbour. The anti-U-boat patrols were more successful though, and in April *Tuna,* Lieutenant D S R Martin, sank *U 644* off the Shetlands, and *Truculent,* Lieutenant R L

Alexander, got *U 308* off the Faroes in June.

Unhappily, there occurred another submarine disaster at this time. *Untamed,* Lieutenant G M Noll, failed to surface after an exercise and although she was contacted by the anti-submarine yacht *Shemara* and was able to pump out oil in an endeavour to gain buoyancy, after twenty-four hours nothing more was heard of her and the entire crew were lost. As so often happens in submarine disasters, the weather became unsuitable for divers to work very shortly after the accident, which hampered rescue plans.

Early in September, *Tirpitz,* and seven destroyers together with *Scharnhorst* which had come north from the Baltic, sailed from Alten fjord and raided Spitzbergen. This was the only time when a German force of any size made a sally and was not engaged. *Tantalus* was our nearest submarine and was sent to patrol off Barentsburg but saw nothing. This effort by the German heavy ships served to emphasize the threat to our communications with north Russia and coincided with the completion of the trials and training of our own midget submarines. It was, therefore, a propitious moment to bring these craft into operation against the most formidable ship the enemy could put to sea.

It will be remembered that plans to build midget submarines were put into operation by Admiral Horton as soon as he had had time to settle into his command. It was a very great disappointment to him not to be in the position later to control these submarines on their maiden attack, but his work had not been wasted. He had created a new arm of great potential, and the Submarine Command was itching to demonstrate what it could do, particularly after the disappointing attack by human-torpedoes on the *Tirpitz* at Trondheim the previous summer.

The new attack on the *Tirpitz* was carried out on 22 September. Four out of six midget submarines penetrated into Alten fjord, and three went on into Kaa fjord in which the *Tirpitz* was lying. Two succeeded in exploding charges under the hull of the battleship which put her out of action for many months. To reach Alten fjord from their base in the United Kingdom the midget submarines had to be towed by large submarines over 1000 miles. To get to the *Tirpitz* they had to proceed under their own power for another fifty miles, passing through minefields, navigating intricate fjords vigilantly patrolled by the enemy, and make their attack despite nets and other defences in confined waters affording little chance of escape.

Six midgets took part in the attack of which four, *X 5, X 6, X 7* and *X 10,* penetrated into Alten fjord. *X 10* was obliged to abandon the attack owing to defects when only within six miles of her objective. This craft was recovered by our own forces after she had hidden in a bay for some five days but had to be sunk within 400 miles of home. Of the two which did not reach the fjord one had to be sunk on the outward passage owing to defects, the other broke adrift from her tow about 200 miles from the entrance to Alten fjord and was not seen again.

Of the three which managed to get through Alten fjord and thence into Kaa fjord, one, *X 5,* may not have succeeded in making her attack. Wreckage, probably from this craft, commanded by Lieutenant Henty-Creer, was discovered by German divers on the day after the attack about one mile to seaward of the *Tirpitz.* There was no knowledge of any survivors. The two midgets which definitely succeeded in attacking the *Tirpitz* were *X 6* and *X 7.* They were commanded by Lieutenant Donald Cameron, RNR, and Lieutenant B C G Place, RN, both of whom were awarded the Victoria Cross. These two boats did not return, and the majority of their crews were taken prisoner.

The attack was made between 8 am and 8.30 am on 22 September. *X 6* went through the boat gate entrance in the net defences astern of a small coaster. She had, however, been sighted by the *Tirpitz.* The alarm was raised, hand grenades were thrown and a pinnace started dropping depth-charges. *X 6* went on and passed under the bridge of the battleship and dropped one charge. Having gone under the ship she did not turn to starboard in time and ran into the nets on the far side before she could make a second run to attack. She was obliged to go astern and in doing so bumped against the *Tirpitz.* Immediately she released her second charge and then surfaced alongside the battleship. The commanding officer next saw his crew safely out of the boat and scuttled his craft. All were picked up and taken on board the *Tirpitz. X 7* negotiated the nets around the battleship but only got inside with a few minutes to spare before the time when the first explosions from charges of the other successful midgets might be expected to go off. However, she managed to drop one charge under the funnel and another under the after turret. *X 7* was only some 400 yards to seaward when the explosions began. The force so damaged the midget that she was put out of action. She surfaced about an hour later and was immediately hotly engaged by gunfire and sunk. Lieutenant Place and Lieutenant Aitken escaped from the midget, the latter using DSEA. Of the others nothing was known.

The explosions lifted the *Tirpitz* five or six feet out of the water. Damage extended from amidships to aft. Numbers of the ship's company on deck aft were flung into the air and several casualties resulted. After settling down the ship took on an immediate list to port of about five degrees which was later adjusted by trimming. More than 100 casualties were caused by panic firing, and destroyers and small craft went into action up and down the fjord. Immediate and skilful action on the part of the captain of the *Tirpitz* in warping his ship quickly from the original position saved her from very considerable damage. All the same, photographs taken between 23 September and 5 October showed *Tirpitz* to be surrounded by thick oil which covered Kaa fjord and extended for over two miles towards the sea. The photographs also showed several small ships alongside which were probably needed to supply the damaged battleship with power and light. *Tirpitz* was still in the same berth at the end of the year and obviously in need of docking in a German shipyard.

In October the Admiralty decided to start sending convoys to Russia again. The matter was studied at Submarine Headquarters and it was decided to try concentrating patrols inshore along the northern coast of Norway rather than send any submarines as escorts. This meant taking some submarines away from the anti-U-boat patrols but all agreed that this must be accepted.

While these arrangements were being put in hand, an enterprise probably unheard of in most civilian circles, took place. It really deserved better success, but things never went right. In November an attempt was made with Welman craft to attack shipping in Bergen harbour. Four officers: Lieutenant J F L Holmes, RN; Lieutenant B M Harris, RNVR; Lieutenant C A Johnson, RN, and Second Lieutenant Pedersen of the Norwegian Army made the attempt. The Welman craft were taken to a point just off the coast by MTBs and thence they proceeded to a small bay to lie up for a day. Owing to unexpected activity by Norwegian fishermen, the craft were discovered and the alarm raised. However, on the following evening, Second Lieutenant Pedersen left in his Welman followed at fifteen-minute intervals by the other three. Pedersen was captured and the three others finding it impossible to penetrate the defences, scuttled independently, and went ashore. Later the three English officers met at a pre-arranged rendezvous and were eventually rescued on 5 February the next year.

The year 1943 in home waters ended in a thrilling manner though not entirely from the submarine point of view. *Scharnhorst* came out from Lang fjord on the northern coast of Norway on 25 December, but was not sighted by our submarines. Again this was not really very surprising bearing in mind the conditions obtaining in mid-winter in those latitudes. Under a new admiral and captain, *Scharnhorst* intended to attack a convoy, though not to be brought to action by warships. However, her plan was rudely interrupted by Admiral Fraser (now C-in-C) with the Home Fleet, in a brilliant action off the North Cape, and she never got back to harbour. Like the *Bismarck* action, the submarines, while rejoicing that such a major warship had been sunk, deplored the ill-luck which deprived them of any active part in the achievement.

MEDITERRANEAN 1943

The year began with a high level conference at Casablanca where a full offensive strategy was initiated. In these conditions there is always less for submarines to do. The hey-day of submarine work is when all our surface forces are neutralized or on the defensive; it is then that the submarine stands out as the weapon which can hit the enemy. Nevertheless while the real harvest for our submarines in the Mediterranean was beginning to pass its peak, there was still much to be done.

In the early hours of 3 January the harbour of Palermo was the target for an attack by British human torpedoes. Five chariots, each with their crew of two, were embarked on deck in watertight containers in the submarines *Trooper*, Lieutenant J S Wraith, and *Thunderbolt*, Lieutenant-Commander Crouch. Just

before midnight on 2 January they were launched outside Palermo. The two carrying submarines withdrew, leaving *Unruffled*, Lieutenant J S Stevens, a third submarine, to act as recovery ship. One chariot had to abandon the attack owing to mechanical failure and was picked up six hours later by *Unruffled*, another sank from an unknown cause before reaching the harbour. The driver of a third, tore his diving suit in getting through the net defences and was drowned but the second member of the crew drove on and finally blew up the chariot. He escaped the explosion and was taken prisoner. A fourth chariot fixed its charge to the 8500 ton liner *Viminale*. The subsequent explosion so damaged the ship that she had to be towed to Messina, and later in the year when seemingly out of danger, the vessel sank. A fifth chariot exploded a charge under the new cruiser *Ulpio Traiano*, 3362 tons, and sank her. This chariot crew also fixed limpet mines to the destroyers *Gregale*, *Ciclone* and *Gamma*, but they were discovered and the charges removed. All members of the successful chariots were taken prisoner. Lieutenant R T G Greenland, RNVR, and Sub-Lieutenant R G Dove, RNVR, were each awarded the DSO.

On 4 January, *P 48*, Lieutenant M E Faber, was reported overdue from her patrol area in the Gulf of Tunis. Anti-submarine conditions there were possibly the most vigorous that our submarines had yet encountered. Rome radio falsely claimed four submarines, though one of these may possibly have been *P 311*, Cayley's boat which was lost in December 1942. The losses were hard to bear, but 21 January brought the submarines of the Mediterranean Command their estimated total of shipping sunk to 1 000 000 tons.

Submarine warfare seemed to take on a more open phase in January 1943. In some ways this was due to the arrival of the Eighth Flotilla at Algiers. Captain Fawkes having brought *Maidstone* to Algiers soon after the successful landings on the North African coast, not long after his arrival had collected together the largest submarine flotilla ever formed in the history of the British Navy. There were in all thirty-eight boats and as the majority were the new improved *S* Class, the flotilla was particularly well equipped. While at Gibraltar, the *Maidstone* flotilla had been likened to the 'nursery slopes' preparing new submarines for the front line patrols of the middle and eastern Mediterranean, but now she had moved to the front line herself. The French took advantage of the new state of affairs and part of the *Maidstone* flotilla consisted of French boats which had come over to the side of the Allies. Names familiar in 1940 came to life again, such as *La Perle, La Sultane, Casabianca, Arethuse* and *Orphe*.

Besides what might be described as orthodox submarine work beginning with the sinking of the Italian U-boat *Malachite* by the Dutch-manned submarine *Dolfijn*, our own submarine *Splendid*, Lieutenant McGeogh, sinking two valuable enemy tankers, *Sahib*, Lieutenant Bromage, sinking *U 301*, and *United*, Lieutenant J C Y Roxburgh, sinking the destroyer *Bombardiere*, there followed a 'mixed bag'. *Turbulent*, Commander Linton, shelled a moving train on the Calabria coast; *Rorqual*, Lieutenant-Commander Napier, shelled a railway

bridge near Spartivento, and *Parthian*, Lieutenant M B St John, bombarded a resin factory when operating in the Gulf of Kassandra, *Shakespeare*, Lieutenant M F R Ainslie, laid the foundations of a most successful war for this submarine and himself with a long list of successes including attacks on escorted convoys and bombardments. Indeed few submarines completed patrols without firing some torpedoes and carrying out at least one bombardment. These were typical of the variety of reports reaching Malta, Algiers and Beirut at that time. Once again, however, the inevitable losses crept into the story. *Tigris*, now commanded by Lieutenant-Commander G R Colvin, and *Turbulent*, Commander J W Linton, did not return to Algiers from patrol.

The loss of *Turbulent* was particularly felt through the Navy. It is believed she had been mined. Captain G B H Fawkes in his report said: 'The grievous loss of this outstanding submarine on her last patrol before proceeding to the United Kingdom to refit is most keenly felt.' Commander J W Linton of *Turbulent*, already possessing the DSO and the DSC was awarded the Victoria Cross on 26 May posthumously. From the outbreak of war, until *Turbulent's* last patrol, he was consistently in command of submarines and had sunk one destroyer, twenty-six supply ships and carried out numerous bombardments. In all it is estimated he had accounted for over 100 000 tons of enemy shipping.

Admiral Submarines wrote these words of this great submarine commanding officer: 'The whole Submarine Service has cause to be proud of Tubby Linton's achievements and we all owe him lasting gratitude for his unstinted help, sound advice and wide experience which he so readily and unfailingly passed on.' Following on this loss, *Thunderbolt* (originally *Thetis*), Lieutenant-Commander Crouch, was overdue. *Trooper* reported hearing a torpedo explosion in her area, then depth-charging followed. It seems that *Thunderbolt* was sunk following a successful attack on the enemy.

Churchill, on one of his visits to the Mediterranean, took the opportunity at this time to visit the Eighth Submarine Flotilla. The outstanding spirit he found there, bearing in mind all that he had seen in the three services now in victory mood, was an inspiration to him. It is recorded that when he left the Algiers flotilla his mind passed to the inevitable losses which must follow, and he was greatly moved.

Addressing the submarine crews of the Eighth Flotilla, he spoke these words: 'Officers and men of HMS *Maidstone* and submarine crews of your flotilla, how proud I am when I go around and see you all. I have been with different branches of the Forces and have been in North Africa before. I have visited most of the battleships and many of the cruisers, but this is the first time I have had the pleasure of visiting a submarine depot ship. Now I can tell you how very closely I follow you in your ventures and the pleasure and relief I share with you at each sinking of the enemy shipping. Of all the branches of men in the Forces there is none which shows more devotion and faces grimmer perils than the submarine. I should like you to know that very often your

exploits and deeds cannot be told because of secrecy. Not alone do I watch these feats of yours in this war, they are followed closely by the whole Cabinet. Great deeds are done in the air and on the land, nevertheless nothing surpasses your exploits.'

Besides Churchill's visit, other honours were shown to the Eighth Flotilla. On one occasion General Mark Clark invited Captain Fawkes and a party of twelve officers and men to his headquarters at Oujda. On arrival the party found an Honour Guard had been paraded to honour the British Submarine Service. Those present will never forget this impressive scene and found it difficult to express adequately their appreciation of General Clark's action.

During April the Axis armies in North Africa were steadily pushed back and desperate efforts were made by the enemy to reinforce their beaten army of North Africa. Once more the submarines sailed, this time in their greatest numbers, to take toll of any targets offered. The attacks on merchantmen made a very long list which cannot be detailed here. Mention must be made though of *Safari,* Commander Bryant, who did the most damage; one signal alone from Bryant told of the destruction. of a 5000 ton armed merchant cruiser, a 3500 ton water carrier and a 3000 ton merchant ship driven ashore and finished off with a final torpedo the day following the attack. Enemy warships also came in for attention; *Unshaken,* Lieutenant J Whitton, sank a torpedo boat, and *Unbroken,* Lieutenant Mars, blew a minesweeper to pieces. *Unbending,* Lieutenant E T Stanley, was also among the submarines with particularly good records at this time.

This full scale submarine effort in April must have made the German High Command think very hard. On 5 March, Hitler had issued a directive which in itself was a tribute to their work. He wrote: 'Tunisia is strategically of primary importance. The retention of Tunisia is a matter of supplies. The Straits of Sicily must team with patrol and escort vessels.'

Sadly, though perhaps not surprisingly, *Sahib, Splendid* and *Regent* did not return from patrol. *Sahib,* Lieutenant Bromage, sank an enemy transport north of Messina and then was caught by anti-submarine forces and had to scuttle. The commanding officer and all the crew except one survived and were taken prisoner. *Splendid,* Lieutenant McGeogh, also had to scuttle after heavy depth charging off Capri; again the commanding officer and the majority of the crew survived. *Regent,* Lieutenant W N R Knox, had a difficult patrol in the Straits of Otranto and was sunk by Italian anti-submarine craft. All three submarines were lost in the first week in May and were a heavy toll for only a few days.

These sacrifices were recognized by the Commander-in-Chief who said in a signal to the Admiralty: 'Desperate eleventh hour efforts of the enemy to reinforce his armies in Tunisia necessitated concentrating our submarines on supply routes and harbour entrances thereby increasing their vulnerability.'

On 7 May Tunis and Bizerta fell and it was at this time that the Commander-in-Chief, Mediterranean, made one of his best-known signals. In launching operation 'Retribution', namely the prevention of evacuation from Tunis by

the enemy, he said: 'Sink, burn and destroy; let nothing pass.' The submarines went about the job with tremendous enthusiasm and in doing so took greater risks than ever before.

A message from the Prime Minister congratulating the Royal Navy on its work in the Tunisian campaign was published on 13 June. In this message Churchill gave certain facts which had impressed him during his recent visit to North Africa. Our submarines had sunk forty-seven ships; and our surface forces forty-two ships; totalling 268 600 tons. Aided by the air the grand total was 137 ships with a tonnage of 443 400 tons, this represented 32 per cent of the shipping initially available at the beginning of the campaign in Tunisia. A message was also received by Captain Fawkes from Commander-in-Chief, Mediterranean, as follows:

'I have read with interest and gratification your summary of the achievements of the Eighth Flotilla during the last six months. It is particularly appropriate that this report covers precisely the period from the initial entry into the North African theatre, to the expulsion of the Axis from the Continent. To the great victory which has been achieved, and of which we are reaping the fruits today, the submarines have contributed a vitally important share; how important is perhaps only realized by those whose profession is the sea. I am sure that the greatest source of satisfaction that can come to you, the commanding officers and ships' companies of the submarines of the Eighth Submarine Flotilla is the knowledge that the Navy itself realizes the full extent of the contribution that has been made to the battle by the Mediterranean submarines. Their achievement has been great and the price has not been light, but the standard which the Submarine Service sets itself has been more than maintained. I request that you will make the above known to the commanding officers and ships' companies of the submarines of the Eight Flotilla.'

Maidstone had had the honour of wearing the Flag of Admiral Cunningham, Commander-in-Chief, Mediterranean, for the past six months and continued to do so for the best part of a year. During the whole of this time the depot ship was at Algiers.

While the Allied armies re-grouped and rested and the planners put together the scheme for the invasion of Sicily, the submarines went looking for trouble wherever they could find it. Once again, this produced a mixed bag, *Parthian*, Lieutenant M B St John, bombarded a railway at the foot of Mount Olympus. She was rather over-daring and was machine-gunned, one rating being killed. *Safari*, now commanded by Lieutenant R B Lakin, got amongst the coastal shipping; *Sickle*, Lieutenant Drummond, sunk *U 303;* and *Shakespeare*, Lieutenant Ainslie, bombarded an airfield in Corsica. *Unruly*, Lieutenant Fyfe, sank the Italian submarine *Acciaio; United*, Lieutenant Roxburgh, got the *Remo;* and *Trooper*, under the temporary command of Lieutenant-Commander Clarabut, added the third submarine to be sunk in one month, the *Pietro Micca. Simoon*, Lieutenant G D N Milner, sank the destroyer *Gioberti* and *Rorqual*, Lieutenant-Commander Napier, returned to her job of minelaying. Both *Safari*

and *Severn,* Lieutenant-Commander Campbell, landed troops in Sardinia. These are but some of the events in the crowded three months of May, June and July.

Meanwhile the Algiers flotilla had one more thrilling experience. The King visited *Maidstone* and ·inspected the whole flotilla. One thing particularly caught His Majesty's eye, this was the number of officers and men wearing decorations. He told Captain Fawkes how pleased he was to see this.

By now the more serious business of the invasion of Sicily had been taken in hand. All available submarines of the three flotillas, the First, Eighth and Tenth took part. Beacon submarines were allotted to beaches to guide the assault craft and then they joined others at various points around the coast. In all forty-seven Allied submarines were employed but the 'bag' was small. Indeed, the Commander-in-Chief described the submarine part in the invasion as disappointing but added that this was due to the reluctance of the enemy to come out and face the situation. *Simoon,* Lieutenant G D Milner, got a hit on the destroyer *Gioberti,* but nothing much else came by our patrols. The Sicilian campaign was over by 18 August, and already submarines had begun to go further afield. *Parthian,* Lieutenant G A Pardoe, RNR, had sailed to return to her proper flotilla at Beirut and intended to do a patrol in Greek waters on the way. Unfortunately, *Parthian* was lost on this patrol. The Algiers flotilla also lost a very efficient submarine when *Saracen,* Lieutenant Lumby, was forced through severe depth charging to scuttle his boat off Bastia. The commanding officer and crew were taken prisoner. Added to these losses, the Greek flotilla at Beirut had despatched the submarine *Katsonis* to land a representative of the exiled Greek Government on an Island in the Aegean. *Katsonis* did not return and later it was learned that two British and eighteen Greek survivors had been taken prisoner.

The next step in the war was the invasion of Italy, and the Salerno landings. *Shakespeare* was sent ahead to reconnoitre the beaches, and in doing so discovered a recently laid line of mines off a chosen beach. She also acted as a navigational beacon for the Allied landings, and the remaining submarines from the Eighth and Tenth Flotillas were disposed to prevent interference by enemy naval forces, which in fact was not forthcoming. At this juncture on 3 September, we arranged an armistice with Italy and our landings took place on the same date. A few hours before the Armistice *Shakespeare* had sunk the Italian submarine *Velella* but after the armistice, a signal was sent to all submarines not to attack Italian men-of-war and merchant ships coming south to surrender.

Later when the Italian surface forces came over, and particularly when at our orders their main battle fleet anchored off Malta, the eyes of all those serving in submarines turned towards these ships with mixed feelings. Here were the targets they had been chasing for months and years. This fleet had never ventured far, or often, but if only it had done so, there surely must have been a harvest for the submarines.

In addition to the men-of-war, a vast fleet of Italian merchantmen came over to the Allies in the same way as the main fleet, and about eighty vessels answered the call of the Allies to join them. In the general mêlée the submarines played their part in directing the ships where to go. *Unrivalled,* Lieutenant H B Turner, had the most spectacular story to tell. When off Bari, Turner decided to enter the harbour. There he found four merchant ships wrecked by the Germans, but the others he organized into a convoy. He found that none of the captains knew where to go, none could speak English and no ship could signal. Nevertheless he took them along with him, later being joined by *Unruly,* and eventually arrived at Malta. Surely a strange sight even in these strange times!

By the middle of September we were ashore at Salerno, and Naples fell on 1 October. Nothing came the way of our submarines in the further landing operations but they played their part making beach reconnaissances and acting as navigational marks for the assault craft.

At the end of September a small private war was carried out by *Sportsman,* Lieutenant R Gatehouse, and *Seraph,* Lieutenant Jewell, who were given the job of catching what they could when the enemy evacuated Corsica. They had a great time sinking landing craft which were escaping with troops and also other small targets.

With Italy as co-belligerent, this change in scene involved the Islands of Rhodes and Leros in operations by the Germans to capture them from their late ally. Submarines were sailed for patrol position in the Aegean. No great prizes came their way. The majority of shipping employed by the enemy was small and much cargo went by air. *Torbay,* Lieutenant Clutterbuck, got a 300 foot floating dock and a small trooper; *Unsparing,* Lieutenant A D Piper, RNR, sank an R-boat and a trooper; *Seraph,* Lieutenant Jewell, caught a seaplane on the water, and in sinking three caiques picked up a German officer and thirteen ranks. *Sokol* (Polish manned) sank an anti-submarine schooner and an E-boat and in her case when sinking three schooners killed 200 Germans, taking no prisoners. *Unruly,* Lieutenant Fyfe, hit a destroyer, and *Ultimatum,* Lieutenant Kett, RNR, sank *U 431,* which generally rounded off a very good year's work. These successes were typical of the times and they showed one new aspect of submarine operations very clearly by the number of anti-submarine craft attacked and sunk. Two years earlier the standard of anti-submarine efficiency was very different and the submarines had not fully acquired the technique of attacking them; nor perhaps the confidence. Things had altered considerably in the closing stages of 1943. The lead had been given in August by *Safari,* Commander Ben Bryant, who had demonstrated that minesweepers, anti-submarine yachts and trawlers were vulnerable to gun attack and had played havoc with them in the Tyrhennian Sea.

Another aspect of submarine warfare had changed, due to an order from the captains of flotillas to the effect that submarines need now no longer proceed submerged in daylight.

As ever, submarine operations were attended by losses. Both *Trooper*, Lieutenant J S Wraith, and *Simoon*, Lieutenant G D N Milner, were lost in the Aegean.

By the end of the year it was obvious that the task of our submarines in the Mediterranean was shortly coming to a close. There was a rapid run down of the Algiers flotilla and many of the boats proceeded to the Far East. The depot ship *Maidstone* went to Alexandria to refit. That *Usurper*, Lieutenant D R O Mott, was lost off Spezia during the last month of the Eighth Flotilla's operations made a sad ending to a splendid record.

Looking back from the early days of 1941 we had come a long way and with the end of 1943 the war in the Mediterranean so far as our submarines were concerned, was nearing its end.

FAR EAST 1943

For some time Acting-Captain Gambier, in the *Lucia* at Colombo, had looked forward to the return of the Dutch depot ship *Colombia*. He was depending on this ship now that *Adamant* had returned to Kilindini following the sinking of the *Hecla*. However, all his hopes were to be dashed to the ground.

On 27 February, the *Colombia* was on coastal passage from East London to Port Elizabeth escorted by the corvette *Genista* and one aircraft. She needed docking and it was decided to sail her by day only, so that continuous air escort could be provided until she reached Simonstown where a dock was available for her. Nothing stronger than one corvette could be found for surface protection as there were six escorted convoys at sea in the Indian Ocean. When a sighting report of a submarine was received from a training aircraft, extra aircraft were sent to cover *Colombia*, and a South African minesweeping trawler was ordered to join the corvette. Just as the first of the additional aircraft arrived, the *Colombia* was struck by a torpedo and sank in half an hour. Neither the aircraft nor the surface ships saw anything of the submarine. This was a further bitter blow for the building up of the Eastern Fleet submarine force. In fact, matters did not go at all well in the early part of 1943, so far as the Submarine Command was concerned, *P 615*, Lieutenant C W Lambert, on 17 April when on her way round the Cape, was torpedoed by *U 123*, 120 miles south of Freetown and this left the patrolling of the Malacca Straits as before, solely in the hands of the Dutch submarines operationally controlled by us if, and when, they were available. There had been one patrol carried out in this month by an American submarine in the Malacca Straits but she found targets scarce and the Commander-in-Chief, United States Fleet, decided that a second submarine would not be sent.

The situation at Colombo during the next three months was very unsatisfactory. There were only four submarines under our operational control on the station. Of these, three were Dutch and one British. *O 21* was engaged on special operations from Australia until September, *O 23* was operational but due to leave Ceylon in September for refit in the United Kingdom, and only

O 24 could be counted on as a permanent unit. *Rover,* the British contribution, was undergoing a prolonged refit in Bombay.

At last on 27 July the Admiralty instructed the Commander-in-Chief, Mediterranean, to release eight long-distance submarines to the Eastern Fleet. This order was almost simultaneous to a plea from the Commander-in-Chief, Eastern Fleet, asking that the projected submarine reinforcements should be substantially advanced.

The submarines detailed to go east were: *Severn, Tally Ho, Templar, Tactician, Trespasser, Taurus, Surf, Simoon.*

Simoon was, unfortunately, lost in the Aegean before sailing and *Trident* joined the concentration instead. *Trident,* Lieutenant Newstead, got away from Aden by 4 August and making good passage went straight on patrol during which, on 29 August, she sighted the Japanese cruiser *Kashi* which was entering Sabang, Sumatra; here there was evidence of good hunting to come.

Perhaps encouraged by this, on 4 September the Admiralty decided that all new construction, all refitted *T* Class and *S* Class submarines, and ultimately the new *A* Class, with the exception of a few ear-marked for training and operations in home waters, should join the Eastern Fleet.

With so many submarines on their way to Ceylon it was essential there should be a modern depot ship in Eastern waters to receive them. Already the overflow from the old depot ship *Lucia* at Colombo was being accommodated in a China river steamer, the *Wuchang.* Accordingly in November *Adamant* was released from Kilindini and by Christmas she had taken over depot ship duties at Trincomalee, Ceylon; *Wuchang* joined her from Colombo but *Lucia* was not fit to move. When *Adamant* arrived, Captain H M C Ionides took over command of the ship and also relieved Captain Gambier in command of the submarines.

The year ended with at any rate one success, when on 12 December, *Taurus,* Lieutenant-Commander Wingfield, sank the Japanese U-boat *I 34* off Penang.

HOME STATION 1944

Interest at home was now greatly centred on those submarines preparing to go to the war in the Pacific. Nevertheless, there was still much work to be done on the Home Station particularly off the Norwegian coast. Convoys to Russia continued, but submarines did not always form part of the close surface escort. Close patrols were maintained along the whole length of Norway because by now *Tirpitz* had sufficiently recovered from her wounds to be able to try and make a trip back to Germany for a full refit. In the early months of the year *Tirpitz* did not move south, but the submarine patrols were not unproductive. On 11 February, *Stubborn,* Lieutenant A A Duff, hit a convoy of seven ships with four torpedoes. Thirty-four depth charges were dropped but she managed to avoid serious damage. Two days later, however, after attacking another convoy, a prolonged attack on her by anti-submarine craft during which seventy depth charges were dropped, crippled the boat.

Stubborn was able to evade her attackers and later, after air cover had been arranged, destroyers came over to within 24 miles of the Norwegian coast and *Stubborn* was taken in tow, arriving home without further trouble. Meanwhile, attention had been drawn to another area where *Taku,* Lieutenant A J W Pitt, hit three ships in the Haugesund approaches, they were *Rheinhausen,* 6300 tons, *Harm Fritzen,* 4800 tons, and the *Bornhofen,* 3000 tons.

By the middle of March there seemed to be a certainty that *Tirpitz* would move, but having crowded the coast with submarines the information proved to be a false alarm. Nevertheless, the submarine concentration was entirely justified, as early in April *Tirpitz* was seen to be doing local exercises. This drew a strong reaction from the Fleet Air Arm who attacked the ship and did considerable damage. *Syrtis,* Lieutenant MH Jupp, keeping a close patrol in the Bodo area in support of their operation was lost. By now the days were getting very long and the odds were against the submarine once more.

With the *Tirpitz* well bombed by the Fleet Air Arm, the X craft crews looked around for other targets. This time the shipping in the port of Bergen was selected. *Sceptre,* Lieutenant I S MacIntosh, towed *X 24* to the approaches to Bergen on 14 April. Lieutenant M H Shean took *X 24* undetected into the Bergen fjord and found his first objective, the Laksvaag floating dock, flooded down and empty. Shean dropped two charges under the dock each with a four hour setting, and got away. The rendezvous with *Sceptre* was kept to plan, crews were changed, and the craft successfully towed back to base. Photographs later showed a 7000 ton merchantman sunk and extensive damage to the quay and the coaling facilities though the floating dock had somehow survived. Shean was given a DSO for his courage in carrying out this hazardous task.

Sceptre was again in the news this year. In May the submarines operating in the Bay of Biscay were paying special attention to the iron ore traffic being run between Spain and the occupied French ports. On 21 May *Sceptre* torpedoed the *Hoch Heimer* and two days later got the *Haldur,* both carrying iron ore. By a coincidence *Upstart* in the Mediterranean had sunk the *Saumur,* a similar ship. These three successes were a very severe blow to the ore trade and proved to be a deterrent to future sailings.

In the Spring of 1944 arrangements were made to transfer certain of HM ships to the Russian Navy. The submarines came in for a quota, and *Sunfish, Unison, Unbroken* and *Ursula* were prepared at Rosyth. Russian crews came over to take them to north Russian ports. The taking over by the Russians was typical. The submarines were examined with the greatest suspicion and innumerable questions asked; however, the boats got away to the scheduled time. On passage to North Russia *Sunfish* did not conform to the agreed route and was promptly bombed and sunk by one of our Liberator aircraft. At this very time the use to which these submarines could be put by the Russians, was emphasized to them by two boats of similar types, when *Ula,* Lieutenant R M Sars, Royal Norwegian Navy, with a Norwegian crew, sank a U-boat, *U 974,* right inside Skudenese fjord in spite of it being escorted, and the British *Satyr,*

Lieutenant T S Weston, got another U-boat, *U 987* off Lofoten.

Just after the Russians had sailed with our four submarines, the Admiralty informed the Fleet that it was established that a number of German U-boats were fitted with extensible air inlet and exhaust trunks, in a single shaft, which enabled them to proceed on the engines, charge batteries and ventilate the boat, when at periscope depth. This gear was called 'Schnorkel'. The trunk was hinged to the deck at the after end of the conning tower, usually the port side, and when not in use lay flush with the deck. The diameter of the trunk was about 14 inches, it could therefore probably be detected at short range by radar. The Germans were also reported to be developing an improved Schnorkel with air intake only, the exhaust being discharged into the water to eliminate smoke. Thus the apparatus which had been discussed by submarine personnel for more than fifteen years had come into being and was being used against us.

The invasion of the Continent now filled everyone's minds. Naturally, all submarines wanted to play their part in this, the greatest amphibious operation of all time. Unfortunately, there was little submarines could do. Two X craft were used as beacons to guide assault craft but other than this there was no specific task. However, so great an operation was certain to cause much enemy movement along the coast of Norway and the Biscay seaboard, so all available submarines were disposed accordingly, but no great harvest came their way.

The surprise of the Normandy operations was the appearance of German human torpedoes and a type of X craft. At one time twenty-seven reports of these craft were received in one day, this was followed by thirty-one sightings the next day. However, with the experience of our own similar craft at our disposal we were able to see that no damage came to British ships. The only success which the Germans had, was to score two hits on the French cruiser *Courbet,* but the vessel was already sunk as a blockship.

On the Allied side, our own X craft team decided to have another attack on Bergen. *X 24* was again selected with *Sceptre* as the towing submarine. All went according to plan. This time the floating dock was successfully destroyed and Lieutenant H P Westmacott, who was the diver, received the DSO.

On 12 September Rear-Admiral G E Creasy relieved Rear-Admiral C B Barry at Submarine Headquarters. Admiral Creasy was not a submarine officer but had had wide experience of submarine warfare as Director of Anti-submarine Warfare at the Admiralty and also as adviser to the United States Navy on anti-submarine operations.

With our armies well ashore in France, the field of operations for the submarines was rapidly closing in. However, there was still the *Tirpitz* in Alten fjord. Events would certainly hasten her efforts to reach home and the submarines were again disposed accordingly to catch her. *Tirpitz* succeeded in moving in late October to Tromso keeping well inside the islands and under heavy escort. Here the submarines could not get at her, but Lancasters of Bomber Command now took a hand and on 29 October made an attack

without suffering serious casualties. Although it was thought that *Tirpitz* was hit, photographs showed her still afloat and upright. Accordingly another attack was decided upon and on 12 November the Lancasters sank her. So ended *Tirpitz*. Once again a great prize had evaded the Submarine Command.

These autumn days saw the liberation of Calais and our assault on Walcheren and naturally attention was drawn away from submarine operations but these still went on. *Sceptre* got two supply ships running for home off the south-west corner of Norway; *Venturer*, Lieutenant J S Launders, had the job of taking stores to members of the underground movement in Norway and got a U-boat, *U 771*, on the return journey. Whenever a ship came outside the protection of the Norwegian leads she ran the gauntlet of the submarines.

With troops and stores being hurried back to Germany, *Rubis* made four more minelays in their path, beginning on 24 September and ending on 19 December. These operations brought to a close the work of this wonderful submarine. In reporting her record to the Admiralty, Flag Officer Submarines said:

'The following month saw *Rubis'* last patrol of the war. Leaving Lerwick on 15 December, Capitaine de Corvette Rousselot, DSO, DSC, laid his last cargo of mines off Jaederens on the 19 and on Christmas Eve of the year berthed his submarine at Dundee. This minelay was a particularly brilliant one as it was necessary to dodge a north-bound convoy of landing barges while actually laying the mines and resulted in the sinking of *UJ 1113, UJ 1116,* the minesweeper *R 402* and the supply ship *Weichselland* (3583 grt). *Rubis* was overdue for refit and Admiralty decided that owing to the strained condition of submarine refitting resources and the fact that it would take at least six months to fit her for further operational service, she was not to be taken in hand.'

Flag Officer Surmarines also paid fitting tribute to this gallant French ally in his covering letter to *Rubis'* last patrol report:

'Since the French submarine *Rubis* joined us in April 1940 she has been attached to various flotillas where she has always been most welcome and her outstanding ability admired by all who met her. She has carried out twenty-two minelaying operations and seven patrols. Four of the minelaying operations and the landing of Agents in Norway were carried out by Capitaine de Corvette Cabanier, DSO, and eighteen minelaying operations and the probable sinking of a 4000 ton tanker by torpedo were carried out under the command of Capitaine de Corvette Rousselot, DSO, DSC, formerly her First Lieutenant. These operations were conducted in all conditions of weather and in the face of the great hazards of enemy mining and both surface and aerial anti-submarine activity. On every occasion *Rubis* carried out her mission successfully despite the fact that towards the end of her time mechanical defects were repeatedly occurring. (*Note—Rubis* was completed in 1932 and under the 1927 programme.)

'The full score of her successes cannot yet be assessed but her captain and company have undoubtedly shown by their skill and determination what fine results can be achieved in a submarine fitted with very little of what is

regarded as normal equipment for a modern submarine ...
'The absence of the *Rubis* will be keenly felt not only by the Ninth Submarine
Flotilla, but by the whole British Submarine Branch. The crew are now enjoy-
ing a very well earned leave in their own homes.'
Analysis of post-war records shows that *Rubis'* actual score was: of 683 mines
laid, mines sank 14 supply ships of 21 410 grt, damaged 1 supply ship of 1683
grt, sank 7 anti-submarine/minesweeper vessels, and damaged 1 U-boat. A
supply ship of 4360 grt was sunk by torpedo.
So *Rubis* passed out of the war picture.

THE MEDITTERANEAN 1944
Events moved so fast in the Mediterranean in 1944 that a submarine could
find a completely changed situation after being at sea three weeks on patrol.
Also the type of work changed. There were many Allied personnel in terri-
tories about to be liberated who needed to be brought off. Operations were
carried out particularly on the Greek coast to bring off loyal men who had
either worked for us or would play an important part during the actual liberation. Some Italian submarines were used for this work and the *Axum* was
lost off the west coast of the isthmus of Corinth on one of these special
trips.
The French submarines which had joined us took over patrols off Toulon.
This was the only operational base for U-boats in use by the enemy in the
Western Mediterranean. It must have seemed strange for these Frenchmen to
be looking at their home country through the periscope, and heartbreaking
for them not to be able to land. But they knew liberation was near.
The landing at Anzio on 22 January ended the calls on our submarines to act
as beacons. As early as February, the First Submarine Flotilla, which had been
based at Beirut, Syria, since the summer of 1942, now ceased to operate from
this French port and after a brief stay at Alexandria returned to Malta. Beirut
came to be regarded as the finest submarine base of the war. When the base
closed the record of the flotilla's achievements on the score board had risen
to an estimated figure of 1 436 400 tons of shipping sunk, 431 932 tons damaged and thirty important bombardments carried out.
In April there had been a mutiny in the Greek Navy. At Malta the Greek captain of the flotilla declined to serve under the Greek Commander-in-Chief of
that time, Admiral Voulgaris. He was arrested protesting his faith in the new
EAM Government. Greek submarines remained in harbour until the National-
ists had been sorted out from those in favour of EAM.
The field of operations for our submarines was so small by this time that the
appropriate areas could be well patrolled without any strain. There were two
main areas, namely off the French Riviera and in the Aegean, and it was the
latter waters which provided the best opportunities for the submarines to use
their guns as so many caiques were pressed into service by the Germans to
bring away from the islands troops and stores.

Those who know their Riviera well will find it strange to learn that in May, *Upstart,* Lieutenant P C Chapman, fired two torpedoes into Nice harbour, bombarded the goods yard at Cannes and set fire to a seaplane hangar at St Raphael. So much went on, and often in rather a small way that it is not possible to record the individual successes of each boat. *Ultor,* Lieutenant G E Hunt, *Untiring,* Lieutenant R Boyd, and *Universal,* Lieutenant C Gordon, were among the successful submarines in the western basin of the Mediterranean while *Unsparing,* Lieutenant Piper, RNR, *Unswerving,* Lieutenant M D Tattersall, RNVR, and *Sickle,* Lieutenant J R Drummond, found targets in the Aegean. The French submarines working with us did quite well but there was no one outstanding French boat in the Mediterranean like *Rubis* in the North Sea. *Casabianca* and *Curie* were perhaps the best and operated close inshore off their own homeland.

Up to now, *Ultor,* Lieutenant Hunt, had made a reputation for accurate firing, and reporting of the result. Between 20 and 27 June Hunt capped a splendid series of patrols. He left Maddalena on 16 June to operate off Monaco, Cannes and Nice; his fifteenth Mediterranean patrol. Hunt describes this patrol as the 'most eventful, arduous and successful of all'. On 20 June *Ultor* destroyed an 'F' lighter off Cannes. A week later she encountered a 3000 ton merchant vessel escorted. There was a corvette ahead, destroyers on the side from which the attack was being made, and one on the further side. Hunt got within 1000 yards, fired four torpedoes and obtained two hits, sinking a naval auxiliary and a merchant vessel. Depth charges streamed down at once but Hunt was away and escaped damage. Three and a half hours later he sighted an auxiliary minelayer of 2600 tons, the *Alice Robert,* and a tanker in tow of two tugs screened by a destroyer and a corvette ahead, three destroyers and an escort vessel disposed on the bows and two R-boats astern. There were five aircraft overhead and the eleven escort vessels were weaving about all the time. Hunt got in to 1500 yards and sank the *Alice Robert.* Again the depth charges rained down. This time there were over one hundred but Hunt managed to evade them all. For this patrol he was awarded the DSO to add to his DSC and bar. Under Hunt *Ultor* had a wonderful record. Sixty-eight torpedoes had been fired of which thirty-two were hits or 47 per cent. This was the highest proportion of hits made by any submarine commander up to that time. The nearest approach to Hunt's figures was Ben Bryant's in *Safari* with fifty-one torpedoes fired, twenty-three hits, or 45.1 per cent.

In June, *Unsparing,* Lieutenant A D Piper, RNR, *Vampire,* Lieutenant C W Taylor, and *Vivid,* Lieutenant J C Varley, all came back from the Aegean having fired almost all their gun ammunition. These patrols heralded the end of operations and it is again sad to record that *Sickle,* Drummond, who reported that she had shelled a shipyard at Potamos in Mitylene, did not return; she was mined on her last patrol. *Vivid* managed to squeeze in one more patrol and sank the only refrigerator ship in the hands of the enemy, the *Tanais,* while the Greek *Pipinos,* patrolling very near home, sank the Italian destroyer

Calatafimi operated under German control. With this success the work of submarines in the Mediterranean, except for some very small actions against caiques was rounded off. By the late summer the whole of the French coast was in our hands and in the Eastern Mediterranean the Germans evacuated Athens on 12 October. Accordingly on 8 November the Admiralty ordered submarine patrols in the Mediterranean to cease.

Vox, Vivid, Virtue, Voracious, Vigorous and *Visigoth* were despatched post haste to the Pacific war to help with anti-submarine training. All the remainder were distributed mostly at home, also to help train anti-submarine vessels. A few submarines remained at Malta.

THE FAR EAST 1944

With a modern depot ship (*Adamant*) at Trincomalee, submarine operations really got going in the Malacca Straits. To tell this tale fully, long lists of submarines would have to be recorded and there is little doubt that some officers will feel disappointment that mention has not been made of their boat, or even the exciting action they had with some small patrol vessel or anti-submarine craft. There are numberless tales, well worthy of recounting, but which cannot for obvious reasons all be recorded here. From time to time certain boats made outstanding reputations. Among these was *Tally Ho*, Commander L W A Bennington. On her third patrol in the Malacca Straits she torpedoed and sank the 5700 ton cruiser *Kuma*. She was fiercely counterattacked but steered towards the shore instead of out to sea and hoodwinked her attackers. Later she was attacked by a Japanese torpedo boat on the surface at night. The enemy's first attempt to ram failed but at the second attempt she scraped along the port side breaking open the port ballast tanks. Fortunately, the enemy was also damaged by the collision and Bennington cleverly managed to dive despite the damaged tanks and got away. On his next patrol Bennington sank the Japanese U-boat *IT 23*. *Templar*, Lieutenant D J B Beckley, followed this up a fortnight later by damaging the 7000 ton cruiser *Kitigami*.

Stonehenge, Lieutenant D S Verschoyle-Campbell had a particularly exciting first patrol. When being hunted and depth charged by anti-submarine vessels, an agitated torpedo-man fired her stern tube without orders and, luckily, sank one of her attackers, the Japanese special minesweeper *No 4*. The consternation in the surface ships enabled her to make good her escape! Unfortunately, *Stonehenge* was lost shortly afterwards, having sunk the 1000 ton naval auxiliary *Choko Maru*.

Although the Japanese were our enemies, they did not cause our submarines as much trouble as the temperature. Conditions in the Far East in our submarines were extremely trying. *Surf*, for example, returned from her first patrol of eighteen days at sea with the entire crew suffering badly from prickly heat and with five cases of heat stroke, in spite of having the good fortune to have a doctor on board for the trip. It was arranged that submarines would

Plate 12

HMS Medway, First Submarine Flotilla: Captain S M Raw, with his staff and senior
submarine commanding officers. Standing, left to right: Lieutenant R S Brookes;
Lieutenant-Commander H C Browne; Commander A C C Miers; Lieutenant R M Favell;
Lieutenant L W A Bennington. Seated: Commander J W Linton; Commander H P de C Steel;
Captain S M Raw; Commander T W Marsh; Commander E F Pizey

Visit of Winston Churchill to Algiers, here seen with Captain G B H Fawkes and
officers of the 8th Flotilla

Plate 13

Commander B Bryant and officers of HM Submarine Safari

Lieutenant G E Hunt and the crew of HM Submarine Ultor

retire from their patrol positions occasionally for a day and spend it on the surface to give a break from the long hours in high temperatures; motor rooms of submarines could reach as much as 120 degrees F. The worst part of these conditions was the humidity, and applications were soon coming in to the Admiralty for improved de-humidifyers and air conditioning.

During the early months of the year the flotilla built-up steadily with *S* and *T* Class and in March *Maidstone* arrived at Trincomalee from Alexandria. Captain L M Shadwell who had been sent ahead from the United Kingdom, immediately took over from Captain G B H Fawkes. All the *S* Class submarines came over to *Maidstone* leaving the *T* Class with Captain Ionides in *Adamant.* In April Captain Shadwell went to Fremantle, Australia, where he conferred with Admiral Christie, United States Navy, and made arrangements to base British submarines on Fremantle at a later date. Captain Shadwell explained to Admiral Christie that another British depot ship, the *Wolfe,* would arrive in Ceylon during the summer and this would release *Maidstone* to bring a flotilla to Australia.

The policy in the Far East at this time was to hold the Japanese in the Malay Barrier and to attack in the Pacific. This made it worth while to take advantage of the shallow waters around most of Sumatra, Java, Borneo and the Malay Peninsula. Nearly all the modern boats could lay mines from their torpedo tubes and a big programme was carried out. At the same time prisoners captured from junks confirmed suspicions that the Japanese were using all the bigger junks they could lay hands on to carry rubber, timber, tin, rice and tea. This afforded tremendous scope for using the gun and matters got to such a pitch that submarines sailed with gun ammunition stowed in every possible place, including under the wardroom table! These practices caused some consternation in circles at home responsible for the safety of ammunition, its stowage in proper magazines, and regulations regarding excessive heat. The story goes that rounds stowed behind the engines caused most anxiety but all survived and many killed Japanese.

Quite a number of airmen were picked out of the sea or rescued from force-landed aircraft by our submarines. It was not pleasant to ditch in shark infested waters. Sourabaya and Port Blair came in for most of the airmen's attention.

Some of our patrols went up the Burma Coast but the most productive area was the Malacca Straits and especially off Penang, where *Telemachus,* Commander W D A King, got a Japanese submarine, *I 166* in July. Another boat carrying out a successful career at this time was *Stoic,* Lieutenant P B Marriott, who previously had commanded the captured U-boat *Graph.* Also Lieutenant-Commander E P Young, who was the first RNVR officer to command a submarine, made successful patrols in *Storm* including a spirited attack on small craft in a harbour on the Burma coast, when he steamed on the surface into confined waters and used his 3 inch gun with great effect.

By August the war in the Pacific was moving fast northwards, and preparations

were already being made for the invasion of the Philippineswhich took place in October. The depot ship, *Wolfe,* Captain J Slaughter, arrived at Trincomalee, Ceylon, in August and accordingly Captain Shadwell sailed in *Maidstone* with six *S* Class and three *T* Class submarines for Fremantle. Our submarines based at Fremantle were under the operational control of the United States Commander Submarines, South-West Pacific, Rear-Admiral R W Christie. From here the *S* Class went principally to the Java Sea and Macassar Straits, while the *T* Class sometimes went through the Karimata Straits and up as far as the Gulf of Siam. Exmouth Gulf, nine hundred miles north of Fremantle, was used as an advanced fuelling base because, although Fremantle was an improvement on Ceylon from the climatic point of view, and co-ordination of operations with the American submarines was made easier when operating from the same base, Fremantle was no nearer the hunting ground.

In fact the submarines were 1500 miles from the edge of the first patrol areas and spent one week at sea getting there. Our men soon saw the reason for the huge size in submarines which the Americans had built. These American 1800 ton boats were able to stay at sea for sixty days without undue discomfort. Indeed they were helpful in replenishing our submarines with fresh vegetables and stores, which they did by meeting at a pre-arranged position on the surface in daylight, the vast space of the Pacific making this a perfectly reasonable operation. Mail was also transferred in this way.

These meetings emphasized the contrast in size between our boats and the American's, and although our *S* Class were so much smaller they were at an advantage in one respect, because they were able to carry out diving patrols in really shallow waters. Such patrols are always hazardous because of the added danger from mines and *Stratagem,* Lieutenant C R Pelly, did not return from one of these operations.

Once again the long list of submarines operating and the numbers of craft attacked by torpedo and gun, principally the latter, make good statistics but difficult to incorporate in a book. Many merchant vessels were sunk, junks destroyed, mines laid and special operations to land agents and Commandos were carried out. Highlights were a success by the Dutch submarine *Zwardvisch,* when she torpedoed a German U-boat off Sourabaya, the most easterly position in which any German U-boat had been found. She also sank a Japanese small surface minelayer, the *Itsukashima,* on the same patrol. *Terrapin,* Lieutenant R H Brunner, sank the special minelayer *No 5* and *Trenchant,* Lieutenant-Commander Hezlet, sank *U 859,* another German a long way from home. By an extraordinary coincidence *Trenchant* had left Portsmouth and *U 859* had sailed from Kiel on the same day earlier in the year. *Trenchant* also took two chariots to Puket Harbour where they sank a 5000 ton merchant vessel. Both crews were recovered. Finally, *Tantulus,* Lieutenant-Commander H S Mackenzie, achieved fame when she returned to Fremantle on 6 December from her first south-west Pacific patrol after fifty-two days at sea, covering 11 500 miles and spending thirty-eight days north of the Malay Barrier.

HOME STATION 1945

Before coming to the details of this last year of the war, it appears to be an appropriate moment to review the submarine strength. Our position at the beginning of the war was shown in the chapter on 1939 and 1940, and again the rapid expansion was enlarged upon in the chapter on 1941, immediately after the German attack on Russia. Two and a half years later the British Submarine Branch had reached its maximum figure. There were in all eighty-eight strictly British operational submarines; in addition nine Allied were working under our operational control, of which half were British built boats. Forty-three submarines were under orders to be built, some of which although half completed were cancelled during the six months January to June. It may seem rather extraordinary that our submarine strength never reached 100 operational boats during the greatest war in history, but it must be remembered that the submarine was not our primary arm as it was in the case of the Germans.

At Home there were two very large flotillas in the Clyde. Ben Bryant, now captain of the *Forth*, ran the working up flotilla. In January 1945 he had fourteen new boats to handle; six *S* Class, six *T* Class, one *V* Class and the first of the *A* Class. To keep things happily turning over in the patrol areas, three *V* Class and one *T* Class were also in the flotilla for operations, but of course, total numbers varied for Home Station patrols as the boats worked up, became operational, did a patrol or two at home, and then sailed for the Far East. Captain Ingram had the other big flotilla in the Clyde based on the old *Cyclops*. These boats did the anti-submarine training for the escort groups. Captain Gambier, home from Ceylon, had the Allied Flotilla at Dundee. There were one or two submarines in what might be called the old familiar places, Blyth still had three for training, and at Blockhouse there were four during this particular month of January.

The above review brought in the mention of the *A* Class. War experiences had shown that the *T*s were too slow and unable to dive deep enough, so a new class, the *A*s, was designed to overcome these deficiencies. Their speed was 18½ knots on the surface and 8½ knots submerged. They were 281 feet long. Preparations were made to go to mass production with this type, replacing the *S* Class as well as the *T* Class. Forty-five were ordered in all but none were completed in time to be tried under action conditions. The main armament was six 21 inch bow tubes and four 21 inch stern tubes. One 4 inch gun and one 20mm anti-aircraft gun were fitted. These boats carried reloads for all the torpedo tubes and could embark twenty-six mines instead of the sixteen torpedoes. New innovations were radar which could be worked from periscope depth, and a night periscope.

The situation in Norway, due chiefly to the withdrawal of enemy aircraft, enabled the Home Fleet to operate much closer to the coast than hitherto, with the result that waters which had up to this time been the sole prerogative of the submarine became a surface ship hunting place. German destroyers

making their way home were attacked by surface forces off Narvik before running for the shelter of shore batteries. Russian convoys ran without much trouble and one return convoy in January, consisting of thirty ships, got home without a loss. Even coastal forces came into the picture and operated up the fjords. Here there was no place for submarines in large numbers and as has been seen from the dispositions, at home we were concentrating on working up boats for operations in the Pacific. Nevertheless, a few patrols were carried out with success. The Norwegian submarine *Utsira* torpedoed a U-boat and a 2000 ton merchant vessel sixty miles north of Trondheim and the British *Venturer*, Lieutenant J S Launders, claimed a supply ship.

Although times were easier there was still a sting in the enemy's tail and in February German aircraft and U-boats again tried to interfere with Russian convoys. Our few submarines off the Norwegian coast saw nothing of the U-boats which was not surprising as the enemy were chiefly off the Kola Inlet where they torpedoed two Russian destroyers and a corvette. Escort carriers, now going all the way round with the convoys, drove off the bombers. But after the convoy had arrived and the U-boats were returning to their base on the west coast, *Venturer* detected an enemy submarine while both he and the German boat were still dived. Launders stalked the enemy and when he was 2000 yards away he loosed four torpedoes aimed by asdic, hitting with at least one. This was a brilliant effort and on surfacing, Launders saw large patches of oil, some wooden wreckage and a large iron cylinder, which was the evidence he needed. We now know this was *U 864*. This satisfactory attack really brought to a close the submarine work on protection of North Russian convoys. While figures are often hard to picture in reality, they at least show the extent of aid given to our ally in which our submarines played their part by helping to protect these convoys. Since August 1944 when full scale convoys were resumed to North Russia, 1 342 581 tons of cargo had been carried successfully, consisting of 29 588 vehicles, 553 fighter aircraft, 1322 tanks, 2249 railway wagons, 487 locomotives, 451 tenders, 316 guns, 106 marine craft, 251 cranes and 811 216 tons of general cargo. In addition 245 549 tons of oil, fuel and spirit had been transported. All branches of the Navy had played their part in this great work; while the biggest prizes did not come the way of the submarines it is fair to say the memories of many submarine officers and men, when looking back on this war, will first turn to those long winter days and nights somewhere in the neighbourhood of the North Cape.

By April, the war at sea in Home Waters was virtually over, and there was hardly anywhere left for the submarines to go. Even the Biscay ports were being blockaded by surface ships, one of which made the signal: 'Lovely weather but nothing to shoot at', and the Home Fleet seemed to spend all its time steaming up and down the coast of Norway. In the Atlantic the escorts were claiming sixty-five U-boats sunk in one month. However, our submarines managed to end their work with a kill.

Tapir, Lieutenant Roxburgh, remembering *Venturer's* success, heard a U-boat

coming home to Bergen submerged. *Tapir* on a working up patrol was also submerged, Roxburgh waited off the entrance of the fjord, believing the enemy would surface before entering the narrow waters. Sure enough, *U 486* made this fatal error, and was hit by *Tapir's* salvo. The U-boat sank with all hands.

British submarines were still off Norway when between 1 and 5 May the Home Fleet carried out their last operation named 'Judgment'; however, nothing came of it, either from the surface ship side or the supporting submarines.

At 1324 on 8 May the Admiralty made the following signal:

'Germany has surrendered unconditionally, cease fire has been ordered for 22.01 GMT.'

So the war was over at Home.

The Submarine Command was proud to receive this warm appreciation from Sir Max Horton, their former Flag Officer Submarines:

'I cannot let this day of thanksgiving for Victory in Europe pass without sending my warmest congratulations to you on the continued splendid work and success achieved by our submarines. There is nothing of which I am so proud as my long association with The Submarine Service. I would be so grateful if you would convey to all concerned my admiration and good wishes.' May 1945

THE FAR EAST 1945

Dispositions in 1945 were based on the idea that the Pacific war might continue for quite a long time yet. The greatest numbers of our submarines were based at Trincomalee. Here there were two large flotillas. The Fourth Flotilla, under the command of Captain H M C Ionides, in *Adamant,* was made up of eleven *T* Class and the Second Flotilla under Captain J E Slaughter in *Wolfe,* had sixteen boats, mostly *S* Class augmented by three *V* Class and two older boats, the latter five being employed in anti-submarine training. Captain Ionides exercised overall operational control of the two flotillas. At Fremantle, Captain L M Shadwell with the Eighth Flotilla in the *Maidstone,* had under him seven *S* Class, three *T* Class and four Dutch boats with three *V* Class's for anti-submarine training. Thus in all there were forty-four boats taking part in the Far East war.

Our submarine concentration in the Far East now divided between Trincomalee and Fremantle was in fact conforming to the general plan for the surface forces. In January there were two distinctly separate surface fleets. The Eastern Fleet under Admiral Sir Arthur Power based on Ceylon, and the Pacific Fleet under Admiral Sir Bruce Fraser based on Sydney, Australia. These two Admirals made their position clear in two messages. Sir Arthur Power stated he had three main objectives:

1. The denial of the Indian Ocean to the Japanese and therefore the cutting of supply lines to their armies in Burma and the garrison in Andaman and Nicobar Islands.

2. The destruction of the enemy war potential especially oil and shipping, shore and harbour installations.

3. Close support of the Army in Burma.

Sir Bruce Fraser's message was quite different, since the British Pacific Fleet was to operate under the Americans. He made a signal to Admiral King, the Chief of Naval Operations United States Fleet, simply stating the British Pacific Fleet was ready for duty 15 January, 1945.

Admiral Power's objective fell primarily on the shoulders of the destroyers and submarines of the Eastern Fleet. The Malacca Straits was still the major area of operations but submarines went well north in the Indian Ocean as well. Such names as Akyab, Moulmein, Mergui, became much better known than hitherto, and it is fair to say that the subsequent success of our arms in Burma, and the condition of deprivation and scarcity which it became known later that some of the Japanese garrisons experienced, were striking testimonies of the effectiveness of the work. This work was chiefly directed against small coastal vessels. The enemy had no ships of any reasonable size to spare or risk on the Burma and Malay coast, so the gun continued to be the most used armament of the submarine. Though this necessary stranglehold on the enemy was made, it was unspectacular at the time, and the DSOs were far fewer and more difficult to earn in this campaign than any other in the war. All the same there was plenty of excitement from time to time. *Shakespeare*, Lieutenant D Swanston, on a first Far East patrol, attacked a convoy off the Andaman Islands on New Year's Eve and sank the supply ship *Unryu Maru*, 2500 tons. Later, on 3 January, he aimed at a 700 ton merchant vessel, but all torpedoes missed. Accordingly he surfaced, the vessel being unescorted, and attacked with his gun. After the fourth round the enemy returned the fire but the submarine kept up a high rate of firing and soon scored two hits. At this juncture Swanston saw what appeared to be a submarine chaser coming through the Straits between the Islands, so turned away to dive, but by this time the merchant vessel was only 1500 yards away and scored a direct hit on the submarine which penetrated the pressure hull and caused some flooding. Diving was stopped and the gun crew resumed action, this time knocking out the merchant ship's gun. By this time the submarine chaser had taken up the duel, but Swanston managed to get out of range. From 9.30 am until 6.30 pm *Shakespeare* had to make her way towards home on the surface in full daylight. Japanese aircraft made twenty-five attacks, using bombers, seaplanes, fighter-bombers and fighters. The submarine was further damaged by these attacks and several men were wounded, but in return this dauntless crew shot down one aircraft in flames and damaged four others. For the next two days *Shakespeare* was free from the attention of the enemy but not daring to break wireless silence, she had to beware of our own forces. Finally, however, she made a successful contact with the submarine *Stygian*, Lieutenant G S Clarabut, who took her in tow.

What were laughingly called Wolf Pack tactics were used more and more frequently: *Trenchant*, Commander A R Hezlet, and *Terrapin*, Lieutenant R H Brunner, went out together on 13 January and did havoc among small

craft, completing their combined effort by the sinking of the minelaying tender *Sakuru Maru* by *Terrapin*. In January, eight other submarines all brought back reports of large numbers of coasters sunk and the toll of disaster to the enemy included the destruction of lighters, piers, and installations, much of which were destroyed by demolition charges. Minelaying also went on regularly by both *Rorqual* and *Porpoise*, Acting Lieutenant-Commander G H B Turner, until the latter, after having patrolled off Penang, did not return to base. She was the first of her class of minelaying submarines completed in 1933 and had laid 465 mines in the war.

The submarines at Fremantle meanwhile were going out for longer periods and covering much longer distances. *Sirdar*, Lieutenant J A Spender, for example, stayed forty-nine days at sea, twenty-nine in the Maccassa Strait and the Java Sea area. *O 19* on one of these patrols got into trouble, but our Dutch friend struggled back to Darwin with just a cupful of oil left for her diesels. *O 19* had sunk a 3000 ton supply ship but the escort had very nearly got her.

To the Fremantle submarines, the Sunda Straits and the Lombok Straits will be everlasting memories. The former separate Sumatra and Java and the latter separates Bali and Lombok, just to the east of Java. These two passages formed the only practicable entrances to the combat area. Very strong tides run through them and naturally they were heavily patrolled by the enemy. Once safely through, the Pacific Fleet submarines had the better of the bargain compared with the Trincomalee boats, as targets were often large, and here and there there were really big prizes. *Tantulus*, Lieutenant-Commander H S Mackenzie, for example, on 11 February, sighted two battleships, but was forced to dive by aircraft. In passing, *Tantulus*, claimed the British submarine time record on this patrol which lasted fifty-six days, thirty-seven of which were spent north of the Malay Barrier.

As the year progressed, the submarines from Trincomalee made the best of their opportunities. *Trenchant* and *Terrapin* went out again in company and this time suddenly surfaced together close to a submarine chaser and before the enemy really knew what was happening the chaser was sunk. There was only one survivor. Other submarines helped air sea rescue operations and carried out special tasks, landing and bringing off Commandos, mostly with the object of bringing back prisoners for interrogation. Some submarines were feeling the disappointment of so seldom firing their torpedoes; however, *Seadog*, Lieutenant E A Hobson, used two very effectively when destroying an important loading pier. Now and again a good target did come along, for example, on 10 May *Statesman*, Lieutenant R G Bulkeley, and *Subtle*, Lieutenant B J Andrew, working as a pair, sighted a cruiser and a destroyer in the Malacca Straits steering north. *Subtle* attacked but the target turned away just in time and all torpedoes missed. The counter attack was heavy and did considerable minor damage, but a sighting of this sort was just what Admiral Power was hoping for and he set off from Ceylon immediately on hearing of

the enemy report. Also the fact that the enemy had been reported by our submarines, was fully in accordance with the dispositions which had been maintained for so many months. Unfortunately, for Admiral Power something
turned the enemy back, possibly a reconnaissance plane. *Subtle* reported the
same force on 12 May steering south, and it fell to the good luck of Captain
M L Power, who was to the southward of the enemy with four destroyers, to
take advantage of this second very important signal. He attacked at night, all
four destroyers carrying out a concerted attack independently from each
quarter. The attack was brilliantly successful, the cruiser being sunk and the
destroyer damaged. We now know the cruiser was the 10 000 ton *Naguro.*

Two days earlier, the last minelaying operation of the Far East war by British
submarines was completed by *Rorqual.* This lay was made north-west of
Batavia in anticipation of the evacuation of the Malay barrier by the Japanese.
Rorqual returned to the United Kingdom and paid off. She was the only survivor of the original six ships of this class. *Seal, Grampus* and *Narwhal* were
lost in 1940. *Cachalot* went in 1941 and *Porpoise* had just been lost in 1945.

Early in April *Adamant* and her submarines moved to Fremantle leaving *Wolfe,*
with sufficient numbers at Trincomalee to finish the war on the Burma coast
and in the Malacca Straits. At Fremantle a busy fortnight was spent adjusting
the flotillas between the two depot ships *Adamant* and *Maidstone,* the latter
taking principally *S* Class, arrangements having been made to build up her
numbers to twelve.

On 20 April *Maidstone* left Fremantle for the Philippine Islands. She called at
Sydney, then Manus Island and arrived at Subic Bay, the American base in the
Phillipines on 20 May. Her submarines had left for patrol from Fremantle and
rejoined their depot ship at Subic Bay. Thus *Maidstone* was operating submarines from Subic Bay only twenty days after the arrival of the British
Pacific Fleet at Leyte, in the Philippines Admiral Fraser, the British Commander-
in-Chief, having brought the fleet there on 1 May.

In June, Captain Ben Bryant arrived at Fremantle and took over from Captain
Ionides. He was greeted by good news.

Trenchant, Commander A R Hezlet, operating from *Adamant* at Fremantle
had achieved an outstanding success by torpedoing the Japanese cruiser
Ashigara of 10 000 tons and carrying 8 inch guns. The attack was made at the
north-east entrance to the Banka Strait between the Island of Banka and
Sumatra. Having passed under an Allied minefield Hezlet fired eight torpedoes
of which five hit. The cruiser sank almost immediately. Sir Bruce Fraser described this as a magnificent performance in shallow confined waters, a most
difficult position for submarine operations. *Stygian,* Lieutenant-Commander
Clarabut, was in the vicinity at the time and rightly received a share of the
credit by drawing off and engaging the attention of the destroyer escort. Hezlet
received a bar to his DSO and also the immediate award of the United States
Legion of Merit, the latter presented to him by Rear-Admiral Fife, USN, who
specially asked that *Trenchant* should proceed to Subic Bay where she arrived

on 20 June. *Trenchant* ended her tremendously successful war career by sinking the Japanese special Minesweeper *No 105* near the Lombok Straits later in August.

One more special event in the submarine story has to be recorded. In the first week in July *Bonaventure,* Captain W R Fell, arrived at Subic Bay from Australia having come out via the Panama Canal with her X craft. He placed his command at the disposal of the United States Seventh Fleet. The United States Commander immediately directed that they were to be employed:

1. To cut the cable from Singapore to Hong Kong;
2. To attack simultaneously Japanese heavy cruisers in the Johore Straits, Singapore.

On 27 July *Spark, Stygian* and *Spearhead* left Brunei, Borneo, and *Selene* left Subic, Philippines, each with a midget submarine in tow. The first two midgets were to attack the cruisers and the last two to cut the cable. D day was to be 31 July.

On that day *XE 4,* Lieutenant M H Shean, RANVR, succeeded in cutting the Hong Kong to Saigon cable, and the Saigon to Singapore cable. The operation was perfectly executed, a foot of each cable being brought back. The job was done in over forty feet of water, much deeper than expected, although hampered by tide and rough weather. Shean gained a bar to his DSO already given for his Bergen operation of 14 April 1944.

XE 5, Lieutenant Westmacott, RN, made a gallant attempt to cut the Hong Kong Singapore cable. Three and a half days and nights were spent inside the defended waters of Hong Kong and the dangerous passage between them and the open sea was made four times. The attempt failed, but Westmacott was given a bar to his DSC.

The attack on the cruisers at Singapore was made by *XE 3,* Lieutenant Fraser, RNR, towed by *Stygian,* and *XE 1,* Lieutenant Smart, RNVR, towed by *Spark. XE 3* found her target, the *Takao,* in Johore Strait nearly aground and only at the midship section was there just sufficient water for *XE 3* to place herself under the cruiser. For forty minutes she pushed her way along the seabed before getting into position, during which time she became jammed under the cruiser for fifteen minutes. The diver, Leading Seaman J J Magennis, found that the hatch could not be opened fully for him to get out and he had to squeeze himself through the narrow space available. The limpets he could only place with great difficulty owing to the foul state of the ship's bottom and the pronounced slope. Fraser released his main charge successfully. After withdrawal from the target. Magennis once more left the midget to release some limpet carriers which had fouled the hydroplanes. Once more he got back safely inside. For this magnificent attack both Fraser and Magennis were awarded the Victoria Cross.

XE 1 was to have attacked the second cruiser two miles further up the Strait than the *Takao,* but she was delayed by having to avoid surface craft during her approach. This put her ninety minutes behind time on *XE 3* when she

should have been ahead. Lieutenant Smart realized he could not make his attack and get away before the time limit for the whole operation expired so he attacked the *Takao* as well. He was awarded the DSO.

By now the end of the war was near and Japanese forces were on the retreat everywhere. *Stubborn*, Lieutenant A G Davies, picked off an old Japanese destroyer of 750 tons, a first class attack against a difficult target. The survivors refused to be rescued, to avoid capture. *Trump*, Lieutenant-Commander A A Catlow, and *Tiptoe*, Lieutenant-Commander R L Jay, working together, caught a convoy, *Trump*, hit a 6000 ton ship, and *Tiptoe*, working ahead of the line of advance of the convoy, got in a successful attack on a 4000 ton ship.

On 6 August the first atom bomb was released on Hiroshima; the second followed on the 9 on Nagasaki. Six days later the Admiralty signalled: 'HM Government has announced that the Japanese have surrendered'. A day later, on 16 August, an Admiralty General Message said: 'The surrender of the Japanese Empire brings to an end six years of achievement in war unsurpassed in the long history of the high tradition of the Royal Navy.'

Although the war was over, some submarines had a long way to go to reach their base. *Statesman* was one of these, and on 18 August, so far as records go, she fired the last torpedo of the war. The target was a derelict which was better out of the way, and was destroyed with one well aimed shot. The brothers J D Martin and K H Martin were also out working together in their commands, *Solent* and *Sleuth*. They too did not meet with any success, but achieved fame by being the last boats to return to base where they arrived on 22 August. *O 19*, our Dutch friend, came into the news from another cause. This boat had done so much, right from the beginning of the war in the Far East, and it was with surprise that the news was received that she had run aground on the Ladd Reef in the middle of the China Sea. Nothing could be done to save this famous boat, and the United States submarine *Shad*, had the sad business of bringing home a brilliant crew without their ship.

At the end of August *Maidstone*, having collected her flotilla together, sailed for Hong Kong and entered the port with the relieving force, under Admiral Harcourt, with *Indomitable*, *Venerable*, *Swiftsure*, *Euralyus* and destroyers of the British Pacific Fleet. *Maidstone* went alongside the dockyard and the submarine secured in the basin to supply power to Hong Kong through the dockyard generating station. It was a fitting climax to the war at sea for the submarines that this flotilla should be part of the relieving force for Hong Kong, which island had always had such a very close association with the Submarine Service.

THE SUBMARINE BALANCE SHEET
September 1939 to August 1945
The balance sheet of the Submarine Branch of the Navy is difficult to compile. Inevitably there must be omissions even with enemy documents from which to check facts, and also for security reasons much has necessarily to be withheld. However, some statistics can be arrived at and are shown in the following table, although nothing in the form of figures can represent the effort and full effect of the submarine operations.

Warships	Sunk		Damaged	
Battleships	0		2	
Cruisers and Pocket				
Battleships	6		10	
Destroyers	16		2	
Submarines	35		6 *(approximately)*	
Minor war vessels	112		35	
Merchant ships *(By theatres of war)*				
Home	84	270 000 tons	16	69,000 tons
Mediterranean	361	1 157 000 tons	86	435,000 tons
Far East	48	97 000 tons	7	14,000 tons
Mining by Submarines				
Home	23 merchant ships		1 U-boat	
Mediterranean	12 merchant ships		1 destroyer, 3 torpedo boats, 1 corvette	
Far East	3 merchant ships			

Perhaps the most outstanding figure in this amazing table is the thirty-five enemy submarines. It should also be remembered that mining successes are most difficult to compute and there were countless special operations and bombardments running into hundreds of separate episodes, many well worthy of individual treatment in the submarine story.

For this we lost 74 British submarines manned by British crews totalling 341 officers and 2801 ratings. In addition 50 officers and 309 ratings were made prisoners of war. These numbers equal almost exactly the total strength of the Submarine Service in September 1939.

To conclude this chapter, it might interest readers to know, with all they have heard and much still untold, that *the men of the Submarine Branch have never, in either peace or war, represented more than three per cent of the entire personnel of the Royal Navy.*

ENEMY SUBMARINES SUNK BY BRITISH SUBMARINES DURING THE SECOND WORLD WAR

British Submarine	Commanding Officer	Date	Enemy Submarine	Station
Salmon	Bickford	4 12 39	U 36	H
Porpoise	Roberts	16 4 40	U 1	H
Parthian	Rimington	6 6 40	Diamante	M
Cachalot	Luce	20 8 40	U 51	H
Thunderbolt	Crouch	15 12 40	Tarrantini	H
Rorqual	Dewhurst	31 3 41	Capponi	M
Triumph	Woods	27 6 41	Salpa	M
Torbay	Miers	5 7 41	Jantina	M
Severn	Campbell	7 8 41	Bianchi	M
Upholder	Wanklyn	5 1 42	Ammiraglio St Bon	M
Unbeaten	Woodward	12 1 42	U 374	M
Thorn	Norfolk	30 1 42	Medusa	M
Ultimatum	Harrison	14 3 42	Ammiraglio Millo	M
Unbeaten	Woodward	17 3 42	Gugliemotti	M
Upholder	Wanklyn	18 3 42	Tricheco	M
Saracen	Lumby	3 8 42	U 335	H
Tigris	Colvin	9 11 42	Porfido	M
Saracen	Lumby	6 12 42	Granito	M
Sahib	Bromage	21 1 43	U 301	M
Tuna	Martin	7 4 43	U 644	H
Sickle	Drummond	21 5 43	U 303	M
Truculent	Alexander	4 6 43	U 308	H
Unruly	Fyfe	13 7 43	Acciaio	M
United	Roxburgh	15 7 43	Remo	M
Trooper	Clarabutt	29 7 43	Pietro Micca	M
Shakespeare	Ainslie	7 9 43	Velella	M
Ultimatum	Kett, RNR	31 10 43	U 431	M
Taurus	Wingfield	12 11 43	I 34 (Japanese)	FE
Tally Ho	Bennington	15 2 44	IT 23 (Japanese)	FE
Satyr	Weston	15 6 44	U 987	H
Trenchant	Hezlet	23 9 44	U 859	FE
Telemachus	King	17 7 44	I 166 (Japanese)	FE
Venturer	Launders	11 11 44	U 771	H
Venturer	Launders	9 2 45	U 864	H
Tapir	Roxburgh	12 4 45	U 486	H

The following officers and men were awarded the Victoria Cross for service in submarines during the Second World War:

Lieutenant-Commander M D Wanklyn, VC, DSO, RN, of Upholder for service in the Mediterranean, 1941.
Lieutenant P S W Roberts, VC, RN, of Thrasher for service in the Mediterranean, 1942.
Petty Officer T Gould, VC, of Thrasher for service in the Mediterranean, 1942.
Commander A C C Miers, VC, DSO, RN, of Torbay for service in the Mediterranean, 1942.
Commander J W Linton, VC, DSO, DSC, RN, of Turbulent for service in the Mediterranean, 1943.
Lieutenant D Cameron, VC, RNR, of X 6 for service in Kaa Fjord, 1944.
Lieutenant B C Place, VC, DSC, RN, of X 7 for service in Kaa Fjord, 1944.
Lieutenant I E Fraser, VC, DSC, RNR, of XE 3 for service at Singapore, 1945.
Leading Seaman J J Magennis, VC, of XE 3 for service at Singapore, 1945.

Plate 14

The Snort mast being raised

Plate 15

The Snort mast in the lowered position: looking towards the stern of the submarine

Chapter six
How a conventional submarine works

DIAGRAMS ON THE WORKING OF A SUBMARINE

The sectional drawing shows a 1941 improved *T* Class, which is the type selected as a basis for the diagrams which follow. The *Ts* were large, overseas submarines and they operated with great success in the Second World War. Designed primarily for work in the Pacific they were found to be equally suitable when operating off the Norwegian coast and even in the more confined area of the eastern Mediterranean.

The diagrams are simple to understand and when taken in conjunction with the descriptions and the photographs they provide the basic knowledge required for an appreciation of the history of submarines.

Diagram 1 shows the actual submarine proper and how the casing is put on top of it to walk on and provide sea-keeping qualities. The watertight bulkheads are shown and all the hatches which pass through the pressure hull. This *T* Class submarine is 273 feet in length, has 1300 tons displacement on the surface and 1575 tons displacement when submerged.

Diagram 2: Propulsion and battery charging. This diagram illustrates how the submarine is propelled when on the surface by diesel engines, and when submerged by electric batteries, or diesel engines with the addition of a 'Snort' mast. In the diagram the passage of air to the diesel engines for surface running is shown passing down the Conning Tower through the control room to the engine room. When the submarine is under the water no air can pass down the conning tower, so the electric motors must be used, except if the Snort mast is raised, when sufficient air can pass down this tube to the diesel engines for slow running. The Snort mast (shown on plates 3 and 4, and on diagram 2) was not introduced into British submarines until after the Second World War.

Although the use of solid injection diesel engines is generally standard for all submarines, a variety of types on this principle is used. For example, in the *T* Class which has been selected for the diagrams, the submarines built at Vickers Armstrongs were fitted with two sets of six-cylinder four-stroke solid injection Vickers engines. The Cammel Laird boats were given Sulzer engines, and Scotts fitted supercharged MAN engines; all the engines giving speeds of 14 knots. The various types were fitted so that experience could be gained with each design.

Nearly all submarine batteries are made by the Chloride Battery Company of

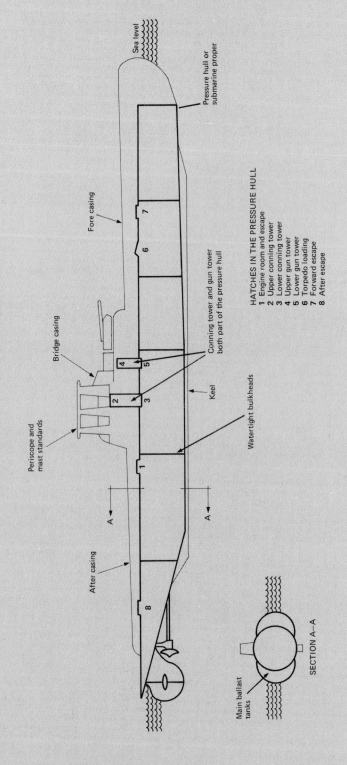

Diagram 1. GENERAL CONSTRUCTION
pressure hull, hatches, casing, superstructure, keel

Sea level

Pressure hull or
submarine proper

Fore casing

Conning tower and gun tower
both part of the pressure hull

HATCHES IN THE PRESSURE HULL
1 Engine room and escape
2 Upper conning tower
3 Lower conning tower
4 Upper gun tower
5 Lower gun tower
6 Torpedo loading
7 Forward escape
8 After escape

Bridge casing

Keel

Periscope and
mast standards

Watertight bulkheads

After casing

Main ballast
tanks

SECTION A—A

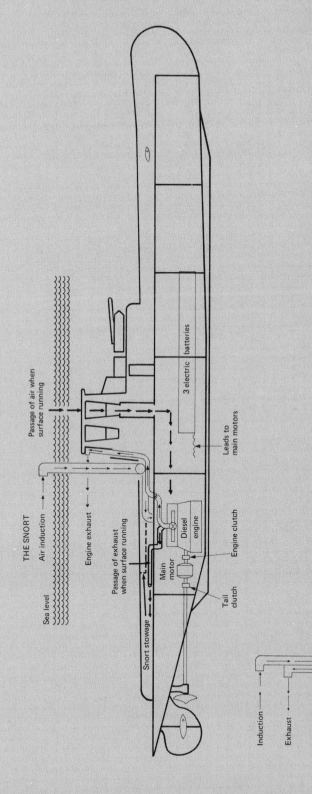

Diagram 2. PROPULSION AND BATTERY CHARGING

THE SNORT

Sea level

Air induction →

Engine exhaust →

Passage of air when surface running

Passage of exhaust when surface running

Snort stowage

Main motor

Tail clutch

Diesel engine

Engine clutch

3 electric batteries

Leads to main motors

Induction →

Exhaust →

EARLIER ARRANGEMENT

Manchester. All submarines have three batteries of 112 cells each, and as no cell, no matter how big, can produce a voltage greater than 2.4, the total voltage of each battery will average about 270 volts. The three batteries are joined in parallel to make one large source of electric power. Each cell weighs half a ton and operates in the same way as a car battery or wireless wet battery, the chief characteristic to the layman being that a cell requires 'topping up' with distilled water from time to time. This is because through electrolysis the cell gives off hydrogen in two parts and oxygen in one part, which when combined form pure water. In the case of the submarine's battery with 336 cells of half a ton each, a large quantity of distilled water is required. If a patrol is to be a long one, particularly in hot climates, something like five tons of distilled water must be embarked for topping up on patrol. These batteries drive the electric motors which consist of two armatures on each shaft. The armatures can be arranged to be in parallel or in series, normally known as 'grouper up' or 'grouper down' because of the position of the grouper switch. When the armatures are in series because of the drop in potential the propellers can be run very slowly enabling the submarine to patrol at no more than about 1 knot. When the batteries are 'run down' they must be recharged and normally this is done with the submarine on the surface. A propeller can be disconnected on one shaft and allowed to trail, the engine connected to the motor and the latter turned by the engine as a dynamo. This operation may take as much as eight hours. It is possible when running on the surface using both propellers and also when dived and using the Snort mast to put a small charge in the batteries.

The maximum speed submerged of most submarines of late war construction is 9 knots but many achieve only 8. Much depends on the hull form and as a large number of submarines are fitted with saddle tank main ballast arrangements which do not give a streamline hull formation, speeds are generally low. (Some very high capacity batteries have given certain submarines an underwater speed of over 16 knots for short periods.) High underwater speed cannot be maintained for long as at that speed the battery is soon exhausted and it must be remembered that normally a submarine when dived cruises at no more than about 2 knots. If a high speed were to be used for some hours the batteries would run down and the submarine would have to surface to charge. This condition is now qualified by the use of the Snort.

Submarines having a Snort mast can be propelled by the diesel engines when dived, but not below 'periscope depth' which is the height of the mast. Fresh air can pass freely down the Snort to the engines, the top of the mast being above the surface of the sea. The mast is about 14 inches in diameter. If waves lap over the open end of the mast, a float valve shuts momentarily to prevent water entering the submarine. When the Snort is not required to operate it is lowered and lies horizontally along the casing just aft of the bridge. The raising and lowering of the mast is worked by an oil pressure system. When the Snort mast is not in use and lying horizontally, it fills with water, and when

first raised for use it is still filled with water, so this is then drained down through a valve into the submarine. When the diesels are started, the induction valve into the pressure hull is opened and the submarine can take in the fresh air for the engines.

Complementary to the Snort induction mast, is a pipe to take the exhaust gases from the engines into the sea just below the surface. This pipe, which is about 9 inches in diameter, is fixed permanently to the after bridge standard. The exhaust pipe when not in use, also becomes full of water, but when needed for the submarine to Snort, the water is blown out into the sea from the reduced air pressure system. The valve to the exhaust from the diesels is then opened and the exhaust pressure from the engines keeps the pipe free of water, and the gases can then be dispersed just below sea level.

Allowances for the difference in 'trim' have to be made as the Snort mast and exhaust pipe either fill with water when not in use, or are emptied of water before use. These adjustments are made in the internal compensating tanks of the submarine.

Diagram 3: Diving. Two distinct operations are necessary to dive a submarine, but in practice they are done concurrently. Firstly the buoyancy must be destroyed and secondly the submarine has to be forced under the water by the hydroplanes while the propellers drive the boat forward. There are two pairs of hydroplanes (sometimes referred to as horizontal rudders) one pair forward and one aft. The after hydroplanes are locked in the horizontal position when not in use, but the foremost hydroplanes which are smaller are 'turned in' to lie vertically against the casing when the submarine has surfaced, and 'turned out' when diving. In normal conditions the propellers would probably be going at half-speed ahead when diving the boat.

The destruction of the buoyancy is controlled by flooding the Main Ballast tanks which in the majority of designs over the years have been 'strapped' to the outside of the pressure hull. When dived a submarine is balanced in water just in the same way as an airship is balanced in air and the boat when 'in trim' can hover with both propellers stopped, and be controlled with ease at a speed of one and a half knots. These conditions cannot be achieved solely by flooding the main ballast tanks as this is not sufficiently accurate. Consequently, Internal Auxiliary and Compensating Ballast Tanks are provided inside the pressure hull by means of which the boat can be trimmed. These allow for a play in trim of about thirty tons of water.

In the case of a submarine which has not been to sea for a day or two, calculations are worked out to adjust the trim for any changes in weight which may have taken place. For example, torpedoes, oil fues and stores may have been embarked and the number of men and the weight of their personal gear changed. To allow for these changes, water is pumped out of, or taken into, the internal compensating tanks according to the calculations. When the submarine then proceeds to sea, and the main ballast tanks are flooded the boat

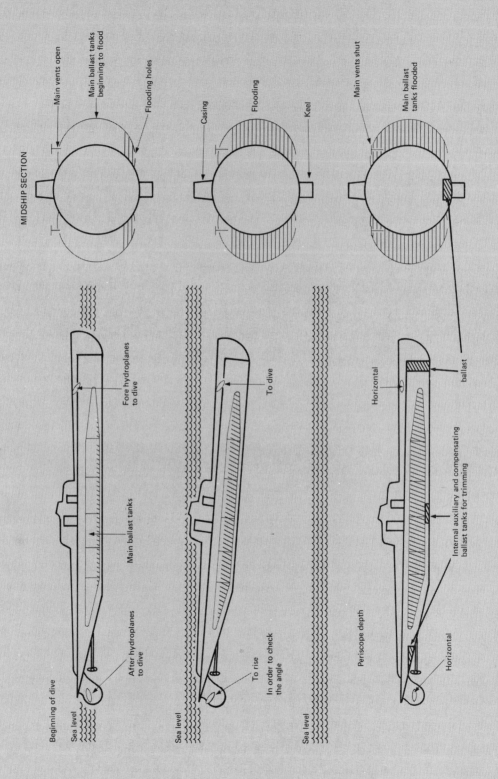

Diagram 3. DIVING

MIDSHIP SECTION

Main vents open
Main ballast tanks beginning to flood
Flooding holes

Casing
Flooding
Keel

Main vents shut
Main ballast tanks flooded
ballast

Beginning of dive
Sea level
Fore hydroplanes to dive
Main ballast tanks
After hydroplanes to dive

Sea level
To dive
To rise
In order to check the angle

Sea level
Periscope depth
Horizontal
Internal auxiliary and compensating ballast tanks for trimming
Horizontal

Plate 16

Cruising at periscope depth using Snort. The top of one periscope is seen to the right of the Snort

The two periscopes showing both the high power or search periscope and the low power or attack periscope. Both periscopes are raised higher than would be normal in a calm sea.

Plate 17

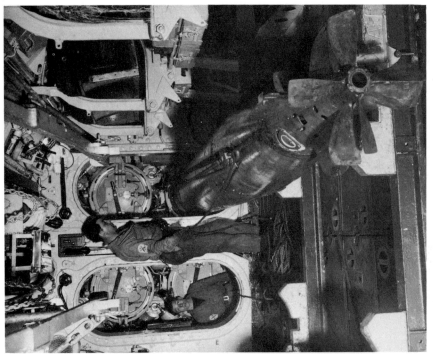

The torpedo tube space and the torpedo stowage compartment, showing a torpedo being loaded into a torpedo tube

Embarking a torpedo

Plate 18

An artist's impression of an attack by a submarine. In the picture three supply ships are being screened by two trawlers on the near side and a trawler and two escort vessels on the far side. The submarine is outside the screen in this case, but British submarines frequently attacked from very close inside the screen. From a drawing by Commander S E Axten, RN (Retd)

Plate 19

The submarine beginning to dive, showing the air leaving the main ballast tanks

The submarine surfacing, showing free water draining from the bridge and casing

Plate 20

The Control Room showing the Captain at the Periscope, the Navigator standing beside the
Chart Table and men operating the wheels which control the position of the hydroplanes

Plate 21

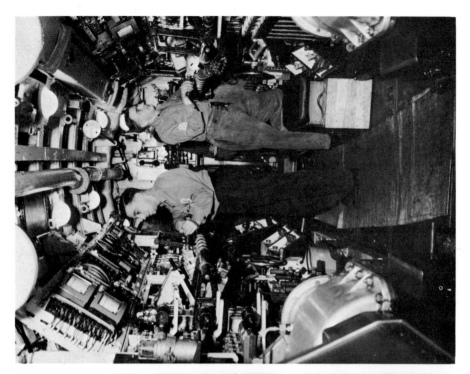

The Motor Room

The Engine Room

Plate 22

Officers in the Wardroom

The Seamen's Mess

Plate 23

Watch diving. An artificer takes over the after hydroplanes

The Fourth Officer working the 'Fruit Machine'. The Asdic operators are seen in the background

should be 'in trim'. Naturally the trim may not always be exactly right due to changes in the density of the sea water which is not constant everywhere and also to the difficulty of assessing small weights such as bilge water. These small inaccuracies will become quickly apparent when the submarines dives for the first time and speed is reduced to 1 or 2 knots. The boat can then be trimmed quite quickly and perfectly using the internal compensating tanks, and once this is done no further adjustments may have to be made for some hours.

On first diving a submarine goes to 'periscope depth' for trimming. If the surface sea is heavy and the waves are felt at that depth then the boat will be taken deeper until tranquility is found in order to trim her.

The change from diesel propulsion to electric motors is made instantly on the order to dive.

All captains have their own slight variations for giving this order. The word of command is combined with pressing a 'klaxon' hooter twice which resounds throughout the boat, and the submarine is dived instantly by the 'Watch' on duty. The remainder of the crew go to their diving stations and those on the bridge scramble down the conning tower, the captain last. He shuts the upper hatch after him. Due to the height of the conning tower there is plenty of time for those on the bridge to go below.

Diagram 4: Surfacing. This shows how the submarine returns to the surface. Compressed air is the 'life-blood' of submarines and is kept in groups of small bottles tucked away in the bilges throughout the length of the boat. Some submarines have as many as fifteen to twenty of these bottles. Pressure in the system is about four thousand pounds per square inch but this can be reduced to less than fifty pounds for domestic and internal use throughout the boat.

The operation of surfacing is normally carried out from periscope depth and after having first opened the lower conning tower hatch. The full force of the high compressed air is then admitted to the tops of the main ballast tanks and the water blown out. The operation is assisted by the hydroplanes with the boat going ahead probably at half-speed.

As soon as any water is blown out of the main ballast tanks the submarine has positive buoyancy and will immediately start to rise to the surface. In practice only a small amount of high compressed air is allowed into selected main ballast tanks so as to conserve this supply of air, and as soon as the conning tower is out of the water and it is safe to open the upper conning tower hatch, air pumps, using fresh air, blow the remaining water out of the main ballast tanks and bring the submarine to full buoyancy. This latter operation may take five or more minutes.

Once the upper conning tower hatch is open the diesel engines can take over driving the submarine from the electric motors. Air compressors can be used to replenish the high compressed air expended when surfacing and if necessary the electric batteries can be recharged.

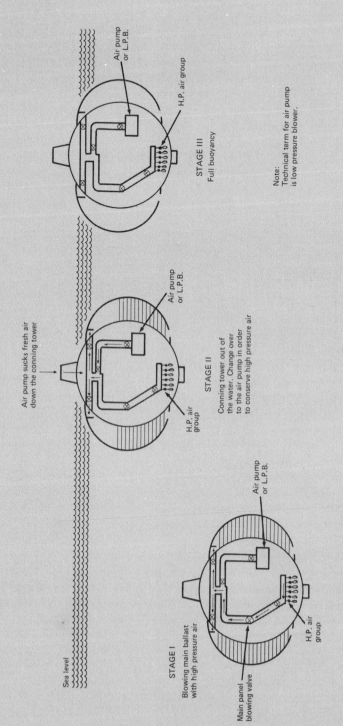

Diagram 4. SURFACING

Sea level

Air pump sucks fresh air down the conning tower

Air pump or L.P.B.

H.P. air group

STAGE III
Full buoyancy

Note:
Technical term for air pump is low pressure blower.

Air pump or L.P.B.

H.P. air group

STAGE II
Conning tower out of the water. Change over to the air pump in order to conserve high pressure air

Air pump or L.P.B.

Main panel blowing valve

H.P. air group

STAGE I
Blowing main ballast with high pressure air

Diagram 5: Periscopes, Wireless, Asdic and Radar.

The Periscopes. In comparison to the earliest designs, periscopes have been improved out of all knowledge. All submarines have two periscopes which pass through supporting standards on the superstructure external to the pressure hull. The length of the periscope allows a submarine of the *T* Class to dive to a depth of 32 feet where tranquillity is generally to be found and at the same time the surface can be viewed. Such a depth means that the majority of ships can pass right over the submarine without piercing the pressure hull so that the possibility of accidents is reduced. One periscope is normally monocular and uni-focal giving normal vision. It is known as the Low Power Periscope and is used in the final stages of an attack and for this reason it has a very small top so that little 'feather' will be shown when close to the enemy. The other periscope, the High Power Periscope, is binocular and bi-focal and includes range finding and sky searching arrangements. The diameter of this periscope is over 9 inches and tapers to about 5 inches at the top. On a clear day objects can be seen through it at ten miles range. Periscopes are raised and lowered by wire pulleys operated by oil pressure rams and where the periscopes pass through the pressure hull there are special glands which are designed to resist external sea pressure.

The Wireless. The great limitation in submarine work is that it is not practicable to transmit wireless waves under the water. If it is necessary to make a wireless signal from a submarine of this type the Seaguard Radar Mast has to be raised and a small aerial attached to it is held clear of the water. This aerial has only a limited range and for those reasons it is not practical for a submarine dived to keep in continuous touch with the shore, or Commander-in-Chief afloat, in the same way as large aircraft are in touch with their Control throughout a flight. One way in which the submarine when dived can keep continuous touch is for a ship on the surface fitted with Asdic to be in the vicinity, then the submarine can communicate with the ship by Asdic and that ship can wireless the message in the normal way. When on the surface a submarine's wireless can be worked in the usual way and is world wide.

The Asdic. The Asdic (introduced in the inter-war years) makes a contact with underwater objects by sending out supersonic sound waves. These can be directional and the echo off another object may be heard up to a range of two miles. All submarines of this period use Asdic for underwater intercommunication and listening. The maximum range for this is ten miles. The sound waves are sent by an oscillator housed in a special dome which is fitted beneath the hull of the submarine. These waves are reduced to sonic frequency and amplified, in much the same way as wireless waves, into the operators' earphones.

NOTE—There has been much controversy over the derivation of the initials ASDIC. This was in fact the code name given to the work on this invention by the Anti-Submarine Department of the Admiralty. Naturally they chose the letters ASD and they added the two letters IC for no better reason than to make a suitable code word.

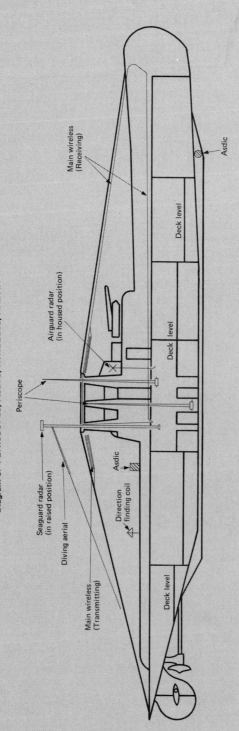

Diagram 5. PERISCOPES, ASDIC, WIRELESS, RADAR

Main wireless (Receiving)

Asdic

Deck level

Deck level

Airguard radar (in housed position)

Periscope

Seaguard radar (in raised position)

Diving aerial

Asdic

Direction finding coil

Main wireless (Transmitting)

Deck level

The Radar. When circumstances permit a submarine can 'view' the surface by projecting radar aerials, one for Airguard and one for Seaguard (introduced in the latter part of the Second World War). This is very convenient in low visibility and at night. On the other hand the commanding officer has to remember that radar fitted aircraft and surface ships may detect the submarine's masts, and thus there may be many circumstances when the commanding officer would prefer not to use his radar. When on the surface submarines use radar in the same way as surface ships.

It must be understood that at the same time the snort mast, periscopes, and wireless masts when raised are all subject to detection by enemy radar.

Diagram 6: Armament—Torpedoes, guns and mines.

The Torpedo. The torpedo is 22 feet in length and 21 inches in diameter. This diagram shows the various places where torpedo tubes can be fitted and they need not always be inside the submarine. A torpedo can remain without deterioration even in such an exposed position as in the casing outside the submarine proper. A torpedo fired from such a position will run quite correctly after being there for a fortnight. None of these external tubes can be reloaded as it would not be practical to carry out this operation at sea. Normally all torpedo tubes inside the submarine are provided with re-load torpedoes.

The torpedo is fired from the tube by a short burst of compressed air from inside the submarine. Thereafter it runs under its own mechanism. Torpedoes attain a speed of over 45 knots in a few seconds and can run at this speed without variation for a distance of about five miles. Arrangements are also provided whereby the torpedo keeps at a given depth, steers a given course and if it fails to hit the target, sinks itself at the end of its run.

The operation of loading and firing is related closely to the trim because of the change in weights, a torpedo weighing one and a half tons. When the torpedo is first loaded into the tube the rear door which has been open to admit the torpedo is shut and the portion of the tube not occupied by the torpedo is flooded with water from an internal tank provided for this purpose. This allows the bow door to be opened without an inrush of water altering the trim. When the torpedo leaves the tube, momentarily the submarine is light, but the water rushes in so quickly that the lifting of the bow of the submarine is checked. As the weight of the water in the torpedo tube is less than the combined weight of the torpedo which has left the tube and the water which surrounded it, arrangements are made whereby automatically an extra amount of water is allowed to flow into a special internal tank to compensate exactly for the discharge of the torpedo. After firing, the bow door of the tube is shut and the water in the tube drained down to the tank from which the tube was flooded during the loading operation. When this has been done the rear door can then be opened and another torpedo loaded in.

The Guns. Submarines of this type normally carry a gun but it is never larger

Diagram 6. ARMAMENT
torpedoes, guns, mines

Starboard foremost hydroplane
in surface turned in position

Two external
torpedo tubes

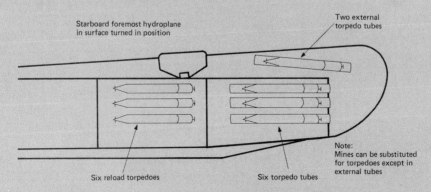

Six reload torpedoes

Six torpedo tubes

Note:
Mines can be substituted
for torpedoes except in
external tubes

Two stern external
torpedo tubes

4 inch gun

Supports for portable
anti-aircraft gun

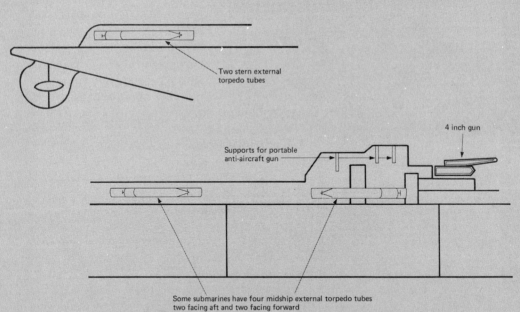

Some submarines have four midship external torpedo tubes
two facing aft and two facing forward

than 4 inch calibre, because it would be too difficult to manage if the gun had to be provided with a separate shell and charge of cordite, making two things to load before it could be fired. In addition all big submarines carry anti-aircraft guns. In some boats to save 'top hamper' these are hand guns brought up from the conning tower when needed and fitted on to supports on either side of the bridge.

Mines. These are specially constructed for laying by submarines using the torpedo tubes. The same method and mechanism is employed for firing the mines from the tubes as for firing the torpedoes. Submarines can carry about twelve mines and lay one at a time from each tube.

Plate 7. This drawing shows the submarine making an attack, which is the main purpose of its being. Attacking requires good judgment, quick thinking and calm nerves. Targets may zigzag, may be screened by destroyers and aircraft and they may alter their speeds. In all this the submarine captain must direct his boat so that he can fire his torpedoes ahead of the target in order that they will hit by the time they reach it. The torpedoes have to be set at a depth which is appropriate. The estimated speed and the course of the target has to be arrived at by observation through the periscopes and by taking ranges and plotting its course. Though the captain is provided with very up to date instruments to help him in all this, he has to calculate correctly, manoeuvre the submarine, while at the same time avoid being seen by aircraft or heard by escorting destroyers, which in an attack like the one shown in this picture, is a problem. The captain must also remember that once the torpedoes have been fired the enemy will know that there is a submarine in the vicinity and the submarine must expect to be hunted and probably depth charged. The captain has various means of getting the submarine away from his pursuers. He can go any course he selects and any depths he considers appropriate, he may move at any speed which he judges the best in the circumstances, or if the depth is satisfactory he can stop all machinery and movement and lie quietly on the bottom. Almost every submarine captain has his own ideas of what is best to do when he is attacked by surface craft. Principles are laid down but what is actually carried out is left to the man on the spot. Submarines do not always have to attack fully escorted targets, and those which are partly un-protected or on rare occasions totally unprotected, leave the submarine captain a comparatively simple problem.

A WALK THROUGH A *T* CLASS BOAT

Plate 2 shows a submarine of the *T* Class, in section, trimmed and submerged to periscope depth. For the explanatory walk through, the submarine must be considered to be on the surface, and in harbour. The normal way to enter when in harbour would be by the torpedo loading hatch, in the fore part of the boat, and leading down into the *torpedo stowage compartment.* There is another hatch forward of this in the same compartment which is used solely

in connection with escape. The conning tower hatch is not used for entering the submarine when it is in harbour.

On entering the torpedo stowage compartment there will probably be seen four torpedoes stowed in racks and two in trenches under the deck. These are provided as a reload when the first six, already in the tubes, have been fired. The torpedo tubes themselves are in the *torpedo tube space* forward of the stowage compartment, and separated by a watertight bulkhead.

Leaving the stowage compartment and walking aft through a second watertight bulkhead are all the *living spaces* for the officers and crew except those of the stoker mechanics. First of all is the seamen's mess, then the petty officers' and engine room artificers' messes and finally the wardroom. In the ratings' messes there are bunks for every petty officer and the majority of the men. Everyone has a locker and these are used for sitting on as well as for stowing possessions. Each mess has one small table, and a locker for mess utensils. The wardroom is small and cramped considering that three executive and one engineer officer live here. Each officer has a bunk with curtains, but there is only limited drawer space and wardrobe accommodation. A table is in the centre round which settees are built into the side of the submarine. This table has to be used for both work and meals. In addition to the settees, sometimes an easy chair is squeezed in. In a corner of the wardroom is a depth-gauge especially fitted so that it can be seen at any time what depth the submarine is keeping. Lavatories, or 'heads', for officers and petty officers are included in this compartment.

The next compartment aft of all these living spaces and reached through a third watertight bulkhead, is the *control room* which is really the heart of the submarine. In a corner of this is the captain's cabin, and it is natural that this and the wardroom should be placed to connect with the control room so that officers are readily to hand. The captain's cabin is extremely small and contains his bunk, clothes accommodation, a chair and a very small table. In the control room there are so many wheels and pipes and electric leads that a newcomer would wonder how anyone could understand them all, but with experience and familiarity the tangle of machinery sorts itself out quite easily. There are levers for opening the valves which flood the ballast tanks to dive the submarine, and more levers which send high-compressed air into the same ballast tanks to drive the water out and surface the submarine. The control room also contains the steering wheel and two operating wheels or levers for working the hydroplanes, one for forward hydroplanes and one for the after hydroplanes. In addition there are oil pressure rams used in the raising and lowering of the periscopes and radar mast. Also placed as conveniently as space permits there are the attack instruments, the chart table, the asdic operating control for working the underwater signalling and hearing device, and the radar plots. In the control room as well are shallow and deep diving gauges, the master Sperry gyro compass and a maze of electrical switchboards and leads. At the after end of the control room is the dividing panel on the other

side of which are the radar and W/T offices. In many submarines the galley also finds a place opposite this. Underneath the control room are large electric batteries which begin below the living spaces forward, and continue as far as the W/T office. They weigh over 150 tons.

Moving further aft through the fourth watertight bulkhead is the *engine room* where there are normally two large diesel engines used for propelling the submarine on the surface. These engines cannot be used submerged because they require fresh air and in the submarine shown in the sectional picture there is no method of passing fresh air to the engines when the submarine is under water. In the latest types of submarines air can be provided by the Snort mast which gives enough air to the submarine's engines for them to run with the boat submerged, but if the submarine goes below periscope depth, which is also the depth of the Snort mast, this mast cannot be used and so the engines have to be stopped and the submarine run by the main motors. Oil fuel and lubricating oil for the diesel engines are kept in tanks along the bottom of the submarine, distributed throughout the length of the vessel. At the after end of this compartment are the main motors which drive the submarine submerged, and get their electric power from the batteries. Overhead, at the forward end of the compartment there is a hatch leading on to the upper deck for the use of the engine room staff when in harbour. It is the largest hatch in the pressure hull as big engine parts may have to pass through it, and also it is fitted as a DSEA (Davis Submerged Escape Apparatus) hatch. In this compartment is the lavatory for the seamen and stoker mechanics.

Further aft and through the fifth watertight bulkhead is the *living space* for the stoker mechanics, which is similar to that of the seamen. In the tail of the submarine there is a *steering compartment* which holds an engine for working the rudder, and a wheel for steering by hand if the steering engine fails. Overhead in this compartment is the after escape hatch.

Returning to the control room will be seen two ladders, one leads up the conning tower onto the bridge through the upper and lower conning tower hatches, and the other leads up to the gun again through two hatches on to the casing forward of the bridge.

The Bridge itself is built up from the casing and contains a chart table, watertight compass, fog syren, engine-room telegraphs and a voice pipe for speaking to the control room. The two standards for the periscopes project up through the bridge deck. Running completely round the standards is the main wireless. Overall from the bow across the top of the standards and down to the stern is a strong 'jumping wire'. This is to protect the submarine from enemy sweep wires and other hazards when dived. A radar mast also projects through the bridge but is kept lowered when not in use.

The gun forward of the bridge is 4 inch calibre and is the main gun armament, and aft of the bridge on a special platform in this submarine is a 20 mm anti-aircraft gun.

THE OFFICERS AND CREW OF A *T* CLASS SUBMARINE

A submarine of the *T* Class would have a crew of about 5 officers and 58 ratings. The numbers are never exactly the same, as every submarine has some slightly different characteristic. Of the officers, the position of the Captain is self-explanatory. He has been 'through the mill', starting as a Fourth Hand then becoming Navigator and after some years of service, First Lieutenant combining Second-in-Command. The Captain has undergone a special course before being placed in command generally of a small submarine at first and finally he achieves his ambition of commanding a large submarine, by which time he has probably reached the rank of Lieutenant-Commander, and he has had many years' experience of submarines. He is then probably in his late twenties or early thirties, as by the age of thirty-five he is considered too old for patrols in the event of war. In addition to youth, he must have courage, a high sense of responsibility and sound judgment coupled with enthusiasm to serve in this specialized branch of the Navy. He must have the complete confidence of his officers and men, as their safety and well being depend on him.

Immediately under the Captain is the First Lieutenant. He is also the Executive Officer of the submarine and has the special duty of keeping the 'trim'. When there are any changes in weights in the boat or a weight is moved from one place to another, then the First Lieutenant makes an adjustment of salt water in special internal tanks provided for this purpose to allow for these changes. He must see that the submarine is always perfectly balanced horizontally when dived. The organization of the ship's company and all details of their work and welfare are arranged by the First Lieutenant. The cleanliness of the boat and the general efficiency of the men and the submarine are his responsibility.

The Navigating Officer or Third Hand, as he is referred to colloquially, is normally a young Lieutenant. He does not have to take a special course for underwater navigation but he has to be rather a 'Jack of all Trades'. He is in charge of keeping the charts corrected to the latest information, he looks after the compasses including the Sperry gyro, and also the chronometers. He is in charge of communications, that is to say, the wireless and radar, and in addition keeps the Confidential Books which include the signalling cyphers and codes, and he attends to the general correspondence of the submarine.

The Fourth Officer controls the armament, that is the torpedoes and the guns. He may also take charge of the asdic if this is not taken over by the First Lieutenant which is sometimes the case. It is a considerable position for a young officer but early responsibility is one of the main attractions of submarines. He works the instruments used in making an attack, the principal one of which is called the 'fruit machine', which automatically works out the director angle in the firing of torpedoes. The duties of Third and Fourth Hand may sometimes be reversed.

All large submarines carry an Engineer Officer. He may be a Lieutenant-Commander (E), a Lieutenant (E) or a Branch Engineer Officer. He is specially

qualified to be in charge of internal combustion engines, and submarine engineers have an amazing knack of getting diesel engines to run under the most difficult conditions which often have to be faced in submarine life.

The Senior Rating is the Coxswain. He is a Seaman Rating and in a large submarine would be a Chief Petty Officer. The whole ship revolves around him. The Coxswain controls the men, makes out the routine, and looks after the provisions and rum. He is also specially qualified in first aid and is the one rating who may officially give morphia. In various compartments underneath the living spaces the Coxswain stows his stores and generally has on board enough provisions to last everyone three months. He has the special duty of being responsible for the DSEA. A Petty Officer known as the Second Coxswain assists him in all duties, and has the additional responsibility of looking after the outside of the submarine, including the wires and ropes for berthing.

There are four specialist Petty Officers each in charge of their own departments. The Torpedo Anti-Submarine Instructor (TASI) is in charge of the torpedoes and asdic, the Electrician controls the main batteries and the main motors, the Radio Electrician is in charge of the radar and wireless machinery, and the Petty Officer Telegraphist who is the senior wireless operator, normally supervises the communications department. The TASI is assisted by an Underwater Control Rating (UC) for the asdic side of the work, he is generally a Leading Seaman and holds the specialist rate of either UC1 or UC2. In a large submarine there is an Electrical Artificer who is a Chief Petty Officer and the Senior Electrical Rating. He attends to the gyro compass and supervises the departmental Petty Officers generally on all electrical matters. He has qualified through a five year electrical apprenticeship.

Some twenty Seaman Ratings, nearly all of whom have qualified in one of the specialist branches, make up the Seamen part of the crew working under these Petty Officers.

The Senior Engine Room Rating is the Chief Engine Room Artificer. He is assisted by three other Engine Room Artificers (ERAs). Theirs is the responsibility of keeping the big diesel engines in perfect condition and each is in charge of an Engine Room Watch. In addition there is the Outside ERA who works outside the engine room and is in charge of the machinery for flooding and blowing all the external ballast tanks, and he works these important controls at Diving Stations under the First Lieutenant. He is also responsible for seeing that the compressed air bottles are kept charged, and that the auxiliary machinery outside the engine room is kept in efficient order. All five are highly skilled artificers who have begun their careers as engineers, serving a full five years' apprenticeship.

There is one Chief Petty Officer Stoker Mechanic in the crew of the submarine. He is in charge of the Stoker Mechanics who number about twenty-five and is assisted by a Petty Officer Stoker Mechanic. Apart from this he has the special duty of 'putting on the trim'. That is to say, he floods internal

tanks with salt water or pumps water out of them as ordered by the First Lieutenant when weights in the submarine are changed. He is also responsible for the fresh water carried in the submarine and the working of the distilling plant fitted in the latest boats.

The submarine is divided into three Watches, Red, White and Blue. Each Watch has an Officer of the Watch and one third of the boats' crew is on duty under him. Any one Watch could if necessary dive and surface the submarine. When 'Diving Stations' is ordered all three Watches are on duty.

It can easily be seen that each man must have a perfect knowledge of his job to make up a really efficient submarine crew. There is great comradeship in crews even in peacetime and the proximity in which the officers and men live bring them all more closely together than in any other branch of naval life.

JOINING SUBMARINES

To join the Submarine Branch of the Navy except during war Executive Officers volunteer when they are Sub-Lieutenants. It is essential that they should do this at an early age, as they should become commanding officers in peace time when they are about twenty-seven. In war they would be in command even younger. Sometimes officers have to be conscripted to make up numbers, but the volunteers have always exceeded the conscripts by three to one and it is seldom that a conscript fails to volunteer after a few months in the Submarine Branch. Service in submarines is divided into set periods. Period one lasts three years during which time an Executive Officer would rise to First Lieutenant. One year is then spent in General Service usually in a big ship. The second period in submarines covers about two and a half years, beginning as First Lieutenant and followed by three months Commanding Officers' Course and one and a half to two years in command. Officers are then given a two year rest period in General Service to learn Fleet work by which time they have usually risen to the rank of Lieutenant-Commander. On returning to submarines for the third period their time in command is limited only by age. Officers were withdrawn from active command at the age of thirty-five during the war. After this age they either return to General Service or serve in a senior appointment connected with submarines.

Engineer Officers join as young Lieutenants, or if they are Branch Officers they join at as early an age as possible. Their big ship time and service in submarines is controlled differently from Executive Officers, and generally in relation to individual circumstances.

It is happily agreed throughout the Navy that fully qualified submarine officers are most valuable when their time comes to serve in surface ships, since they have learnt to take responsibility at a young age and in the case of Executive Officers, they have invariably had considerable practical experience of ship handling, navigation and torpedo work, coupled with a close understanding of the sea and weather. With these qualifications acquired at an early age it is not surprising to learn that a large number of our admirals served in

submarines in their earlier days.

Submarine Ratings also volunteer, and again if numbers are not sufficient they are conscripted. The Service has always been 95 per cent volunteers. There are three manning depots in the Royal Navy: Portsmouth, Chatham and Devonport, and each of these depots has a submarine quota. Men can only join when they are fully trained in whatever non-substantive branch they have taken up, and the younger the better. Also they must have a standard of conduct of at least 'Good'. Some specialist branches can only provide their quota when the men are of Petty Officer rate, these are the Engine Room Artificers. Generally other rates work their way up while in the Submarine Service to become Petty Officers and Chief Petty Officers. Some specialise in torpedo work or asdics, while others work their way to the top executive rate and become Submarine Coxswains. All submarine ratings do five years in their first period, and then they are at liberty to volunteer for further service or to return to surface ships. A man who wishes to be a Submarine Coxswain cannot reach this high rate in his first five years except in war time.

Chapter seven
Some questions answered about submarines

It would seem appropriate here to cover some of the questions which people ask about submarines. 'Submariners' themselves are liable to assume that the public know more about these vessels than they actually do.

Many of the questions which are asked today by the public about submarines are the same ones which were being asked fifty years ago, so taking some at random it is hoped they may cover most of the questions the reader wishes answered, which have not already been covered by the diagrams.

1. How deep can a submarine go?

During the fifty years covered by Part 1 of this book, hulls have been built stronger and stronger and therefore submarines have been able to go to a correspondingly greater depth. The depth gauge in a *T* Class submarine is marked down to 350 feet but no one knows how much deeper some submarines may have been in war either to avoid attack or because of damage which took them to a greater depth before full control had been restored.

2. Why cannot a submarine have a window?

When underwater, generally speaking, it is not possible to see any distance at all. In clear Mediterranean water, if the submarine is not more than forty or fifty feet deep, and one looks through the periscope while the lens is underwater, it is possible to see the shape of the submarine up to about the bow, but probably not to the extremity of it. This can only be done when the sun is overhead or nearly so. In waters around our coast here in England, one could not see more than a few yards. In these circumstances there is no point in giving a submarine a window in the pressure hull apart from the fact that the depth charge and similar weapons entirely preclude the idea.

3. Is it rough under the water?

Except when the sea is remarkably rough and the depth of water not very great, it is calm as soon as the submarine is under the trough of the waves. Generally speaking, if the centre of the submarine is at about forty feet depth, and there is quite a big sea on the surface, the submarine is absolutely still and no motion will be experienced until the submarine is taken almost to the bottom of the sea where it is possible there may be a ground swell. In our peculiar North Sea, where the depth may not be more than 100 feet, and where in rough weather the sea is very sharp and steep, it may, however, be difficult to find tranquillity. In fact the submarine may 'pump' up and down and roll slightly when beam on, and certainly in rough conditions it is not practicable to sit on the bottom as the ground swell is too great. In open seas, below the surface, tranquillity can soon be found and one often hears a sigh of relief

from the crew when the submarine dives.

4. What about the air in a submarine?

The air in a submarine which the crew breathe is another point on which people ask many questions. It seems odd, to say the least of it, that some five officers and sixty or seventy men can go on breathing the same air for several hours. In point of fact they can do so. The air in which we live contains approximately 79 per cent nitrogen, 21 per cent oxygen and ·03 per cent carbon dioxide. We exhale normally 80 per cent nitrogen, 16 per cent oxygen and 4 per cent carbon dioxide. The increase in carbon dioxide in the atmosphere of a submarine during a long dive, though causing slow poisoning, does not begin its work very soon. Long after it is impossible to strike a match or smoke a cigarette through lack of pure oxygen, human beings can work, and more important, can think in such conditions. In a submarine not until air has been breathed for some fifteen hours need there be any distress, and in these days with the Snort mast which can bring air down to the submarine when the vessel is at periscope depth, there is no necessity for the submarine to surface at all to replenish the air. If, however, no fresh air is available for a long time there are means provided for easing the position which can be used at the commanding officer's discretion. Chemical canisters are fitted in the ventilating trunking which absorb the carbon dioxide gases and, complementary to these, candle oxygen generators are supplied which help to replace the loss of the four to five per cent oxygen from the air. One canister and one candle are kept at each end of the boat. The canisters are about one foot square and the candles about eighteen inches long and four inches in diameter. In tropical climates submarines are fitted with air conditioning plants which keep the temperatures tolerable and also de-humidify the air to a great extent.

5. What about the fumes in a submarine?

There are fumes in the submarine but in modern vessels they need not be dangerous. They were dangerous when petrol engines were used. Modern submarines have very fine ventilating systems and if these are correctly run the danger from gases can almost entirely be avoided. In early submarines white mice were used to detect carbon monoxide and indeed they were part of the engine room equipment when petrol engines were used to propel the vessels on the surface. These mice were kept in cages low down so that the gas did not rise to human mouth level before the mice had given warning. White mice were preferred to brown because they were tamer and easier to handle and mice were preferred to other animals because they breathe quickly. They have to breathe quickly to keep up their body temperatures as their bodies are roundish and their capacity for cooling is great. Happily, for very many years now, there has been no need to use them!

The gas, however, for which submarine officers and men have the greatest respect is hydrogen. This is the most potentially dangerous gas made in submarines today. When an electric battery is being charged or is discharging at a high rate, hydrogen gas is given off as well as oxygen gas. The proportion of

the two gases are: hydrogen in two parts to oxygen in one part. When the hydrogen in two parts is mixed with the oxygen in one part the result is H_2O which is pure water, but when separated they remain as gases and the hydrogen gas is very explosive. This hydrogen is dispersed by very carefully thought-out ventilating systems, especially for the batteries, but it may occur either through some fault in drill or faulty operation of a fan, or in some obstruse way, that there are pockets of hydrogen around the battery. If the smallest light from a match or spark from an electric switch happens in the vicinity, then an explosion is almost certain. As might be expected the hydrogen explosion is very violent.

There is also another gas which can be a danger to submarine people. This is chlorine. If salt water is mixed with sulphuric acid, the latter being the liquid which is in the electric batteries, then chlorine gas is given off. The fact that the submarine spends its life almost entirely under the water, and that in the batteries there are many tons of sulphuric acid, tend to make a risky situation. It is easy to understand that a quantity of water going down the conning tower hatch might find its way to some of the cells of the battery, but gas masks are proof against chlorine gas. With careful checking of the ventilating system and proper attention to the water-tightness of the batteries, accidents from these gases should not occur.

6. Why does a submarine have guns?

Most submarines have 3 inch or 4 inch calibre guns except those specially designed for high speed under water, which carry no guns. The primary reason for a gun is so that if a submarine is unable to dive it has some means of defending itself, also the gun has proved to be a useful weapon for offensive operations. In the last war, particularly in the Pacific, the gun was used against small supply ships, light shore targets such as railways, light anti-submarine craft and a numerous variety of targets where a few shells caused temporary damage and annoyance. With aircraft constantly on patrol over the sea in war, submarines are also supplied with anti-aircraft guns, but the best defence against air by a submarine is to dive and usually the AA guns are only used if the submarine is unable to do so.

7. What happens to the gun when the submarine dives?

The answer is it gets wet, but some of the mechanism is taken below when the submarine dives and is only brought up when the gun is going into action.

8. Why are there holes in the casing?

If there were no holes in the casing then air pockets would occur when diving and it would be difficult if not impossible to get the submarine underwater. It is essential therefore to have large holes everywhere along the casing so that the air gets out quickly as the water rises up over the submarine. Following on this, in a very heavy sea it is not practical to dive the submarine straight into the sea because the casing does not flood properly owing to the big waves, so the submarine has to be turned and dived down the trough of the waves. This is a tricky manoeuvre but submarines dive so quickly that there

is no special danger from it. Those who understand about buoyancy and the centre of gravity will be interested to know that at a particular moment during this operation, the centre of buoyancy and the centre of gravity coincide and the submarine has no righting moment, but this step is quickly passed by the rapid diving of the boat.

9. Can a submarine dive in fresh water?

When built, submarines are normally designed to dive in sea water of a density 1.027. The auxiliary and compensating ballast tanks are provided to allow for changes in trim from the empty condition without torpedoes, ammunition, and bunks and only ten per cent fuel up to the full condition, loaded with a complete outfit of torpedoes, full of fuel and all ammunition on board. If the submarine moves into either very salt water of a density of about 1.030 or into fresh water of density 1.0, then the capacity of the auxiliary tanks is strained and there may not be enough latitude to enable the submarine to operate. If a submarine is known to be going to operate in almost fresh water, then the boat may have to leave some of her torpedoes and stores behind and start with very full auxiliary tanks. Then when the fresh water is encountered there is sufficient water in the auxiliary tanks to pump out to enable the trim to be maintained. Conversely, if the submarine is going to operate in very salt water, extra weights may have to be embarked so that the voyage can be started with the auxiliary tanks almost empty and when the very salt water is encountered there are plenty of empty tanks into which the salt water can be taken to maintain the trim.

10. How long can a submarine remain at sea?

With the advent of the Snort, it is not uncommon for a submarine to be at sea for months and to cover a distance of many thousands of miles. Human endurance, food and fresh water are all agents which play their part when considering this question. However, endurance of submarines at sea is becoming more a matter of oil, both fuel oil to run the engines and lubricating oil for the working parts and bearings. For an engine in good repair it is normal to carry 3½ per cent lubricating oil to 96½ per cent fuel. With long running, away from the depot ship, the percentage used one to the other may vary — thus one may run out ahead of the other and reduce the calculated time the submarine can remain at sea.

11. What difficulties are there in the domestic side of submarines?

In war, food and water is always a difficulty on long patrols. Bread is taken on board wrapped in special paper and remains edible for about a fortnight. Fruit is carried, but not many fresh vegetables, except potatoes, so great reliance has to be placed on dehydrated vegetables, every day lime juice is issued to make up for lack of Vitamin C. The submarines have refrigerators, so meat can be stored for quite a long period, and in addition large quantities of tinned food is embarked to last the patrol.

Fresh water has to be rationed most carefully, and, generally conserved for drinking. Most submarines however could arrange for a fresh-water sponge-

Plate 24

The first depot ship: HMS Hazard with a Holland boat alongside

A modern depot ship: HMS Forth with seven large submarines alongside

Plate 25

To Spithead

Entrance to
Portsmouth
Harbour

'Promotion Point'

Instructional
Escape Tower

Haslar Creek

Fort Blockhouse: HMS Dolphin. The home of British submarines for over fifty years

Plate 26

Building the first British submarine, Holland 1

Plate 27

The launch of a T Class submarine

A submarine of the T Class

down for the crew about three times a week. (On war patrol many of the crew grew beards to save the necessity of shaving.) Post-war submarines have two distilling plants, and each plant can make fifteen gallons of fresh water in one hour. Water consumption for all purposes (in twenty-four hours) is normally about 225 gallons, so the distillers can provide fairly comfortable conditions for the crew, even if the situation on patrol precludes their being run for very long periods. In peace time there are not many restrictions. Supplies of food can be replenished and everyone can wash freely, big submarines being fitted with a shower.

Lavatories are different from the usual ones at sea because the exit in a submarine must be below the surface of the sea, whereas in an ordinary ship it is just above. There is a special pan which can be flooded with salt water. It has a valve opening through the hull of the submarine to the sea and by passing compressed air to this pan the contents can be forced outside against the pressure of the water. It is a little complicated to operate this arrangement correctly because it requires two or three manoeuvres done concurrently and exactly right. Normally the lavatory must not be operated below a depth of 200 feet.

12. Are cigarettes and alcohol allowed in submarines?

If fresh air is coming into the submarine through the Snort, smoking is permitted all the time, but when dived without using the Snort no smoking is allowed. After about twelve hours diving without any replenishment of fresh air no smoking could take place in any case because there is not enough oxygen to light a match or allow a cigarette to draw.

Rum is carried as it is in every naval ship but in submarines it is only issued at the commanding officer's discretion at selected times. One time which is avoided is just before surfacing, as the rum, coupled with fresh air, soon goes to men's heads.

13. What happens in a case of illness?

In a case of illness in peace time, the patient is landed or transferred to a surface ship at once. In war, if it is permissible to break wireless silence, then the commanding officer can call up his headquarters and suitable arrangements are made. If, however, the submarine is on an important patrol, which in no circumstances must be interrupted, and wireless silence cannot be broken, then the captain and the coxswain do their best with the aid of a medical chest and medical books. The principle should be, that as long as the submarine can be operated, which is practicable with even half of the crew, there must be no turning back, and if a man should happen to die it must unfortunately be accepted.

14. Why do people join submarines?

There are a variety of reasons. It is essentially a volunteer service and this tradition has been maintained almost entirely without break throughout the years. Officers join for the opportunities it offers to youth in adventure and early command coupled with the enjoyment of small ship life. There is a

slightly higher specialist pay than in other branches which has some attraction. Many of the same reasons apply to the ratings where instead of early command they have early responsibility and enjoy the comradeship shared by all.

The questions which may be asked about submarine escape and salvage it is hoped will be covered by the chapter devoted entirely to this subject.

Chapter eight
The building and support
of conventional submarines

THE BUILDING OF CONVENTIONAL SUBMARINES

Like all ships built for the Navy, submarines are designed on the basis of 'Staff Requirement'. That is to say, the Naval Staff work out what type of vessel they consider is required when opposed to another Power. Not only will the types of ships against which we might find ourselves at war come under careful study, but also the distance of their bases from ours, and many other important factors. For example, T Class submarines were designed primarily in case of war against Japan, when our bases at Hong Kong and Singapore were many thousands of miles away from the Japanese bases off which our submarines had to patrol. Thus the Ts had to have long endurance and good habitability, and had to be able to keep up a reasonable surface speed during a long ocean passage.

After the Staff Requirements have been approved in the Admiralty, it may be decided to build a few of the class in the Royal Dockyards of Portsmouth, Devonport and Chatham. The others will be put out to tender among the big shipbuilding firms. Only a few of these specialize in the building of submarines, in addition to their large surface ship construction, and naturally these few have the contracts. It is necessary for a shipbuilding firm which constructs submarines, to train some employees with special knowledge of that type of work, and therefore those who do this, hope to have a fairly constant flow of orders, so as to keep at least a nucleus of their skilled men on continuous engagement.

The firm which has built most submarines for the Royal Navy is Vickers Armstrongs which, when the first 'Holland' boat was built in their works at Barrow-in-Furness in 1901 was called Vickers Son and Maxim. This firm are world renowned experts in submarine construction with a long list of successful boats to their credit. Other notable firms which have played a great part are Cammell Laird of Birkenhead and Scotts of Greenock.

None of these firms make all the parts required and have to obtain a great deal of machinery from other engineering works. For example, periscopes are made by Barr and Stroud, compasses by the Sperry Gyroscope Company Limited, propellers by John Thornycroft and Company, batteries by The Chloride Electrical Storage Company, and many other such instances. Thus in the building of one submarine there may be a dozen or more firms employed in supplying machinery and parts.

In peace time a submarine takes at least two years to build, but in war, firms of the calibre of Vickers Armstrongs can cut down the time to about one year.

Great work has been done by British shipbuilding firms and the engineering works which provide machinery. It must always be borne in mind that their responsibility is to ensure that no material failures will overtake the boat, and in this they have gained the full confidence of all who sail in submarines.

Submarine naval officers and ratings do not normally see the laying down of the keel of a boat. The first person to see the submarine under construction is the engineer officer, and he will form part of the ship's company. According to whether it is peace time or in war, he will join a month or more before the vessel is launched, and at this ceremony he may still be the only person directly concerned with the future operation of the boat. The launching ceremony itself is similar to that of any surface ship. The lady launching the submarine stands on a raised and decorated platform; the ribbon releasing the customary bottle of champagne is cut, and the bottle breaks against the bow of the submarine. At this moment of christening the submarine is given a name or number, and with the words 'May God bless her and all who serve in her' the boat begins to slide down the stocks, gathering speed, until she takes to the water for the first time.

At the time of launching the vessel is little more than a shell, but construction has gone ahead to the extent that all compartments forward of the engine room have their bulkheads fitted, and no more machinery or furniture can go into these compartments except through the hatches and bulkhead doors. For example in some of the bigger submarines, in which a fairly large wardroom table may be required, if it is desired to have this table all in one piece, it is necessary to place it in the wardroom very early on, during the pre-launching period, otherwise later on it will not be possible to embark it.

After the launch a large part of the top of the engine room compartment called the coverplate, is removed and both the main engines and the main motors are installed. The main batteries follow, cells being hoisted on board through both the fore and engine room hatches. At this period large numbers of experts bring to the boat, for fitting into their places, a vast array of pipes and electrical gear and auxiliary machinery. To walk through the boat at such a time gives one the impression that it will be impossible to sort everything out into a compact and spotlessly clean unit of Her Majesty's Fleet. Indeed this condition prevails until quite near the completion date, when suddenly a transformation takes place.

Normally the captain (or commanding officer) of the submarine joins the engineer shortly after the launch. He is followed by a handful of key ratings, and this small party spend some months learning their submarine, as she is being completed, so that when about six weeks before the boat is ready for the first machinery trials and the whole ship's company arrive, they are in a position to teach the remaining officers and men their duties. As soon as the whole crew have joined, the boat is said to be in 'Commission', and the captain may fly his Commissioning Pennant from the top of the mast. The White Ensign is not flown because the submarine is still the property of the builders

who fly their own flag.

The first dive is carried out by the naval crew in one of the basins in the building yard. First of all the main ballast tanks are flooded, generally one pair of tanks at a time, but the submarine will not go underwater completely because at this time there is no water in the internal auxiliary tanks. Salt water is next flooded into these tanks, little by little, until the submarine slowly sinks under water when she is exactly 'trimmed' and made to balance perfectly. The amount of water in the auxiliary tanks is then carefully measured and entered in a book, called the 'trim book', together with other details of the amount of oil fuel, stores and torpedo gear then on board. From that time onward a trim can be put on the boat by use of the internal auxiliary ballast tanks, allowing for any change of weights which have taken place since the last trim. Thus when the main ballast tanks are flooded the submarine can be dived and will be very nearly truly balanced in water, the final adjustments being made after the boat has been levelled off at periscope depth. The first trimming which has just been described is called the 'statical trim'.

After all the machinery has been fully tested in position by the builders, the crew begins to take over under the supervision of the builders until everyone is satisfied. After this the boat proceeds to sea for running and diving trials. It is now that the builders' flag is flown actually at sea, but the naval officers navigate the boat for the company. Finally, when the boat has dived in the open sea and run at her full speed successfully over the measured mile she is brought back to the builders' yard. Here without ceremony the submarine captain signs for the ship on behalf of the Admiralty, after which the builders' flag is hauled down and the White Ensign hoisted. Almost at once the submarine sails for a quiet port, generally in Scotland, where for some weeks the boat can be worked up to an efficient fighting machine. Finally she sails for her operational base where there are always many pairs of interested eyes to observe the arrival of the new member of the flotilla.

SUBMARINE SHORE BASES AND DEPOT SHIPS

Of all men-of-war the submarine is the least self-supporting. Every aspect of life at sea in a submarine points to the necessity for a base for both the boat and the crew when they are not actively employed at sea. Submarines therefore have shore bases and depot ships. Both are necessary, but the depot ships are more important as they give mobility to the submarines all over the world. These depot ships only proceed to sea as the strategical situation demands and they are not only accommodation ships, but the modern ships are in the nature of a small dockyard for the maintenance of submarines.

The first depot ship for the British submarine fleet was HMS *Hazard*, a gunboat. This ship formed a depot for the original five submarines of the Navy which were built at Barrow-in-Furness, in late 1901. The *Hazard* was launched in 1894, was 250 feet long (about the length of a medium sized submarine of today), she had a complement of 120 officers and men, and was armed with

two 4.7 inch guns, four 3 pounder guns and five 18 inch above-water torpedo tubes. Her displacement was 1070 tons, again typical of a modern submarine.

This ship was the forerunner of many whose names are household words amongst submariners, but do not hold the same interest elsewhere and therefore are not described in detail. Some of these ships were old cruisers such as *Thames, Forth* and *Mercury,* all built in the late nineteenth century and which served as depot ships in ports around our coasts until the First World War. As the policy was then to employ submarines in the defence of several of our ports at the same time, in the place of mines, and also to prevent a ship standing off a port and bombarding it, the number of depot ships in the early days greatly exceeded those in service in later years.

By 1911 two ships, the *Adamant* and *Alecto* were laid down as actual submarine tenders or small depot ships. They were only 935 tons but were useful for accompanying submarines on cruises and exercises, also at the same time the first large depot ship to be built as such, was begun. This was the *Maidstone,* a ship of 3600 tons which was completed just before the First World War. Quite rightly the emphasis in the construction of this ship was on living accommodation for the submarine crews, and repair facilities, but it seems rather stretching a point today when it is realized that the ship was designed without any armament.

During the first war some improvization had to be resorted to, and at times merchant ships were taken over and converted. One of these was the *Titania* which was purchased from the Clyde Shipbuilding Company in 1915, and another the *Lucia,* an ex-German Hamburg-America liner of 5800 tons which had been captured in 1914.

The modern depot ships such as the *Forth* and *Maidstone* were completed just before the last war and are 9000 ton ships, nearly 500 feet long and carrying eight 4.5 inch guns, pompoms and many smaller arms. These ships are equipped with large heavy and light machine shops, a foundry, coppersmiths', plumbers' and carpenters' shops. There are large specially constructed torpedo rooms and workshops, electrical repair shops and plant for charging submarine batteries. They have a complement of 502 officers and men including 64 repair staff and 43 spare submarine crew. These ships can each house the crews of six *T* Class submarines and carry out almost every large repair required by a modern boat.

The *Adamant,* 12 500 tons, the largest of the depot ships built especially for that purpose was completed during the last war, when as well as the depot ships already serving, merchant ships had again to be adapted to meet the demand of the increased submarine flotillas. Very big liners of 20 000 tons were brought into service, and one of these, the *Montclare,* continued as a depot ship long after the war.

Each large flotilla of submarines, unless attached to a shore base, must have a depot ship in which each officer has his own cabin and the ratings have their own messes and accommodation, so that the submarine crews can make the

depot ship their home.

The shore bases may vary according to the strategical situation at the time, but the permanent submarine headquarters and school, HMS *Dolphin,* remains at Fort Blockhouse which lies at the western side of the entrance to Portsmouth harbour from Spithead. The selection of this fort as a submarine base appears to have been prompted from a conclusion reached in 1904 that submarines would supersede the mine in the defence of our ports. At that time it was decided to establish flotillas of submarine boats at Portsmouth, Sheerness, Plymouth, Queenstown and Milford Haven; the last two never achieved permanency and only Portsmouth has survived as the *real home* of submarines.

Every submarine officer and rating knows Fort Blockhouse intimately. Here the Flag Officer Submarines normally flies his flag and has his offices. All major decisions on submarine matters are made within its walls. Everyone who joins submarines reports to Fort Blockhouse and every officer and man has to qualify at the Instructional School here. Most of the big social events and official ceremonies connected with submarines take place in this home of the Submarine Service.

History relates that the defence of the entrance to Portsmouth harbour was first considered in Edward IV's reign when the erection of towers on the western side was begun. Henry VIII completed the towers, and later Queen Anne made further improvements. By 1714 the shape of the Fort was much as it is today except that from its eastern wall, projecting across the harbour mouth, was a heavy iron chain used in the defence of the port, and on the western side there was a drawbridge over the moat leading to a handsome gate, part of which can still be seen today.

Early in the seventeenth century the Fort was finally completed, the walls being raised to their present height. Much history is centred round the ancient bastion, covering the wide activities from the olden day refitting of ships in Haslar Creek, which runs along the northern boundary, to the gibbet, used for hanging-out criminals, and from the exploits of the press-gangs who swooped on neighbouring Gosport when the local taverns were full, to the never-to-be-forgotten sight of the *Victory,* tacking out of the harbour on the way to St Helens roads, where she waited for Admiral Lord Nelson to be his flagship at the Battle of Trafalgar.

During all the years which the Fort has been the home of the Submarine Branch of the Navy, many buildings have been erected and piers have been constructed and improved, so that in the post-war period there is hardly a space left inside the Fort which does not serve some integral purpose. Every building is called after a submarine depot ship or tender. Names familiar to sailors such as *Thames, Pandora, Bonaventure* and *Vulcan,* mark the various blocks which house the submarine crews of officers, coxswains, chief and petty officers and all ratings. There are extensive workshops, torpedo stores, battery sheds and a large power station. A second and new tower for

instruction in submarine escape, 100 feet high, has been erected and stands above all else, forming a new navigational mark for vessels approaching Spithead from the east.

There are two chapels in the Fort. One is very small and built on top of the eastern ramparts overlooking the harbour entrance, and the other is a large modern one near the old drawbridge tower. There is a Chaplain of the Fort and one in every depot ship. Both in peace and war these men have a special responsibility in serving a branch of the Navy where risks are taken above those normally met. All connected with submarines have a debt to pay the Chaplains whose influence in an establishment or ship can be very great.

The submarines attached to Fort Blockhouse berth in Haslar Creek alongside the pier running the length of the northern side of the Fort. Years ago, when submarines were not much over 150 feet in length, there was adequate space, but now, with submarines nearly twice this length, conditions are cramped and only half a dozen boats can lie alongside at any one time. There is another pier further up the creek to take the overflow in numbers but if peace time requirements grew, the congestion in the creek would be a problem. The turn into Haslar Creek from the main channel in the harbour is over 90 degrees if coming from seaward. This is a difficult manoeuvre at the best of times but with a large submarine turning across a strong tide, a high standard of seamanship is required. Little wonder that a spit of land stretching out from the north-east corner of the Fort is commonly called 'Promotion Point' on which some careers have been wrecked!

Besides Fort Blockhouse, Plymouth has always been a base for submarines, generally with a depot ship in support. Portland, where so much anti-submarine training takes place, has also been a home for submarines, again generally supported by a depot ship.

Abroad, the Mediterranean Fleet was never without one or two flotillas based on Malta, partly on shore and partly in depot ships. Also, in the days when the Navy was in strength in the China seas, there was always a large force of submarines in those waters with two depot ships primarily based on Hong Kong.

All shore bases and depot ships are commanded by a Captain who is himself a submarine specialist. He also commands the attached submarine flotilla and is assisted by a Commander (Submarines) and a team of other specialist officers covering all branches of the Navy. In addition there is always a non-specialist Commander for executive duties in the base or depot ship.

In a large submarine flotilla working with the fleet, the smooth running of the organization needs careful dove-tailing from the operations room, under the Commander (Submarines), through all the specialist departments. All must play their part to make a really efficient flotilla.

Plate 28

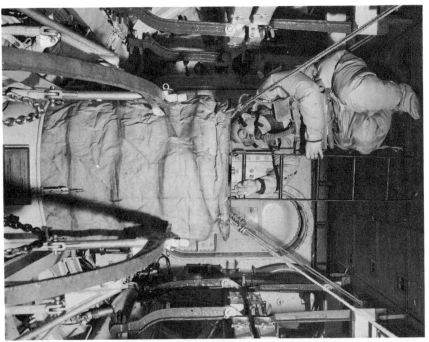

The Twill Trunk lowered from the fore escape hatch, showing a rating wearing an early type immersion suit and a DSEA

An instructor with pupil practicing in the use of DSEA

Plate 29

Raising a sunken submarine by mechanical lift

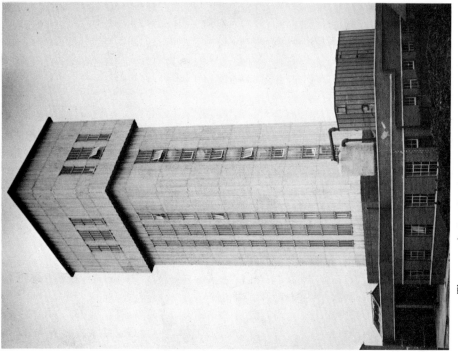

The escape instructional tower at Fort Blockhouse

Plate 30

A submarine of the A Class, HMS Andrew, of this class, made the first crossing of the Atlantic underwater, by use of the Snort, arriving at Portsmouth 16 June 1953, the day after HM the Queen reviewed the Fleet at Spithead

Plate 31

HM Submarine Thermopylae

Chapter nine
Accident, escape and salvage: the first fifty years

From the day when *A1* was lost in the approaches to Spithead nearly fifty years ago, controversy has arisen over the whole range of submarine work, and this has been stimulated whenever a disaster has occured in times of peace.

In submarine work, accidents have occurred from time to time, both by the very nature of the craft, and the fact that risks have to be taken when training with weapons of war.

It is reasonable that those who are not familiar with submarines should find it difficult to understand clearly what causes the accidents, why it is not always possible to save those trapped in the boat, and what can be done to raise the vessel. Naval officers and men who have not served in submarines are sometimes as mystified as many of the public, and there are occasions when experts in the Submarine Service themselves search for answers to the many questions which immediately arise on such occasions.

The object of this chapter is to give sufficient background to enable people to have a better understanding of these matters, and first of all it must be realized that very considerable thought has been given to all aspects of submarine disaster by some of the finest brains in the country, and that action has always been taken immediately, to save life whenever possible.

It was in 1851 that the first underwater disaster occurred from which lives were saved. As this event has a bearing on the whole problem, it is worthy of mention here.

The 1851 disaster concerned a submarine built by Wilhelm Bauer of Germany. It was of light metal construction and sank in comparatively shallow water in Kiel harbour. This boat was not a man-of-war but purely an experimental craft. The story goes that the vessel lost buoyancy through flooding, and rested on the bottom of the harbour, thereby trapping Bauer and his two companions who were inexperienced seamen. The disaster was known to others on the surface and it was not long before a ship fitted with metal grabs attempted to lift the boat bodily from the sea bed, this being deemed practicable owing to the small size of the submarine and her location.

On hearing the grappling irons touch the plating of the boat, Bauer realized that there was every possibility of the thin plating being torn apart when these irons got a hold and tried to take the weight, and then he and his two companions would be drowned. Accordingly, he opened two flood valves in the bottom of the boat with the object of flooding up the compartment until the pressure inside equalled the pressure outside. He reasoned that the hatch could then be opened and the three men would be carried to the surface.

On seeing the water coming into the boat the two seamen immediately shut off the valves and held down Bauer by force to prevent him continuing with the operation. Realizing that his only chance of survival was to flood the compartment, Bauer argued with his companions and eventually managed to convince them that what he intended to do was their only hope.

Once more the valves were opened and the water flooded in. The space being small, the water soon rose and Bauer knew that shortly the pressure inside the boat would equal that of the water outside, and then the hatch could be opened. By now the three men were standing up to their necks in water, but their heads were in the air which was being compressed into a small volume at the top of the compartment. Also by now, Bauer's two companions realized that this space would never fully flood with water unless the compressed air was allowed to vent out of the boat. Confidence had been restored.

At this moment, however, the light construction of the boat came into play. The hatch above them, without any action on their part, flew open and the bubble of compressed air rushed out of the opening, taking the three men with it. In the space of a few seconds they found themselves on the surface where all three were picked up by surface craft, and survived their ordeal.

This little story is loaded with important information and it will be seen, as the reader progresses through this chapter, that Bauer's escape followed nearly all the principles on which our present ideas are based.

ACCIDENT

Looking back on past accidents, the reasons sort themselves out fairly clearly. The submarine is an easily vulnerable vessel and operates in peace time under conditions approximating to war. The boat must be exercised in attacking screened targets and be exposed to the risk of a sudden change of course by the surface ships, and if the judgment of the commanding officer is faulty, the submarine may be rammed while submerged. Such a risk, however, is remote because the commanding officer is experienced and has made his way to his responsible position through a very testing number of years. For greater safety, though, conventional submarines now have a diving depth due to long periscopes, which will allow all except the deepest draft vessels to pass over the boat without danger to the pressure hull. Again when operating a submarine under attacking conditions, some failure in drill may bring the boat to a dangerous position. Failure to keep the depth ordered, through a sudden change in trim, is a situation which must be dealt with very promptly and this difficulty may be created by very rough seas, or by a sudden and unexpected angle taken on by the boat. These are factors which have a potential danger but do not trouble an experienced and well trained crew who are kept to a pitch of efficiency equal to such circumstances. In fact, in a first-class boat, unexpected happenings are corrected instantly and treated in the course of every day routine without any bother. Nevertheless a few such accidents have occurred during exercises, when for example L 24, while submerged, was lost

in collision with HMS *Resolution* in 1922. Bearing in mind, however, that British submarines are at sea day after day, training and exercising, both at home and abroad, the incidence is remarkably small.

There have also been accidents during trials periods. This is always a testing time, but if every possible step is taken to double check that orders are carried out, and also that no mistakes have been made in the detailed assembly of the more important machinery, there would be no risk at all. Refitting is also a time when special care has to be taken as sometimes only a skeleton crew are present, and for example, if ballast water has to be moved, the same precautionary drill must be observed as if the boat was in full commission. Water is a relentless enemy, and at no time can a crew take liberties with it. *H 29* was sunk in Chatham dockyard when moving main ballast water without first shutting the engine room hatch.

Almost every day somewhere in the world a *surface ship* collides with another. These ships have many hundreds of tons buoyancy, some have thousands of tons. Thus, when the water pours into the hole made by the collision, it is by no means a probability that the vessel will sink. This is not the case with the *submarine,* as it is a low buoyancy ship and has no more than 250 tons in hand. Even a small hole very soon admits 250 tons of water and once this has taken place the boat will sink. It follows then that if a submarine meets with a collision when steaming on the surface, it is quite likely that she will sink. Here again, drill may save the boat, but much depends on the position of key ratings at the moment of impact, and this again is dependent on the time of day or night and similar factors. The shutting of the water-tight compartment doors is all-important, but so often this cannot be done in time, or two compartments are holed so that the submarine's buoyancy is bound to be destroyed. Immense thought has been given to this problem of surface collision when navigating such a low buoyancy ship, and particularly to the importance of the operation of water-tight doors. The problem in a surface ship proper, is fairly simple, because it does not tax the fighting efficiency of that ship to install power-operated doors. Indeed, this may be desirable from the fighting efficiency point of view, but in a submarine, where space is at a premium, such considerations have to be ruled out. Moreover, the more times a bulkhead is pierced by pipes and machinery rods passing through it, the weaker it becomes, and the strengthening of bulkheads to withstand high pressure is already a difficult problem.

From the point of view of the surface ship, it must be emphasized that if a submarine is encountered in times of low visibility, many quite experienced seamen simply do not understand what they are seeing, or even in which direction the object is moving, until disaster is upon them. This may be due to such a little of the submarine being visible above the waves, and the unfamiliar shape of her bridge. When one reflects that surface ships are navigated by all manner of people, including small Chinese coasting firms, Arabs in dhows, and ships in which the helmsman is sometimes left to fend for himself, it is not

surprising that situations arise where danger from collision may be present.
Generally speaking early and prompt action by the commanding officer of
the submarine should avert all possible chance of a collision.

Examples here are *Poseidon* which collided with a small Japanese steamer off
north China, and more recently, *Truculent* which collided with a small Swedish steamer in the Thames estuary at night.

It is difficult to say whether a submarine disaster has ever been directly caused
by failure of material. Sometimes the material may have been asked to do too
much, but this is unlikely except in war.

Gases in submarines have caused accidents, and a severe hydrogen explosion
could bring immediate and fatal disaster, but such a possibility should be
eliminated, at least in peace time, by correct drill and constant checking of
the battery ventilating system.

To sum up, it can be said that there is no greater risk in submarine life than
in many other walks outside the office chair, provided at no time is there ever
any relaxation of drill and care.

ESCAPE

Training. The first sight which greets anyone approaching the submarine base
at Fort Blockhouse is a huge new tower which is 100 feet high, and has been
built so that realistic training in escaping from sunken submarines can be
given. Let it be understood that the chances of a submarine accident are slight,
but if a submarine is sunk in the open sea, the chances of survival are small,
although much time, thought and money is, and has been, expended in reducing the hazard. The tower is at the same time a very good navigational mark
for ships manoeuvring in the Spithead area and, so far as all true submarine
men are concerned, that is the place it takes in their minds and daily life. No
more erroneous impression could be given, than that the main thoughts of
submariners are on how to get out of a boat from the bottom of the sea.
Indeed one can say that if anyone serving in submarines experiences relief
when the boat surfaces, then he is not a good submarine man. The true submariner is only really happy when the boat has dived, when all is peace and
quiet, far away from the troubles and bustle of modern life ashore. With the
advent of 'snorting' the quiet may not be achieved in the same measure as in
days gone by, but the reaction must be the same in the minds of all true
submarine men. No matter how interested the public may become in the subject of escapes from submarines, it must be placed in its proper perspective.
Learning about escaping from submarines in the course of training is treated
in the same way as learning about the engines and the electric batteries. At
no time does this section of training gain greater importance than the other
subjects. Sensational headlines in the newspapers are bound to impinge their
words on people's minds, and the enormous new tower at Blockhouse does not
help to place this subject in its true perspective, but let it be remembered,
those who live this life are the least concerned in their minds with the subject,

and are the first to wish for their attitude to be adopted throughout the country.

Investigation by Committees. At times special Committees have been formed to consider the question of escape from a sunken submarine. There have been two of particular note. The first was the Nasmith Committee formed in 1939 under the Chairmanship of Admiral Sir Martin E Dunbar-Nasmith, VC, KCB. Among those called to give advice were Messrs Siebe Gorman and Company Limited, experts in deep diving, whose staff from the works at Tolworth, Surrey, under the management of Sir Robert Davis, have always done so much in this field for the Submarine Service. Subsequently, during the Second World War, the Admiralty formed the Experimental Diving Unit at the Tolworth works under Lieutenant-Commander W O Shelford. This unit worked with Messrs Siebe Gorman and Company Limited, for over three years.

The second Committee was formed in 1946, this time under the chairmanship of Rear-Admiral P Ruck-Keene, CBE, DSO. He was assisted by a very large team of experts. Shelford was co-opted to the Committee, together with two very experienced submarine commanding officers, namely Bennington of *Tally Ho* fame, and   Rimington, who did such outstanding work in *Parthian*

The work of the 1946 Committee was particularly valuable because its members were able to make a full study of escape based on the evidence from submarine survivors from the Second World War, of various nationalities. They interviewed the survivors of 32 submarines: 12 British, 15 German, 3 United States, 1 Danish and 1 Norwegian. Their deliberations have resulted in the 100 foot tower at Fort Blockhouse.

Past Methods of Escape. At the time when the 1946 Committee sat, there were in the British Navy two recognized methods of escape. Both these methods were assisted by the use of the Davis Submerged Escape Apparatus, commonly called DSEA and it must be emphasized that this apparatus was not a method of escape in itself, but an adjunct to it. The apparatus consists of a mouthpiece connected by a flexible tube to a rubber bag, and attached to this rubber bag is a metal container charged with oxygen under pressure. By this means, the wearer is able to breathe under water during ascent. The bag has to be charged with oxygen at a pressure equal to that of the water at whatever depth from which the escape is to be made. On the way up, the apparatus automatically releases some air from the breathing bag as the pressure of the water decreases. Splinterless goggles are worn to protect the eyes, and the nose is shut by a clip, so that breathing is only done through the mouthpiece. The apparatus acts as a lifebelt once the man has arrived at the surface. To use the gear successfully it is necessary to operate one or two valves, and finally to remove the mouthpiece when on the surface after escape. In the difficult circumstances generally obtaining at the time of an accident, the necessary actions have proved a disadvantage though many successful escapes have been made by using the DSEA.

One method of escape was by the *Twill Trunk*. Submarines so fitted, had two

hatches in their pressure hulls, one at each end of the boat specially designed for escape purposes. With the submarine on the bottom, the survivors in the forepart of the boat collected by the fore escape hatch, and similar action took place aft. These two separate sections of the boat were then sealed off by water-tight doors and valves. In each section the Twill Trunk was lowered from the hatch, making a complete funnel about two feet in diameter stretching from the hatch to within a few feet of the deck. This having been done DSEA sets were put on to prevent breathing CO_2 and Nitrogen under pressure while flooding up. The flooding was done as quickly as possible. It took about ten minutes at 100 feet and longer at shallower depths. The amount that the water rose in the compartment varied with the pressure to which the air had to be compressed. This action naturally equalized the pressure inside and outside the boat. When this was done, an officer or senior rating dipped under the bottom lip of the trunk which by now was full of water, as the air inside it had been allowed to escape to the surface through a special vent. Having taken off the hatch clips it was a comparatively easy job to open the hatch, and the man could then make his ascent to the surface, or else he could return to the other men by the same way as he had come, giving those waiting in the compartment the assurance that the hatch was open, and making his own escape later. Each man could then take his own time to escape through the trunk, one at a time.

The second method was by the *Escape Chamber*. This involved incorporating escape locks in the design at either end of the submarine. By this method the lengthy flooding of the whole compartment could be avoided. Not more than *two* men could enter the small chamber at once and having done so they closed the door behind them and put on their DSEA sets. All their subsequent movements could be observed through a glass inspection port. Their companions outside then flooded up the chamber. As soon as the pressure inside the chamber equalled that of the outside water, the pocket of air at the top of the chamber was vented and the two men opened the escape hatch and proceeded to the surface. Having observed them leave the chamber, those remaining in the boat then shut the escape hatch by hand mechanism, and drained the water out of the small chamber, after which the door could be opened and the process repeated till all had escaped. The last two men could operate the flooding mechanism inside the lock before making their escape.

Evidence of Survivors. The evidence of the survivors from the submarines, who were interviewed by the Ruck-Keene Committee, was illuminating. For one thing, as far as the survivors could recall, it appeared that only about 16 per cent of all those who were alive immediately after the accident occurring to their particular submarine, made escapes. In most of these cases survivors told tales of great heroism and endurance displayed during efforts to bring the submarine itself to the surface.

Another very important point which the evidence brought out, was that of the 16 per cent, as many men survived the actual ascent without using Davis

apparatus, as with it.

Reasons for Failures: 1. Efforts to save the ship. There is little doubt now that the 84 per cent of men believed to be alive at the time of the disaster, and who never made their escape, gave their lives in attempting to save the whole ship. Analysis of this evidence showed that this is where the time factor counts. In making attempts to bring the ship to the surface the crew would have to give the vessel positive buoyancy. Unless the boat had been holed very low down, so that the application of air pressure could immediately empty the compartment of water, efforts to gain buoyancy would take too long and this is undoubtedly what had happened in the past. A large number of men remaining in a confined space for some hours increases the carbon dioxide in the air so much, that after a dozen hours or so the men become considerably affected by the poison. Some may be incapable of further effort, others can only continue under the greatest strain. The air we breathe in, contains approximately 79 per cent nitrogen, 21 per cent oxygen and only 0.03 per cent carbon dioxide. The air we breathe out, contains approximately 80 per cent nitrogen, only 16 per cent oxygen and an increase up to 4 per cent carbon dioxide. It is this increase of carbon dioxide which troubles men confined in a small space with no means of replenishing with fresh air. Given the number of men and the area in which they are confined, scientists can tell in what state those men are likely to be after a certain number of hours in those conditions. It is most important to remember that the concentration of CO_2 in the compartment increases when pressure is admitted during flooding. In fact, for every additional atmosphere of pressure, the CO_2 concentration is doubled. It is therefore reasonable to say that there may well have been many cases where men delayed so long in their gallant endeavours to surface the submarine that, when at last they abandoned the effort and decided to make their escape, they were too far poisoned by carbon dioxide at atmospheric pressure to do so, or else they became unconscious when flooding up took place. The *Thetis* disaster was an example of CO_2 poisoning and again during the War when Lonsdale in *Seal* called his men to the control room for prayers nineteen hours after being on the bottom, only six could respond; this was primarily due to the presence of carbon dioxide in considerable quantity. This points to the fact that unless it is obvious that early efforts to give the boat buoyancy will be successful, no attempt should be made to do so, and the attention of everyone should be directed to making an early escape before the carbon dioxide is present in dangerous quantities.

2. Effect of breathing CO_2, Nitrogen or Oxygen under pressure. It will be remembered there were two standard methods of escaping. In the first method with the Twill Trunk, it is necessary to flood up the whole compartment. In doing this, the air is compressed and two factors come into play. Firstly the carbon dioxide concentration increases rapidly under pressure and immediately becomes more lethal. Secondly, when the pressure of the air is increased by the flooding, the blood absorbs more nitrogen from the air than normal.

The amount absorbed is directly proportional to the increase in pressure. For example, at 250 feet depth there is seven times as much nitrogen in the blood of a diver than there normally should be. This excess of nitrogen must be released slowly and that is why a diver comes to the surface in stages, the length of time he takes being conditioned by the time he has been breathing nitrogen under pressure, and the depth from which he is ascending. A large compartment in a submarine being flooded up under the Twill Trunk method will subject men to breathing nitrogen under pressure for a long time as the compartment cannot be flooded quickly enough. Those men who have DSEA can use them to overcome the above two troubles because the set has an air-purifying arrangement in it to help remove excess CO_2 which would otherwise accumulate in the bag when breathing out, and by wearing the set they can also eliminate the possibility of breathing nitrogen under pressure. However, it has since been established that there is also danger from breathing the pure oxygen under pressure, from the DSEA, and in fact over a depth of 60 feet men may get convulsions or full blackouts from this effect. The interval of time before these reactions take place, differs in each man, but generally an increase in depth lessens the time factor. There have been successful escapes in isolated cases by using the Twill Trunk method combined with wearing the DSEA, but they have been in comparatively shallow depths where the dangers described above are greatly reduced. Although under certain circumstances this method might still have to be resorted to, it is definitely not advisable over a depth of 150 feet.

Admiral Ruck-Keene's analysis certainly confirmed that some of the disadvantages of the Twill Trunk method were overcome by the second escape method, namely the fitting of the small Escape Chamber. The two men using this chamber could flood it up quickly, thereby greatly reducing the possibility of oxygen poisoning from the DSEA. Nevertheless if the submarine was deep the time allowance when they could breathe pure oxygen under pressure without getting into trouble remained very small. There was also some reason to believe that potential danger existed by having two men in the chamber at once. Not only did this entail the chamber being larger than was ideally suitable, but sometimes a fit man had been prevented from making his escape by his anxiety to stand by his mate who was not in such good condition either mentally or physically.

In both methods, the Twill Trunk and the Escape Chamber, it appeared there was possible danger from using the DSEA for the actual *ascent*. Evidence showed that a man reaching the surface with his DSEA on might not be in a state to remember the final stage of his drill, namely to remove his mouthpiece, with the result that when the oxygen ran out, he suffocated.

Conclusions. From the conditions and circumstances described above, three clear conclusions emerged:

1. Before escape, which should be early, men should be kept at atmospheric pressure and the excess of carbon dioxide removed by purifying the air.

2. An escape chamber must be used, but this should be as small as possible to reduce the time needed to flood up, and thereby minimizing the length of time under pressure. As only *one* man should escape at a time, this small chamber is suitable.

3. The DSEA set should not be used.

To put the first conclusion into practice, work was done on improving the air-purifying arrangements. Machines for this purpose already fitted in all submarines, were now to be run by electricity. In a sunken submarine it was also thought necessary to have alternative driving power such as compressed air, or better still to have some method of purifying by chemical means without using any mechanical contrivance requiring power.

The second conclusion required no special research. The chamber was to be very small, capable of holding one man only, and fitted with an ejector ram to push the man out if he failed to take this action himself.

With regard to the third conclusion, men were to be taught to make a 'Free Escape' without using an apparatus (except a ring or life-jacket to give them buoyancy) and it is to teach this technique that the large tower at the Submarine School has been built. It consists simply of a steel tower 100 feet high and 18 feet in diameter, strengthened to hold 100 feet of water. At the bottom there are chambers to simulate the action of flooding up in a sunken submarine, one being exactly the same design as the future fitting in all boats. At intervals up the side of the tower are air locks to enable instructors to observe men making their ascent and if necessary pull a trainee into a lock if he is in difficulty. Free escapes can be practised at all depths before a man makes a full scale escape from the chamber at 100 feet. This is done by means of a small diving bell in which a man can be lowered to any depth, increasing the depth as his training progresses.

To make a 'free escape', a man begins his ascent with compressed air in his lungs and he need never worry about inhaling because he has more air in his lungs than normal. He keeps his mouth open during the ascent and allows the compressed air in his lungs to escape out of his mouth as the air expands due to the lessening pressure which he experiences on his way to the surface. If a man making a free escape holds his breath he will burst his lungs due to the air in them expanding and having no exit. This might appear to make the method a dangerous business, but it will be remembered he has first been well drilled in this method at the Submarine School. The tower at Fort Blockhouse completed in 1952, was not the first of its kind. One had been used in the United States where very large numbers of whole submarine crews have made escapes from 100 feet.

The particular advantage of the 'free escape' apart from it being the surest method, is that there is as far as possible an equal chance for all, a vitally important factor. Whenever escape is dependent to a certain extent on a particular type of gear being available to every man, there is always the danger that there will not be enough 'sets' to go round. Circumstances are such that

it is almost impossible to ensure enough 'sets' of special gear in every corner of the boat to be sure that each man is provided with one. With the 'free escape' no gear is required and every man, provided he can get near one of the two escape chambers, and it is reasonable to expect that those alive should be able to do this, knows that he has an equal chance with all the others, of escaping.

These arrangements have not been arrived at without considerable risk to some of those connected with the work. At Messrs Siebe Gormans during the war, the three naval officers, Rainsford, Donald and Davidson, together with Professor Haldane, all subjected themselves to tests in order to gain first-hand experience. Since the war, Dr Wright of the Naval Physiological Department has been decorated for making simulated ascents by the 'free' method from depths up to 300 feet which demanded considerable courage and devotion to duty. Davidson also received an award for his work generally in connection, with physiological effects in submarine work.

Operation Subsmash. As soon as a submarine fails to make its appointed signal announcing that it has surfaced and also fails to answer any signals made to it a very special organization comes into force. It is obviously unnecessary to go into details of this organization and all that need be said is that every possible step is taken immediately to find the submarine and bring the rescue ships to the position. The name of the operation is 'Subsmash'. Obviously what is needed is a means of finding the submarine as quickly as possible and to this end a special type of marker buoy has been made.

Two buoys are provided for release by a submarine if, for any reason, it is unable to come to the surface after diving. Their purpose is to mark the position in such a manner that aircraft and searching vessels can easily locate it, and thus be on hand to rescue survivors. Each buoy is kept in its stowage, in the casing of the submarine outside the pressure hull, by two wooden doors. These doors are kept shut by a metal toe. The toe can be moved by rod mechanism to release the doors which can be operated from any main compartment in the submarine. As soon as the doors are free the buoy rises, due to its buoyancy, pushing the doors wide open as it ascends.

The buoy is constructed of light metal alloy and composed of a series of capsules enclosed in an annular structure and it has been ingeniously designed to combine strength, compactness and buoyancy adequate to support warning devices. A flashing light unit is installed, and the buoy is equipped with a radio transmitter.

The requirements for the submarine marker buoys are as follows:

1. To be strong enough to withstand the rigours of submarine conditions, yet at the same time be light and small enough to be carried in the superstructure.

2. To be visible at a reasonable range to aircraft and searching vessels, both by day and by night.

3. To remain afloat and anchored to the distressed submarine in all weather conditions and,

4. To transmit some form of distress signal.

The annular structure of the buoy can be likened to a drum within a drum. The buoyancy is given to it by packing with water-tight pressure-resistant metal capsules the space between the outside of the inner drum and the inside of the outer drum. There are 216 of these capsules, which are of a light alloy and are about six inches long and of about two and a half inches diameter.

Good riding qualities are given to the buoy by attaching the mooring line to a mild steel stirrup, which is pivoted on the sides of the buoy and hangs downwards like an inverted bucket handle. The upper surfaces of the buoy are painted with Day-glow special composition which has a high daylight visibility range, and around the top is a crown containing twenty-four reflecting road studs. A flag-mast with a red nylon flag is carried on the top.

The interior of the inner drum is reserved for the light and warning apparatus. The flashing unit is housed in a pressure-tight container of cast light alloy. The light, which automatically switches itself on and off when the buoy is released, is powered by two 21 amp/hour batteries in parallel, which gives a minimum life of 42 hours, and during test had an actual effective life of 52 hours. A 2.5 watt light gives a range of 3500 yards in good visibility conditions.

As regards the transmission of a distress signal this is a complex problem, for it necessitates striking the balance between a number of desirables, including lightness, homing qualities, and the ability to transmit signals which can be picked up by receiving apparatus operating in widely different frequencies, such as are standard in ships of different types.

As soon as the signal 'Subsmash' is made, a large number of ships and aircraft proceed to the probable scene of the accident. One of the most important vessels is HMS *Reclaim,* the Navy's special diving vessel. Unfortunately, there is only one of this type of vessel and she cannot be everywhere in the world at once, and even in home waters she may be a great distance away from the position of the submarine. It is ideal to have this ship on the spot if possible, because besides special medical arrangements she carries the finest divers in the world and has amenities such as decompression chambers. In this connection the provision of air hoses to supply fresh air to, and equally important to exhaust foul air from, sunken submarines is dependent on divers being available, and conditions of depth, state of sea, strength of tide and clarity of water all being favourable.

Inside the submarine, although the escape must be made as soon as possible for the reasons already described, judgment must be used to determine the most favourable moment from all points of view. Considerations such as the tides, whether it is day or night, and the proximity of rescue craft must all be weighed carefully; the bias, however, must always be on early escape.

Note. An additional aid to men who have escaped is provided by immersion suits. These are watertight suits covering the whole body including the head. They are stowed through the boat in sufficient numbers to give each man a

reasonable chance of having the advantage of one. The suit is put on just before the escape is made, and as soon as the man reaches the surface he blows it up. It not only gives him plenty of buoyancy but protects him from cold and it is fitted with a light to indicate his position at night. Improvements are constantly being made, and while a man will also wear a life-jacket or ring of which large numbers are provided, in time it may be possible to incorporate this in the suit itself. A man can be assured of a life-jacket or ring, and can be fairly certain of having an immersion suit as well. Whatever happens his chances of a successful escape in no way depend on whether he has a suit: it is entirely an aid to survival once he is on the surface.

Escape by Mechanical means. A method of escape used by the Americans is a Rescue Bell which was operated with success in the case of their submarine *Squalus*. The bell itself is a large structure capable of holding ten men; the crew consists of two divers. It is used with a specially fitted hatch in the hull of the submarine with a large flat seating on which the bell rests, and it will stand pressure up to that which any modern submarine will stand. The bell hauls itself down to the submarine, from a special diving ship, by a 'down haul' wire, which a diver has previously attached to the submarine's hatch, and is clamped down by holding-down bolts which ensure a watertight joint. The escape hatch in the submarine can then be opened and eight men can enter the bell. The cycle is then reversed and the bell comes to the surface under its own buoyancy. No man at any time has been under pressure above atmosphere nor has anyone got wet.

The matter of having such a diving bell in the British Navy was considered but it must be remembered that the weather conditions around our coasts are very different from those on the other side of the Atlantic, and might prevent the operation of the bell. Also, knowledge that a Rescue Bell is available could make men delay making an early escape and this might well be to their disadvantage.

In 1952 a film was shown in this country in which an Italian submarine was sunk and the crew escaped by means of a one man buoy, released from the submarine rather like the releasing of a marker buoy. This buoy could be hauled down to the submarine by those inside after each man had made his escape. This captured the imagination of film goers, but the amount of space the buoy and its mechanism took up in the boat, bearing in mind there was one at each end of the vessel, would be unacceptable in the British Navy as it would seriously affect the fighting efficiency of the submarine, and after all the submarine is first and foremost a warship.

SALVAGE

Among the most interesting and intricate subjects which confront men who have to do with ships, is the salvage of sunken vessels. Ships sunk in land-locked harbours, in shallow water or where there are no strong tidal streams normally do not present any great problem to the salvage expert. Those in

great depths in open waters, and where currents run strongly, present immense difficulties requiring great skill to overcome them, and often calling on those taking part in the operation to face considerable hazards. Of all ships which may fall to the Admiralty Salvage Department to raise, the submarine is considered by many to be the most difficult.

Whatever method is adopted in raising a sunken submarine, the fundamental principle is the same. The lifting force applied must exceed the total underwater weight of the structure. This lifting force may be in the form of *buoyancy* or *mechanical effort*.

A *buoyant lift* may be obtained by removing water from a sufficient number of compartments by pumps or blowing it out by compressed air. An alternative method is to attach buoyant vessels externally to the sunken vessel by means of chains or wires. One such appliance is the salvage pontoon or 'camel'. This is a cylindrical drum which can be sunk to the depth of the vessel on the bottom of the sea and subsequently given buoyancy by injecting compressed air. If sufficient of these are attached to the ship which is to be raised, when they are given buoyancy and rise to the surface, they bring the vessel with them. As all surface ships are buoyant vessels they too can be used, but in a different way, provided they are in tidal waters, as will be explained later.

Mechanical effort involves the use of heavy cranes or special lifting vessels fitted with heavy tackles. To lift the sunken vessel, wire slings must be passed under the ship at least at both ends if not in the middle as well. Some of these slings may have to be passed under the ship by divers, according to how the vessel is lying.

When news is received that a submarine is sunk, the possibilities of salvage are widely discussed. No guiding rule can be given, as the circumstances are invariably different in every case, but the main considerations are the weather, the water, including the depth, tidal effect and visibility. The weight of the structure to be lifted also has to be considered, and the power available, including the capacity of pumps and air compressors, the strength of cranes and wires, and the personnel, including the experience of the divers and the number available. Only experts can sum up these factors, and as the weather is often unpredictable their summary can seldom be other than conditional. Added to these points is the fact that a modern large submarine fully flooded weighs over 900 tons.

It is not the purpose of this book to give a detailed account of the various methods of raising a submarine outlined above; however, a brief idea of the actual work to be done will give the reader a better chance to follow these matters when they arise.

There are three forms of normal *buoyant lift.*

1. Raising on Compressed Air. By this method water is removed from the wreck in sufficient quantity to give it positive buoyancy by injecting compressed air. First of all an endeavour is made to expel the water from the main ballast tanks, which it will be remembered are external to the pressure hull.

Normally, with the exception of one tank on either side, all these tanks have holes in the underside permanently open to the sea. An air hose pushed into these holes in turn will soon drive the water out provided the vent valves at the top of the tanks were shut, which they should be. For the remaining two tanks which have valves in the underside and which might be shut, divers must make the necessary holes in the tanks for the application of air and to allow the water to escape. This would also have to be done if the submarine was lying on its side and therefore masking the holes in all the tanks on one side of the vessel. Getting rid of this ballast water gives about 120 tons buoyancy, so that it is still necessary to gain a further 780 tons. This is done by applying the compressed air to the inside of the submarine itself. Here all manner of unknown factors come into play. For example, if the submarine is tilted in any way particularly longitudinally, the air will collect at the upper end, this may slightly raise one end and the effect of that will be an air pressure inside the boat in excess of the water pressure outside. If this excess becomes too great it may lift hatches, vent the air and the vessel will then return to the sea bed along its whole length once again, possibly capsizing in the process. Often it is not known which bulkhead doors are open and which are shut. That further complicates the problem as it may not be known to what extent water is being driven out of the boat if an air hose is applied at one end only. In fact, before such an operation is attempted it may be necessary for a diver to enter the wreck and ascertain the full facts. This is in itself a hazardous business. Experienced salvage officers are not encouraging when this method is discussed.

2. Raising by means of Camels. Camels are cylindrical in shape and built of steel. Admiralty camels have an outside diameter of 13 feet 6 inches and an overall length of 32 feet. Each has a lifting capacity of 80 tons. At approximately 8 feet in-board from each end is a hawse pipe through which can be passed chain or wire slings for making the connections to the wreck. In the case of a submarine with a weight of 900 tons at least twelve camels would be required, unless it was possible to expel the main ballast water by compressed air, as explained above, thereby gaining some 120 tons of buoyancy, in which case only ten camels might be sufficient. Whenever possible it is best to pass slings right under the submarine and attach them to the camels. If the submarine is undamaged structurally and it is lying so that the bow and stern sections are clear of the sea bed, the slings may be slipped over each end and worked into appropriate positions in relation to the centre of gravity. Either seven or nine inch circumference flexible steel wire can be used or 2½ inch studded link chain cable.

The Admiralty camels can be operated to a depth of thirty-five fathoms or 210 feet. If the wreck is deeper than this, an alternative to securing the camels actually alongside the wreck, is to set them in tiers above it. When given buoyancy, the camels will lift the submarine off the sea bed. After this both the camels and submarine can be moved progressively to shallower water where

the depth will allow the camels to be secured eventually alongside the wreck for the final lift to the surface.

3. Raising by Tidal Lift. A sunken submarine can be slung under one or more specially strengthened surface craft and raised by an amount depending on the range of the tide. The largest Admiralty vessels suitable for this operation are 180 feet long with a beam of 39 feet and 17 feet depth. Using this method a number of wire hawsers are drawn under the submarine and secured to bollards or clamped across the decks of these craft at low water. The 1200 tons of ballast, is then pumped out, drawing the wires taut and slightly lifting the wreck. As the tide rises, the surface craft lifts the submarine from the bottom and both are towed to shallower water. At the next low water the process is repeated until the wreck dries completely as the tide recedes. This method is very slow unless there is a good rise and fall of tide.

There is only one form of raising by *Mechanical Effort.*

This can only be attempted in relatively sheltered waters. Floating cranes or other surface vessels fitted with special hauling machinery and tackles are necessary. Cranes can only be used when absolute tranquillity is assured because on an exposed site, by reason of their high superstructure and the high lifting gantries, if there was any swell they might easily capsize.

The Admiralty Salvage Department during part of the post-war period had the use of two German lifting vessels. These vessels, the *Energie* and *Ausdauer,* are constructed with ballast tanks to enable them to be trimmed and they have double but independent stern gantries from which lifting tackles can be suspended. Each vessel can take a stern load of about 600 tons but the depth at which they can be operated is limited to thirty fathoms or 180 feet.

In dealing with a submarine on the bottom, the bights of four nine inch wires must be drawn under the bow and stern, two at each end. The lifting vessels have to be moored so that their gantries can take the wires which have to be so spaced at either end of the wreck to conform to the width between the gantries.

To raise the submarine, eight winches in the two lifting vessels are used, four for hauling the wires which have been passed over the gantry heads, and four for pulling the other ends of the wires along the upper decks of the two lifting vessels. To reeve these wires and keep the various vessels employed in position through all states of tide and weather conditions, requires extremely expert handling. It is easy to say how the operation should be done but quite another thing to carry it out. For example, in the case of *Truculent* sunk in the Thames estuary in 1951 the operation using *Energie* and *Ausdauer* took three months. This was a very fine feat and could hardly be bettered.

The above brief survey of the more usual methods of salvage can only give an idea of what is needed to salve a submarine. The subject could easily fill a book in itself. It is hoped, however, that the foregoing paragraphs will have convinced the reader of the intricate problems and great difficulties involved, if a submarine is to be raised from the sea bed in open water.

Chapter ten
The post war period, 1945-1958

The end of hostilities brought a situation similar to that of 1918, and it was necessary to scrap the majority of the current submarine building programme. Further, a large number of orders for boats had already been placed with firms and most of these had to be cancelled. Besides this, many submarines then in commission were well past their age of normal service and others were worn out with hard running. In 1945 therefore some forty-five boats were scrapped and over fifty orders to building firms were cancelled. Among the boats which were scrapped were two *L* Class and some *H* Class, these veterans having ended their days giving anti-submarine training to Atlantic convoy escort groups. Of the boats which were cancelled the majority were *A* Class, but the few which had been completed were retained and rebuilt with streamlined upper decks including enclosed fin conning towers 26½ feet high. It was appreciated that these boats would only be a stop-gap until the submarine of the future came into being. Also a few *T* Class were kept, some for operational duties and others for training.

While these reductions would have taken place in any event at the conclusion of a major war, it was obvious that the last year of the war had brought to light new developments. These would so affect the pattern of things to come that a pause would be necessary to study them before a new and sound programme of peace time construction could be decided upon.

When our armies were advancing across Germany in 1945, much information fell into our hands and later on, unconditional surrender having been extracted from the enemy, all types of their naval ships were available for scrutiny. In the submarine sphere it was found that the Germans had concentrated on underwater speed. This was a natural development, as every knot faster means a great deal to a submarine which is being hunted. At the beginning of the war depth charges were always dropped over the stern of the anti-submarine vessel when the ship had gained position almost on top of the target. Towards the end of the war, due to the increase in underwater speed of the submarine, the anti-submarine vessel could not afford to wait until she was over her quarry, so throwers were designed to hurl charges from the stern of ships right over the tops of their bridges, so that these missiles struck the water ahead of the attacking anti-submarine vessel. Every submarine captain knows that precious knots and seconds not only give him the opportunity of placing himself in a more favourable position for his attack, but when the time comes for him to leave the scene, he can put that extra distance between himself and his assailants which will enhance his chances of evasion. In rough seas, when the

target or anti-submarine vessel may be forced to reduce speed, even more advantage can be taken of added underwater speed. There was no doubt in the minds of everyone in the Navy as a whole, and of the Submarine Command in particular, that underwater speed was a primary factor which must be developed. The Germans had never lost sight of this fundamental need throughout the war.

With these facts in mind, the primary interest lay in the captured German submarines, and extensive trials were carried out to test their performance. Their high speed battery boats, Types XXI and XXIII, showed that 17 knots submerged was obtainable. Some of our operational *T* Class were converted and achieved similar speed submerged. In all the high speed battery boats both German and British this maximum speed could only be maintained for short periods, otherwise the batteries would have run down to unacceptable limits.

Concurrently experiments were carried out with a German hydrogen peroxide driven submarine, their Type XXVI, more commonly known as a Walther boat and named after Dr Walther who had worked on this design for some years. This boat was known by our submariners as *Meteorite,* and not only were submerged speeds of up to 22 knots attained but endurance trials gave figures of 8 knots maintained for twenty-four hours. Thus the Germans had been on the threshold of a submarine programme which, through the high submerged speed of their boats, could have put the effectiveness of the Allies' anti-submarine forces into question.

The principle of the Walther boat was to use hydrogen peroxide in a highly concentrated form. This liquid was named 'Ingolin'. When Ingolin is passed over a catalyst it gives up its oxygen content and this process generates heat. On its release from the Ingolin the oxygen is burnt with a sulphur free fuel and water injected into the combustion chamber. The resultant steam is passed through turbines to drive the submarine. This engine took the development of the submarine one step nearer the 'true submarine' which would remain submerged indefinitely.

As a result of all this, two experimental boats were built with a British design of hydrogen peroxide engine. They were *Explorer* and *Excalibur.* They were unarmed and were built for speed trials only. Unfortunately they took a long time to complete and did not make an appearance until 1958, but when they did, submerged speeds up to 25 knots were achieved. They proved very useful in giving experience of high speed submarines to our anti-submarine forces.

As well as benefitting from the knowledge of the German high speed battery boats, we incorporated into our own submarines the Snort Mast. This was originally a Dutch invention which the Germans were the first to put into practical use and introduced into their U-boats in the latter half of the war. This gave German submarines greatly increased endurance submerged and eliminated the need to surface to charge batteries.

During this time British and United States submariners were in touch at all levels, so it was known in general terms about the developments in the United

States Navy on the atomic side of underwater propulsion from which we would eventually benefit. It was felt however, for the time being it was more expedient for Britain to put some new construction in hand on an improved conventional or standard type of submarine and the *Porpoise* and *Oberon* Classes were designed.

Eight *Porpoise* Class and thirteen *Oberon* Class were approved for building from 1955 onwards. *Porpoise,* the first of this class was laid down on 1 August 1955, at Scotts yard at Greenock and the last of the class was laid down on 12 February 1958 at Vickers. All eight were completed by 11 February 1961. The first of the *Oberon* Class was laid down on 28 November 1957 and *Osiris,* the last of the thirteen of this class on 26 January 1962. All in this class were completed by 11 January 1964. The building of these boats was shared between Scotts, Vickers, Cammell Laird and Chatham Dockyard.

Both these classes were designated 'Patrol Submarines'. They form the conventional part of the British submarine fleet today. Their design is very similar. They are bigger than the *A* Class, displacing 2030 tons on the surface and 2410 submerged. They are 241 feet long and have a beam of 26 feet. Eight 21″ torpedo tubes are fitted, six in the bow and two in the stern, and they carry twenty-two to twenty-four homing torpedoes. Propulsion is by diesel electric on the surface and when schnorkelling, and electric when submerged. Submariners often refer to them as the 'diesel electric boats' rather than use the term 'conventional'. Surface speed is 12 knots and they can attain 17 knots submerged. The crew consists of sixty-eight, of which there are six officers and sixty-two ratings.

The operational qualities of these boats show a great advance on anything in the submarine service in the Second World War, and by improved schnorkel arrangements they can remain submerged for several weeks at a time. They are very silent underwater in spite of two screws, very considerable attention having been paid to cavitation noises.

Every kind of modern technical device to improve their operational capability has been provided. Sonar, in its most modern form for underwater listening and high definition radar to detect enemy search radar when on the surface or schnorkelling, make them difficult to track down. These boats go all over the world and have gained experience of the Arctic, the Pacific and especially hot climates such as at Singapore. Their travels have prompted scientists to obtain permission to go on these cruises, with the particular object of studying oceanography.

So far as the submarine itself is concerned this history ends on a clear cut line as Part Two will so plainly show. However, the main operational principle of conventional submarine work in war remains, namely this type of vessel still has the unique advantage of being able to remain unseen and to operate entirely unsupported deep into enemy waters.

The future will not alter the fact that the principles of submarining remain; notably, that to dive a ship the buoyancy must be destroyed, and the reverse

process must be achieved to surface. Yet throughout the past and also in the future, as long as men put to sea in submarines, the governing force will always be the human one, and the success or failure of this vessel will remain in the hands of the commanding officer and his crew.

Note. Homing torpedoes were first embarked in British submarines in 1953. They homed on the cavitation noise of the target.

PART II
THE NUCLEAR AGE

Plate 32

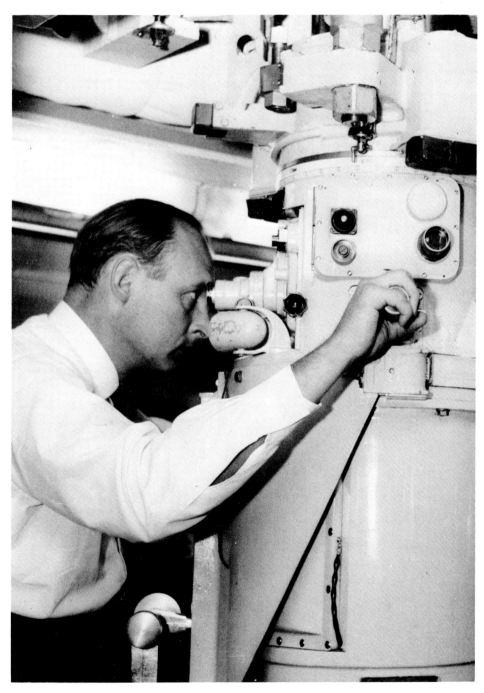

Commander B F P Samborne the first captain of Britain's first nuclear submarine
HMS Dreadnought at the search periscope

Introduction

by Vice Admiral Raikes,
Flag Officer Submarines and Commander
Submarine Forces Eastern Atlantic (NATO)

In following the British submarine into the Nuclear Age Commander Lipscomb has taken a stride into history. For, by now, the nuclear powered Fleet submarine has become the lynch pin of sea power, the 'Capital ship' of the World's most powerful navies. Although balanced naval forces are still essential, in the final reckoning it is the Fleet submarine which holds the trump card. Thus the maritime forces of NATO (wherein the US Navy plays prominent part) have not been slow to realise that the greatest threat at sea to merchantmen or men-of-war is the Soviet nuclear powered submarine armed with an anti-ship missile. Momentous thoughts indeed in 1954 when Part I of this book was written, but fact in 1974.

None of this denies the essential part still played by carrier borne aircraft or other units of a balanced naval force, but it emphasizes the fact that the submarine is now very much the weapon of the stronger power and because of this they are perforce pitted against each other — submarine versus submarine.

In 1976 it will be 75 years since the launching of the first British built submarine — the *Holland I* — and progress must surely be called staggering. The submarine in the nuclear age has the most remarkable flexibility in what it can do, when, where and how. This book will, I hope, bring to the public a feeling of familiarity with our latest recruits in the struggle for sea power, and, knowing them for what they are, I hope our friends and allies will welcome them with open arms when these fine submarines come visiting so that they become part of the everyday scene creating a sense of security rather than storing doubts about reactor safety.

We can only dismiss the warnings of the various statements by Admiral Gorshkov, the head of the Soviet Navy, at our peril.

As Commander Lipscomb introduces you to the nuclear age where the Polaris missile and its huge parent submarine remain our sure deterrent shield, he opens a window for us to look out into the broad horizons where the fleet submarine has such an exciting future. Read on — and the author has my full support in bringing you along with us. It is, after all, the submariners who do the job and they are mightily proud men.

Chapter eleven
The advance

DREADNOUGHT AND THE FLEET SUBMARINE

While the post-war experiments and the Patrol Submarine building programme was keeping the submarine service equipped with good material, there was always in the forefront of the minds of submariners a feeling that the Navy should be making at least a start ourselves in nuclear propulsion, on which the United States Navy had already made a good deal of progress.

To set the scene for the nuclear age in British submarines a review is also needed of developments in the United States in this first post-war decade, because so much of our development was based on American progress.

In America the naval building yards and experimental establishments had survived the war undamaged, so that whatever decisions were arrived at in naval strategy, there was nothing to stop the necessary action being taken. The United States also had the financial resources. Immediately after the war, like ourselves, she scrapped the old boats, in her case seventy and she cancelled the building of another ninety-two. This left the submarine branch of her navy with a little short of one hundred fleet type.

Her naval policy was to base her fleet on the aircraft carrier. For this she needed radar pickets to warn the carriers of the approach of an enemy attacking force. Towards the end of the war she had suffered heavy surface casualties in radar picket destroyers, and therefore decided to convert some submarines to carry out this role underwater, particularly for those aircraft carriers which carried the nuclear armed aircraft. She also developed a missile carrying submarine. The missile was named 'Regulus' and was carried in a hangar, rather like the German V1 rocket and launched it in a similar way. This latter development introduced an entirely new role into submarine warfare. Earlier, submarines had been capable of firing their guns at targets along the seaboard of an enemy country, but never had they been capable of firing a nuclear armed rocket deep into enemy territory.

America also carried out experiments with captured German submarines and like ourselves examined them particularly with reference to underwater speed. As a result of these trials, America designed the *Albacore,* to do hydrodynamic research. Similar to British experimental submarines, *Albacore* was unarmed. What they found out from this design was that a short, fat, streamlined hull gave the best underwater speeds and a single screw was much better than twin screws. *Albacore* achived a top speed of 35 knots.

With their facilities for research, they also began a programme to examine nuclear propulsion for submarines. This programme was in the hands of a

naval officer who was both submariner and engineer. He was Captain Hyman
Rickover who started on this project in 1946. He had at his disposal much preliminary work by Dr Ross Gunn of the Naval Research Laboratory and Dr
Philip H Abelson of the Carnegie Institute. The idea of a nuclear reactor took
root at Park Ridge, Tennessee and for the rest of the 1940s Rickover fought
relentlessly to overcome formidable opposition, and even hostility from some
quarters, which resulted in initial lack of money and materials. But he never
gave up and in spite of opposition early in 1950 it was clear that his work was
going to be successful and the first hull to carry a nuclear reactor was laid
down. Meanwhile Rickover had been passed over for promotion, but when
his work showed that a nuclear reactor was definitely a certainty and the construction of the submarine to carry it was speeded up, he was promoted to
Rear Admiral. His amazing achievement altered all naval thinking both in the
United States and here in England. Rickover's name will go down in submarine
history with those of Fulton, Laubeuf and Holland.

Admiral Rickover's dream came true when on 17 January, 1955 the USS
Nautilus slipped from her building yard at Groton, Connecticut and moved
out to sea and made the now famous signal 'Under way on nuclear power'.

The size of the nuclear reactor and its shielding meant that *Nautilus* had to
be 320 feet long and displace 3539 tons on the surface, in fact a ship the size
of a cruiser. She was fitted with only six bow torpedo tubes but her vast size
meant that she could carry three reloads.

Much has been written about this remarkable vessel, but for the purpose of
this review it is sufficient to say that here was the first 'true submarine' which
need never surface for about two years, other than to meet the limitations of
the human element. A necessary embodyment to effect this achievement was
the CO_2 'scrubber' for air purifying, coupled with machinery for the generation of oxygen.

Inside, *Nautilus* was unrecognizable to the ordinary submariners. They saw
bunks for all her ten officers and ninety-five ratings, air-conditioning, washing
machines, a library and laboratories. These were only some of the vast improvements in comforts and technology compared to the old conventional
submarine.

With speeds of up to 20 knots on the surface and 23 submerged, she happily
cruised at 16 knots underwater to Puerto Rico, a distance of 1381 miles. All
submarine records had been broken and she was a complete success.

At this point world events began to influence strategic thinking in both
America and Great Britain. In 1953 the Russians exploded their first nuclear
weapon, and in 1957, just two years after *Nautilus* became operational, they
put their first sputnik into orbit. Americans and British alike realised that
the security of both countries had once again been threatened. No longer
could the United States fleet be built around the aircraft carrier, now so open
to detection wherever they might be on the oceans, and the whole strategy
of carrying nuclear headed bombs in aircraft carriers was called into question.

Not only this, but the safety of the land based strategic bomber force was placed in doubt.

There was now a vital need to look for another means of carrying the nuclear strike which would be beyond the means of detection and would be totally reliable. A 'Second Strike' was needed, which would mean that if any nuclear armed country considered destroying another country by this weapon, it would know that within minutes of attack, the aggressor would itself receive the full power of nuclear destruction.

Some forward thinking had been done on this problem in the United States but without any priority. A young admiral, William Rayborn, had been given the task of 'developing a strategic missile and submarine to launch it, within ten years'. Rayborn was of the same make-up as Rickover and with the danger clouds so clearly on the horizon, he went ahead with the submarine and its missile with the greatest priority.

It was now time for Great Britain to act and take her place in this nuclear age and for the Navy to mount its first steps on the ladder to nuclear propulsion by ordering a reactor to be developed at the Ministry of Defence Research Station at Dounreay, Caithness, Scotland. That this was done was due to a great extent to the pressure from Admiral of the Fleet, Earl Mountbatten, who was First Sea Lord from 1955 to 1959. He was advised by Admiral Sir Wilfred Woods, Flag Officer Submarines at the time. These two officers both felt strongly that British sea power could not be allowed to fall so far behind any other maritime nation, and the answer lay both in the submarine and nuclear power. This argument was accepted, and it was not long before the British Navy's first nuclear submarine was authorised. The contract to build the submarine was given to Vickers Armstrong and the building of the reactor plant went to Rolls Royce and Associates.

At home, just as in the United States, the world situation influenced the timetable for construction both of the submarine and the reactor. All went well with the former and by 12 June, 1959, the first hull section of the submarine was ready to be placed into position. This was done by HRH The Duke of Edinburgh at a 'keel laying' ceremony that day.

Things however were very different at Dounreay. The development of the reactor was proving to be a very slow business and there appeared to be no hope of a breakthrough which would speed up completion. Something quite drastic had to be done if the Chiefs of Staff directive, namely, that to meet the strategic requirements the Navy should have a nuclear submarine operational as soon as possible. Earl Mountbatten, by now Chief of the Defence Staff, solved the problem by an agreement between Britain and America, made in 1959 which enabled the Admiralty to purchase a complete American nuclear power plant including the reactor.

This would be a replica of the plant in the USS *Skipjack*, which had been developed from the experience gained from both *Albacore* and *Nautilus*, and was the prototype of a massive nuclear submarine building programme for

the American fleet.

Skipjack had been designed with a blunt nose. She was shaped rather like a rugby football. Outboard she was stripped of the normal casing and upper deck fittings, but retained the large fin on which were fitted the forward hydroplanes. She was built a little smaller than the *Nautilus* and provided with only one propeller like the *Albacore*. When the agreement was made, *Skipjack* had just completed trials during which she had achieved an underwater speed of about 35 knots. Her development on these revolutionary lines meant that one more major step had been taken in submarine history. The purchase by Great Britain of a similar power plant meant that the whole after section of our first nuclear submarine would be American, but this was not the first time the Navy had taken such a step. After all, way back in 1902, we had purchased from America the complete plans of the Hollands, our very first submarines. To complete the propulsion unit of our first nuclear submarines it was felt necessary to install auxiliary power. So the diesel engine, the snort mast and batteries were still to be incorporated even in the most modern nuclear submarines, primarily to provide the source of electrical power needed to support the reactor systems when the reactor itself is shut down. This 'conventional power' facility could also be coupled in to drive the main screw when necessary for manoeuvring on the surface and for short passages which would not justify the 'flashing up' of the reactor to its critical state.

It was decided that this first British submarine of the new era would be named *Dreadnought* and become the ninth man-of-war to bear this famous name and one which was synonymous with great changes in the Navy.

From this moment all the expert technical knowledge of Vickers Armstrongs, who it will be remembered built the *Holland* Class at the turn of the century, and had had fifty years experience of submarine building, was put to the test, but as ever Vickers proved equal to the task. Concurrently Flag Officer Submarines had to arrange for the training of the crew, which was carried out partly in the United States and partly at home. Then again an operational base had to be chosen and equipped and because of *Dreadnought* drawing nearly 30 feet, those harbours which she might have to frequent had to be dredged to the required depth.

The *Dreadnought* story would take a book in itself to tell fully, but for the purpose of this general history suffice it to say that she was laid down on 12 June, 1959 and launched by Her Majesty the Queen on 21 October, 1960, the anniversary of Trafalgar Day. Next, early in 1962 the Skipjack reactor was loaded onboard and late in the same year it was made 'critical'. Finally on 17 April, 1963, *Dreadnought* was commissioned, and the greatest step forward in the history of British submarines had been taken.

In the United States of America Admiral Rayborn's work had rapidly come to fruition. Apart from his personal drive, unlike Rickover, he had had no opposition. The construction of the 'Missile' had raced ahead, so much so that on 20 July, 1960, a year ahead of the expected schedule, a selected United

States submarine fired two missiles while submerged. They were named Polaris missiles. The experiment had been entirely successful. Both missiles hurtled down the 1100 miles of the Atlantic missile range and arrived on target with perfect accuracy. Meanwhile the 'Polaris submarine to carry the missile', the other part of Rayborn's directive, had raced ahead in construction and was already doing trials. These went along so fast, including the first firing of a Polaris missile by this submarine now fully operational, that on 15 December, 1960, well over two years before *Dreadnought* took her place in the British Navy, the USS *George Washington* had sailed from Charleston for a long patrol somewhere in the North Atlantic. In this monster of 6700 tons and 382 feet long, carrying sixteen Polaris missile launching tubes amidships, the nuclear deterrent was 'in being' and the 'Second Strike' a reality.

Concurrently the Americans were continuing with their nuclear submarine programme, based on the outstanding success of *Skipjack*. By 1959 the USS *Tullibee* had made her appearance as the first 'hunter killer' submarine, designed to hunt and destroy enemy submarines. She was followed by two whole classes of similar nuclear submarines being authorised, no less than thirty-two *Permit* Class and thirty-four *Sturgeon* Class. The resources of the United States were immense.

Here, in the British submarine service, steps taken for a programme within the means at our disposal, were very heartening. *Dreadnought* had been a great success and our knowledge was leaping ahead. With the experience of the Skipjack power plant, confidence in our own ability was now so strong that *Dreadnought* was treated as a prototype of a class of nuclear submarines designated 'Fleet' submarines or 'hunter killers'. This was the *Valiant* Class. The submarines were to be entirely British, both in design and in the building of the reactors. This leap into the nuclear submarine era is of such importance that it is appropriate to dwell on some of the detail.

Submarine	Laid down	Completed
Valiant	22 January 1962	18 July 1966
Warspite	10 December 1963	11 April 1967
Churchill	30 June 1967	15 July 1970
Conqueror	5 December 1967	9 November 1971
Courageous	15 May 1970	16 October 1972

An improved design of four were laid down or ordered as follows:

Swiftsure	6 June 1969	17 April 1973
Sovereign	18 September 1970	July 1974
Superb	January 1971	Building
Sceptre	1972	Building

The first five are 285 feet long and have a beam of 33 feet. They displace 3500 tons on the surface and 4500 submerged. The submarines are armed with six 21 inch bow torpedo tubes and carry homing torpedoes. Their single

propeller drives them underwater at about 30 knots. All these Fleet submarines were provided with one addition to their propulsion systems. This is a retractible electrically driven outboard motor known as the 'eggbeater' which swivels and provides an effective manoeuvring aid when the main drive is stopped during evolutions such as berthing. Later this was also to be included in the Polaris submarines.

The building was put in hand at Vickers Armstrongs and also at Cammell Lairds, another firm with long submarine building experience.

The original five have a crew of eleven officers and about eighty-eight ratings, the other four when commissioned will be manned by thirteen officers and about ninety men.

It was stated at this time that the primary duty of the *Valiant* Class was to operate against enemy submarines.[1] For this purpose these fleet submarines can cruise submerged beneath our own convoys, an ideal position for providing protection for them, and a capability undreamt of in days gone by. Secondly they also perform the age-old duty of sinking the enemy's surface ships. Thirdly they carry out the special feature of their forebears by operating close to the enemy's bases entirely unsupported. Besides these roles, they can transport assault and reconnaissance parties, but here it must be emphasized that even in the last war the use of a submarine in these tasks had to be carefully weighed in relation to its other duties. It has to be a very important mission for such a valuable ship to be risked which in itself has such immense power, capable of actually turning the balance of sea power against the enemy.

The Fleet submarines with their high underwater speed handle rather like aircraft, using a powered control column for changing depth and turning, in which latter evolution they bank like an aeroplane. All this is accomplished with an endurance virtually unlimited, but generally they are expected to be at sea for two months at a time.

The living spaces are slightly restricted in comparison with Polaris boats, but in other respects they are completely comparable, having ample fresh water, laundry facilities, exercise machines, library, cinema and every man his own bunk. Normally officers and ratings have two periods of four hours on duty in each twenty-four hours, more commonly known as a one in three routine. Among the eleven officers are four engineering and electrical specialists and sometimes a medical officer. Of the eighty-eight ratings there are approximately forty-eight engineering and electrical, twenty-eight seamen and communications and the remaining twelve ratings are divided between stores, medical, cooks and stewards. The complement of Fleet submarines may vary in the future according to the restructuring of the various submarine trades involved.

Sometimes because of its steadily increasing capabilities and offensive power, the submarine has been alluded to as the capital ship of the future. With the *Valiant* Class this forecast became a reality and the stature of the British submarine has now risen to the highest position it has ever held in the Navy. As

1 The use of the Fleet submarine is more fully described in Chapter XIII in the light of later experience.

an example of one of its capabilities, in 1967 *Valiant* steamed the 12 000 miles home from Singapore, non-stop submerged, in 28 days. In this the Inertial Navigation System, whereby the submarine knows its exact position at all times, played a significant and successful part.

With this advance in the British Submarine Service it was felt that Great Britain in her traditional role of a great sea power, was ready to play her part in the deterrent and provide an aid to the 'Second Strike'. This was particularly opportune as, in common with the United States, our own strategic bomber force was coming to the end of its era.

On this occasion, Prime Minister Harold MacMillan requested a meeting with the President of the United States, John F Kennedy and this took place at Nassau in December 1962. At this vital meeting the following points were decided; that the United Kingdom should have five[1] Polaris submarines to carry the latest A3 Polaris missiles; these submarines should be British designed and built, but that the whole weapons system and equipment, except the warheads, would be purchased from the United States; the warheads would be entirely British. These five submarines, officially known as Ships Submersible Ballistic Nuclear, (short title SSBNs) were to be deployed at the earliest possible date. This was another turning point in British submarine history.

POLARIS SUBMARINES

The Missile. The Polaris missile is a two-stage ballistic rocket with nuclear warheads and its own inertial guidance system. It has a maximum range of 2500 miles and although launched from a submerged submarine it can reach any land target on earth with an accuracy measurable in yards.

In order to achieve this accuracy, exact knowledge of the position of the target must be known, coupled with the precise position of the submarine, and its behaviour in respect of its diving trim and attitude at the moment of firing. The speed and course of the submarine must be exactly recorded.

All this vital information is provided in the submarine by the target information computer tapes and a continuous supply of information from the Ships Inertial Navigation System (SINS). There are two firecontrol computers which, with this data, continuously calculate the necessary flight instructions and supply the answer to the missiles which are permanently at the ready in their firing tubes.

As soon as the missile is launched, its flight is controlled by its own inertial guidance system, and when this calculates that the nuclear warheads will reach their target in a free fall ballistic flight, the warheads separate from the second stage motor and go on to the target.

Action. To deploy this fantastic weapon 'at the earliest possible date', to quote the Government's directive, meant that the year 1963 would have to be one of quick decisions, made with the utmost clarity of thought, to put in motion

1 One Polaris submarine was cancelled by the Labour Government subsequently, as an economy in the administration Defence Policy.

the building of these five Polaris submarines agreed at Nassau. This was a tremendous responsibility for those concerned, since on these decisions made under pressure of time, the major part to be played by the British Navy in defence of the free world would depend, and that part was in the hands of the Submarine Service.

It was decided to set up a Polaris Executive. The officer selected to command it was Rear Admiral Hugh Mackenzie, at that time the Flag Officer Submarines, and a submarine officer of great experience and distinction. The first of the quick decisions was to make an immediate start on the design of the submarines, now reduced to four in number. Two of the building contracts were given to Vickers Armstrong and two to Cammell Laird. The first of the class was to be built by Vickers.

Next, arrangements were made for the necessary Royal Navy, Civil Service, British weapon system contractors and shipbuilder's staff, to be trained in the United States. Thirdly, it was decided to build the operational support base in the west of Scotland at Faslane in the Gareloch, and to create an armament depot at Coulport in Loch Long, close at hand, and an immediate start was made.

The choice of Faslane and Coulport needs some clarification. There are certain fundamental needs which have to be taken into account in the case of nuclear powered submarines. Firstly, due to their great size, they should be based in deep water harbours and within easy distance of the open sea. Secondly, because of the nature of their power units, it was important they should be remote from populated areas, though sufficiently close to give the ships' companies adequate shore facilities. Thirdly, because of the special weapons and equipment, it must be practicable to ensure the utmost secrecy and security. No naval ports along the south coast of England, except possibly Devonport, fulfilled these requirements.

The situation facing the Polaris Executive was this. During the Second World War, submarines had used the west coast of Scotland extensively as bases. The principal of these was at Rothesay which with Loch Long and the Holy Loch, formed a complex, not only for operational submarines but for contractor's trials, working up and crew training. When the post-war construction programme of patrol submarines was authorised it was clear that the creek at HMS *Dolphin*, Gosport, could not provide the necessary support. The two war-time depot ships, *Adamant* and *Maidstone* were moved to the Scottish base, subsequently moving to the Gareloch, the former taking over the *Porpoise* and *Oberon* Classes as they became operational. *Dreadnought,* when commissioned, was to be attached to *Maidstone* which was receiving modernisation to handle nuclear submarines, and was expecting to welcome her first charge in the spring of 1963. Besides this, an extension to the Gareloch base for the *Valiant* Class fleet submarines was already in hand, although the first of these was not expected to be complete until 1966.

From all these considerations it was really an obvious choice to extend the

Gareloch base to meet the requirements of the Polaris submarines as well.

The complex of the Faslane base was divided into three areas, the dockyard, the barracks and the logistic support and training area. The dockyard area contained jetties, the floating dock, alongside facilities including workshops, a nuclear effluent disposal plant and an electrical generating station to provide power to the submarines, other than their own. The barracks area was design- to accommodate 250 officers and 1500 ratings and included indoor and out-door sports areas, clubs, shops, dental and medical departments, a cinema and a church. Close by were married quarters for both officers and ratings. The logistic support area contained all the stores buildings which housed spare spare parts, bulk food, paints, gases and oil fuel, to name a few items. Besides this there were in the area the training quarters, which included the Polaris school and the propulsion plant control trainer.

Further north in Loch Long, the base at Coulport was commanded by an officer of the Director General Supplies and Transport (Navy) and manned almost entirely by civilians. It stored and maintained the Polaris missiles. It had its own jetty for transferring the missiles to and from the Polaris sub-marines, and this was termed the Armament Depot.

That part of the design of the complex which could be seen by the general public was submitted to the Scottish Fine Arts Commission and approved by them.

Just for the record, the Americans had asked for a base for some of their nuclear submarines on the west coast of Scotland, so Holy Loch was handed over to them, where they are today, a completely separate entity.

The next year, 1964, was marked by the visual signs that things were happen-ing. Additions to the Faslane base and the depot at Coulport began to take shape. Construction of a floating dock was begun and at the building yards the 'keels' of the first two submarines were laid. Progress was so fast, that by the end of the year equipment was being installed in the Polaris school at Faslane, which included a complete instructional missile system. Observers from the banks of the loch saw houses being built for officers and men and a school for the children and much else besides to make the whole base thor-oughly functional.

The next two years will be remembered by the Submarine Service for the dedicated work put in by all concerned to adhere to the Government directive. For most men it meant a complete subjugation of all personal interests and this was done willingly and cheerfully.

1966 was noted for the launch of the first of the class at Vickers Armstrong by Her Majesty Queen Elizabeth, The Queen Mother who named Britain's first Polaris submarine *Resolution* on 15 September. All present felt the significance of the moment when *Resolution* glided gracefully into her true element. To have brought this submarine to this stage with all its complications in design and material, of which most were entirely new even to Vickers, was a truly splendid achievement. She has a length of 360 feet and displaces 7500 tons

on the surface and 8400 submerged. Her armament is sixteen Polaris A3 missiles and six 21 inch bow torpedo tubes. She has a surface speed of 20 knots and over 25 knots submerged.

In February 1967 Cammell Laird brought the second Polaris submarine to readiness for launching and Mrs Healey, wife of the Defence Minister at that time, named the vessel *Renown*.

Events now raced ahead, one following another in quick succession. *Resolution* carried out her contractors trials in June. The additions to the Faslane base were ready to receive her and the floating dock was operational. The Command Communication system was 'on the air' and the missile depot jetties at Coulport were completed. Then came the great day when *Resolution* was accepted into the Fleet on 22 October 1967.

It is difficult to describe the extent of brain power, judgment, clarity of thought and sense of urgency, right across the board in so many departments, which had contributed to this undoubted success. The fact was, *Resolution* was there for all to see, on time and in perfect operational condition. It is perhaps appropriate at this moment of submarine history to record that Faslane was formally commissioned and appropriately named HMS *Neptune*. Before the year was out Vickers had the third submarine ready for launching. She was named *Repulse* and was launched by Lady Joan Zuckerman.

All Polaris submarines have to go to the United States to carry out the operation of firing a Polaris missile down the range at Cape Kennedy. This was successfully accomplished by *Resolution* in early 1968 and was followed by a short period of final training at HMS *Neptune*. Then in July of this momentous year, Great Britain's first Polaris submarine sailed for patrol and British sea power had again taken its rightful place in the defence of the free world.

Revenge, the fourth Polaris submarine had taken the water at Cammell Laird's yard in March of this same year and was named by Lady Law, wife of Admiral Sir Horace Law, a former Flag Officer Submarines. When *Revenge* was completed on 4 December, 1969, Admiral Mackenzie had been relieved by Rear-Admiral A G F Trewby as Chief Polaris Executive and he was able to report to the Cabinet that the Government directive had been successfully carried out.

This chapter would not be complete without naming those who were principally responsible for the historic advance of the British submarine into the nuclear age. The following diagram of the 'family tree' in its simplest form shows eight Heads of Departments. The roman numerals in brackets after each Department refer to the officers named in the list following. The work done by these very skilled officers could not have been brought to a successful conclusion without support from the highest quarters. Those in these positions at this time were: Sir Clifford Jarrett, Secretary of the Admiralty; Vice Admiral Le Fanu, Controller of the Navy (later First Sea Lord); Lord Carrington, First Lord of the Admiralty.

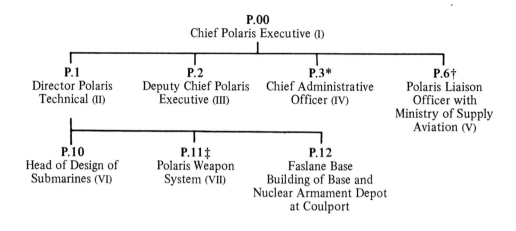

P = Polaris
* The Senior Civil Servant — The coordinator by which the whole organisation fitted into initially the Admiralty, then the Ministry of Defence and Government Departments.
† Responsible for procuring the nuclear warheads.
‡ Procurement from US of Polaris weapon system and installation in submarines.

	THEN	NOW
I	Rear Admiral H S MacKenzie	Vice Admiral Sir Hugh MacKenzie
II	Mr Rowland Baker, RCNC	Sir Rowland Baker
III	Captain J R McKaig	Admiral Sir Rae McKaig
	Captain P R Higham	Rear Admiral P R Higham
IV	Mr R N Lewin (4 years)	
	succeeded by Mr F Nailor	Professor at Lancaster University
V	Rear Admiral F W Dossor	
VI	Mr S J Palmer, RCNC	
	Mr H W Tabb, RCNC	
VII	Captain C W H Shepherd, RN	Rear Admiral C W H Shepherd
VIII	Captain Leslie Bomford	

Chapter twelve
Nuclear submarine shore support

FASLANE – THE CLYDE SUBMARINE BASE

When the Polaris Executive handed down the blueprints of the submarine base at Faslane in such quick time, they had to do so not only in the light of their submarine experience but also with considerable imagination and forethought; would it be able to stand the test of time and would it be used in the way they visualised? The answers are that it has stood the test of time very well and its functioning can scarcely be faulted. It would have been a miracle if there had been no shortcomings, but what there have been have resulted chiefly from circumstances which have developed during its first ten years of extence by reason of world changes and government defence policy.

The basic requirements of a nuclear base have been stated in Chapter XI and it is difficult to know where to begin a more detailed description of this vast complex, but in these days of violence and political intrigue, perhaps the security comes first, for without this in its highest degree the base could not exist. With this in mind the site chosen on the eastern shore of the Gareloch is an elongated stretch of land, and on the western side is the mile wide loch with a range of wild Scottish hills running down to the water's edge on the opposite side of the loch. This range separates the Gareloch from Loch Long, adjacent to Holyloch, where the American base is. A coracle could easily be spotted coming too near the base from seaward. On the east side of the site is a railway and more hills devoid of habitation. The base area being elongated, the two ends are narrow, so there are only two entrances. The whole is surrounded by a security fence. The area covered by the base is about a mile long and a quarter of a mile wide.

To enter even officially is no mean feat and to move within it involves innumerable checks, special passes and often explanations. To the unsuspecting, all this might appear to be sufficient, but on turning a corner, two or three Royal Marine Commandos, recently returned from tough duty in Northern Ireland, may appear as from nowhere. So from this aspect the Executive chose the site well and the Base Security Officer has taken full advantage of it.

Faslane is first and foremost a support base and the nuclear submarines lie alongside while changing crews and undergoing maintenance. They come first in every particular. The workshops are at their service twenty-four hours out of every twenty-four. These are very large and among their capabilities they are fitted with all the test equipment for sonar systems and there are special facilities for doing repairs on nuclear power plants. There is also a plant for treating radio-active waste so as to make final disposal a safe and economical

process.

The twenty-four hour service also applies to the stores, and the first lieutenant of a Polaris submarine when preparing for patrol has only to whisper that he needs this or that and it is supplied within the time that he is ready to receive it. To do this, the mechanics of moving stores and transporting them represents the last words in logistic thinking, and those who provide this service are rightly proud of their part in the organization.

It is at Faslane where the officers and ratings selected, attend the Polaris School. Here everything which they will meet in connection with the missile is repeated, so that when they go to a boat they are not confronted with anything unexpected. Besides this, when in harbour, complete Polaris teams from boats can brush up their drills ashore and 'work in' any new members who will be with them on their next patrol. Control centres with their computers and SINS are all there, manned by a team of experts to instruct in everything from a practice operational run to the most complicated repair in a SINS gyro.

In a way there is something rather sombre in all this and it contrasts with the 'Attack Teacher', in the building next door, where all the commanding officers of Polaris and Fleet submarines, both old hands and new, together with the learners—'the Perishers'—are taught how to attack targets such as a transport, a surface man-of-war or a submerged submarine.

All submarine commanding officers have always enjoyed the attacking. Ever since Launders in *Venturer* sank *U 864* when both were submerged, firing by asdic, there has been an added fascination in this type of attack and an increasing need for its development. Now in these days with fast nuclear driven submarines, coupled with every scientific device available, this attack calls for greatly increased skill and the Faslane Attack Teacher provides all that is required to practice it. As with the Polaris Teacher, the commanding officer has his own crew in the Teacher operating in the identical positions they occupy in the boat. Here the difference from the old days is almost unbelievable. In the pre-Second World War Attack Teacher there was room only for the commanding officer and the problems set were somewhat limited. In fact on occasion, if a new pupil was doing too well, he could at least be slightly put off by the surreptitious use of a watering can with a fine rose, so that the next time he raised the periscope his vision was limited by rain!

Now the commanding officer has an additional and equally absorbing interest, as the submarine has become very much more part of the fleet than ever before, and he is taught in continuation of the course, his part in tactical 'games' as part of a task force. Only since Fleet nuclear submarines came into being has the submarine moved so far away from its own domain and become very much part of the Navy as a whole. Indeed that part played by submarines is rapidly becoming the most important part of all. In recording this as one of the major developments of the last twenty years, it may be news to some to learn that in 1942 Sir Dudley Pound, the First Sea Lord, wrote in a

minute: 'It is for consideration whether every convoy should have either a battleship or a submarine attached to it'. Submariners took careful note of the word 'either'.

The task of working up and training submarine crews steadily became so complex with the modern advances and the sophistication of the equipment now involved, that it was too burdensome a commitment for the squadron staffs who, hitherto, had been responsible for these aspects of operational readiness. Accordingly, on 1 January 1974, a submarine sea training organization (headed by the Captain Sea Training) was established at Faslane. Henceforth, all submarines recommissioning after refit and on major crew change, were to be attached to CSST for work-up before joining their operational squadrons. At the same time the CSST took over responsibility for running the Attack Teacher, the Royal Naval Polaris School, and the Nuclear Power Control Trainer.

To run this base with all its installations large numbers of civilians are needed, most of them scientific and technological experts. In many ways this is a new feature. It is an amalgamation of naval and civilian personnel. It all works very well and is a pattern for the future elsewhere. It would be a pity here not to include the WRNS, as efficient and decorative as ever, many of whom work in the Attack Teacher.

Space does not allow a full description of every activity at Faslane and it is only possible to mention some and regretfully pass on. There are Medical and Dental Departments equipped with everything modern. In an arcade there are shops, a bank, a post office, a cinema, a newsagent and of course a barbers shop. The recreational facilities are vast and ultra modern, centered on a Sports Drome with a magnificent gymnasium and swimming bath. Besides the usual football grounds and tennis courts there is a 0.22 rifle range, a trampoline and an artificial ski slope. There are two thriving clubs, one for sailing and the other the junior ratings club, the Trident, the running of which is an example to others. Two things are missing. Because of the lack of grass there is no rugby ground and because there is not sufficient level ground there is no cricket pitch!

To complete the picture, besides large messes and cabin blocks for officers and ratings inside the complex, there are large estates outside for married quarters. All this is well designed and includes garage space, this last item setting an unprecedented problem as there are about 1500 cars at Faslane. Ownership does not go by rank or rating as all can afford them.

The Church of St John the Evangelist is just outside the Naval Gate and is shared by all denominations. There is an Anglican Base Chaplain, a Chaplain, Church of Scotland and an Officiating Chaplain, Roman Catholic. In addition there are two small chapels which were incorporated into the original design. There is no special rig for church; sometimes men have no time to change.

It was said at the beginning that it would have been a miracle if there had been no shortcomings. There are two which apply today but may not tomorrow.

The Polaris Executive understood that the requirements for accommodation for the Fleet submarine crews would not be great, as the habitability of these submarines had improved so much compared with the conventional submarines, that many men would prefer to sleep on board when in harbour. In the event this has not been so. Again, the training and working up of conventional submarines has moved to Faslane to a great extent because the facilities for this are so good. To add to this Faslane has been found to be particularly suitable for additional tasks, one recent one being the development of the Mark 24 torpedo. This has meant accommodating technicians for whom no provision had been made. The other shortcoming is that the splendid recreational facilities are not fully used. The broad answer to this is that the submarines are so busy, and some spend so much time away that many men who would like to take advantage of all that is there are just unable to do so. However it is hoped that the British submarine fleet will grow and this being so the provision of so large a recreational concept will have been justified.

From this account it may appear that Faslane is solely a nuclear submarine base, but for the time being some conventional submarines augment the Fleet submarine operational squadron, and this year, Royal Netherland Navy submarines attached to the Royal Navy are also based here.

The whole of the Clyde Area is commanded by Commodore Clyde. This includes Coulport as well as Faslane. The Commodore is Captain of HMS *Neptune,* the naval element of Faslane, and is also Superintendent of the civilian element. This is a unique command and much of it is virtually on an active service basis at all times.

Faslane exudes an infectious spirit of liveliness and activity, coupled with a sense of purpose in all it means to the Navy as a whole and to the Submarine Service in particular.

THE DOUNREAY SUBMARINE PROTOTYPE

Up at Caithness, Rolls Royce and Associates were steadily putting their immense technological knowledge to the needs of the Submarine Service with special reference to the reactor prototype. The Dounreay Establishment had been named HMS *Vulcan,* another well known name in submarines. *Vulcan* is the Navy's nuclear propulsion test and training establishment. It is owned by the Ministry of Defence (Navy) and is commanded by a resident Captain Superintendent. Rolls Royce and Associates have a contract from the Ministry to maintain and operate the Dounreay site on their behalf. Specific responsibilities under this contract include the operation and maintenance of the submarine reactor prototype, maintenance of the reactor simulator used for training submarine crews, and the post-irradiation examination of fuel elements from spent reactor cores.

The Dounreay submarine prototype itself is a replica of that part of a submarine's hull which contains the reactor and the propulsion machinery, together with their associated control panels and stations. Part of the hull is

surrounded by a large tank of sea water which is an extra layer of biological shielding for the reactor and, in addition, reproduces the physical environment in which production plant will operate and provides a heat sink for the energy cooling system.

The entire prototype is housed in a large building which includes the technical and administrative control centres needed for its operation.

Chapter thirteen
The submarines

POLARIS SUBMARINES: A WALK THROUGH

To walk through a Polaris submarine as compared with a *T* Class boat, as described in Part I, leaves two very clear impressions. The first is that in the Polaris submarine, there is embodied so much in technical advancement, that the difference between the two types of boat is comparable to the change from sail to steam. The second impression is equally clear. There remain many characteristics familiar to all submariners, and the fact that the basic principles of submarining remain unaltered, whatever the vintage.

Those things which are much the same and give the second impression, are concerned with the fundamental laws of the submarine. There must be ballast tanks to destroy the buoyancy so that the vessel can submerge. There must be high pressure air available to blow out the water from the ballast tanks in order to surface. Hydroplanes are necessary to control the submarine when diving and surfacing as well as when submerged. Two periscopes, one 'search' and the other 'attack' were provided in submarines sixty years ago and the same applies today. Thus to the submariner of many years standing it is only necessary to cast a quick glance overhead to recognise a high pressure air pipe, or to go into the control room and see a periscope raised, still by a hydraulic ram, to feel partly on familiar ground.

Again in the control room the main flooding and blowing panel, which in days gone by was worked by a petty officer artificer with a spanner, today is worked by a similarly skilled petty officer operating electric switches. One also finds that though there are now three backing up systems which come into play in case of failure, what pleases the 'Old Timers' is to see the hand-lever alongside a vent by which the rating on duty there can open or shut the valve by hand. Inevitably a sailor walks through the control room carrying two cups of tea. This warms the heart as well as the body — no change here!

Lastly on this theme, forward in the torpedo space the torpedo tubes have a very familiar look, and the Mark VIII torpedo of the Second World War is still there holding its own, though not for much longer. When Whitehead invented the locomotive torpedo in the late nineteenth century, thereby providing the means to use a submarine as a warship, he could hardly have thought that the child of his genius would still be alive in 1974.

Those things which are so completely and utterly different, and give the first impression, are the size and amazing innumerable technical changes which embrace propulsion, navigation, fire control, weapon launching, communications and sonar, to give the broad headings under which these can be grouped and

the components of which are among the most advanced scientific productions of the last decade.

It should be remembered that all submarines differ in some details and so certain features described in the following 'walk through' may not necessarily be found in a submarine of the same class.

The submarine is built in the form of a central cylinder with conical ends. There are three decks in the central section and two decks at either end. The vessel is so big that the main passages can be down the centre of the boat instead of at one side. Therefore there are working components and accommodation on both sides of each deck, which has never happened before.

The submarine is entered by a main access hatch about half way between the forward hydroplanes and the fin. The top of the hatch passes through the casing which is all round the submarine and is free flooding. The lower end of the access hatch passes through the pressure hull and a ladder leads to the top deck of the three, deck 1. The main wireless office is here and the sonar room. Going down one more deck and moving forward from here to a position just abreast the forward hydroplanes is Number 35 bulkhead, from where the forward conical section begins. There are 147 bulkheads in the submarine but only half a dozen are important to this description, number 35 being one. Forward of this bulkhead there are only two decks.

Here on deck 1 is the ratings' recreation space and the library. Never before has any one part of a submarine been devoted entirely to recreation. When a film is being shown — and they get the best ones — two thirds of the ships' company can be accommodated. Below this on deck 2 is the torpedo loading space at the rear of which is the hydraulic torpedo loading gear. This is a more simple operation than in the *T* Class as the tubes are placed horizontally in two groups of three instead of the groups being vertical as the beam of a Polaris submarine gives the necessary space. Underneath 2 deck are the forward main trimming tanks and special tanks for torpedo compensating to adjust the weight when they are fired.

In this conical end there are two more interesting things. They are two CO_2 absorption units and four oxygen generators which are subsidiary to the main plant which is in the after part of the submarine, and in this part of the boat overhead, is the torpedo loading hatch and the forward escape hatch.

Returning through Number 35 bulkhead on 1 deck is the junior ratings' dining hall on the starboard side, with the pantry, galley and garbage ejector opposite on the port side. About two thirds of the ship's company can be fed at one time in the dining hall.

Immediately aft of the junior ratings' dining hall on 1 deck and passing through a bulkhead, is the senior ratings' dining hall. In some submarines there is a screen in the forward bulkhead of this space so that when the cinema is showing the senior ratings can see it from their own compartment, though it is rarely used. Opposite on the port side is the senior ratings, lounge, bunk space and wash room.

Below this on 3 deck are more senior ratings' bunks and the main junior and senior ratings' bunk space together with their wash rooms and showers. Each has his own locker and curtain so that he can be absolutely alone if he wishes and his own punka luva and separate reading lights. All officers and all ratings sleep in sleeping bags.

Underneath 3 deck is the main battery which provides current at 480 volts and where necessary this is reduced to 115 and 24. Fresh water tanks are also here and two compensating tanks.

Now going up the ladders from 3 deck to number 1 and moving aft is the control room. In some respects the control room in this submarine is very like that of a *T* Class boat. The difference is in the concentration of control. Instead of three wheels, two for hydroplanes and one for steering the submarine is manoeuvred with control columns which look as if they had been borrowed from an airliner. Pushing forward or pulling back will cause the submarine to pitch down or up and a twist will cause the submarine to bank into a turn. There are two control positions and in front of each is a 'blind flying panel' with gyro and electronic inertial attitude displays, which, again, are reminiscent in some ways of the instrumentation of an aircraft cockpit. The two control positions can be divided either between a two man team (for example during evolutions) when one man will take the fore planes and the other the after planes, or for patrol routine, when control of both sets of hydroplanes and steering can be channelled into one control column, so that all manoeuvring functions be carried out by one man on his own, and, as an ultimate refinement, the system can be put into autopilot.

There is a central position between the two pilots where the officer of the watch sits. Whereas in the *T* Class if the electrics failed, the hydroplanes or the steering were immediately put into 'hand', in the Polaris submarine if this happens a hydraulic system can take over and if this should fail then there is an air pressure system.

There are four places in the pressure hull where tubes and masts pass through which project above the fin when raised and house in the submarine when not in use. In all submarines two of these are periscopes. Submarines differ with regard to the other two but generally they are one radar mast and one electronic counter measure mast.

Other tubes and masts which are fitted in the fin are the schnorkel induction and exhaust masts, wireless masts and the satellite navigation mast.

The main control panels for the diving system have already been mentioned. They look very neat and compact with their electric switches. The attack instruments are improved as might be expected but look much the same at first sight. Sonar is a leap ahead into the scientific world compared to the asdic. Its plot occupies much the same place as the asdic plot of byegone days but naturally it is bigger. The same goes for the radar plot which is also in the control room. There is an ample chart room but this is in fact just outside the previous compartment and opposite the wireless office. At the after end of

the control room and cut off by a light bulkhead is the navigation centre which holds the Inertial Navigation System (SINS) and aft of this the second important bulkhead Number 72.

Immediately under the control room on 2 deck is a space where the two periscopes and two other masts pass and around these are the captain's cabin, the wardroom, the officers' cabins and washrooms all on the port side. Opposite on the starboard side are the ship's office, the coxswain's office and the sick bay. Below all this on 3 deck are some junior ratings' bunks placed around the enclosed 'wells' into which the lower ends of the two periscopes and two other masts stow when the submarine goes below periscope depth. Here too on the after side of the space is the all important missile control centre.

Below this part of 3 deck is Number 1 auxiliary space where amongst a variety of machinery are the hydraulic pumps for raising and lowering the periscopes and various other masts. The midship port and starboard compensating tanks have been fitted in here as well.

These two compartments abutting Number 72 bulkhead really contain the brains of the missile system, since by their computers the navigation centre and the missile control compartment continuously feed information to the missiles. This information consists of the exact position of the target and of the submarine, together with the latter's course and speed and also the behaviour of the submarine as regards trim and attitude.

From 72 bulkhead to 99 is the missile compartment, where only those who have actual business there are allowed to go. Here all sixteen missile tubes are ranged in two groups of eight to house the missiles which need this combined height of all three decks when embarked. Their vital statistics are a length of 9.5 metres, a diameter of 1.4 metres and a weight of approximately 16 tons. In this compartment, the largest in the submarine are also a health physics laboratory, a weapons office and a technical office.

From the missile compartment Number 99 bulkhead, there is quite a small section to Number 108. This is Number 2 auxiliary machinery space which contains the system which allows the submarine to remain continually dived. On deck 1 is the air purification room. The plant here removes the carbon dioxide by dissolving it, while deck 2 has the cooling and conversion room with plant which replenishes the oxygen by generating it from an electrolytic process. Again in this compartment on deck 3 are the two main diesel generators. Men working in this space say it gets rather warm. With all this machinery no doubt it does.

From 108 bulkhead to Number 118 is the all important nuclear reactor. Engineers who keep watch on this have had special training for their very responsible job and are a team similar to the Polaris specialists. A tunnel runs through this compartment instead of decks; it is specially shielded from radio activity and other hazards of a nuclear plant.

Moving aft from here on deck 1 is the manoeuvring room, down one deck is the switchboard room, and on deck 3 below, the turbo-generator room.

Immediately aft of this between bulkheads 134 and 147 is the engine room, on three levels, and here are the two distilling plants each with an output of over 5000 gallons a day, which is quite sufficient for the reactor systems and the domestic services. Showers are always available for the ship's company and the laundry is never starved of fresh water. From 147 the submarine becomes shaped like it does forward to the dome bulkhead and there are two decks only. The motor room is here on the two levels and overhead is the aft escape hatch. For the technically minded there is a diagram and explanation of how the engines work, given in Appendix III.

Having come as far as this, all the 400 feet of the boat, there is a feeling of almost mental saturation, far too much to describe in the space of part of a book, but certain points can be clarified and may go some way to clear the minds of students in these matters.

First of all, by reason of the nuclear plant and the machinery which has been mentioned, for the first time man has been able to place himself beyond the need of the earth's atmosphere for unlimited periods while submerged.

Secondly, by reason of the immense reserve of electrical power which the nuclear energy source allows the submarine to generate, scientists have been given the scope to improve the sonar, passive and active, in a medium such as the sea, to an extent which puts the submarine at an advantage in relation to other ships.

Thirdly, some of the machinery and instruments have not been mentioned but it can be said that the vast size of the Polaris submarine offers plenty of space for any device which scientists may produce and which can assist the submarine in its operation, for example navigating under ice.

Fourthly, it should be mentioned that the shielding arrangements on nuclear reactors in Royal Navy submarines at least, are so efficient that when the boat is submerged and has a depth of sea water above it cutting off the natural radiation of the earth's atmosphere, the radiation levels to which the crew are then subjected from their own power plant are less than the radiation levels which are experienced when walking around on our ordinary business on the public highway.

It is the Royal Navy experience that long submerged patrols in nuclear submarines, whether they are fleet submarines or Polaris submarines, produce no unusual psychological results. Outsiders who have an opportunity to meet the crews, are particularly struck by this total normality on their coming ashore.

One interesting physiological aspect however is that when submerged in a submarine for up to two months with no opportunity to go up on the fin to look around, men become used to focusing the eyes at no distance greater than about sixteen feet and quite often substantially less, therefore at the end of a patrol officers and ratings alike are advised not to drive a motor car for at least twenty-four hours until their eyes are adjusted once more to focussing at longer distances.

POLARIS SUBMARINES: THE OFFICERS AND CREW

In the equivalent section in Part I it was possible to cover adequately the subjects of officers and crew in a few pages. This would be quite impossible in 1974. Today, just as the leap into the nuclear age has so profoundly affected the submarine in material and technology, so have these conditions imposed the need for officers and crew to undergo far more advanced mechanical and technical training than ever before, and so greatly increased the numbers needed to man a nuclear submarine, more than double those of a submarine of twenty years ago.

Of the two classes of nuclear submarines the Polaris and Fleet types, the Polaris has been selected to complement the 'Walk Through' described earlier. The description follows the pattern adopted in Chapter VI and opens with the numbers in personnel and their duties. In a Polaris submarine the crew consists of about 13 officers, 54 senior and 75 junior ratings.

To be Captain of this submarine it is necessary to hold the rank of Commander. The Captain must have had at least one previous submarine command, possibly a patrol submarine, and he may have been Executive Officer of a Polaris or Fleet submarine.

He will have completed a nuclear course at the Royal Naval College Greenwich, a Polaris course at Faslane, and a special submarine conversion course, as Polaris submarines have features different from Fleet and Patrol submarines.

Immediately under the Captain is the Executive Officer who is a Lieutenant-Commander. He will have completed the same technical courses as his Captain and he will have commanded a Patrol submarine. Also he will have had some Polaris and Fleet submarine experience.

Next on the Executive side is the Navigator who is usually a Lieutenant and a navigation specialist. He will have done the first two technical courses and he will have been Navigator of a Patrol submarine.

There are two more Seaman Officers[1], both Lieutenants. These are the Torpedo and Sonar Officer, and the Communications Officer. There is also a Supply Officer (who may keep a watch at sea as a Seaman Officer).

Six other officers can be grouped under the heading of Technical Department. On the propulsion and ship's system side there are four technical officers, a Lieutenant-Commander and Lieutenant Marine Engineer and a Lieutenant-Commander and Lieutenant Weapons Electrical Engineer. They will have all completed a long nuclear course at Greenwich and an operator's course at Dounreay, HMS *Vulcan*. One of the Electrical Officers will also look after weapon systems other than the Polaris system. In some cases, one of the two senior (Lieutenant-Commander) engineer appointments may be filled by a full Commander although this is unusual nowadays.

This being a Polaris submarine there are two officers for these special duties, a Lieutenant-Commander who is the Polaris Systems Officer and a Lieutenant

1 In passing, for the information of 'Old Timers', the term 'Seaman Officer' has been introduced during the last decade.

or Sub-Lieutenant assistant. These two officers will have done the basic Polaris submarine course and the long Polaris training course at Faslane. Last, but not least, there is the Surgeon Lieutenant. He will have done the submarine entry course at HMS *Dolphin* including the 100 foot tank, a course at the Nuclear Medical School, a Medical Officers' health physic course and a short run at Dounreay.

The Senior Rating in a Polaris submarine is a Fleet Chief Petty Officer and is known as 'Fleet Chief of the Boat'. He has assumed the duties of the Coxswain as the senior Senior Rating in the submarine and can be drawn from any branch.

Over the years there has been a considerable change in the nomenclature of certain skilled rates. For those who are not fully familiar with these changes it has been felt appropriate to enlarge on some of those which will be referred to in the description of the crew.

There have been artificers in the Navy since 1853 when Shipwrights became the first category to be established. For this good reason the term artificer has been retained and there are four artificer categories concerned with submarines. The following are their titles and duties:

The Marine Engineering Artificer. Operation and maintenance of all types of propulsion machinery. Responsibilities include mechanical and hydraulic systems and ship hull maintenance.

Control Electrical Artificer. Specialises in electronics and light electrical and mechanical engineering. Maintains sonar fire control, internal communication and compass equipment and computers which answer data for guided missiles.

Ordnance Electrical Artificer. Maintains electrical generators, motors and control equipment. Responsible for missile launchers, diving equipment, torpedoes and torpedo tubes.

Radio Electrical Artificer. Maintains radio and radar equipment including television. Responsible for transmitters and receivers which control weapons and assist navigation.

Nomenclature and duties of the other technical qualifications are self explanatory.

Thus, following the same route used in the 'Walk Through' and beginning with the torpedo space, here are a Petty Officer Torpedo and Sonar Instructor and an Ordnance Electrical Artificer 1st Class with his appropriate Leading hands and Junior rates. In the sound room itself there is a Petty Officer Underwater Control 1st Class and his team of Underwater Control and Sonar operators. In the adjacent compartment, the computer-filled sonar console space, there is a Control Electrical Artificer 1st Class and one or more Control Electrical Artificers, with appropriately trained mechanics to assist them.

Coming now to the galley, there is one Petty Officer Cook and he has four or more cooks of other rates to assist him. In the wardroom there is a Petty Officer Steward and he too has three other stewards to assist him. Also here in the midship part of the submarine, the stores space, the ship's office and

the sick bay are all provided for with Petty Officers and men of appropriate rates and training.

Moving aft, the technical side is again in evidence, and in the radar office, a Petty Officer Radar Plotter 1st Class presides over at least four radar plotters. Close by, the wireless office is a hive of talent and manned by a Chief Radio Supervisor and under him some ten radio operators of varying rates. Here also is a Radio Electrical Artificer 1st Class with a supporting team of technicians.

By now the walk has come to the control room. Besides the Seamen Ratings necessary for handling the steering and the hydroplanes, here there are men of all ranks and of many callings. These include Marine Engineering Artificers (Propulsion), Control Electrical Artificers, again with supporting ratings of varying rates. In the navigation centre there is a Control Electrical Artificer 1st Class and a Radar Electrical Artificer 1st Class and they are both supported by very strong teams of Petty Officer and Leading rate standards. The talent collected in the control room does not end here, as the Missile Control Centre is manned by a Chief Control Electrical Artificer and he again has a strong team of Petty Officers and other ratings to run the computers and associated instruments.

The missile compartment itself has two very senior Ordnance Electrical Artificers to man it, together with a number of Petty Officers and Leading hands, all technicians.

This ends the operational side of the manning and as the rest of the boat is concerned primarily with propulsion we come now to the domain of the engineers. In the manoeuvring room there is a Fleet Chief Engineer Artificer and numerous Marine Engineer Artificers and Control Electrical Artificers. The motor room, the main machinery space, the switchboard room and the turbo-generator room are all manned by appropriate Chief Petty Officers, Petty Officers, Leading rates and mechanics.

Together with the officers this is a long list, but it serves to show what it means in manpower to put this large nuclear submarine to sea on operational duty. While it is comparatively easy to list the men and their duties it has to be remembered that all have had to be trained, some over very long periods. For example, Senior Seaman and Engineer Officers will have been 70 weeks doing their courses before they can rise to the top positions. Chief and Petty Officers do a minimum of 17 weeks and all junior members of a crew do up to two months nuclear submarine training. Cooks and stewards manage with the least time, namely 5 weeks. The organisation to keep all this going so that the nuclear submarine fleet is always fully manned is a wonder of its own.

POLARIS SUBMARINES: ROUTINE ON PATROL

The life of a Polaris submariner is the most orderly in the Navy. It has well defined cycles which are rigidly adhered to. Every Polaris submarine is complemented for two crews known as the Port and Starboard crews. With the operational requirement to maintain at least one Polaris boat at sea on patrol

all the time, (bearing in mind that one probably will be out of service in refit) it is obvious that a Polaris submarine's time in harbour must be kept to the minimum. With two crews this is possible.

The patrol cycle begins when the signal is made that the new commanding officer has assumed command. This means that his crew is 'on' and takes over and prepares the submarine for the next patrol. As it is vital that the submarine leaves for its station at the appointed time, the 'off' crew augments the 'on' crew for as long as is necessary which is roughly a fortnight. To get on patrol requires an immense amount of hard work, not only from the 'on' crew, but the 'off' crew, and the whole base, including the first rate stores organisation, the experts in the machinery shops and the final checking up on training.

Towards the end of this preparation time officers and ratings experience a feeling of urgency to get to sea. This is very understandable and it comes as a relief in many ways to wives and families when the parting is over as they can then begin looking forward to their return again from patrol and the joy of another long leave.

The first few days of the patrol are taken up with getting to the appointed station and generally settling down. Only a handful of those on board are aware of the submarine's position and as far as families and friends ashore are concerned the submarine has disappeared for a couple of months. In the submarine not only is radio silence strictly observed but the boat remains dived for the entire length of the patrol, as the first consideration is to remain undetected.

The question which everyone ashore asks is 'What do you actually do all day?' The submarine is organised on a three watch basis so one third of every twenty-four hours is looked after by being on duty. Then there is time taken up by sleeping and eating. Probably quite a lot of every twenty-four hours is spent in the privacy of the bunk space where most men read a great deal. The permanent and exclusive bunk provided for each man is a great asset and means everything to him. By normal submarine standards the living conditions in a Polaris submarine are palatial, and in the communal living space the overall impression is of peace and quiet, with only the normal sounds such as ventilation and auxiliary machinery. Sometimes the quietness and stillness makes it difficult to believe the submarine is at sea and on operational duty.

As with most basically routine ways of life, food assumes an exaggerated importance. On the whole cases of complaint are few, as the fridges and provision stores have been carefully stocked to provide good quality and variety. In practice only a very fussy eater would be unable to find satisfaction from at least one of the choices available at each meal. Although the spaces in the submarine are larger than in any other class, exercise facilities are really non-existent, so the problem of dieting has to be considered by almost everyone. This can become almost an obsession with some men. In practice few put on weight during a patrol. As regards drinking, spirits are available in the wardroom and the senior ratings' mess but consumption is very modest and this

goes for the beer which is available to everyone.

On the domestic side, as explained in the 'Walk Through' account, there is always enough water for washing and showers and for laundry purposes. Liquid waste is easily disposed of by collecting it in various tanks and pumping it overboard when it is safe to do so. Solids are dealt with by compacting them into sheet metal containers. These are then discharged overboard from an ejector.

The removal of the carbon dioxide from the air and the replenishment of the oxygen has also been dealt with in the section on the 'Walk Through' and the result so far as living in the submarine is concerned is that it seems to be rather dry air. It does have a certain indefinable smell about it. Families speak of clothes smelling 'Nuclear Submarine'. The characteristics of the smell are made up of everything on board such as oil, hot machinery, cigarette smoke and cooking; even electronics appear to have an odour of their own!

Great care has to be taken to ensure that the atmosphere problem is not increased unnecessarily. For instance, aerosol sprays are forbidden, so are paints and metal polish. Shoe polish is also on the list of 'NOs' and quite a number of the officers and men wear sandals at sea.

Most of the ship's company bring some sort of hobby with them but the occupations which fill more of the time than any others are reading, watching films and playing cards and board games. Besides the main library there are additional small ones all over the submarine and in these paperbacks are easy to stow, and all manner of old magazines. Films are so plentiful that a new Films are so plentiful that a new one can be shown every day. The base film library reserves the most recent releases for the Polaris submarines and great trouble is taken to make sure that everyone has a chance of seeing them. There is a second showing for watchkeepers who missed the first one and if the film is very popular it is sometimes repeated at midnight. One amusing factor which has emerged from this is that when the submarine returns and the wife or girl friend asks to be taken to the latest film, almost always her submariner has already seen it.

The most important of all amenities for all on board is the weekly family-gram. The news from home has to be condensed into forty words. Families are issued with special forms before the submarine sails and much time is spent fitting in all that needs to be said.

Officers and men have an option on what particular news they wish to receive or have omitted. Besides the family-gram, members of the 'off' crew compile a broadcast of local news at the base and in Helensburgh and this too is sent once a week.

The internal contribution is principally in two forms. From time to time records and tapes are relayed around the living spaces and a newspaper is produced at intervals. The latter would be inexplicable to anyone not in the submarine's crew as it is chiefly concerned with life aboard and personalities. This is in no way a serious document and in fact its subleties and general

humour are in a class of their own.

Night and day become a slight problem on a two month patrol when dived all the time. In a way they are rather unimportant, but it is easy enough to tell which is which by the domestic routine and an actual impression of night is formed by switching passageway lights to red during night hours. This is done in the control room too, in order to preserve night vision if the submarine has to go to periscope depth. Broadly speaking days of the week have little significance but routine events such as Church and Captain's rounds remind everyone at least once a week in each case what day it is. From time to time on patrol the whole crew are made aware of what their presence in the ocean is all about by a full Polaris weapons system readiness test being carried out. This is originated by Headquarters or the Captain.

Missiles Operational Procedure. First of all it should be understood that each tube has three access doors through which the missile can be reached by technicians if need be. Each missile has its own built-in computers and precision control guidance system for flight control; each missile carries three warheads. There are many safety checks which are automatically performed by the computer while the missile is in flight so that a missile which has not flown properly will not arm.

Regular exercises are carried out to give all personnel involved the necessary practice in the complex missile operation procedures but there are a very large number of safeguards designed to ensure that the ultimate release of the missiles cannot be achieved accidentally or by a madman or group of madmen. Indeed a computer can stop the whole operation if there is a fault in the system or the drill.

First there is a message broadcast on the ship's address system from the radio room, 'There is a flash message on the broadcast'. A couple of seconds later when the radio room have seen a particular identification they report again on the main broadcast, 'The flash message is a firing message'. At this point the diving officer of the watch pipes 'Action stations missiles'. Nobody knows, not even the Captain, whether it is a simulated or actual firing instruction. The first message, the firing message, consists of a group of codes. This message is taken by two officers, usually the Executive Officer and the PSO who cross check data held in separate safes to which only they have access. After this authentication the two officers report to the Captain in the control room, 'The signal authenticates the message is a weapons system readiness test' OR ... It is only when the two officers make this report to the Captain that he knows whether or not it is a simulated weapons test.

'Action stations missiles' having been ordered on first receipt of the firing message, the boat is now piped to set condition 1SQ for weapons system readiness test. The procedures begin. In the control room and manoeuvring room (engine room) the submarine's depth, attitude and speed are adjusted to the optimum conditions for a Polaris launch. In the missile compartment, under the command of the assistant Polaris systems officer, the technical staff

are preparing the missile suspension system for the 1SQ launch condition, while the overall Polaris systems officer, with his team in the computer filled missile control centre are programming for the launch sequence. From another safe, the Captain draws two boxes of missile arming keys. These he passes to an officer who takes them to the missile compartment and hands them to the assistant Polaris systems officer. There is one key to each missile tube and until they have been inserted and turned the missile launching system cannot function. While the assistant Polaris systems officer (APSO) in the missile compartment and the Polaris systems officer (PSO) in the missile control centre receive a stream of verbal reports and watch the electronic indicators change to indicate the rapidly advancing readiness state of the weapons, the Polaris systems officer reaches under his desk to two small safes each with a combination lock. In one there is the black trigger which is used for exercises, in the other is the red trigger which would be used for an actual missile release. The Polaris systems officer positions his trigger on the end of its length of coiled flex close to his hand.

Finally, the PSO receives from APSO the report, 'Launcher ready 1SQ'. The PSO then checks his own displays and when they indicate total readiness of all parts of the Polaris system he passes a message to the Captain, 'Missiles in 1SQ'. Two final safety checks remain. Round the Captain's neck on a chain is a key to which only he has access. He places it in a keyhole in a missile readiness indicator panel but he does not turn it. Over the submarine's general broadcast he himself has to pass the message, 'PSO from Captain, you have my permission to fire'. On a separate intercom circuit to the PSO the Executive Officer, standing in the control room with the Captain, confirms the Captain's own message, 'You have the Captain's permission to fire'. Only then does the Captain turn his key to complete the final circuit and in the control room and in the missile control centre two green indicators light up. If it was 'for real' the missiles would begin to fire as the PSO pressed the red trigger.

Sometimes it seems ages since the submarine sailed. When all of a sudden, the realisation comes that the last few days of the patrol have arrived and it is then that time drags. For some this is a time for reflection on their responsibilities of the last two months. All through the patrol there has always been a possibility that some defect might occur in some important system or complicated equipment.

It is here that the full measure of experience, training and ingenuity would come into play. Now all that responsibility would be over in a couple of days and thoughts turn to families and friends. Not all the crew will be able to join their wives and friends immediately, as after a brief dockside meeting, many key members will be engaged in connecting up shore supplies of power, water and so on and preparing to shut down the reactor. There will be the missiles to disembark at Coulport too. When completed the homecoming crew will hand over to the other crew and then there will be a four day long weekend before they return to help the new 'on' crew. By then the patrol just com-

pleted will be fading from men's minds and thoughts will be turned to the prospect of long leave and three months as 'off' crew.

THE FLEET SUBMARINE. A COMPARISON: WEAPONS, AND EMPLOYMENT WITH THE FLEET

Many people have searched their minds for an analogy which would help in understanding the roles of the Polaris and Fleet submarines. Perhaps the nearest current suggestion is that the former is the bomber and the latter the fighter but in fact this is not a true comparison and very probably there is none.

The two roles are perfectly clear. The Polaris is a platform for a strategic missile, while the Fleet submarine is what its name implies, part of the fleet.

The Polaris submarine cannot deny command of the sea in any area, it cannot protect shipping, nor can it exercise any authority in the purely technical realm of sea power.

The Fleet submarine, on the other hand, provides a powerful offensive for the exercise of sea power. It can be used tactically and strategically providing a major force in the maintenance of the command of the sea. By virtue of its high underwater speed, its independence of external fuel and its ability to operate undetected, never disclosing its whereabouts, the possible presence of a Fleet submarine is a powerful factor which has to be taken into account by any Government seeking to change the balance of maritime power in any area of the world.

Its other roles are many: in particular (1) it can act unsupported against surface ships in controlled waters; (2) it is complementary to aircraft in anti-submarine operations in that the Nimrod aircraft 'locates', the Sea King helicopter 'pin points' and the submarine 'destroys'; (3) by itself it is also an extremely good anti-submarine vessel, greatly aided by its ability to carry the best sonar due to its size, its powerful nuclear reactor and its submergence; (4) it is capable of firing a variety of weapons from its torpedo tubes in support of a task force; (5) in carrying out these roles its silence is an advantage which no other vessel with the fleet possesses.

In peace time the primary work of the Fleet submarine is to practice attacking, shadowing, evading and reconnaissance. A balance has to be found between the exercise of these roles on individual anti-submarine work or combined work with the fleet.

The Fleet submarines could be fully employed on the above duties all the time but there are other calls on them as well. Occasionally the Americans ask for a submarine to work with them for a time and this is very essential from many points of view. Visits to foreign countries are fitted into the programme when possible and these are not so numerous as everyone would wish. Again a submarine may be required for quite a long period when a certain weapon has to be tried.

Employment with the fleet has opened a new phase in submarine operations.

Plate 33

Porpoise and Oberon Class conventional submarines alongside HMS Dolphin in early 1975

Trafalgar Day 1960. HMS Dreadnought immediately after being launched by Her Majesty the Queen at Vickers Armstrong's, Barrow

Plate 34

An aerial view of Faslane, HMS Neptune, the nuclear submarine support base

The Fleet submarine Warspite operating with a helicopter

HMS Swiftsure
starboard side view

MAIN ACCESS HAT

REACTOR COMPARTMENT

1 Rudders
2 After hydroplanes
3 Engine room
4 Escape hatches
5 Manoeuvering room
6 Air conditioning space
7 Control room
8 Junior ratings' mess
9 Wardroom and officers' cabins
10 Senior ratings' mess
11 Torpedo tubes
12 Hydroplanes

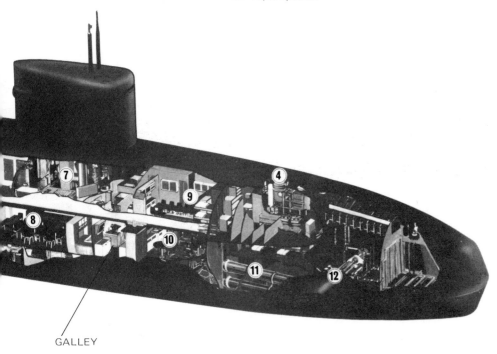

GALLEY

Plate 35

The Wardroom in HMS Valiant

The navigator checks his charts in the Control Room of a nuclear submarine.

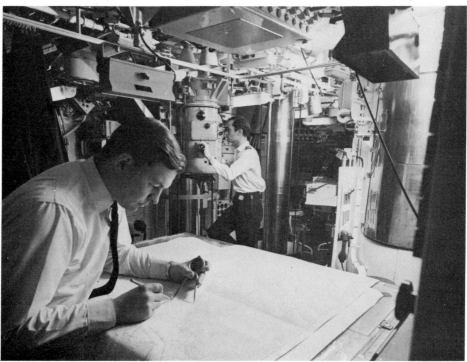

Plate 36

HMS Valiant. Steering and hydroplane control

Maintaining radar watch in the navigation area of HMS Sovereign's Control Room

Plate 37

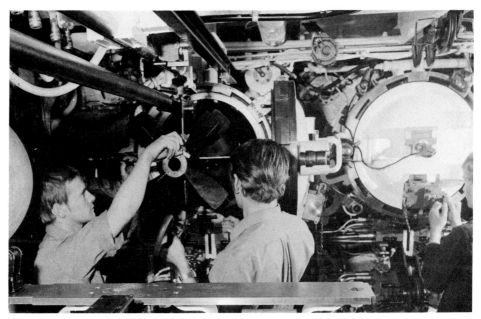

Loading a torpedo in the fore ends of a Fleet submarine

The Officer of the Quarters torpedo tube systems control panel in the forward ends of
a Fleet submarine

Plate 38

The systems control console in a Valiant Class Fleet submarine

Another Fleet submarine: the launch of HMS Churchill with one more building

It was *Dreadnought* which pioneered this when she went to the Far East in the second half of 1973. She spent more than six months away from British waters on a voyage which took her more than 40 000 nautical miles.

Dreadnought sailed from Faslane on 11 June to join the helicopter cruiser HMS *Tiger,* the *Rothesay* Class anti-submarine frigate HMS *Rhyl* and other fleet and fleet support units in the Far East.

For much of her time *Dreadnought* exercised under the operational control of Flag Officer Second Flotilla, Rear Admiral R P Clayton, maintaining company with the surface warships by continuous underwater cruising speeds in excess of 20 knots.

The Admiral gave a press conference about the operations and there is no doubt that what he said set the pattern for more and harder fleet exercises in 1974.

Admiral Clayton said that *Dreadnought's* patrol in company with the helicopter cruiser HMS *Tiger,* the anti-submarine frigate HMS *Rhyl* and other surface warships and fleet support vessels was the first time this type of group operation had been staged. He spoke about the strategic importance of having such a powerful force moving around together, especially in such areas as the Indian Ocean and went on to describe the success of the group deployment as 'Absolutely marvellous: something which, if only we'd had enough fleet submarines, we ought to have been doing years ago'.

'At least we've started', he commented, 'and certainly speaking as a non-submariner its the best thing that I've ever done. I think it has great hopes for the future. As soon as you have a Fleet submarine working with surface ships it enables you not only to keep yourself in training all the time, but also to develop procedures for working together and making the best use of the tremendously powerful potential you have with a Fleet submarine'.

With the new technology of Fleet submarines providing the commanding officer with such extended capabilities, all that he lacked was a torpedo weapon to match the sophistication of the rest of his equipment. This is now provided by the Mark 24 Torpedo, code-named Tigerfish, which has entered service in 1974. It provides a highly effective capability against submarines of all types. The development programme has included hundreds of successful test firings, using experimental, pre-production and final production models of the new weapon.

Tigerfish is some 21 feet long and 21 inches in diameter, and is propelled by low noise, contra-rotating propellers, designed at the Admiralty Research Laboratory, Teddington. Its electric propulsion system is powered by batteries of advanced design.

During its run to the target, Tigerfish remains connected to the firing submarine by a wire link, which is paid out both from the torpedo and the submarine. This method allows the wire to remain stationary and free from strain. The wire link enables the course of the torpedo, its depth and an appropriate mode of acoustic homing to be selected or changed as necessary

while the torpedo is on its way. When its sonar equipment has made acoustic contact with the target, the final phase of the attack is entirely automatic, the weapon homing on to the target in the already selected mode.

Explosion of the torpedo's powerful warhead is initiated either by a conventional impact fuse, or by a proximity fuse developed initially at the Admiralty Underwater Weapons Establishment, Portland. In the event of a near miss, the proximity fuse ensures the detonation of the warhead at the nearest point to the target.

Lead contractor for Tigerfish was Marconi Space and Defence Systems Ltd, under the direction of a special team in the Navy Department of the Ministry of Defence. Scientific support came from the Admiralty Underwater Weapons Establishment.

Significant design and development work was also carried out by the Plessey Company and other contractors, and Plessey is sharing in the assembly of the torpedoes. Final preparation for issue to submarines is being carried out by the armament depot at Coulport.

There are three variants of Tigerfish — the warshot, the exercise and the dummy. The warshot is the fully operational battle weapon. The batteries in this version were developed and manufactured by Chloride Industrial Batteries Ltd. The exercise version becomes buoyant at the end of its run for ease of recovery, and this version contains special instrumentation and recording equipment for post-exercise analysis. It is powered by a rechargeable battery made by SOGEA Batteries Ltd. The dummy is used to prove handling, stowage and discharge arrangements, as necessary, in advance of the deployment of the other, more expensive versions.

All three versions are in full production, a task currently being shared between Marconi and Plessey, with the involvement of other specialist firms. Submarines now have this very sophisticated and powerful weapon, something which will remind submariners of 1974.

Other sophisticated weapons are in an advanced state of development such as the USGW (under surface guided weapon), which is also fired from the torpedo tube but travels above the sea to its target.

Chapter fourteen
HMS Dolphin

THE SUBMARINE COMMAND

Ever since Admiral Sir Charles Little, when he was a Sub-Lieutenant, took over Fort Blockhouse in 1904 the Fort has been the principal base for the Submarine Command. It is true to say that the second paragraph on page 179 in Part I, is equally applicable today, twenty years later. So much seems the same right down to the last brick, but there will never be a last brick at Blockhouse! Buildings have been built, pulled down and rebuilt, and new buildings constructed ceaselessly for seventy years, and in this year no less a place than the Admiral's Offices are wrapped in scaffolding.

In the last twenty years, accommodation for officers and ratings has changed very much for the better; the Submarine School has been greatly enlarged and the main gate moved to the furthest extremity along the sea wall leading to Haslar and Alverstoke. A large portion of the playing field has had to go for building land. Many of the names on accommodation blocks and offices reminding submariners of depot ships and tenders of byegone days are still in use, typical of these are Hazard and Alecto. Also some new names, this time of officers, have made their appearance, notably Horton, which has been given to the Submarine School.

In the wardroom, Colonel Wylie's pictures depicting sailing ships, which were the original bearers of names associated with submarines, run before the wind from north to south in their large canvasses. In the hall and the ante-room specially painted portraits include those of Admiral Sir Max Horton and Commanders Wanklyn and Linton, both holders of the Victoria Cross who sadly did not survive the last war.

One part of Fort Blockhouse has not changed. This is the pretty rose garden which has survived stony soil and strong sea breezes for forty years or more. Across the road opposite it is something new, namely the Submarine Museum, which now houses most of the important relics, and is a great credit to the Curator, Lieutenant-Commander Frere-Cook. As always the little chapel on the battlements is looked after with loving care and a page of the Book of Remembrance turned daily.

From his office by the main pier the Flag Officer Submarines overlooks Haslar Creek where conventional boats of the First Submarine Squadron dominate the scene, though not very many at a time — so different from the days when five or six boats lay alongside each other in double trots, and half a dozen more secured further up the creek by the Instructional School.

The Admiral controls this increasingly important Command and deals with

policy, administration including personnel, bases and refitting. He also controls all operational programmes, which involves trying to sort out the jig-saw
puzzle of balancing operations with leave periods, training, maintenance and
refitting.

The submarine operations and training are covered in their respective
separate sections, but refitting in the nuclear age has assumed such large proportions and is so much the concern of the Flag Officer Submarines, that it is
necessary to add information on this subject. It was decided to provide nuclear
submarine refitting facilities at Rosyth, Chatham and Devonport.

Nuclear refits involve techniques and standards far in advance of those required for refitting conventional machinery. This applies both to Fleet and Polaris
submarines.

Rosyth was chosen to be the first nuclear refuelling and refitting dockyard
chiefly because of its relative remoteness from built up areas.

Mr Rowland Baker RCNC, later Sir Rowland Baker, was placed in charge of
the constructional development and Rear Admiral T C Ridley was appointed
technical adviser. Admiral Ridley later became Admiral Superintendent
Rosyth. It was these two who pioneered the whole complex of a nuclear refuelling and refitting base. In doing so they knew that if the plan was not right
then the answer would not be right and this required considerable foresight
and judgement. The facilities included nuclear core handling, nuclear refuelling
rigs and the design of a nuclear clean area. All the testing and trials arrangements had to be capable of sending a nuclear submarine to sea 'as good as
new'.

The nuclear refuelling station opened in June 1967 and was the first 'custom-
built' one in the western world. *Dreadnought* refuelled and refitted there in
1968 to 1970. This operation involved the highest technical ability. As well as
being the first, many of the techniques were being developed as the work progressed, and not the least of the worries was the health and safety of all
personnel taking part.

Meanwhile the Polaris Executive on which Sir Rowland Baker was the Technical Director, decided that Polaris submarines should be handled solely at
Rosyth. This was a natural sequence to the developments which had taken
place. Also Rosyth was best suited to take these very large submarines because
of its deep water approach, which meant that tides need not be taken into
consideration.

Apart from a date line which was a vital requirement, the refuelling and refitting of the Polaris submarines immediately brought further special problems, involving unique management and organisational techniques owing to
the absolute necessity, (because of only having four boats), of completing in
approximately one year, a task which would normally take two years or more.
In the event, when *Resolution* the first Polaris submarine came in for the first
refit, the whole job was completed in just over six months, for which the
Project Manager, Mr Charles Deane, was awarded the OBE.

Added to all the technical problems with which Rosyth Dockyard had to deal, there was the training of workmen in special techniques for both fleet and Polaris submarines. This has to go on more or less continuously to allow for wastage and so on. Once again let it be said that we learnt a good deal from the Americans, and in this case it is only fair to say that they learnt quite a lot from us too.

Chatham first built submarines in 1908, their first boat was *C17*. Ever since then Chatham boats have always been well built. Chatham has one disadvantage, namely the tides. Polaris submarines could not have been handled there because of the tidal docking and undocking complications, together with the large rise and fall of the tidal passage to and from the open sea. It would have been regrettable, to say the least, if all the expertise at Chatham and the tradition of all the work done there over the years had been overlooked. In fact the reverse has been the case and a complex has now been built there specially for refitting Fleet submarines, largely based on the experience of Rosyth.

The complex was opened on 29 June 1968 by Vice Admiral Sir Horace Law, a previous Flag Officer Submarines, at that time Controller of the Navy. This was an undertaking of major proportions, and like Rosyth it had to be finished, come what may, by a certain date. Some account of this is therefore necessary and the names of those construction firms which successfully completed the job recorded.

The development of Chatham Dockyard as a refitting yard for nuclear Fleet submarines was carried out under the direction of the Ministry of Public Building and Works. The programme involved the creation of a large complex very similar to much of Rosyth with very specialised mechanical and electrical plant facilities above and below ground. The basis was designed round docks 6 and 7 and consisted of a ten storey block housing offices, accommodation, welfare offices, security check points, workshop and storage area, and a health physics specialist department. Dominating the whole is an exceptionally large cantilever crane. This cost over £300 000, weighs about 1500 tons and is 160 feet high.

There were a number of unexpected difficulties in clearing the site, as old crane supports were found firmly embedded and yet the foundations had to be sunk to 100 feet before sufficiently firm ground to hold the whole structure was found. Much of the complex is in tunnels underground and all the complicated arrangements for handling nuclear reactors necessitated specially designed workshops and storage spaces. That this was all accomplished against a tight time scale was due to the excellent co-operation of all concerned with the Ministry and specially John Mowlem and Company Limited who designed the complex and carried out the main construction, assisted by Messrs Andrews, Weatherfoil and F H Wheeler.

Devonport. Before the main refitting and refuelling yard was designed and completed at Rosyth there was some hard thinking whether this should be at Devonport. In addition to the reasons given earlier the decision to go north

was also prompted by the difficulty at Devonport in acquiring the necessary ground. However, like Chatham with its years of naval history behind it, Devonport is now equally modern in every sense, and indeed more so because an operational squadron of nuclear and conventional submarines has been based there for sometime. Refitting and refuelling facilities for nuclear submarines are now being provided there too. In fact in 1974 Devonport, now called HMS *Defiance,* is a growing submarine base and a very important link in the chain of naval strategy.

JOINING SUBMARINES AND TRAINING: A GENERAL REVIEW
The Captain Sea Training has already been referred to in the section on Faslane in Chapter XII. His responsibilities of working up new submarines or new crews is only part of the whole training organisation. There is a big organisation at HMS *Dolphin* which has always been the 'home' of basic training and so it remains today.

Up to the nuclear age submarine training progressed in the gradual evolutionary way as boats became larger and submarining advanced. But since the advent of the nuclear age the whole of submarine training has suddenly become a vast and abnormally complex subject, and the greatly enlarged crews require a very high degree of technical ability and scientific knowledge.

Training is divided into two parts: that of the submarine personnel; the other with the fleet. The submarine squadron at *Dolphin,* together with those at Faslane and Devonport play an equal part in this in providing a mixed conventional and nuclear powered flotilla to meet the multitude of commitments which are presented from training and trials to C-in-C fleet tasks.

The training and trials with the fleet is a very heavy commitment, and as ever, the anti-submarine surface forces, the Fleet Air Arm and the RAF strike forces, need submarines all the time to co-ordinate with their own training. On the personnel side it is almost impossible to set aside submarines solely for personnel training as in days gone by, and only the officers' 'Perisher' course utilises boats earmarked especially for their needs, but these are drawn from conventional submarines of any squadron as the submarine programme dictates at the time and both officers and ratings have to gain their sea experience mostly under semi-operational conditions. Besides this, due to shortage of man power, trainees generally find they are 'part crew' and carrying out full submarine duties, rather than being 'additional for training'.

In broad terms, basic submarine training at *Dolphin* and at sea lasts about three months, at the end of which ratings get their submarine badge. This is something all are very proud to have and it is a great incentive to all new entries to get this as soon as possible.

Today the Submarine Service is sixty per cent volunteers and the remainder are conscripted. Lack of volunteers is understandable since naval careers in the surface fleet, or Fleet Air Arm, offer so much that is equally attractive. It must be said too, that the 100 foot tank at the Submarine School is a slight

Plate 39

HMS Resolution, Britain's first Polaris submarine, passing HMS Dolphin, the home of
British submarines

The torpedo tube line up in the fore ends of a Polaris submarine.

Plate 40

The Control Room of Resolution. In the background between the Captain (left) and Navigating
Officer is the Steering and hydroplane control

HMS Resolution. Steering and hydroplanes control

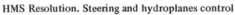

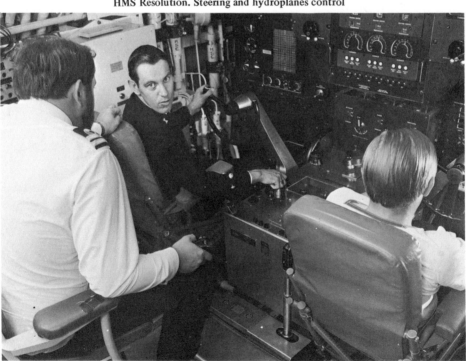

Plate 41

The missile computers of Resolution

The sonar watch closed up on the Type 2001 equipment of Resolution

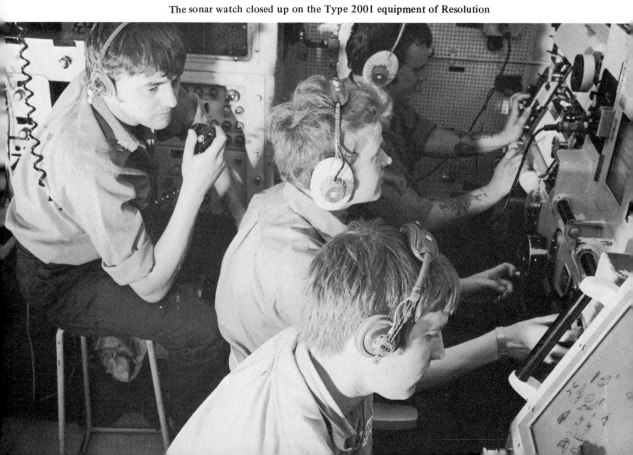

Plate 42

The missile systems control panel in the missile compartment of Resolution

The Polaris submarine
starboard side view

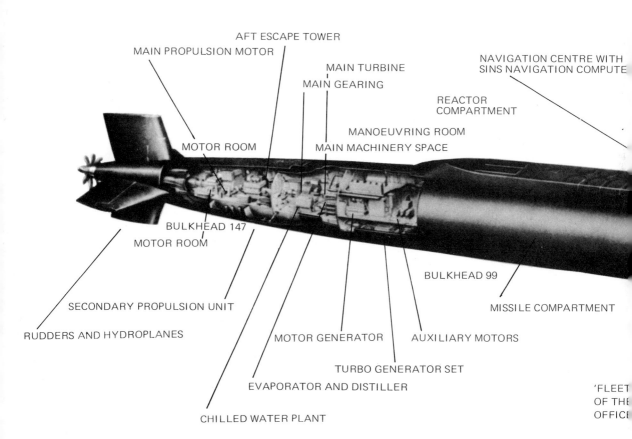

AFT ESCAPE TOWER

MAIN PROPULSION MOTOR

MAIN TURBINE

MAIN GEARING

NAVIGATION CENTRE WITH
SINS NAVIGATION COMPUTE

REACTOR
COMPARTMENT

MANOEUVRING ROOM

MOTOR ROOM

MAIN MACHINERY SPACE

BULKHEAD 147

MOTOR ROOM

BULKHEAD 99

SECONDARY PROPULSION UNIT

MISSILE COMPARTMENT

RUDDERS AND HYDROPLANES

MOTOR GENERATOR

AUXILIARY MOTORS

TURBO GENERATOR SET

EVAPORATOR AND DISTILLER

CHILLED WATER PLANT

'FLEET
OF THE
OFFICE

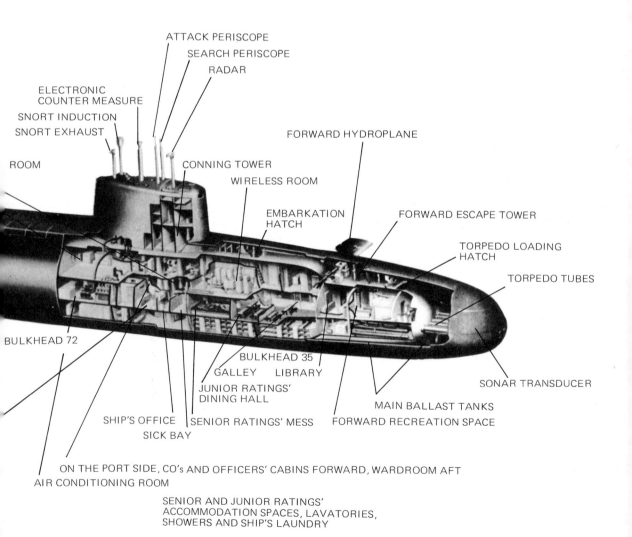

ATTACK PERISCOPE

SEARCH PERISCOPE

RADAR

ELECTRONIC
COUNTER MEASURE

SNORT INDUCTION

SNORT EXHAUST

FORWARD HYDROPLANE

ROOM

CONNING TOWER

WIRELESS ROOM

FORWARD ESCAPE TOWER

EMBARKATION
HATCH

TORPEDO LOADING
HATCH

TORPEDO TUBES

BULKHEAD 72

BULKHEAD 35

GALLEY   LIBRARY

SONAR TRANSDUCER

JUNIOR RATINGS'
DINING HALL

SHIP'S OFFICE   SENIOR RATINGS' MESS   FORWARD RECREATION SPACE

SICK BAY

MAIN BALLAST TANKS

ON THE PORT SIDE, CO's AND OFFICERS' CABINS FORWARD, WARDROOM AFT

AIR CONDITIONING ROOM

SENIOR AND JUNIOR RATINGS'
ACCOMMODATION SPACES, LAVATORIES,
SHOWERS AND SHIP'S LAUNDRY

Plate 43

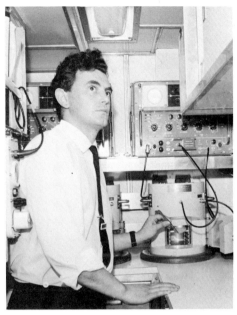

Commander Grant, commanding officer of Resolution's Port crew, inserts the key into the
Polaris systems panel in the Control Room, confirming 'Captain's Permission to Fire'
for a missile exercise

The health physics laboratory of Resolution

The Missile Control Centre in Resolution during a simulated missile firing exercise. In the
foreground is the Polaris Systems Officer holding the trigger grip which would be used to
launch the missiles in the event of a live firing

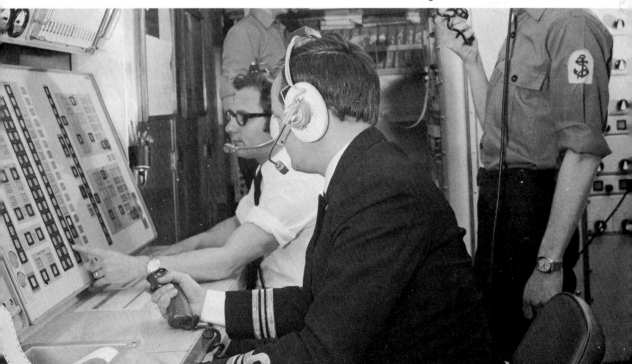

Plate 44

Chefs in the galley prepare lunch for Resolution's 143 man crew

Off-watch ratings relax over a game of chess in the forward recreation space of Resolution

deterrent, and there are rare cases where a conscripted officer or rating is temperamentally unsuited. Submarine service must be for a minimum of five years, and the fact remains that at the end of that time an average of ninety-seven per cent of those who have been conscripted wish to re-engage for further service in submarines, and of this the Submarine Service is rightly very proud.

All officers when they join the Navy, be it through the Scholarship Scheme, the Royal Naval College Dartmouth, or the University Cadetship, must sign that they are willing to serve in submarines if required to do so. This applies to Short Service entries as well, but these are precluded from commanding submarines.

Ratings can join the Navy from any school in the United Kingdom from as young as 16 years old and all have to sign that they are willing to serve in sub-marines. Young men are now entering submarines at 17 or younger immediately following their new entry training. Some boys at the naval schools, such as Shotley, (HMS *Ganges*), volunteer for submarines at 16, and go almost straight to a conventional submarine provided the boy is averagely intelligent. Unfortun-ately a few of the other young entries may have come from overcrowded schools and find difficulty in reading and writing, but this defect can be quickly remedied provided the boy is really keen.

Entry to the Navy is available to men up to the age of 33 depending on cer-tain qualifications and aptitude. Thus the Submarine Command may find itself with men between the ages of 20 and 33 joining, and quite a number of these may be artificers.

So far as joining submarines goes, it can be said that officers and ratings have one thing in common, namely that in practice there is no age limit. Volunteers will always be considered in the light of their past history and qualifications. Nor for long service officers and ratings is there any bar to those in the Sea-man Branch from reaching the coveted top, namely the submarine commanding officer. The rating attains this through the 'Upper Yardman' scheme by which he can become an officer provided he is selected between the ages of 17½ and 24.

A Few Particulars. During the latter half of the 1970s it is probable that the whole structure of submarine entry and professional training will undergo far-reaching changes. However as the purpose of this second edition of *The British Submarine* is to span the years 1954–1974, priority is being given to the outline and pattern of submarine training and entry as it has evolved so far following the leap from exclusively conventional submarines to the ex-treme complexities of the nuclear powered Fleet and Polaris submarines.

The Submarine School of today has evolved from the hutted training unit of days gone by to a highly impressive complex, with lecture rooms, demonstra-tion rooms and complete working sections of many of the submarine's basic systems, other than the Polaris and nuclear reactor sections. Of these two the former is centred at Faslane and the latter divided between Greenwich

and Dounreay.

New entry ratings do their training in three parts: *Part I* is a comprehensive introductory course lasting for four weeks. Whatever his calling, whether sonar operator, engineer or cook, he learns how a submarine works, what the safety rules are, and what is expected of every man in terms of team-work, inter-reliance and care. He also goes through his submarine escape training in the 100 foot water tower. At the end of Part I each entrant is streamed into Polaris, Fleet or Patrol class submarines, before going on to Part II which is technical training appropriate to the class of submarine for which he has been selected. *Part II* is also run by the Submarine School, some courses lasting as long as thirty weeks. During this time stokers, (now called marine engineers) go to HMS *Sultan,* which is the ratings engineers' school, radio operators go to HMS *Mercury* which is the RN communications establishment, and Polaris System technicians visit the Polaris school at Faslane. Whatever length of time these technicians visit the Polaris school at Faslane. Whatever length of time these courses have taken, at the end, trainees go on to *Part III* which is their sea training. Now for the first time they draw submarine pay. As has been mentioned earlier, few find themselves supernumeraries and most have to combine doing their job under supervision as well as overall sea training. The final test to become a fully qualified submariner takes place after sixteen weeks sea time with an oral examination arranged by the submarine's commanding officer. In the case of the Polaris submariner, he has to wait for his oral examination until after his first patrol. This is when all who pass these final hurdles are awarded the coveted submarine 'Dolphins' badge and put up their HM Submarines cap ribbon.

The fact that during this early training ratings have acquired special knowledge of one class of submarine, does not prevent them going to different class boats later on during their submarine time.

Training for officers follows much the same general lines as that for ratings up to the end of Parts I and II during which they too go through the 100 foot escape drill. They also follow certain specialised lines right from the start of their training. After this they have a stiff examination before a Squadron Board, and it is at this point that those who are successful are awarded their submarine badge. After this, officers switch about a good deal, too complicated to record here with advantage, and of course they do their Part III sea time. Officers' courses can be quite long, especially the engineers who do a long time at the officers engineering training establishment at Manadon. Also those working with the propulsion plant have the longest training, covering seventy-one weeks in all including thirty-two at Greenwich and ten at Dounreay.

This is all a far cry from the first fifty years of submarine history. For seaman officers however, there is one thing which never changes. This is the submarine commanding officer's qualifying course, the legendary 'Perisher'. This still remains the ultimate test of a hopeful submarine officer's fitness to become one

of the elite, the submarine CO. And it should be added here that there is one new facet in the requirements of a modern CO, namely that with the submarine becoming more and more part of the fleet, he has to be able to operate with surface forces, a technique which is still in its infancy.

Summary. In years gone by things were comparatively simple, now the complications are so great that there has to be 'continuation training' when boats are refitting, or crews are standing by boats building, so that officers and men can practice their jobs at the advanced electronic simulators, in the manoeuvring rooms at Faslane, and at the one-man control simulator at HMS *Dolphin*, to mention just part of it.

Finally, though certain basic things in submarines can never change, the modern technology and the many new demands which are made upon the talents and experience of the modern submariner calls for an academic and technical training unheard of two decades ago.

ESCAPE

Twenty years ago the 100 foot tank at Fort Blockhouse had just been built and the free escape method had been adopted. Some of the theory of the medico-physiological aspects of diving and the performance of the human body under severe conditions of high pressure oxygen, nitrogen and other gasses have been described in Part I and as this is a subject of very wide implications, a full acount of the last twenty years of further research regretfully cannot be added in Part II. However, as this short account of these latter years is given a certain amount of technical information is necessary, which it is hoped will meet the needs of most readers.

Following the *Truculent* disaster of 1950, a Standing Committee On Submarine Escape (SCOSE) was set up to assist in implementing the findings of the 1946 Ruck-Keen Committee. The most important finding of that committee was the recommendation to use a one man escape chamber, the theory being that the time during which a man remains under pressure must be reduced to a minimum, and a time of three minutes at 300 feet was considered the borderline.

Ten years passed during which the Royal Navy Physiological Laboratory built up an exhaustive volume of information covering possible escapes down to 600 feet. By 1960 design work on *Dreadnought* had reached an advanced stage and it was necessary to come to some decisions in the light of nuclear submarines, their operating depths and the depths at which escape might be practicable. It was decided that operations in the waters of the Atlantic Shelf should be considered and that at depths greater than this, individual escape would be impracticable and there could be no attempt at salvage.

Initially 600 feet was taken as a maximum target for possible escape as this was the maximum depth that research appeared to show would be practicable. At this point the SCOSE clearly needed more support, so it was decided that another review should be carried out in order to benefit in every way from

the ten years of highly technical research. A Committee was formed this time under the Chairmanship of Captain J S Stevens, DSO, DSC, an extremely experienced submariner. The meeting began in May 1963 and reported in November. By this time *Dreadnought* had been completed and there were other Fleet submarines under construction. Also four Polaris submarines had been ordered. This meant the matters under review were really urgent and the Committee made the following recommendations:

(i) Trials and development aimed at increasing the depth from which successful buoyant ascent was possible should be vigorously pursued.

(ii) That one man escape towers be fitted in *Porpoise* and *Oberon* Classes and that in future this method should be the primary method of escape.

(iii) Very close liaison with the United States should be established on escape methods, particularly so bearing in mind that the loss of the USS *Thresher* nuclear attack submarine on 10 April 1973 had led to much re-thinking on escape policy by the US Navy Deep Submergence Review Group.

Captain Stevens' Committee ended their report with sound principles which as ever need restating. They drew attention to the fact that submarines were primarily military machines designed to have the greatest efficiency in war. Lavish provision of escape or rescue equipment must inevitably reduce war potential and increase liability to destruction by the enemy. Something less than ideal escape arrangements must therefore be accepted and first priority must be given to accident prevention by sound design and construction, with high levels of compliance with design requirements and crew training.

The work of the Stevens Committee, coupled with the advent of nuclear submarines in the British fleet, and the reminder of dangers so clearly shown by the loss of the *Thresher,* brought about an intense effort to examine fully the three main questions posed:

(i) Could exposure times be found short enough to avoid the dangerous effects of nitrogen narcosis, oxygen poisoning and decompression sickness at, say, 20 atmospheres?

(ii) If such time existed, could men tolerate its imposition?

(iii) Could these conditions be achieved with reasonable freedom from excessive complications in a submarine under disaster conditions?

A full programme of trials was initiated. They were fascinating in detail but can only be summarised here. Experiments were carried out with animals and later on with human volunteers in simulated escapes down to 400 feet. As a result of these, trials were carried out in 1965 from *Orpheus* in the warm waters of the Mediterranean, when members of the Submarine Escape Staff from *Dolphin* surfaced from 500 feet. The success of these trials was clearly due to the short time from the start of pressurisation to arrival on the surface and in the case of the 500 foot trial the time was only 85 seconds.

Then came the really great moment when in 1970, instructors from the training tank in *Dolphin,* made ascents from *Osiris* off Malta from 600 feet. These dives were world records which were the culmination of many previous years'

work by Lieutenant-Commander L D Hamlyn, who was awarded the OBE. Lieutenant-Commander M Todd superintending the trials was awarded the MBE. All this had been made possible by improved escape towers and inflation suits resulting from the dedicated work of the Royal Naval Physiological Laboratory, members of the Royal Corps of Constructors and the instructors of the training tank in *Dolphin.*

As shown in the section 'A Walk Through a Polaris Submarine' the escape towers pass through the pressure hull to the inside of the submarine. The upper hatch is kept tight by heavy clamps, similar to the conning tower hatch, which can only be freed by an operating lever. For escaping the clamps are disengaged and the hatch is held shut purely by sea pressure, in the idle position, so that when the pressure in the chamber equals that of the sea water outside the chamber, the air in the tower is such that the hatch opens automatically. The tower is equipped with apparatus for supplying clean air at pressure and for flooding from the sea. There is a lower hatch by which the escaper enters the tower, and there is a sighting port so that those inside the boat can see inside the tower while the escape operation is in progress. The tower is lit by a salt water battery and watertight light bulbs.

The yellow immersion suit, which is put on before entering the tower is fastened by a strong zip, and the hood which has a perspex face is passed over the head and has its own zip. This zip is rather stiff and if an escaper on arrival at the surface cannot manage to unzip the hood, there is a rip-strip which by being pulled will release the hood. The suit is fitted with a lifejacket called a stole. Its purpose is firstly to carry the escaper to the surface and then to act as a lifejacket. There is a pocket in the suit which carries a salt water battery supplying power for a light which is on the outside of the suit, and another which carries gloves which the escaper can put on to keep his hands dry and warm when on the surface. He is also supplied with a whistle and polaroid glasses. The arrangements in the tower and mechanical fittings outside it are called the Hood Inflation System, because the hood is the all important factor. The suit in use today is the Escape Immersion Suit Mark 7.

To escape, a man enters the tower through the lower hatch and connects his suit to the Hood Inflation System by a simple push-in plug. Through this he receives air at one pound per square inch above the pressure in the submarine at that time. The lower hatch is then shut for him and the tower is flooded from the sea. The pressure in the tower is then doubled every four seconds until it reaches sea pressure, for example from one atmosphere to sixteen atmospheres in sixteen seconds. The tower is calibrated to achieve this pressurisation rate at any depth without adjustment or action by the escaper. During this phase of the escape the Hood Inflation System supplies air at one pound per square inch more than the sea pressure, first inflating the stole or lifejacket and then through two relief valves it provides air for the hood. However fast the pressure builds up in the tower, the hood remains with a comfortable airlock by which the escaper breathes. When the tower pressure

equals that of the sea, the upper hatch opens, and the natural buoyancy of the escaper then allows him to float upwards. The air connection to the submarine escape air supply disengages and immediately seals itself. The whole operation takes place because of the man's natural buoyancy.

The ascent is instantaneous and is completed at 8.5 feet per second. The escaper breathes naturally as he goes up from the air pocket in the hood which reduces pressure automatically to half pound per square inch above that of the sea. On arrival at the surface the hood is removed and the suit protects the escaper from exposure or drowning.

The personnel inside the submarine then wind the top hatch shut again – they can see what is happening through a direct vision panel in the bottom hatch – the water in the chamber is drained down and it is ready for the next man to enter.

The last man to escape works the mechanism himself and there are special fittings for this.

Sufficient immersion suits are carried for all members of the crew and with some to spare near each hatch. Two complete sets are supplied so that if all the crew are either one end or the other of the submarine all can still escape.

Four hundred practice escapes at sea, over one hundred by volunteers from submarine crews, have proved this to be the safest and best escape method in the world. It is used in its Royal Navy form by many navies all over the world. Besides this, over 18 000 ascents by this method have been made by men under training from 90 feet. In fact, the system has been so well proved that submariners have complete faith in it. Nevertheless, this does not mean that no more work is being done on further research. While 600 feet is now considred to be absolutely safe the continental shelf is much deeper than this in many places and there is plenty of research and experimental work ahead for all concerned.

Chapter fifteen
Strategy

THE BRITISH SUBMARINE IN 1974
AND ITS PLACE IN NAVAL STRATEGY

Updating *The British Submarine* from 1954 to 1974, has so far concerned the advances in material, technology and scientific inventions applicable to the Submarine Service during these twenty years. In this final chapter the intention is to discuss briefly in the light of these advances, the present strategic thinking, and to define the place of the submarine in the resultant naval policy.

Overall British naval policy is based on the Western Alliance, and the British submarine force makes an important contribution to it. It has to be recognised that our island is uniquely dependent on the use of the sea and our relatively large maritime interests. Also it has to be acknowledged that the maritime environment in the next few decades is likely to be a very turbulent one.

In stating these broad considerations on which our naval strategy has to be formed, new factors in maritime affairs have come into play. One is that naval vessels of most countries, however small, are now armed with weapons of such sophistication that few can be ignored. As an example of this, in 1967 the Israeli destroyer *Elat* was sunk by two Styx missiles fired from over the horizon from an Egyptian fast patrol boat.

The principal factor however is the rise and the forward deployment of the Soviet Navy. Their fleet is now greater in size than that of any other nation other than the United States. This is notably so in the case of nuclear submarines, the growth of which has gone quite a long way towards swinging the balance of maritime power in their favour. The deployment of their navy is becoming increasingly world wide, such as their growing naval presence in the Indian Ocean, Admiral S G Gorshkov, the Commander-in-Chief of the Soviet Navy, in one of his eleven papers on sea power, the last of which appear-in 1973, stated:

'Those countries that have strong navies are rich and powerful and those that neglect their navies are doomed to decay.'

In another passage the Admiral looks to the future when he enlarges on the growing importance of the oceans as a source of raw materials and food. He states:

'Whereas in the nineteenth century the big international question was that of dividing up the dry land of this planet, now it is the division of the sea.'

To cover these considerations, British naval strategy in 1974 is primarily formed on the policy of 'Deterrence'. The general pattern is that we should

be capable of providing a 'presence' which would give a low level 'response' to aggression. The aggressor then would have to decide whether to 'escalate' or 'back down'. If he does the former then we would have to bring in a backing of higher quality forces. Depending on the attitude of the aggressor this could mean eventually calling on our allies for more cover. If the reasoning of the potential aggressor is sensible, he will conclude that there is no more advantage to be gained by taking further aggressive action, and our strategy will have deterred.

Our Strategy of Deterrence is designed so that naval forces can interpose where an aggressor appears to be considering hostile intervention to further that country's political aims, and to respond to a call for support in the face of a threat to the security of an ally. In both cases the object is to obtain local or temporary command of the sea. Bearing in mind the dependence of this country on our sea communications, the strategy includes, should the need arise, provision for command of the sea in the vicinity of merchant ship convoys.

The availability of ships in the British Navy to carry out this strategy provides for a 'balanced force' of all principal types. Here, almost for the first time, the British submarine takes its place as a powerful unit of the fleet acting in conjunction with surface forces.

The principal ships are: minesweepers and minehunters, frigates, destroyers, guided missile destroyers, cruisers, and now submarines. In addition the aircraft carrier *Ark Royal* is still operational and the RAF Strike Command provides the all important Nimrod antisubmarine aircraft together with Buccaneers and Phantoms in support of submarines individually and of the 'Balanced Force'. In the case of the submarines, there are twenty-one Patrol and eight Fleet.

In order to maintain our strategy it is necessary to keep up the quality of the fleet. This is done by a rolling programme of new construction which at present includes the Type 42 guided missile destroyers and Type 22 frigates. These ships come into service as the older types retire at the end of their useful lives. Of the large ships, the through deck cruiser *Invincible* is currently building. All new ships are designed to carry the very latest surface-to-air and surface-to-surface weapons and helicopters. There is also a rolling programme to increase the number of Fleet submarines. These submarines are a vital ingredient in the deterrent strategy and a force of at least fifteen is needed.

As each local or world situation develops, the combination of surface ships, aircraft and submarines to mount the necessary 'presence' has to be determined. The principal areas where our interests lie are: Home Waters; the Atlantic; the Mediterranean; and the Indian Ocean. With the Navy reduced to such small numbers, and the commitments so wide, deployment is necessarily thin. This prompted a statement by the Under Secretary of State Defence (Navy) in 1973, in which he said:

'The Navy had adopted a strategy of a very limited "presence" which could be increased by moderately powerful forces'. This still applies in 1974.

In this strategy British submarines have a very important part to play. Their different roles have been fully stated in Chapter XIII but because of the importance of these roles it is as well to repeat them here in brief form. The Polaris submarine is the ultimate deterrent. It provides the final backing to our higher quality forces in the face of a potential opponent and although fully, (normally), committed to NATO, is available to support (unilateral) national policy when supreme national interests are at stake.

The Fleet submarine on the other hand plays a key position in purely naval strategy. It is basically a 'sea denial' vessel and a very good one. Its job is primarily against enemy submarines, secondly against surface raiders and thirdly always being ready to operate with the surface fleet to 'deter'. It has great offensive power through sophisticated weapons. It is relatively invulnerable through its silence and it has very high speed through its nuclear reactor.

In common with us, Admiral Gorshkov also advocates a 'balanced fleet', and in the case of their submarines we are told, they are 'continually sliding down the slipways of the USSR in a steady stream'.

This brings the strategic considerations full circle and back to the Western Alliance. The United States still shows massive strength and much of this through her submarine fleet. At present she can deploy fifty-six fleet submarines and forty-one Polaris boats. Her forward base for both types of nuclear submarines in the Holy Loch in Scotland, is a corner stone of the naval strategy of the Alliance.

We in Great Britain have our obligations, not only to the Western Alliance but to the safeguarding of our own shores. We have had plenty of warning from history of what can happen when we reduce our Navy beyond certain well defined strategical requirements. We have had ample evidence of what enemy submarines can do. In 1917 this country was on the point of surrender, and again in 1944 the German high speed submarines were about to appear and in sufficient time could have reduced this country to a desperate situation. There is so much which concerns us as a maritime nation, and it has been clear for some years that we cannot adequately defend our extensive sea communications without the help of our allies. It is essential however that we should play our full part by contributing in greater numbers of vessels. With the growth of the Soviet Navy, and in particular their numbers of nuclear submarines, our very lifeline could be threatened. We must begin to think in terms of a third Battle of the Atlantic and time is not on our side.

The vessel which can best protect us against enemy submarines and surface raiders is the Fleet submarine and of these, as has been stated, we have only eight. Our present modest building programme at least must be maintained, whatever the cost, and provision made for speeding up in our building yards to increase numbers rapidly in the event of a crisis. These submarines must be supplied with the best and latest weapons, to give them the means to carry out their vital task.

Today the British submarine holds a greater responsibility as a man-of-war

than ever in its seventy years. In the four Polaris and eight fleet submarines, together with a squadron of patrol submarines, we have a well built force excellently maintained. They are manned by the best officers and men in the world, trained to the highest standards and all concerned realise they have a real purpose in the defence of this country, and their keenness and morale could not be better.

What is needed now is the means of fulfilling our naval strategy, by our submarines taking their new found place in the Navy in sufficient numbers to enable them to carry out their vital and decisive part.

UNDER THE WATER: THE PROGRESSION IN SUBMARINE WARFARE
In 1967 Admiral of the Fleet Sir Michael Pollock, GCB, MVO, DSC, ADC, then a Vice Admiral, was Flag Officer Submarines. Before leaving that Command he wrote a paper under the above title. In March 1974 he relinquished active service after having been First Sea Lord, the highest position in the Royal Navy.
That part of the paper which deals with the advance into the nuclear age is reproduced here. Although seven years after it was written Sir Michael considers that what he wrote then to be equally applicable today.
It is with great pleasure that with the full approval of the Admiral of the Fleet these paragraphs are reproduced. They form a fitting climax to this review of the last twenty years of the history of the British submarine.

The Nuclear Powered Vessel.
It is important to understand why the introduction of this method of propulsion was so revolutionary in the field of underwater warfare.

The submarine has always been vulnerable to surface forces because of its need to have contact with the surface of the sea to replenish its atmosphere and recharge its underwater propulsion system.

There had always been a conflict in design created by the different characteristics required when operating on the surface and when operating submerged; the very shape of the hull could not be optimised for both, and because of the limited weight and space available for propulsion, the requirement for speed and endurance was not reconcilable within the same hull for both submerged and surface conditions.

The True Submarine. With nuclear power the true submarine became at last a

realisable prospect. Developments were now possible in air purification and conditioning, to a sophisticated navigation system depending on gyros and accelerometers rather than observations of astronomical or earthly reference points, to new steels, new welding techniques, new standards of precision engineering and greatly improved submerged sensors.

The dream of Jules Verne thus became capable of construction and Captain Nemo's *Nautilus* of fiction became translated into fact and sailed under the United States ensign.

With almost unlimited endurance, with a submerged speed greater than most surface ships under calm conditions and than all in rough weather, wholly divorced from contact with – and hence detection on – the surface of the sea; capable of evading the most advanced sonar by outrunning its carrier; or attacking any ship at a time of its own choosing and, if unsuccessful, of withdrawing and returning to repeat the attack; capable of following a hostile force in periods of tension until required to intervene; here was a new concept of undersea operations made possible by this revolutionary advance in technology and seeming set fair to replace all other forms of maritime power.

Search for a Weapon. Of course it proved not to be entirely so – at least in the early years. The propulsion system proved astonishingly reliable, the vehicle met all demands made upon it. But the weapon was lacking; it was as if the Chieftain tank had been armed with a two pounder gun, the supersonic fighter with a machine gun.

The torpedo, an effective weapon for certain limited purposes, could not, by its very nature, meet some of the future applications which this remarkable war vessel had made possible, and in others could not match the performance of above water weapons.

For the same reasons that sonar is so much less effective a sensor than the comparable above water systems which depend on electro-magnetic rather than sonic emissions, so is the weapon itself limited; the sea is a less homogeneous, singularly opaque and immensely variable medium compared with the ether.

Propulsion: hull: weapons system: the trio which has always dictated the state of the art in submarine warfare. Propulsion was now far ahead of both the others; hull design and systems were adequate to support the new development for perhaps several decades; weapons lagged behind.

So there began in the late fifties a most interesting diversification of the weapons fitted in submarines which lifted them out of the tactical and into the strategic field.

Vehicle for Ballistic Missiles. As the result of the most important diversification, the 'Polaris' ballistic missile system, the submarine at present provides the most invulnerable second strike capability so far devised.

In another application in the tactical field, a threat to the carrier strike force concept analogous to that presented to the battle fleets by the carrier force of thirty years ago is now also in service.

The United States Navy has led the way in the development of the strategic weapon; the Soviet Navy, as a substitute for a sea borne air strike capability, leads in the tactical application.

Following their traditional view that the submarine is primarily an anti-submarine weapon, the British have concentrated on developments in their use in this role.

The Strategic Deterrent. The strategic Polaris ballistic missile system was revolutionary, not only in sophistication and reliability but in the speed in which it was introduced into service.

The system was developed in the astonishingly short period of five years and the first missile was fired from the *George Washington* little more than two years after she had been laid down in early 1958.

The submarine has acquired a new role – that of making a vital contribution to the strategic deterrent, in which capacity its mobility and invisibility render it in the forseeable future virtually invulnerable.

The Tactical Field. In the tactical field, weapon development has been led by the USSR, in pursuit of their traditional role of defence of the homeland – in this case from the potential threat of nuclear attacks launched from the carrier task forces of the Western Powers.

For this role the developed weapon is a cruise type rather than a ballistic missile, although they are also developing the latter for the strategic role.

Diversification of methods of defence has led them to mount such a missile in surface ships as well as submarines, and in the case of the latter, both in nuclear and conventionally powered submarines.

The British Contribution. The British contribution to the developments made possible by the introduction of nuclear propulsion has been in the field of silencing the propulsion machinery and fitting an excellent sonar set which can be used in direct cooperation between surface forces and a nuclear power-ed submarine in defence of a task force or convoy.

Until nuclear propulsion gave the submarine the capability to keep up with a surface force while remaining submerged, and until underwater communications became sufficiently reliable for continuous contact with the surface force to be maintained, close company operations between submerged and surface forces had been virtually impossible, and when essayed, had proved disastrous.

Technological progress has, once again, permitted what was impracticable and concerted operations are now well established practice in the British Navy.

Diversification of Roles. In the course of the last fifteen years the submarine has therefore greatly diversified her roles to make best use of the increased capability that nuclear propulsion has provided.

The traditional roles of attack on shipping, whether merchant or warship, remain with the balance heavily tipped for the moment in favour of the nuclear powered attack submarines.

Patrol and surveillance, blockade and shadowing can all now be carried out

with greatly enhanced efficiency, while to these roles have been added the totally new ones of strategic nuclear deterrence, long range tactical strike at ranges hitherto possible only for aircraft, and finally, increased capability for operation in direct support of surface forces.

The effect of this dramatic improvement in performance and diversification of capabilities is that, at this present moment, the nuclear powered submarine has far outstripped the ability of other forces to combat it; in its varied forms it is becoming the most formidable unit of the maritime power game.

The precise balance between this and other essential ships and aircraft will vary over the years and in different navies, but as advanced methods of detection and reconnaissance, by satellite or other space body, of the earth's surface become more and more effective and continuous, the possibility of concealment will become exclusive to the submarine and the balance of the larger navies will certainly shift towards the deployment of a greater proportion of their weapon systems underwater.

Exploitation of Inner Space. A parallel trend towards a more intensive exploitation of what has been called 'inner space'—that vast proportion of the earth's surface which lies under the sea—will also accelerate the pace of underwater development.

Not only is there great mineral wealth under the seabed but also the largely untapped potential for food production of the sea itself which will be developed as the human race relearns the lesson that early man learnt on land; that it is more profitable to be a farmer than a hunter.

The signposts pointing to this are already clear; whether it be in the diversification of aerospace firms into underwater projects or the growing forest of oil and gas rigs operating on suitable areas of the continental shelves at ever increasing depths.

Current progress in underwater physiology and diving expertise indicates that man may be able to live on the seabed for extended periods and divers to undertake useful work down to 1000 feet.

The commercial impetus of these activities will create a demand for underwater vehicles of many types for a wide variety of purposes. The place of the submarine in the future seems assured.

Submarine Now Weapon of Stronger, Not Weaker Powers. In parallel with the discontinuity in tactics and warlike potential caused by the introduction of nuclear propulsion, has come a comparable break in the historical pattern of submarine development.

Through all its earlier history the submarine was the weapon of the weaker power since it offered the opportunity of operating effectively in areas under hostile control and some possibility of countering an otherwise overwhelming maritime superiority.

It is probable that this is no longer so and that the building, operating and support of nuclear powered submarines is so expensive and technologically advanced a process that they will take the place, held by the strike carrier in

the forties and fifties, as the prestige and power focus only of the large navies of the world.

This will be brought about not only because of the initial monetary cost, but because the highly trained men required to maintain and operate them are not so easily provided and the extensive and sophisticated installations necessary to refit and refuel even one modern nuclear powered submarine represent a formidable capital investment for any country.

Thus the nuclear powered submarine which will comprise the central strike capability of the major navies can only be included in the armoury of a nation with an advanced technology, well educated manpower and the will to devote a substantial slice of both to the operation and support of their maritime forces.

It is significant that, to date, only the USA, the USSR and the UK are building a substantial number of nuclear powered submarines and there is evidence to suggest that the effort and money required to develop and sustain a force of nuclear powered submarines could have a detrimental effect upon the balance of forces in smaller navies.

Maritime Power from Undersurface Warships. It is probable that we have now reached a point in history where the exercise of maritime power will come more and more to depend on the striking power of undersurface warships.

That, within this century, the navies of the world will all operate submerged, seems highly unlikely: the cost effectiveness equation of nuclear power and underwater passage coupled with the problems of entering, training and retaining crews to operate what would inevitably be highly complicated ships, when compared with their surface equivalents, does not produce an attractive answer in the case of merchant shipping.

Trade will therefore continue to move on, rather than under, the sea and surface warships will be needed to protect it from a variety of threats.

The Ultimate Arbiter. It is as one moves up the scale of escalation of threats that the nuclear powered submarine becomes the inescapable deterrent backing which other maritime forces must have in order to exercise maritime control: this is why they are increasingly referred to as the 'capital ship'—that ultimate arbiter on which maritime strategy has always depended.

Held in successive generations by the line-of-battle ship, by the battleship and then by the aircraft carrier, this role of the capital ship will be exercised more and more from under the surface where, for a long time to come, the elements of concealment and hence surprise will still persist, and are now allied to unlimited mobility and developing weapon systems.

The New Capital Ship. As has always been the case, the new capital ship will be expensive and hence few in number for all but the super powers.

The diversification of roles into different hulls, which has already started with the specialisation of the strategic missile carriers, may well continue and this will accelerate the process of designing the hull, propulsion and weapon systems as an integrated whole so that the characteristics and capabilities of each are in balance.

In parallel with the case for installing the nuclear powered submarine as a diversified capital ship of the future, must be examined the continuing requirement for a supporting cast of less expensive and less sophisticated ships as has always been found necessary in the past.

Exploration On The Continental Shelves. The growth of exploration and exploitation activities on the continental shelves, particularly in the shallow areas, will strengthen the requirement for a propulsion system of economic cost for the many underwater vehicles which will be required.

Both for commercial activities themselves and for requirements likely to arise out of them, such as for emergency or rescue services, the submarine will have its part to play.

If agreement should eventually be reached on international regulation of activities on the seabed, there may also be a requirement for vehicles to carry out underwater inspections: here, too, the submarine is likely to be the most suitable vehicle.

Need For Improved Conventionally Powered Submarines. Indeed, there seems every reason to believe that many of the tasks arising from developments in underwater exploitation will best be met by conventionally propelled submarines, since, for many years, they will be cheaper and simpler to build and operate.

This, and military requirements, will depend upon another breakthrough in technology to replace the present diesel/battery propulsions system with one which will offer at least some of the advantages of nuclear propulsion at a far less cost, and perhaps, be capable of operation by less highly qualified officers and men.

There are many potential contenders for this breakthrough: the HTP turbine to which reference has already been made: the fuel cell to replace both battery and charging agent: or even a closed cycle diesel.

Any of these, allied to the advanced hull shapes already in use for second generation nuclear powered submarines, could produce an immense improvement in performance compared with any conventionally powered submarine at present in service or under construction.

So far none have shown sufficient saving in costs when compared with a nuclear plant to make their reduced capability acceptable, but there is undoubtedly a need for a submarine designed on these lines both to supplement the nuclear propelled capital ship of the major navies, and to provide the smaller navies with the essential benefits of a submarine capability without leading to a gross unbalance in the proportion of resources devoted to it.

Submarines Of The Future. Up to the end of the century it is possible to forecast the pattern of underwater warship design with reasonable assurance.

On the assumption that there will be no agreement on a comprehensive disarmament treaty, there will be a continuing need for submarines capable of delivering strategic nuclear weapons.

The vehicle will be a 'true submarine' to avoid all possibility of detection; large, to give crews good living conditions which long patrols demand; extensively automated to reduce the number of crew to a minimum; and designed to survive by concealment and evasion.

There will also be a continuing requirement for a diversified force of 'capital ships' to provide support and backing for surface forces.

These, too, will be true submarines and their role will be to counter other submarines and to provide a major strike capability against surface forces.

The conventional submarines' role will be two-fold. It will remain the essential underwater component of the maritime forces of the smaller navies and, outside the military sphere, it will be used in tasks arising out of commercial exploitation of the seabed.

Until The Third Millenary. It may be argued that the foregoing is no more than the projection of current functions of a maritime power into a generally underwater environment. This is not denied because the functions stem from the roles and the roles from the human characteristics which make warlike forces necessary: by 2000 AD, which is as far ahead as it is sensible to project even such a vision as this, there seems little reason to suppose that either human characteristics or the principles of war will have changed to such a degree as to make some totally new concept credible.

Appendix

Appendix I

Inspecting Captains of submarines
Captain R H S Bacon, DSO
21.10.04 Captain E Lees
12.11.06 Commander S S Hall (Captain 31.12.07)
14.11.10 Captain R J B Keyes, MVO

Flag Officers (submarines)
31. 8.12 Commodore R J B Keyes, CB, MVO
 8. 2.15 Commodore S S Hall, CB (Rear-Admiral 18.7.19)
18. 8.19 Rear-Admiral D L Dent, CBE, CMG
15. 8.21 Rear-Admiral H F P Sinclair, CB
 1. 9.23 Rear-Admiral W S Nicholson, CB
 1. 9.25 Rear-Admiral V H S Haggard, CB, CMG
 1. 9.27 Rear-Admiral H E Grace, CB
 2. 9.29 Rear-Admiral M E Dunbar-Nasmith, VC, CB
 2. 9.31 Rear-Admiral C J C Little, CB
10.12.32 Rear-Admiral N F Laurence, DSO
10.12.34 Rear-Admiral C P Talbot, CB, DSO
10.12.36 Rear-Admiral R H T Raikes, CB, CVO, DSO
15.12.38 Rear-Admiral B C Watson, CB, DSO
 9. 1.40 Vice-Admiral Sir Max K Horton, KCB, DSO, (Admiral 9.1.41)
 9.11.42 Rear-Admiral C B Barry, DSO
12. 9.44 Rear-Admiral G E Creasy, CB, CBE, DSO, MVO
 1.11.46 Vice-Admiral M Mansfield, CB, DSO, DSC
 8. 4.48 Commodore B Bryant, DSO, DSC
23. 8.48 Rear-Admiral G Grantham, CB, CBE, DSO
20. 1.50 Rear-Admiral S M Raw, CB, CBE
 4. 1.52 Rear-Admiral G W G Simpson, CB, CBE
 9. 2.54 Rear-Admiral G B H Fawkes, CB, CVO, CBE
 7.12.55 Rear-Admiral W J W Woods, CB, DSO
12.11.57 Rear-Admiral B W Taylor, CB, DSC
24.11.59 Rear-Admiral A R Hezlet, CB, DSO, DSC
31. 7.61 Rear-Admiral H S Mackenzie, CB, DSO, DSC
23. 1.63 Commodore E J D Turner, DSO
28. 5.63 Rear-Admiral H R Law CB, OBE, DSC
27. 5.65 Rear-Admiral I L M McGeoch, DSO, DSC
28.12.67 Vice-Admiral M P Pollock, CB, MVO, DSC
10.11.69 Vice-Admiral J C Y Roxburgh, CB, CBE, DSO, DSC
 2. 9.72 Vice-Admiral J A R Troup, DSC*
 2. 7.74 Vice-Admiral I G Raikes CBE, DSC

Appendix II
Submarine tree

Completion date of first of class	Type	Length (in feet)	Displacement Surface	Submerged	Hull ballast tanks	Engines
1901	Holland	63.25	105	120	Single	American petrol
1903	A	100	165	180	Single	Wolseley petrol
1905	B	143	285	313	Single	Wolseley petrol
1906	C	143	290	320	Single	Petrol
1908	D	165	494	620	Saddle tank	Vickers diesel
1912	E	178	652	795	Saddle tank	Diesel: Vickers Admiralty
1914	S	148	252	386	Double	Italian diesel
1915	V	148	364	486	Double	Vickers diesel
1915	W	150	320	490	Double	Schneider Lambert diesel
1915	F	151	353	525	Double	MAN diesel
1915	G	186	693	964	Double	Vickers diesel
1916	Swordfish	231	904	1 384	Double	Laurenti steam turbines
1915	H	150	364	434	Single	Nelseco diesel
1916	J	275	1 200	1 900	Double	Vickers diesel
1917	Nautilus	240	1 270	1 694	Double	Vickers diesel
1917	K	340	1 780	2 450	Double	Parsons & Brown Curtis steam turbines
1917	L	231	870	1 055	Saddle tank	Diesel
1918	M1	296	1 650	1 950	Double	Diesel
1918	H improved	171	440	500	Single	Nelseco diesel
1918	R	163	410	500	Single	Diesel (one)
1918	L50	235	960	1 150	Saddle tank	Diesel
1920	M2	296	1 650		Double	Diesel
1920	M3	296	1 650		Double	Diesel
1925	X1	363	3 050	3 585	Double	Diesel
1926	O	296	1 490	1 892	Saddle tank	Vickers diesel

Armament Torpedo tubes	Guns or other	Officers	Ratings	Surface	Submerged	Endurance	Remarks
1x18″ bow	—	2	7	8.5	7	500 at 77	Originally designed without a periscope
1x18″ bow	—	2	9	10	4.5	at 320 at 10	
2x18″ bow	—	2	11	12	6.5	1 000 at 8.75	First British submarine to be fitted with fore hydroplanes
2x18″ bow	—	2	14	12.25	6.5	1 000 at 8.75	Fitted with two periscopes
2x18″ bow 1x18″ stern	Some had a 2 pounder	3	24	14.5	10	2 500 at 10	First British submarine to have wireless included in the design
1x18″ bow 20 mines 2x18″ beam 1x18″ stern	1x6 pounder or 4″	3	28	15.25	9.75	3 000 at 10	
2x18″ bow	—	2	16	13	8.5	1 600 at 8.5	Italian Laurenti design
2x18″ bow	1x2 pounder	2	16	14	9	3 000 at 9	
2x18″ bow	1x2 pounder	2	16	13	8.5	2 500 at 9	French Lanbeuf design
1x18″bow 2 x18″stern	1x2 pounder	2	16	14.5	8.75	3 000 at 9 .5	
2x18″ bow 2x18″ beam 1x18″ stern	1x3″	3	28	15.5	9.5	2 400 at 12.5	
2x21″ bow 4x18″ beam	2x12 pounders	4	38	18	10	3 000 at 8.5	First British steam submarine
4x18″ bow	1x6 pounder	3	20	13	11	1 600 at 10	Built in Canada and United States
4x18″ bow 2x18″ beam	1x4″	5	39	19	9.5	5 000 at 12.5	
1x21″ bow 4x18″ beam 1x21″ stern	1x12 pounder	4	38	17	10	5 300 at 11	
4x18″ bow 4x18″ beam	2x4″ and 1x3″ AA	5	45	23.5	10	3 000 at 13.5	Designed to operate with the fleet
4x18″ bow 2x18″ beam or 16 to 18 mines	1x3 AA or 1x4″	3	32	17	10	3 800 at 10	
4x18″ bow	1x12″ Mark IX 1x3″ AA	6	59	14	8	3 840 at 10	12″ gun
4x21″ bow	—	2	20	11.5	9	1 600 at 10	
6x18″ bow	—	2	20	9.5	15	2 000 at 8	Designed for anti-submarine work
6x21″ bow	2x4″	3	32	12.5	8	4 500 at 8	
4x18″ bow	1 Parnel Peto seaplane, 1x3″ AA	6	59	14	8	3 840 at 10	Seaplane carrier: 2 of complement aircrew
4x18″ bow	100 mines	6	59	14	8	3 840 at 10	Minelayer
6x21″ bow	4x5.2″	6	104	18.5	7.5	12 400 at 12	Cruiser submarine
6x21″ bow 2x21″ stern	1x4″	5	51	13.5	9.5	6 500 at 10	First of post war design for operations in the Far East

Completion date of first of class	Type	Length (in feet)	Displacement Surface	Submerged	Hull ballast tanks	Engines
1929	O improved	283	1 790	2 035	Saddle tank	Diesel
1930	P	289	1 760	2 040	Saddle tank	Diesel
1930	R	287	1 740	2 015	Saddle tank	Diesel
1932	River	345	2 165	2 680	Double	Diesel
1932	S	202	735	935	Saddle tank	Diesel
1936	Narwhal	293	1 750	2 150	Double	Diesel
1938	U	191	630	730	Single	Diesel electric
1938	T	269	1 300	1 575	Saddle tank	Vickers diesel
1940	U improved	197	630	730	Single	Diesel electric Paxman
1942	S improved	217	830	990	Saddle tank	Vickers diesel
1941	T improved	273.5	1 300	1 575	Saddle tank	Diesel: Sulzer Vickers Admiralty
1943	V	204.5	662	740	Single	Diesel electric
1945	A	281.5	1 371	1 620	Double	Diesel Vickers Admiralty
1958	Explorer	225.5	780	1 000		Hydrogen peroxide
1958	Porpoise	295.2	2 030	2 410	Saddle tank	Admiralty 16 VMS diesel
1961	Oberon	295.2	2 030	2 410	Saddle tank	Admiralty 16 VMS diesel
1963	Dreadnought	265.8	3 500	4 000	External	American ISSN nuclear reactor, geared steam turbine
1966	Valiant	285	3 500	4 500	External	British nuclear reactor; geared steam turbine
1967	Resolution	425	7 500	8 400	External	British nuclear reactor, steam turbine+
1970	Churchill	285	3 500	4 500	External	British nuclear reactor, steam turbine+
1973	Swiftsure	272	3 500	4 500	External	Rolls Royce nuclear reactor, steam turbine+

† Approximate
* Governed by the requirements of the crew
+ English Electric geared
Note Complements are slightly flexible and submarines generally take on board additional complement in war.

Armament Torpedo tubes	Guns or other	Complement Officers	Ratings	Performance Surface	Submerged	Endurance	Remarks
6x21" bow 2x21" stern	1x4"	5	51	17.5	9	8 500 at 10	
6x21" bow 6x21" stern	1x4"	5	51	18	9	8 400 at 10	
6x21" bow 6x21" stern	1x4"	5	51	18	9	8 800 at 10	
6x21" bow	1x4"	5	56	22.5	10	13 000 at 8	
6x21" bow	1x3"	4	32	14	10	3 690 at 10	
6x21" bow	1x4" and 50 mines	5	54	16	8.75	7 400 at 10	Minelayer
6x21" bow	—	3	34	12	8.75	4 050 at 10	
10x21" bow 1x21" stern	1x4"	5	51	16.25	8.75	8 000 at 10	
4x21" bow	1x3" 1x12 pounder AA	3	34	12	8.75	4 050 at 10	
6x21" bow 1x21" stern	1x3" or 4" 1x20mm AA	4	32	14.75	9	6 000 at 10	
8x21" bow 3x21" stern	1x4",1x20mm AA	5	56	15.5	8.5	11 000 at 10	
4x21" bow	1x3"	3	34	11.25	10	4 700 at 10	
6x21" bow 4x21" stern	1x4", 1x20mm AA	5	56	18.5	8.5	10 500 at 11	
nil	nil	5	36	7	25+	—	Experimental scrapped 1965
6x21" bow 2x21" stern	—	6	65	12	17	Limited	2 shafts
6x21" bow 2x21" stern	—	6	62	12	17	Limited	2 shafts
6x21" bow	—	11	77	20†	30†	Unlimited*	Fleet prototype nuclear powered, 1 shaft
6x21"	—	13	90	20†	30†	Unlimited*	1 shaft
6x21" bow	16 Polaris A3 missiles	13	129	20†	25+	Unlimited*	Two crews to each submarine one on patrol one stand off 1 shaft
6x21" bow	—	13	90	20†	30†	Unlimited*	Improved Valiant Class
5x21" bow	—	12	85	20†	30†	Unlimited*	Improved Churchill Class

Appendix III
Nuclear propulsion power plant

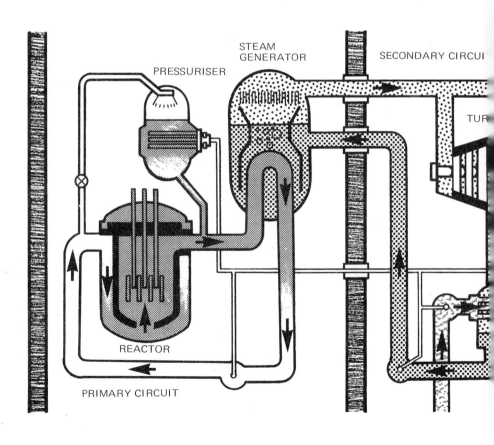

PRESSURISER

STEAM
GENERATOR

SECONDARY CIRCUI

TUR

REACTOR

PRIMARY CIRCUIT

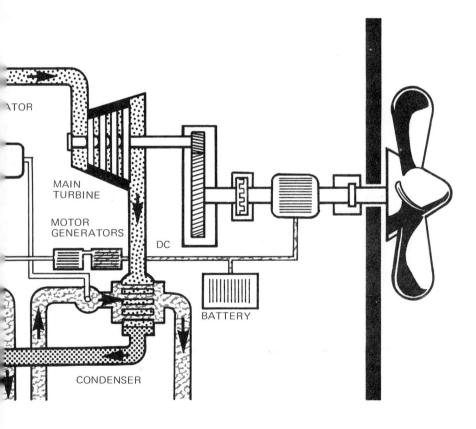

ATOR

MAIN
TURBINE

MOTOR
GENERATORS

DC

BATTERY

CONDENSER

The heart of the nuclear power plant of a Polaris Submarine is a Pressurised Water Reactor. It is a collection of fissile uranium fuel elements arranged in a heavily-shielded pressure vessel. The enormous release of energy produced by fissioning uranium nuclei manifests itself as heat in the fuel elements. The fission rate in the reactor is controlled by special rods which are inserted into the   fuel to absorb fission-producing neutrons.

The reactor, steam generator, pressurizer, coolant pump and pipework form an enclosed loop called the primary circuit. Water coolant is pumped round the circuit, passing through the reactor on its way, where it picks up heat from the nuclear fuel elements. The reactor is so hot however that the coolant would rapidly boil and the steam generated would lead to unstable conditions, were it not for the pressurizer which maintains the system at the correct saturation pressure. It does this by the formation of a steam bubble in the pressurizer vessel, created by electrical heaters inserted through the vessel wall.

After passing through the reactor the hot coolant circulates through the tubes of the steam generator where its heat is used to convert the low pressure water outside the tubes into high quality steam. The now cooled primary water is recirculated through the reactor to continue the heat exchange cycle. The whole primary circuit is housed in a specially shielded reactor compartment to protect the crew from all harmful radiations.

Steam from the secondary side of the steam generator is used to drive the 'ahead' and 'astern' main turbines and they, through clutch and gears, drive the single propeller shaft. On leaving the main turbines the spent steam is condensed in a sea water cooler and returned to the steam generator as water to begin the secondary cycle once again.

In addition to driving the main turbines, steam is used to drive turbo-generators which provide ac electrical power for the submarine: dc power requirements are met by motor generators or batteries. Spent steam from the turbo-generators, like that from the main turbines, is condensed and returned to the steam generators.

Sophisticated automatic and manual controls provide the controlling means for both the reactor and steam generating facilities and, in addition, elaborate electronic and mechanical features assure the safety of the nuclear reactor at all times.

From the point of view of the Captain and the Officer of the Watch, suppose the reactor is working steadily at low pressure and the submarine steaming at 'Slow Ahead'. The Captain orders 'Full Ahead'. The engineer watchkeeper opens more steam to the turbines, more heat is removed from the steam generator, colder water goes back to the pump and then into the reactor.

Colder water is more dense, has more closely packed hydrogen atoms to slow the neutrons. The slower neutrons lead to more fissions and an automatic increase in power just at the time when it is needed.

If the Captain then orders 'Stop' the reverse happens. The throttles are shut, less heat is taken from the steam generator, hotter less dense water goes to the reactor. The neutrons move faster, more get lost and the power dies down to meet the new lower demand. This process is a great advantage for a submarine plant where rapid changes in power may be needed.

Index